WOMEN, RELIGION, AND DEVELOPMENT IN THE THIRD WORLD

WOMEN, RELIGION, AND DEVELOPMENT IN THE THIRD WORLD

Theodora Foster Carroll

PRAEGER

PRAEGER SPECIAL STUDIES • PRAEGER SCIENTIFIC

New York • Philadelphia • Eastbourne, UK
Toronto • Hong Kong • Tokyo • Sydney

Library of Congress Cataloging in Publication Data

Carroll, Theodora Foster.
  Women, religion, and development in the Third World.

  Bibliography: p.
  Includes index.
  1. Women and religion--Developing countries.
  2. Developing countries--Religion.   I. Title.
  BL458.C38   1983   291.4′088042   83-13670
  ISBN 0-03-064108-X (alk. paper)

Published in 1983 by Praeger Publishers
CBS Educational and Professional Publishing
a Division of CBS Inc.
521 Fifth Avenue, New York, NY 10175 U.S.A.
© 1983 by Theodora Foster Carroll

3456789   052   987654321

Printed in the United States of America
on acid-free paper

In fond memory of my parents,
Phyllis Hunt and Wally Carroll,

and for my husband,
John Foster,

and my daughter,
Katrina Heather,

with love.

—Free Spirits All—

CONTENTS

PREFACE

Throughout history women have exerted an unrecognized, but pivotal, influence on the evolution of human thought and on the shaping of attitudes and values. Yet their achievements have taken place in an environment that imposed all sorts of constraints on them and, in most instances, was actually inhospitable to them as persons.

Consideration of the place and role of women in society has assumed a new importance in our time. Theodora Foster Carroll examines four major world religions and their contributions to conditioning the social environment within which women live and work. It is significant that she has placed her analysis in the context of development because, while the influence of religion and of women on development is sometimes acknowledged, these prime factors are the most frequently neglected in development planning.

Much of what the author says may be regarded as an indictment of organized religions—in particular, of their treatment of women. Yet she has distinguished between doctrines as originally stated and practices for which religions are only partly responsible; she shows that some of the inequities from which women suffer arose owing to misguided interpretation of prophetic teachings, while others had their roots in older customs. She goes on to discover an underlying sense of justice and flexibility in these religions. Although religious institutions may often have retarded progress and infringed on women's liberty, it is equally true that they are capable of changing and of being valuable agents of change. Religion has had, and may continue to have, a profound positive effect on the shaping of modern society.

Those who seek to advance world development will appreciate that the key to it is the development of women. Hence, serious students of human change will recognize the importance of this book.

Theodora Foster Carroll brings scholarship and detachment to this study. She reflects the practical and sympathetic eye of a woman who has worked in development endeavors in societies that owe much to the religions she considers. Her study makes a valuable contribution to current thinking about women and development and helps to place the subject in a global as well as historical and social perspective.

Lewis Perinbam,
Vice-president

Canadian International Development Agency

ACKNOWLEDGMENTS

When I first embarked upon this project, I frankly did not know what I was letting myself in for. I only knew that I was very concerned about women, that women were being ignored in the development process, and that religion very definitely had a greater impact on women's development than was being acknowledged. Virtually nothing had been written on the linkage between women, religion, and development, so with blind faith and the very active support and encouragement of my husband, John Foster, I plunged ahead. Thus, my first and foremost thanks must go to him for his advice, sympathy, and help, draft after draft, and to my daughter, Katrina, for her patience, understanding, and love.

Many thanks are due to Norma Dove, Claudette Ducran, and Shakeeb Atallah of the World Bank in Washington, D.C., for their encouragement and help when I was digging for materials, and to my many kind friends in Ottawa.

Special thanks are due to Valeriana Kallab, of the Overseas Development Council, and to Linda Sharpe, my editor at Praeger, both of whom evinced faith in my project and encouraged me greatly.

I would like to thank the librarians at the International Development Research Centre and the Ottawa Public Library as well as René Tragatsch and Jane Archambault of EDPRA Consulting Incorporated in Ottawa for their great willingness to track down material for me. And I would like to acknowledge the tremendous amount of work that Sunday Maclean, Angie Chew, and Teresa Taylor at EDPRA Consulting did in typing and retyping the manuscript, as well as the final editorial contributions of Debbie Schoenholz and Kathy Hagen at Praeger.

Finally, I am most grateful to Lewis Perinbam, vice-president of the Canadian International Development Agency, for writing the preface.

To all these, my thanks and appreciation.

1

INTRODUCTION: RELIGION AND TRADITION

When the role and status of women in development are discussed, the issue of religion and its impact on women's traditional position is typically sidestepped. Because the subject is ultrasensitive and emotionally charged, development planners treat religion as a nonsubject. At meetings and conferences this subject is virtually taboo in discussions about development. But religion, be it Christianity, Hinduism, Islam, or Buddhism, is an all-pervasive force, whether consciously realized or subconsciously assimilated, in the lives of people everywhere; and as such, it should be considered. Its implications for the success or failure of development projects should be discussed.

Religion has governed human actions for eons. In the past it frequently was a society's main source of law and social control (namely, the Ten Commandments, Moses's Laws, the Koran, Buddhism's Five Precepts, and the Laws of Manu), governing and guiding daily life and being a tacit reminder of the power of the invisible world. Unfortunately, religion's high priests and society's power mongers—at times hardly distinguishable from each other—have too often interpreted religion narrowly and in power terms, straining to control and constrain human actions and emotions. It has too often been used to inculcate fear into its adherents when social forces suggest or promote change; and it has been manipulated to drive the less educated or less thinking into automatic obeisance and static acceptance of regulatory ritualism. Undoubtedly, religion has provided strength and sustenance to people in times of hardship, poverty, strife, and need. But it has likewise been used to prevent changes that would lessen those afflictions and benefit these same people.

The ossification of religions and their original tenets, established to accommodate the conditions of bygone times, has had a particularly detrimental effect on women worldwide. Religion—or more

1

specifically, religiosity, folk religion, or popular religion—has been used to excuse the prejudicial treatment of women, to degrade them, and to restrict them to endless childbearing and drudgery.

Naturally, when considering religion in a development context, one must distinguish a religion's rituals, customs, and institutions from its inner truth and most fundamental philosophy. However, as much as one would hope that a religion's philosophy in its deepest, most visionary sense would prevail, it is typically its ritualistic institutions that govern a society's mood. Not only are these more comprehensible to the masses than philosophy, but they are totally acceptable, being essentially "a ritualized and stratified complex of highly emotional beliefs and valuations that give the sacredness, taboo, and immutability to inherited institutional arrangements, modes of living and attitudes."[1]

Ritualization and stratification have largely been responsible for the negative emotional reaction evinced by people, priests, and planners alike when change has threatened to disrupt their established patterns of action or thinking. In essence, social ritualization and stratification have been—and continue to be—responsible for the vast social inertia that retards education, population control, women's advancement, rural development, urban restructuring, and social reforms. And religious stratification and ritualization have so compounded prevailing negativism and inertia as to hamper social change in many economically underdeveloped societies.

This is not to say that religion is incapable of effecting beneficial change. After all, to use a well-worn cliche, the great religions of the world were basically reform movements in their time. Even today the visionary tenets of those faiths could be major instruments in effecting fundamental, beneficial changes if they were exercised in their full generosity of spirit and in accordance with modern conditions and needs. Unfortunately, power seekers, secular and ecclesiastical alike, have ignored or warped those tenets to suit their own designs and enhance their earthly power. They are unlikely to relinquish that power and its trappings unless circumstances—and people —compel them to do so. Since the possessors of power are usually men, they seek and obtain reinforcement from the males of their community. This latter group, being inextricably tied up in the maintenance of both the appearances and actualities of power, is unlikely to compel the power elite to divest itself of power unless moderately assured of acquiring a share of the divested control. It would be the rare group that would force the power holders to yield influence to an unrelated, peripheral group, a hitherto neglected unit of people. Most priests are no more anxious to encourage the full participation of women in religion than landlords are to hand over their land to rural peasants. As a consequence of this group's acquiescence to the attitude of "no change unless it is for my benefit," power holders are able to perpetuate their influence indefinitely. Moreover, where women are concerned, they are also able to elicit passive support—sometimes the most tenacious and inert of all—from the female community. Sometimes this support is extracted by direct intimidation, as by invoking scriptural injunctions or manipulating confessions; sometimes it is elicited indirectly, using the women's menfolk, who are warned to keep their women in order or suffer the consequences. Thus, women who might benefit the most from social reform and economic development end up being the most resistant; fearful of reprisal, intimidation, loss of their own fragile image, or disruption of economic support, they too end up blocking change.

It is time that the subtle and not-so-subtle impact of religion on various facets of development is recognized. Innumerable religious groups exist that oppose change because they fear the consequences of contravening age-old tenets. Equally innumerable politicians and power holders exist who, unbelieving themselves, are unscrupulously prepared to use religion—and its adherents' biases—to gain their own ends and to stay in power. Both perform the disservice of preventing a rational discussion of religion and its impact on development in much the same way as a rational dialogue of population control or disarmament has been hampered. Consequently, policy makers have been reluctant to confront the religious powerful and their supporters for fear of a backlash against their developmental efforts or to disturb the religious beliefs of the masses for fear of causing a revolt. Yet the failure to recognize, research, and discuss the prevalence of religion and its impact on people's lives very often leads to the precise problems that development experts seek to avoid.

The educated elite may be one of the last to encourage the stripping away of the rigid stratification and ritualization of their country's religion, although theoretically they should be the first. On the one hand, they stand to lose the most in terms of power and position. On the other hand, they are genuinely wary of reforming or counteracting popular religion unless they are assured of the masses' support. They may firmly believe in the "purification" of their religion—the disposal of rites, superstitions, and customs that have attached limpet-fashion to it—but still quake at disturbing the religious equilibrium of the masses by proposing radical reforms. Yet, being out of touch with the common people, the intelligentsia. frequently makes the mistake of underestimating the people's needs or wants (contraception being one of the most notable examples) and ends up leading from behind. Then, ironically, it is the masses that, in a pragmatic and unassuming way, provide the initiative and leadership for propagating change, leaving the rulers and religious powerful puffing to justify their tardiness.

At their highest levels, most religions are rational, idealistic, and unopposed to reform. They tend not to be saturated with magic, taboos, and mystical rites. However, most popular religions adopt customs, institutions, priestly interpretations, and community biases; cloak them with religious sanctions; and convert them into immutable doctrines. Social and economic disparity, arising out of poverty, tribal wars, division of labor and agriculture, geographical conditions, and community protection, is likewise given religious and customary sanction that thereupon becomes converted into undying religious tenets.

The unfortunate consequence is that fast-growing populations, desperately needing some of the changes that modernization can bring, cling to inequalities and sapping customs. Without a doubt many prevailing customs and traditional values were not only appropriate for the past but are still suitable for the present. Obviously certain modes of dress are more suitable for one climate than for another. Various folk medicines and treatments gleaned from the past have been found to be as effective as many modern prescriptions. Customary ways of planting and building have been proved to be better for certain types of soils and climates than new, inappropriate, and often untried methods. Rituals of bathing feet and hands before entering places of worship ensure at least partial hygiene where hygienic standards are otherwise minimal. And the ban on eating certain types or combinations of foods guarantees an element of protection against disease and food poisoning where dirty conditions prevail and government standards do not. However, these must be recognized for what they are: economic and social customs initially implemented for people's survival. Although they may have subsequently been given religious sanction, they are not, and should not be regarded as, the religion itself.

Such customs, receiving the emotional support of a religion, provide a source of strength and stability to the community. Removing such values and customs unnecessarily can quickly create a void that destroys the cohesiveness of a community's life and the inner strength of its individuals. Nevertheless, failure to modify the more deadening rituals and attitudes and to loosen their hold on society's various strata can create an impenetrable mass of unreasonable rules that then have the effect of strangling the community.

Policy makers need to distinguish between mere religious sanctions (termed here religiosity) and the fundamental visionary tenets or philosophy of religion. Then, by drawing the basic rational tenets of religion into development planning, they might encourage the reform of outmoded religious sanctions without alienating a religion's adherents. As Myrdal says, "From the point of view of the modernization ideals what is needed is merely the eradication of the ballast of irrational beliefs and related valuations."[2] Unfortunately, dumping the ballast of irrational beliefs is not so simple. Since religion is "part and parcel of the whole complex of people's beliefs and valuations, their modes of living and working, and their institutions, it needs to be reformed in order to break down inhibitions and obstacles to development."[3]

Reform would require not only the elimination of the baggage of eons of misinterpretations and corrupt renderings of each religion's holy writs by religious power holders but also a return to the essential nature and reformist aspect of each faith. Recalcitrant religious leaders may find that if they do not initiate the removal of inhibitions and obstacles the initiative to reform will be taken away from them, thereby leaving their religion weaker in influence among the masses. As K. M. Panikkar, a leading Indian reformer, said: "The fight against such customs leads directly to the reform of religion. It is significant that every movement for religious reform in free society has been against traditionalism."[4] Panikkar believed that as liberal political institutions are adopted by a society, religious taboos, social practices having religious sanctions, and priestly influences are broken down.

Although his sentiments are praiseworthy, Panikkar is perhaps overly optimistic, specifically where his own country, India, is concerned and generally when contemplating the conjunction of religious and political affairs in most countries. While the adoption of liberal political institutions might occasion the breakdown of detrimental religious practices to the benefit of the masses in some states, in the majority the liberalization of political and religious institutions only affects a favored few. The satisfactory coalescing of time, inclination, and the effective enforcement of dynamic legislation might effect reform at all levels; but it is a truism to say that the last usually to be beneficially affected are the women. Religious strictures surrounding women have had a particularly gluelike quality requiring rather longer and greater applications of the solvent of reform than almost any others.

Theoretically, religious sanctions become modified as more people are educated to higher levels, more communications are developed nationwide, more urbanization with its disparate influences results, and more mobility occurs. On that basis the secularization of religion, particularly as it pertains to women, should be occurring rapidly and comprehensively throughout the developing world. But it is not. In part this is because religion's secularization occurs mainly among the educated elite and the urban populace, who comprise only a relatively small proportion of the average developing country's population; and in part it is because the publicly espoused secularization of the elite, government officials, and educated urbanites is merely nominal within their private sanctums. In public an educated official may proclaim secularization. In private he may believe in astrology and numerology, the aphrodisiacal effects of local herbs, and the secluded role of women. This conflict is bound to intrude into his decisions, unless he is quite exceptional and able to divorce his private self from his public self.

This underground attitude partly accounts for why the reform of religion on a more popular and local level is only feebly pursued. An official's basic pragmatism in bringing about gradual change through the back door without unnecessarily disturbing a society's equilibrium also partly accounts for not tampering with religious customs, even if that means leaving 50 percent of the population in a state of servitude to those customs. Whatever the reason—pragmatism, nominal secularization, power—the failure to consider and reform religiosity has had the effect of ignoring a basic cause of underdevelopment. Religiosity has perpetuated distasteful inequalities among men and has assigned women to some of the lowest and most unenviable positions in society.

The inner meaning of religion and the basic doctrines of the old religions need not be interpreted as being inimical to either modernization or women. The great religions were reform movements or attempts to radically change existing patterns of thinking, attitudes, and customs. Their prophets were visionaries who tried to give their respective peoples new commandments to live by. They increased their followers' spiritual awareness and their sense of concern, compassion, and cooperation. The seeds of change and reform, originally implanted in the major religions by their prophets, are still there, perhaps quiescent or buried by the detritus of the ages, but for all that available for the rejuvenation and reform that a rapidly approaching twenty-first-century society needs and demands.

Unlike the original prophets, subsequent interpreters of the great faiths have mangled the basic tenets and directions of those religions. Recently, in such countries as Iran, Cambodia, Pakistan, and Libya and among fanatics scattered worldwide and of many faiths, they have misused the basic tenets to justify biases, unfair practices, and power motivations. They have deliberately disregarded the social conditions and mores under which the great religions were conceived and have compelled their followers—on pain of punishment, spiritual or temporal—to adhere to archaic rules and rituals that are often inapplicable to their present condition. Seldom have they invoked the compassion or understanding inherent in their professed faiths to ensure that successive generations are not tied down or victimized by outmoded concepts. They have contributed to the petrification of their religions and, moreover, to the disavowal of religion by increasing numbers of people who are unobtrusively withdrawing from religious activities. Nowhere have misinterpretations and biases in the name of religion been more vigorously applied than in the case of women.

Fundamentally the great religions preach equality, or at least relative equality. Insofar as the female sex has been concerned, this concept has been well and truly ignored or corrupted. In the name of religion, women have been downgraded, rendered subservient, and relegated to the back room of progress and development. But as long as 50 percent of the world's population is dealt with unjustly, greatly needed economic and social improvements will be only 50 percent accomplished. With problems and population increasing exponentially, one-half of the population could with proper attention and training conceivably help to alter the lemminglike leap of exponential figures. These should no longer be bypassed and ignored by the power brokers of religions or the architects of development.

It is often contended that the issues of women, religion, and custom cannot or should not be dealt with because they are too emotionally ridden and controversial. However, that argument begs the question, Why should 50 percent of the population not benefit from and contribute to development? It ignores the fact that the status quo has already been upset by development, progress, and modernization. What affects one part of society also affects even the most ignored and the least visible. Custom, tradition, and values have all been rocked, even upset, so it becomes pretentious and invalid to say that women and religion as development issues must be ignored to avoid conflict. Certainly, dealing with the two untouchables of religion and women directly and comprehensively will not magically transform development or society, but it could add a hitherto forgotten dimension to issues of human development and thus help nudge social and economic change forward a little faster.

The following chapters will explore the great religions of Hinduism, Buddhism, Islam, and Christianity; the social conditions out of which they emerged and the reforms advocated; their societies' original attitudes toward women; and the subsequent impact of the religions on the female sex. Judaism has not been comprehensively dealt with as it typically does not pertain to Third World countries. Hence, any discussion of Judaism has been restricted to considerations arising from Christianity and Islam. Likewise the animism that prevails in many parts of Africa has been left out, not for want of interest or because it does not have a major impact on the lives of African women, but because of time and space restrictions. These religions, like the subjects of this analysis, have considerably affected the role and position of women in their respective societies; their women's perceptions of themselves; and female evolution, emancipation, and development.

Scientific evidence that religion impedes women's development is distinctly hard to come by. Factor analysis has been used to try to demonstrate that there is a positive relationship between religion and socioeconomic development,[5] but these studies typically are very broad based and refer not at all to women. This is not surprising, since most articles or studies on religion and development essentially concentrate on the impact of religion on the economy or political system of the male. Women are treated very peripherally, as mere afterthoughts. This is true of most major development textbooks, which show index notations for worms and weevils but rarely women.

Fortunately after 1975, International Women's Year, women themselves started to redress the situation by writing about women's integration (or lack of integration) into development from basic, first-hand observation, or comprehensive interviews with Third World women in rural and urban areas.* Persistent and dedicated, they and their writings have gradually persuaded and convinced many development planners, generally men, that there is real economic and social merit in looking more closely at the issue of women's integration into development and even in doing something substantive about it.

Having worked in the international development field for 18 years and having lived in Third World countries for at least 12, this author has seen greater credence being given to the importance of incorporating women into all aspects and levels of development. That is encouraging. But hesitation is still rife, and implementation of that credence still progresses at tortoise pace. Perhaps that reluctance, or reticence, partly stems from a misplaced idea that embarking upon the development of women impinges upon convention and custom, which is tantamount to meddling in the religious affairs of a society.

Women have been surrounded by myths and taboos sanctified and accepted almost as much by Westerners as by their Third World counterparts. They have been hemmed in by religious beliefs and occasionally liberated by them. They have been transmitters of religious values but seldom innovators of new religious directions.

Women and religion have been inextricably tied together for eons. Subconsciously knowing this, development planners have trodden a cautious course to avoid antagonizing women's communities. But need they be so cautious? Increasingly, women from all walks of life are demonstrating that they do not wish to be left out of development; they do not want to be barefoot, ignorant, pregnant, poverty stricken, and in the kitchen. Women, Religion, and Development will

---

*See Selected Bibliography for a brief listing of works by Barbara Ward, Ester Boserup, Irene Tinker, Accola Pala, and Mayra Buvinic.

show that religion need not be an inhibitor of women's development and that it can be used instead as a force for change. If it were, that would be a major departure from the norm; one that would have far-reaching implications for women.

As Perdita Huston points out, the perception of women's status by Third World women is still very much "affected by numerous practices—often based on taboos, superstitions, religious beliefs, or even misinterpretations of religious tenets—that continue to have a stunting effect on their personal development, assertiveness, and participation in the life around them."[6] These beliefs have seriously hurt women physically, psychologically, economically, and educationally. They are demeaning and degrading to women, but insufficient work has been done to remedy the situation. Legislation needs not only passing, but forceful implementation. Attitudes toward women need changing. Education is essential. Especially important is constructive leadership, determined to improve women's lot and self-esteem, at the national level, among development planners, and by women. Only in this way will the best of religion be used and the worst undone.

NOTES

1. Gunnar Myrdal, Asian Drama: An Inquiry into the Poverty of Nations (New York: Pantheon, 1968), p. 103.

2. Ibid., p. 105.

3. Ibid., pp. 105-6.

4. K. M. Panikkar, Afro-Asian States and Their Problems (London: G. Allen & Unwin, 1961), pp. 94-95.

5. Cynthia Taft Morris and Irma Addman, "The Religious Factor in Economic Development," World Development (Oxford) 8, no. 7-8 (July-August 1980): 491-501.

6. Perdita Huston, Third World Women Speak Out (New York: Praeger, 1979), p. 47.

2

OVERVIEW OF HINDUISM
AND ITS IMPACT
ON WOMEN

If I were born a woman, I would rise in rebellion against
any pretension on the part of man that woman is born to
be his plaything. . . . I realized that the wife is not the
husband's bondslave, but . . . as free as the husband to
choose her own path.

Mahatma Gandhi

A discussion of modern Hinduism is virtually impossible without a glance at the civilization of pre-Aryan India.* Many of that
era's religious and cultural influences have passed into the present in
a form hardly adulterated by the intervening centuries. Equally a
deeper understanding of Buddhism† may be gleaned from a look at its
cultural and environmental roots in not only Hindu India but pre-Vedic
India as well.

Until the 1920s little was known of pre-Vedic or pre-Aryan India and even less of their direct influence on and contribution to Hinduism. Only when the ruins of unique civilizations such as Mohenjo-
Daro, Harappa, and Chanhu-Daro were excavated in the Indus River
Valley by Sir John Marshall in the 1920s did a greater comprehension
of the primordial traditions of India's aboriginal inhabitants or non-
Aryans emerge.

Archaeologists puzzled out that those non-Aryan peoples had
been wide-flung, living in the rich Indus River Valley, the Tamil ter-
ritory of the south, and the Bengal region of the east. Furthermore,

---

*Various authors and scholars ascribe wide latitude to the date
of different eras in Indian history.
†See chapters on Buddhism.

they ascertained that the non-Aryans had originated in those areas at least around 2500 B. C. (possibly as early as 3000-4000 B. C.) and were of mixed origin and diverse ethnic composition.

The non-Aryans' intellectual bent led them to produce both the tangible and the intangible. Their Bronze Age art was outstanding, and their architecture, as exemplified by the fine cities of Harappa (in the Punjab) and Mohenjo-Daro (in Sind), was easily comparable to the much glorified Mesopotamian and Sumerian cities. They progressed from the tangible to the intangible by conceiving such concepts as the law of karma,* reincarnation, animal veneration, totemism, female or earth-mother goddesses, deity worship (not unlike the worship of Shiva), and male and female fertility symbols (the predecessors of phallic worship). They also contributed to Hinduism such non-Aryan components as its world-negating (life is meaningless, life is useless) attitude; extreme asceticism, or personal deprivation; puja, or worship, including image worship; yoga, or the techniques and philosophy of meditation; and even atheism.

By 1500 B. C. India was populated by the ancestors of today's Dravidians, who dwell mainly in southern India, and by older primitive tribes. Only a few remnants of the latter, such as the Bihors, still exist in India's diminishing southern and central jungles. It is accepted that the Aryans were influenced not only by Dravidians who, like themselves, were also invaders, but Dasa, Naga, or Dasyus, dark-skinned, phallus-worshipping, primitive aboriginals. Their culture, religion, attitudes, and customs were considerably modified by those early inhabitants of India, and Hinduism itself eventually became an amalgam of those influences.

India's harsh climate and rough geography effectively discouraged prospective invaders for centuries. Ultimately, however, the lack of defenses in the northwest encouraged a nomadic people, the Aryans, to descend upon the north Indus River Valley where, around 2000 B. C., they easily overpowered the established, pacific aboriginal farmers.† Gradually, the invaders settled into an agricultural life with the men herding cattle (and periodically waging war) and the women providing stability by gardening, homemaking, and raising food.

---

*See Glossary.

†Many of India's and Persia's similarities in language, customs, and deities (Mitra, Varuna, and Indra) are directly traceable to the Aryans, who were descendants of Indo-European tribes and who launched their invasions from central Asia. The Persians' description of the Sindhus River inhabitants led to the name India, though Bharata is India's indigenous name.

Despite the conquerors' warlike propensities, they did introduce various useful innovations into India. They ushered in hitherto unknown domestic animals—cows, horses, sheep, goats, and dogs. They launched new eating habits—meat, milk, and soma—and produced horsedrawn chariots. On the intellectual side they produced the samhitas, Hinduism's earliest sacred writings, and developed a modern assembly-line concept, bringing the division of labor into classes and becoming the harbinger of Hinduism's most pervasive social institution, the caste system.

The Aryans also diligently converted the existing matriarchal and matrilocal system into an authoritarian patriarchy and eroded the freedom of non-Aryan women. Thereafter, descent and inheritance, once traceable through the mother's line, and the system of a daughter's husband living with his in-laws were altered. Descent became reckoned through the father,* who was also the sole head of the family, its property owner, and (in India's early days) its family priest. Daughters were ousted from their intimate family and sent to live with their in-laws, who rapidly developed a sense of property in them. Even so, women remained relatively free, especially when compared with women in brahminical and Muslim India or with most rural women of modern India. The wife and mother retained considerable authority over the home, children, and servants; was subjected to little husbandly restraint and scrutiny; and was very much less secluded from society or excluded from knowledge than her descendants.

Initially, the Aryans overwhelmed the non-Aryans, suppressed their religion and cultures, and imposed their own values. But gradually the invaders became progressively Indianized, their customs absorbed and assimilated, their religion modified. Written records of the social and religious practices of the non-Aryan civilizations are scant, having been either nonexistent or callously destroyed by the invaders. However, copious Aryan records illustrate how their own religious and social customs were inexorably fused with and Indianized by the native peoples. This was the beginning of the long-enduring tradition of India, of Hinduism, and of India's intellectual development—the fusing together of incoming concepts and prevailing customs.

The Aryans were warmongering and philosophically creative. They aggressively subjugated the local, black-skinned people and drove them southward, acquired control of the whole northern and

---

*Many English words show a rooting in the Indo-European group of languages and similarity with such offshoot languages as Sanskrit, Latin, Greek, and German. For instance, father and mother are easily recognizable in Sanskrit: pitar and mitar.

central zones of India, and obtained increasingly more pasturage for
their cattle. Yet, they produced vibrant Vedic literature, including
the foundation of Vedanta philosophies, the Upanishads; the graceful
and sacred language of Sanskrit; the ritual of yajna, or sacrifice; and
high theological thought. They were intensely concerned with life's
meaning and the seeking of unity in the totality of the world. To this
end they conceived the all-important religious and philosophical concept of Atman-Brahman, the subjective support of one's own personal
existence and inner self that is combined with the objective experience
of the whole world and the Absolute, the Supreme Reality. As the
Aryans moved away from warfare and anarchy into a more ordered
agrarian way of life, they gradually formed a system of government
that largely endures, in a modified form, in rural India today. Their
creative processes led to many new innovations in agriculture, medicine, anatomy, and formalized religion.

Not least of the new institutions that the Aryans gave to Hinduism and that, enduring, has strongly affected the position of Hindu
women for the last 4,000 years is their division of society by caste,
or more accurately speaking, varna (color). This institution first
emerged around 500 B.C. and appears to have risen out of the Aryans'
firm rules of endogamy and exogamy, which forbade marriage outside
the racial group and also prohibited marriage within near degrees of
kinship. Their rigid enforcement of those rules undoubtedly was influenced by their being outnumbered by a subject, black-skinned, allegedly inferior people. Thus, marriage outside the tribe was originally prevented more for reasons of color or long versus broad noses
than for reasons of status, class, birth, or occupation. When the
Portuguese came to India, they mistakenly translated varna into
castas, meaning class or caste; but, in reality, the first division of
society was based on unadulterated race or color discrimination. In
due course, however, varna became separation and discrimination by
virtue of jati, or birth, and then occupation, with a color taint remaining.

In Vedic India marriage among the Aryans themselves was
comparatively free, being governed only by a few select marriage
rules. Neither status nor marriage was determined by hereditary
status, birth, or occupation. This situation did not last long. By the
time of the heroic age of the Mahabharata and the Ramayana, caste
degrees had rigidified, occupations had become specifically defined,
and marriage rules had ossified. As rules became more entrenched,
the position of women became accordingly more restricted and their
freedom circumscribed. Thereafter, their position and role were to
become inextricably bound up in the caste system and its evolution.

The caste system is venerable. Its origins may be perceived
in the earlier writings of the Rigvedas. Therein the four social divi-

sions of Indian society were portrayed as the four levels or organs
of primeval personage:

> His mouth became the Brahman.
> His arms became the Kshatriya.
> His thighs are the Vaisya.
> The Sudra was produced from his feet. [1]

Yet, despite this original stratification, pre-Aryan and early Aryan
India was not really afflicted by class rigidity. Some social grading,
the minimum needed by a society trying to avoid anarchy, existed,
but even by the end of the fourth century B.C., a fairly fluid social
structure still characterized the two existing groups. The pale-
skinned, conquering Aryans occupied the upper social echelons; the
dark-skinned non-Aryans, the lower. Within each stratum the social
classes intermingled and little separation occurred. However, the
endogamous and exogamous needs of marriage combined with a desire
to keep Aryan bloodlines "pure" moved the system toward caste.
Politics, ambition, and occupation expanded it into an all-pervasive
organism, as Kshatriya and Brahmin vied with each other to hold the
dominant position in Aryan society.

At the outset of the Aryan invasions of India, the Kshatriyas,
the warriors and leaders, were preeminent. Their position satisfied
the inherent warring nature of the Aryans and acknowledged the importance of the Kshatriyas' role in cowing the aboriginals. The second rank of importance was accorded to the Brahmans,* the priests
and educators. Skillful at political manipulation, vital for youth's
education, and essential as society's oral communicators, the
priestly class became increasingly important to and dominant in an
Aryan society becoming less warlike and more settled. As repositories of their race's history, traditions, literature, and religious
and secular laws, and as interpreters of their religion's increasing
complexities (in part created by them), the Brahmins eventually ousted
the Kshatriyas from their supreme place. The Kshatriyas, ex-
hausted by war and preoccupied with administering expanding terri-
tories as well as peaceful agricultural pursuits, resisted this priestly
encroachment for over a thousand years of political see-sawing. Ultimately, their power base floundered, owing to long absences, and
their religious and educational influences declined after the end of

---

*Throughout this book Brahmans, meaning priests, will be spelled
Brahmins in order to minimize confusion with Brahman, the Absolute
Creator-Reality or Supreme-Being; the Brahmanas, or priestly writ-
ings; and Brahma, one component of the Vishnu, Brahma, and Shiva

the seventh century B. C. Finally, they capitulated in the face of their people's religious predelictions and brahminical determination to regain Rigvedic preeminence.

The third caste, the Vaisyas, or Aryan commoners, did not become a formalized division until around Buddha's time. It was composed of merchants, laborers, and free men with a sprinkling of Aryo-Dravidians. Like the other two castes, they were known as the twice-born. By contrast, the often-enslaved Sudras, or fourth caste, consisting of most of the native, non-Aryan, black population, the workers and tillers of the soil, were excluded from both reading or teaching the Vedas, from assuming the epithet of twice-born, and from wearing the sacred thread.

From the outset, the first three castes ostracized the fourth, primarily on the original basis of varna. Social activities (even of the most casual, mundane sort), eating or drinking together, and intermarriage were strongly discouraged to prevent racial contamination and to minimize injury to Aryan ascendancy.

The group that ultimately formed an undesignated fifth division of caste was comprised of the Outcastes (Untouchables, or social pariahs). The first Outcastes were generally native tribes unconverted to Hinduism, war captives, intermarrieds, and slaves. Initially, their numbers were few, but over time their ranks swelled substantially. It is estimated that in India today 45 million to 60 million people are Outcastes. Although renamed Harijans, or children of God, by Gandhi, and despite modern laws, the social situation of most Harijans is still as despicable and despised as ever.

The stratification of Indian society became increasingly rigidified as the power struggle intensified between the Kshatriyas and Brahmins. Stringent rules for governing individuals and society were minutely charted. Freedom—whether of association, conduct, or marriage between the four varna and the proliferating subcastes, or jatis—was denied. The emergence of numerous subcastes was a paradox, being the result of the prohibition against intermingling. Gradually, caste structures, originating as racial bias and metamorphosizing into social mores, were granted the ultimate sanctification—absorption into religious dogma.

Caste strictures and religious dogma served doubly to hurt women. Not only did Hindu thought and scriptures relegate females to a lowly status, but they were assigned the low caste standing of Sudras, irrespective of the caste into which they were actually born. They were doubly damned as women and as Sudras and were therefore banned by decree of the Brahmanas from contact with the scriptures, deities, and Brahmins. Thus, caste and status of women became and have remained inextricably intertwined. It is doubtful whether the position of females will substantially improve until the abuses of caste are

removed. Educating women will not in itself be enough. Strong implementation of legislation to reform the caste system will be more
essential than ever, especially as industrialization has spawned the
proliferation of entirely new subcastes that are based upon recent
technologies and yet are as rigidly defined by caste stricture as occupations of old.

Vedic India saw the Aryan-Indians develop a carefully regulated
agricultural and pastoral society. Land was divided by each village
community among its families to till and "own," which meant that it
could be bequeathed to families' heirs in direct male line (the demise
of pre-Vedic matrilineal descent) but not sold to outsiders. Moreover, it was to be irrigated in common, with the families of the community sharing burdens and benefits on a relatively equitable basis.
Sophisticated and varied handicrafts abounded, causing powerful guilds
to be organized not only to regulate their expansion but to arbitrate
intraguild disputes and guild members' marital problems. Trade in
everything from brides to cows was lively and interest rates usurious.
In time the guild system became the base for the multiplicity of subcastes throughout India and therefore effectively helped to consolidate
the caste system.

Pre-Vedic society was basically matriarchal with matrilineal
descent and inheritance prevailing. Goddesses, particularly earth-
mother types, figured prominently in religious ceremonies and worship. Aryan family life has been depicted as being generally stable
and of good standard, suffering no more than the usual aberrations of
any lively society. Non-Aryan males and females led a life of relative coexistence and equality, while pre-Aryan men and women recognized each other's essential role in performing life-sustaining tasks.
But this sense of mutuality was to disappear with the establishment
of the Aryans' patriarchal society; and the esteem for womankind was
to sink correspondingly. As the concept of patriarchal property grew,
men increasingly exercised their property rights over wives and
children by owning and disowning, bartering, and buying and selling
them. Females and cattle alike were an integral part of a family's
inheritance, to be used or disposed of as seen fit by the family's
patriarchs.

Nowhere were patriarchal rights more evident than in marriage.
The most honorable marriages were those settled by daughter purchase, although a bride's forcible abduction was considered a highly
complimentary event (provided it occasioned no loss of property or
life), since it was likely to be financially advantageous to the bride's
father. But a marriage by mutual consent between bride and bridegroom verged on the disreputable and was firmly discouraged. With
patriarchy's entrenchment, polyandry declined and polygamy sprouted.
That male privilege was not only permitted but actively encouraged,

especially by the nobles for the nobles, with the avowed purpose of developing spiritual merit, transmitting esteemed (male) characteristics to large numbers of progeny, and improving blood lines. Even so, vestiges of polyandry survived.

The more the women lost the power to control their own property, except in very unusual circumstances, the more the Brahmins consolidated their superiority of wealth and position by capitalizing, in effect, on the custom of polygamy. This consolidation was helped along by the Code of Manu, which inveighed against celibacy, the unmarried state, and unfaithfulness in monogamous marriages while condoning and legitimizing polygamy. It used polygamy to guarantee the Brahmins' superiority of wealth and position by stipulating that each wife was to be of different caste and that the wife of the husband's caste was to have precedence. In specifying the duties of husband and wife and the rules of inheritance, the Code leaves little to the wife and most to the eldest son(s) of the eldest wives of the highest castes. [2] Thus, polygamy subverted polyandry, and the Code subverted women's rights. Nevertheless, polyandry, on occasion, would be resurrected—when female infanticide had so reduced the female population of an area and created such a preponderance of marriageable males that it was the viable alternative.

Perhaps pre-Vedic women and, to a lesser degree, Vedic women had greater freedom of action and thought than did their counterparts in other periods of India's history, but they were not free, as modern apologists would have us believe. They had some say in the choice of spouse, and even in the type of matrimony. They could avoid suttee, or wifely immolation on a husband's funeral pyre. As widows, they could avoid social condemnation or relegation to a state of servitude by freely remarrying, unrestricted by religious dictates or social convention. And a few could indulge in polyandry, expand their property base, and retain control over their property with little male interference.

Yet despite the Aryans' strong patriarchal system, Vedic women were initially permitted to participate with men in public feasts, dances, and religious sacrifices; to study varied subjects, including the holy scriptures; and to join in debates and philosophic discussions. Gārgī, one of India's most famous early philosophers, is often cited as an outstanding example of Vedic womanhood, having contributed to the Upanishads and participated in many philosophical debates. A slight suspicion arises as a result of the frequency with which she is mentioned over other women that she may have been one of the earliest "token" women in history.

Undoubtedly, "Women in ancient India occupied a dignified place."[3] However, it would be both overstating the case and spurious to say that they were much freer than their modern Western counterparts. They lacked legal and property rights, since they and their children were in essence chattels to be bought and sold or cast off at the whim of the male having the right of ownership in them. They were buffeted by the prevalence of polygamy, and their position was undermined by the existence of female slaves and concubines in aristocratic Aryan families. Despite some liberties Vedic women were de facto and de jure subject to the patriarchal omnipotence of their family's head male, whether father, son, husband, or uncle. Accordingly, as Aryan culture overwhelmed non-Aryan, some women, unwilling to be completely circumscribed or subjugated, sought out Buddhism and its protected monasteries or other less restrictive religions to continue their higher studies and to maintain a semblance of personal liberty.

The heroic or epic period was epic for Indian women only in that they lost most of their vaunted Vedic freedom and status. This loss was due not only to the ascendancy of the formidable patriarchal system, it was also due to the paramountcy of the Brahmins, who sought to limit the numbers of those seeking education and holy learning to a favored few. Even the Brahmins' own wives were not exempt from such preclusion. Likewise, men almost as much as women, if they came from the "wrong" castes, were discriminated against and excluded from the higher intellectual pursuits. By thus limiting the public's access to education, the Brahmins effectively controlled the populace generally and women specifically.

More than that, the Brahmins portrayed themselves as the central and essential mediators for all religious supplications and deity imprecations. With time the priestly class became imbued with an aura of holiness and indispensability. Their word became law. And so the priests, with the ritualistic sacrifices they performed with increasingly complex dexterity, assumed importance over even the gods themselves.

The Brahmins further reinforced their hold over the people by composing the Brahmanas and appending them to the sacred Vedas. These legends and sacrificial directions—the earliest Indo-European prose extant—proclaimed that the supreme role of the priests and their contrived sacrifices were the masses' ultimate path to salvation. Other paths were effectively dismissed. Deities, once assiduously worshipped, were pushed into the shadows. Sacerdotalism took grip, with the Brahmanas declaring that "a person's salvation depended upon paying fees to officiating priests who perform the appropriate sacrifices and ceremonials."[4]

The Brahmanas initiated various innovations within Hinduism that successfully endured 2,700 years of change and confrontation. First, they assured the Brahmins' paramount position within the caste system. Second, they explicitly stated a belief in reincarnation, which absolutely reinforced the idea of brahminical supremacy. And third, they introduced eating restrictions, including the rules that wives were to eat separately from husbands and were to be the last fed within a family. Interestingly, while beef eating was generally proscribed, it was allowed in exceptional circumstances.

Travelers to India can note that many of those ancient brahminical innovations still prevail despite the fact that laws and education have attempted to change them. Other castes are still regarded as beneath the Brahmins in hierarchy. Intermarriage and social intermingling are still discouraged. The Sudras and Outcastes are still often treated as dirty and lowly and are discriminated against. Segregation by caste may have been legislated away for the purposes of work, education, and transportation, but indecisive implementation of laws and ambivalent education have only made biased attitudes less overt.

Social life is still hedged by various dietary practices. Water cannot be accepted from the defiling hands of a low-caste or "untouchable" person. Fertilized eggs and most meats are rigorously avoided. Beef is taboo except among modern, upper-class, liberal youth, who evade the issue by euphemistically calling the forbidden fare "chicken" or "mutton." Men entertain guests at their dinner tables, but wives are still left to squat as of old before their charcoal chulhas, excluded from socializing. Women still suffer from a higher degree of nutritional deficiency and malnutrition-related diseases than men. And ten times as many female infants as male infants die of nutritional marasmus—the result of males being fed first, most, and best, while females are fed last, least, and on the dregs.

Education and industrialization should, theoretically, lessen the grip of the caste system. But educators even in the upper echelons of universities continue to inveigh against female education and liberal caste associations. They perceive those innovations as being morally debilitating for the individual, the society, and the state. As a consequence they undermine legislative efforts and social-reform measures designed to improve the situation of females and the lower castes. Ironically, their resistance to change has been aided and abetted by industrialization. This has inadvertently spawned the development of entirely new subcastes based upon the new technologies but as rigidly circumscribed by caste strictures. Without a doubt caste as a custom, blessed by centuries of racial, social, and religious dicta, has been difficult to alter, despite legislation, education, and social reforms.

Epic period women were firmly discouraged from embarking on mental pursuits and participating in religious festivities on the grounds that "for a woman to study the Vedas indicates confusion in the realm."[5] This expression was symptomatic of the times that saw purdah (the seclusion of women) begin long before Islam, suttee drastically increased, the choice of mate reduced, and widow remarriage castigated. Priestly exhortations against females, combined with patriarchal authority and economics, helped to degrade their once-proud place in society. Simultaneously used was a universal ruse employed by priests and power mongers since time immemorial—that of extolling the virtue of the "ideal" woman, a being passive and submissive. Sita, the humble heroine of the Ramayana and passively devoted wife of Rama, replaced the vigorous female deities and became the Indian woman's epitome of wifely submission, fidelity, and unquestioning loyalty. Only exceptional women, ladies of high degree or disparaged temple courtesans, by reason of their personality or position, escaped the bonds of prohibition and confinement by acting unconventionally. Others, equally daring, joined the newer religions or sects to escape priestly and patriarchal oppression.

Women's trend toward greater passivity and submissiveness was intensified by the fusion of Aryan and non-Aryan concepts, with non-Aryan negativism and fatalism tending to submerge the vital positivism of the Aryans. Obversely, the fusion allowed Aryan autocratic authoritarianism to submerge non-Aryan cooperation and equivalence. Thus, the ordinary woman or man unwittingly developed negative and submissive attitudes through unconsciously imbibing a plethora of doctrines. They became imbued with maya, samsara, and karma. They embraced moksha and bhakti.* On the higher plane of Hindu philosophy and spirituality these doctrines provide people with a wondrous explanation of life and its struggles. But at the lower level of religiosity and custom, they merely reinforce and justify archaic, untenable prejudices and practices. What has been perceived to be the fatalistic and submissive attitude of the average Hindu woman, the apparent unthinking resistance to change in society or personal life, has its roots in such concepts. The consequences for females, especially of the lower castes, has been and will continue to be especially grim as long as they never have a glimmer of the potential or hope offered by the higher realms of Hinduism.

Much of the resistance to women's emancipation, freedom, or progress can be directly traced to the ongoing influence of the Hindu literary tradition of smitri and sruti on India's people.† The extensiveness and marvelous complexity of the literature, the cost and difficulty of producing it in written form, and the public's illiteracy have combined to reduce Hinduism's literature to a folkloric level of interpretation and myth. Inadvertently, the literature has contributed to

---

*See Glossary
†See Glossary.

making Hinduism a continuing source of barriers to change. Hindus
have been constantly inundated with influences flowing out of Hinduism's
literature, yet few, including today's university-educated youth, are
really cognizant of the content and its impact on their daily lives.

The first sruti, the Vedas, were composed almost 3,500 years
ago. The four collections of Vedic hymns were in the highly developed
oral tradition, imaginative, emotional, and questing. Besides showing the questioning evolution of Hinduism, they provided extensive information about Hinduism's historical development, its early mythology and rituals, and its original deities. Overall, they charted the
rise and fall of females, not least of which were the early goddesses.
As Hinduism's literary tradition evolved through the ages, through
the Brahmanas, the Upanishads, the Epics, the Bhagavad Gita, the
Code of Manu, the Puranas, and the Agamas, the life and status of
Hindu women can be followed. This will be discussed more fully in
Chapter 3, but meanwhile, a detailed discussion of the Code of Manu
and its impact on women is merited here.

The institutionalization and regimentation of the caste system,
the establishment of the primacy of the priests, and the creation of
guidelines for the behavior and functions of Hindu women were, in
the end, irrevocably fixed by the Code of Manu. Before the Manu-
Samhita, no real code of laws had existed in India. The country had
been governed according to the benign or despotic temperaments of
its various and numerous kings, village traditions or the dicta of
panchayats (governing councils of elders), and caste rules. Laws of
the land were basically nonexistent. Thus, those that took on the force
of law were the dharmashastras, the legalistic treatises on social and
individual behavior or textbook rules composed by the Brahmins for
their perpetuation. The most venerable of the dharmashastras was
the Code of Manu, believed to have been divinely inspired and composed by Manu, a mythical ancestor of the Manava tribe, or school
for Brahmins, near Delhi. Initially conceived to ensure "acceptable"
behavior by the Manava Brahmins, the Code evolved into a code of conduct for the whole Hindu community, and it acquired the total force of
law.

The Code became a compulsory social institution that gave stability to Hindu society but simultaneously regimented all actions and
relationships within that society. Through it, Hinduism became
more than a religion and philosophy; it became an established institution, the binding glue of a complex society. The Laws of Manu provided many fine elements of morality and decency: respectful obedience to teachers and parents, unresentful and patient endurance of
evil, reverential eating, fulfillment of promises, and confession with
repentance. However, its main emphasis was the upholding, reinforcement, and refinement of Hindu traditions. It outdid itself in its elabora-

tion of caste and the position of females both within and without the family. The seal on female subjection, degradation, and ignorance was set for untold centuries by the dharmashastras, of which the Code of Manu was preeminent.

In all fairness, the Code also provided for the protection of females, given their dependent state. The unquestioning attitude, passivity, and utter dependence even now evinced in most Indian women, especially those of the rural areas where 80 percent of India's populace lives, directly stem from this constant reiteration of dependency and threat of social disfavor.

Wives in the past could be sold or repudiated by their husbands, though the Code of Manu attempted to modify such behavior by advising husbands against such drastic action. [6] Were women so treated by their husbands, they were nevertheless not automatically released from their husbands' clutches. They were, instead, hedged in by double standards that deprived them of independence, respect, freedom, and status. They could expeditiously be cast aside for being of unprepossessing characteristics, such as having a temper or a fondness for drink, but they could not retaliate if their men were of unsavory character. As women they were expected to remain grateful for neither being cast off nor being deprived of their own personal property by boorish spouses. [7]

A woman's position was further unfairly eroded if she was still barren by the eighth year of marriage, if all her children had died by the tenth, if she had borne only daughters over eleven years of wedlock, or if she had traits her husband disliked. Without any recourse whatsoever, such a woman could find herself superseded by another wife with precedence over her—an intolerable situation, particularly if the succeeding wife was of lower caste, as frequently happened. If the disgraced wife failed to accede graciously, she could either be confined to closed quarters or expelled from her home at her husband's behest. [8] In essence, the most conscientious wife was under tremendous pressure to keep bearing children to attest to the "husband's rebirth," replace deceased children, and produce male heirs.* That her barrenness or proclivity for bearing females might not be her fault was neither here nor there. She and only she had to accept the blame for the failure to produce a suitable family.

On the whole the women of Manu's India were prohibited from taking on gainful work. That prohibition was only lifted to allow wives to take on "blameless manual work," when their husbands had failed to provide them with maintenance for the durations specified by the

---

*See Chapter 4 on Hinduism and population regarding the pronatalistic pressures exerted on women by Hinduism.

Code. Husbands were counseled to provide their wives' maintenance
for eight years when away on sacred duty; for six years of learning
or the call of fame; and three years if their absence was due to pleasure.[9] As might be expected, such wives were supposed to remain
silently and chastely at home, not socializing, not going out, and not
working for gain.

In modern India it is not at all uncommon for husbands and
wives to be separated for long periods of time while he (and, today,
sometimes she) is abroad studying, working, or just traveling. The
wife remains back with her own family—or, occasionally, his—rearing the children, participating in the household, and more infrequently,
working at a paid job. The apparent passive acceptance of such long
separations may, in fact, have its roots in the common heritage of
the Code. Likewise, the attitude engendered by the Code toward working wives, combined with the passivity engendered by Hinduism's
concepts of karma and dharma, may also partially account for the
relatively small number of Indian women who are gainfully employed
in the modern sectors of trade and industry. The traditional attitude
that women do not or should not work may account for the invisibility
of women in statistical analyses and the lack of recognition given to
their back-breaking agricultural work.

The pall of the Laws of Manu still hovers over the majority of
women, rural, illiterate, and steeped in the fearsome mythologies of
historic conventions. Though the extremes of Manu may have been
tempered by legislation, reform, and education, the gist of the rules
still permeates—more subconsciously than consciously—every corner
of the average Hindu woman's life.

In the past, women's perennial state of dependency and inertia
was traceable to the archaic custom of child marriage, which was
given legitimization by force of law. This law, requiring all young
girls to be married before puberty, was originally meant to prevent
intercaste liaisons. Then, the Laws of Manu gave religious sanctification to that ancient custom of child marriage. A major consequence
of this long-established tradition of child marriage was the relegation
of wives to a mentally incompetent, inferior, eternally childlike
status and the consignment of all their affairs, including the control
of their own property, to their husbands. Control was power. Loss
of property control meant loss of not just economic sustenance but
loss of self-worth and dignity. Basically under the Laws of Manu,[10]
a wife, like a eunuch, Outcaste, or slave, could not hold property,
although she was theoretically permitted to keep her dowry and nuptial
gifts and could rule in her eldest son's name until his majority.
Daughters, in terms of inheritance, were treated peripherally. Essentially, they were dependent upon their brothers' largesse and generosity, although in the most fortuitous circumstances they could re-

ceive one-quarter of their father's estate. The most fortunate daughters were those who were unmarried and had mothers with separate property that they could inherit directly without interference from their brothers. Unmarried sisters whose fathers had died could also anticipate a dowry provision from their brothers to ensure their suitable marriage. By contrast, married sisters, being their husbands' properties, could expect at best a few personal trinkets or tokens by way of property or inheritance from their own family.

With the rigid application of the Laws of Manu, women's polygamous and inheritance rights were further reduced. In addition to the wife of the husband's caste having precedence, the larger portion of a man's estate was to go to the sons of his Brahmin wife and thereafter in diminishing segments to the sons of the Kshatriya, Vaisya, and Sudra wives.[11]

Moreover, as a further extension of its property inheritance rules, the Code provided for the inheritance and transmission of learning and caste. Where education was concerned, only a Brahmin of the four real varnas could acquire knowledge through learning and teaching the Vedas.[12] "On account of his pre-eminence, on account of the superiority of his origin, on account of his observance of (particular) restrictive rules, and on account of his particular stratification, the Brahmana is the lord of (all) castes ('varna')."[13]

The downgrading of castes was always ascribed to women, never to men. Even though it was the "twice-born" men who were permitted to marry and beget sons from wives one or more degrees lower than themselves, it was the women who were faulted for the downgrading of caste or the lowering of caste standards for "the fault (is inherent) in their mothers."[14] Even an Aryan woman was blamed for the downgrading of the allegedly superior Aryans if she had had the "misfortune" to marry a non-Aryan, as her offspring automatically inherited non-Aryan status. Needless to say, the children of an Aryan father marrying a non-Aryan woman did not suffer the same downgrading but were accorded Aryan race. This discrimination against the female parent was not unlike the situation that existed many centuries later in countries such as Canada where, until legislation in the late 1970s altered the situation, a child born abroad of a Canadian mother could not inherit the mother's nationality unless declared illegitimate. Indeed, the situation still exists in Canada whereby a Canadian Indian woman marrying a non-Indian man loses her Indian status and native rights, while a Canadian Indian man marrying an outsider does not. And those most opposed to giving the Canadian Indian woman equality are the Canadian Indian men, who recognize that equality would diminish their share of the property pie. It is ironic that some twentieth-century countries still perpetrate the ancient myth that nationality (race, religion, or caste) emanates solely from paternity, a much less provable fact than maternity.

With the evolution of innumerable castes in India, the Code concocted imaginative nomenclatures for the numerous permutations and combinations that sprang up from the licit (and illicit) liaisons between different castes and their variegated offspring. By all accounts, the lower castes were treated abysmally and were even marked, such as with forehead branding, to show their low status. Women were not exempted from such treatment, so if they were from low castes, they were doubly degraded.

The low esteem in which women were held was exacerbated by the belief that the spiritual needs of women were nonexistent. While the Laws of Manu—not entirely unrepresentative of other religious treatises—comprehensively contemplated the lifelong mental, verbal, and bodily acts of males; their likely effect on men's transmigration; and their possible states of reincarnation,[15] women were totally ignored. Their spiritual and mental needs were of no account. Their minds and souls were nonentities, unworthy of consideration, except in one regard: thieving women were threatened with transformation into the female of the undesirable species into which male thieves could be changed. A stealer of linen would be transformed into a frog; a perfume thief into a muskrat; a woman stealer into a bear; a cattle thief into a she-goat; and, among many other inventive creations, a robber of salt into a female cricket.[16]

No consideration was given to women's salvation or to their religious joy and satisfaction. They were only considered as possible miscreants to be yet more held down, threatened, punished, and degraded.

The lack of concern for women's spiritual development was paralleled by an equal disregard for their mental enrichment. The Code of Manu abruptly halted Indian women's early Vedic interest in intellectual pursuits. This will be discussed more extensively in Chapter 3, but it can be said that the Brahmin priests were probably no more obdurate in their opposition to female education than were many of the early Christian clergy who opposed the opening of intellectual pursuits to women and girls. More surprising has been the attitude of prominent figures in this century, such as Tagore in his Chitra[17] and Swami Prabhupada, who have reviled female education. The swami, professing enlightenment, has exhibited little illumination about women. His regressive statements would be amusing if they were not so harmful of attempts to upgrade the debased position of females through education and to alter the public's customary attitude toward female education. The swami believed that the basic principle for peace, prosperity, and spiritual progress in life is a good population in society, which in turn depends on the chastity and faithfulness of its womanhood. He emphasized that just as children are prone to being misled, women are also prone to degradation and should be protected by the elder members of the family. Likewise, he believed that by being engaged in various religious practices, women will not be misled into adultery. Like the sage Cānakya Pandita, the swami had a low opinion of women, their intelligence, and their trustworthiness. He had an equally low opinion of Sudras and those below them.[18]

Despite such overt opposition and lukewarm acquiesence to improve women's position, the emancipation and education of Indian females have progressed. General reform movements culminated in legal reforms and the elimination of the more wretched practices of suttee, devadasis or nautches, strict purdah, child marriages, and ostracized widowhood. Political reform and education of the masses at all levels invoked the participation of members of both sexes who had hitherto been excluded from intellectual stimuli and political pursuits. India's struggle for independence, necessitating the participation of both male and female, demonstrated clearly the latent qualities and abilities of Indian women and produced some outstanding women leaders. The average woman, with the examples of those outstanding women and India's own struggle before her, was emboldened to throw off some of the same shackles of bondage that bound India itself. Yet even today, most Indian women, like the majority of Harijans, have not been able to break finally the greatest link in the chain of bondage, entrenched prejudicial attitudes.

While the Laws of Manu and other brahminical treatises may not be followed in their minutest detail, it would be extravagant to deny that those ancient scriptures still influence and support most spheres of daily Hindu life. As codes of social and moral order for Vedic India, they have been carefully preserved and transmitted through the ages to the present, where they constitute the warp and woof of the complexly woven tapestry of Hinduism's religion, culture, and philosophy. They are not easily eradicated from the minds and mores of the people—nor should they necessarily be eradicated in their entirety. But their continuing hold on India and their most pernicious aspects must be thoroughly scrutinized when proposals for change are bruited.

The failure to take account of the religious factors that pervade Indian life will constitute the neglect of a major factor that can determine the success or failure of not just an individual development project but of India's general development. This is being demonstrated by India's present government, which in its grandiose plans for reform and development, has ignored certain basic facts that have their roots in ancient religious tradition. First and foremost is the fact that, parliamentary laws to the contrary, ancient brahminical tenets prevail, relegating the Untouchables (now designated the Scheduled Castes) to bottom status and, as a corollary to that, the Harijan women to an even more inferior position. Second, the power base designated by the sacred scriptures is not likely to be lightly relinquished by those entrenched in power by tradition or by those who by virtue of their innate favored status have acquired extensive land and property holdings to the detriment of the disfavored, the landless, jobless, and homeless. And third, the once-suppressed minority of Harijans now constitutes a majority among castes, representing 41 percent of the urban population and 48 percent of the rural—a majority with an increasing consciousness of economic, social, and political rights and the concomitant of rising expectations. Since women constitute a majority of the have-nots and oppressed, with equally rising consciousnesses and expectations, they along with the Harijans, represent a formidable storehouse of future trouble and violence. Typically, these groups have been restrained by their religion and their priests from kicking over the traces. But the question now is, How long can they be constrained in a modern world by a religion and its religious leaders who are unresponsive to their burgeoning needs?

The Code of Manu, still pervasively influential today, subtly but definitely shifted the emphasis away from color toward occupation, and so opened up the possibilities for innumerable subcaste divisions. Today, at least 3,000 such subdivisions prevail in India. Further, it lifted Brahmins to a position of permanent paramountcy, reduced the low castes and women to a permanently inferior (spiritual and economic) position, redeemable (in another life) through the salvation of prayer and strict obedience to caste law in this life. Women, however, could anticipate only limited redemption or a long drawn-out process of reincarnation because of their restricted access to spiritual learning and the Supreme Being.

The priests consolidated their power by converting themselves into India's aristocracy, a sacred cult given divine inspiration and an exclusive association above the law. Their aloofness contributed to their mystique—helped by threats of divine and corporal punishments —as did the public's sacred duty to assist in their keep. Their august body was exempted from most fines and punishments normally extracted from the hoi polloi for misdemeanors and crimes. For instance, a Sudra would die for murdering a Brahmin, but a Brahmin's life and wealth were sacrosanct whether he murdered a Sudra or any other non-Brahmin mortal. Amazingly though, the Brahmins used remarkably little physical force or violence to keep their supreme position in India for nearly 2,500 years. The other castes lacked the education or organization to counter the Brahmins. The masses were made inert by their poverty and hard toil in a harsh climate, while women were paralyzed by fear and the enormous burden of complying with the welter of religious and social rules.

Moreover, by avoiding the trap of complacency, the Brahmins ensured the public's compliancy by invoking myths and superstitions and by ordaining trial by ordeal, or lex talionis, to obtain steadfast obedience. Women no less than men, accused of wrongdoing, might only be absolved if their hands escaped unscathed from a basketful of poisonous snakes or if their feet remained uncharred from a trip across white-hot coals.

The Laws of Manu were an extremely important tool. They made millions of Brahmin males the Code's chief beneficiaries and thereby helped to increase their wealth commensurate with their power. Not only were they permitted to institute wife beating (albeit limited), they could charge fees for a thousand and one ministrations—for their temple services and for their home services, including making barren women unbarren. They established temples and acquired numerous land grants from grateful patrons. They specified allowable and forbidden foods in overwhelming detail and obtained tax exemptions from intimidated local officials. Being innovators themselves, they were careful to limit the possibilities of future innovations that foreseeably might jeopardize their status. They therefore condemned in advance all modern innovations liable to contravene the holy Vedas. Their eventual condemnation of women's emancipation, female education, family planning, and contraception is thus not so surprising in the light of their history, although admittedly a few liberal-minded Brahmins were among India's first modern reformers. Inexorably, brahminical prestige, power, and wealth mushroomed; inevitably, as a group they were the rearguard of change.

The popular Hinduism of the Epics and Puranas produced no alleviation of caste rules. Life became a thorny thicket of social prohibitions. Home life, too, did not escape the brier patch. It became progressively governed by a plethora of popular Hindu observances prescribed for meals, birth, death, marriage, washing, toilet, and funerals. It was caught up with purifications and ceremonial bathings, offerings to the manes ("spirits of the dead"), and the sacred thread ceremonies of pubescent boys. Social life was thoroughly circumscribed by eating and drinking proscriptions and by the fear of ritual contamination through association with menstruating, childbearing, or lactating women and the other castes.

The women of the family had the primary responsibility for overseeing the daily rituals and practical observances of Hinduism. And the elder women, brooking no deviation, gradually indoctrinated the girl children into those social and religious mores. Through the rituals and their observances, Indian women, apart from their childbearing function, achieved a modicum of stature in the eyes of their families and community. Acquiring so little stature of self-worth from other sources, it is understandable why they—the older women especially—have been reluctant to relinquish even the most archaic, detrimental customs. Before they can or will embrace a new system, they must be convinced that their already lowly status would not be endangered or further diminished.

However, the status of outcasted women—and men—could not sink any lower than it already had or benefit more from caste reform. Menials, relegated to a lifetime of dirty jobs, were regarded as defiled, contaminated, beyond the bounds of humanity. Being ostracized from all normal social intercourse, including popular religion and the temples, they enthusiastically practiced animism until viable alternatives—Buddhism, Jainism, Sikhism, Christianity, and reformed Hindu sects—were opened to them. Indirectly, they influenced popular Hinduism, lending it many of their animistic practices—horoscopes, astrology, charms, and curses—that the higher castes, despite their denials, have since adopted.

Hinduism's unique caste system, with its commitment to order, dharma, and (sub)caste codes of conduct, has been conducive to providing India with a cultural, political, and social stability and a moral steadfastness it might otherwise have lacked. Without the system, India might have succumbed to chaos and extreme duress in the face of eons of invasion, conquest, exploitation, tyranny, and change. Caste rules established habits of diet and cleanliness for all to emulate in an otherwise disease-ridden, parasite-ridden, sanitation-lacking country and probably, in India's earlier years, contributed to minimizing diseases, famines, and pestilences.

On a personal basis, the caste system provided women and men with a sense of place and belonging, an element of security in and contentment with life, and a feeling, however limited, of self-worth and occupation. It rationalized the differences and inequalities between individuals, thereby leaving them relatively satisfied with their lot. Unrealistic expectations and discontentment were thereby minimized, a most useful condition in a poverty-stricken country where the seeds of rebellion could easily erupt.

However, the caste system, with the combined concepts of dharma and karma, has also contributed to a negativism, a passivity, and a fatalism that permeated—and continue to permeate—the average Hindu woman's life and acted as a drag anchor on the community as a whole. In a society increasingly threatened by overpopulation and its associates of famine, poverty, and disease, such attitudes are not only deadening but irresponsible, as they hinder urgently needed social changes.

Individuals contributing to a dynamic society need to have a sense of individual ability and personal moral responsibility. They need a sense of a universal humanitarian standard over and beyond mere social distinctions and a belief in achievement by the masses and the individual. They need idealism. Instead, caste has created inertia and divisiveness. It has especially rendered women fearful or incapable of seeking change, whether in their social status, educational attainments, or economic position. It has inculcated in women the belief that only death and reincarnation can alter their individual social status and has thus instilled in them a disclaimer of responsibility for their own actions or, more likely, inaction. And these attitudes and beliefs they pass on to their offspring, causing the negative cycle to be repeated.

Caste rules still dictate attitudes and actions that in turn hamper developmental change, for "caste remains central both at the personal level and in the larger social structure."[19] The outcome of this has been the refusal of the majority of individuals to assume responsibility for bettering the lot of their society. They have used caste rules and Hindu philosophy to justify their rejection or listless avoidance of moral and humanitarian claims on their time and energy. And they have justified this lack of cooperation in work or reform on the basis that the specific contacts, associations, and tasks are deemed unsuitable by their predestined role. Sadly, this is seen among many wealthy and well-educated women who, despite little to do at home, steadfastly refuse to involve themselves in helping to improve the lot of poorer, greatly disadvantaged women and girls.

Superficially, women in India are emerging from isolation and ignorance, and the caste system is ameliorating. But for many of India's reformers, anxious to see India achieve its potential and escape its poverty, the pace of change is too slow. Their dismay intensifies when they note that attitudes and habits change little faster among the educated elite than among the rural poor.

A survey of college students of different castes exemplified the slowness of attitudinal and habit change.[20] Of the "twice-born" men surveyed, 56 percent favored traditional caste distinctions and functions. While at the university and away from their parents' or community's orbit, they were prepared to study, eat, and drink with other castes. But once they left the hallowed halls of college, they tended to revert quickly to caste traditions because of family or community pressure, loyalty, social status, and work prospects. In a sense, the caste system can act as an "old-boy" network, which is crucial to graduates in a country of rampant unemployment.

The conservatism of the high-caste men was not equally shared by the "twice-born" women, for only 5 percent approved wholeheartedly of the traditional system. Nor, as might be expected, was it shared by two-thirds of the Sudras and nine-tenths of the Untouchables, who like the women, stood to gain more from the modification or elimination of the caste system than the "twice-born" men. Nevertheless, only a few of the most liberal and reform-minded students indicated that they would dare to contravene the system once they left the protection of academia.

Intellectually, most of the university students interviewed could aver that they "did not believe in the 'traditional division of Hindu society and the code of conduct ascribed to them according to tradition,' as being divisive to Indian society, uneconomic and unprogressive."[21] Yet, emotionally they could not relinquish caste division in marriage along with the appropriate marriage rituals, certain rites of passage (such as the sacred thread ceremony), and various death ceremonies. Nor did they generally rebel against arranged marriages, although many stated that they would allow their own children free choice. Nonetheless, despite their strong feelings for many Hindu traditions, their level of education, and their backgrounds, only a small minority of students knew the origins of Hindu traditions or had read the holy scriptures.

If such students, as an example of India's educated elite, can so readily reassume the cloak of caste and sexual inequality once away from the freedom and protection of a university, how much more difficult it is for the uneducated rural masses, immured in age-old traditions, to break away from custom.

> There is little evidence that modern education leads an appreciable group to a complete or meaningful break with their religion. . . . Further, there is a strong apprecia-tion of tradition and the value it possesses in giving smooth continuity to life and society. There is little indication of a determination to change existing patterns in personal, family or community life; these have proved their worth in the past and are believed to be necessary for the pres-ent and the emerging future.[22]

Reformers, besides being faced with lethargic lack of determina-tion to change existing patterns, are also confronted with the problem that, as India's economic and social order becomes more complicat-ed, the caste structure likewise becomes more complex and difficult to unravel. Amoebalike, it has divided and subdivided to accommo-date Indian society's diverse elements and their functions. But this was contrary to one of the original premises of caste—immutability—since "in ancient India the rigidity of the caste system was predicated upon the presumed finality of the economic structure, then relatively simple."[23] Industrialization and modernization, being the antithesis of a simple, final, economic structure, have exacerbated the com-plexity of caste by contributing to its further subdivision. Traditional racial, migratory, and sectarian castes have become joined by func-tional, occupational, and specialist castes.

Ironically, caste entrenchment has been aggravated by external reform movements—a result of their lay members being unaccustomed to individual action or cooperative organization and thus easily susceptible to divisiveness and subdivision and the lure of (new) security-producing social strictures. Reformers therefore have cause to be anxious about the slow pace of change. If they are to hasten development, which must include women's advancement, they must be prepared to make a concerted effort against the suffocating clasp of the caste system, using all means—legal, economic, educational, religious, and social—at their disposal.

While Hinduism throve and expanded during the Puranic period, its offspring, Buddhism, after an initial forceful impact, became practically nonexistent by 600 A.D. In part its demise was due to its esotericism and inability to furnish the populace with the security of Hinduism's social and ritualistic prescriptions for daily living, but more important, it could not withstand the incessant waves of Islamic incursions that methodically and thoroughly destroyed Buddhism's lifeline—its Sanghas, or Buddhist monastic orders. However, despite the elimination of its prime religious competitor, Hinduism also experienced a weakening through the onslaught of Islam.

Islam's initial border incursions into northern India early in the tenth century gradually intensified in size and ferocity until the whole north was under the Muslim heel. India's geography partially protected the south from the excesses of the fanatical marauders. Its magnificent temples and sculptures largely escaped the brutal destruction and desecration suffered in the north. And southern Indian society and religion were not substantially altered as were northern religious attitudes and social fabric.

India's built-in resistance to unification efforts hampered the Muslims from totally controlling the country and its peoples. Not until the early 1600s, shortly before their ouster by the British, could the Muslim invaders claim rule over a unified India—a feat accomplished by only one Hindu king, Ashoka, in 300 A.D. Similarly, Hinduism's absorptive capacities also hindered full-scale Islamic conversions and total dominance; Hinduism adopted only those commonalities with Islam—an absolute God, a divine world, and an intense devotion within a monotheistic context.

The intense pressures on Hindus to accommodate Islam and to accept at least its external manifestations severely affected the women of northern India. Islam and the Code of Manu combined to further deny females a sense of self-worth or individualism. To this day a purdah mentality obtains in much of the northern region, except where Sikhism prevails, in contrast with the south where women tend to participate more freely in community life, the pursuit of educational goals, and even politics.

The drift of the "new Hinduism" toward new religious insights and concepts made it extremely receptive to external influences and amenable to incorporating some of the finer features of Islam. To a degree this coincidence produced a certain synchronization of outlook and attitude and ultimately another religion, Sikhism, which was a synthesis of Sufism, Islam, and Hinduism.

The founder of Sikhism, Guru Nanak,* a Kshatriya, based the new religion on the religious syncretism of Kabir, who had been influenced both by the Sufi thinkers of Persia and Iraq and by the saints and more intellectual thinkers of Hinduism and Islam. Although initially orally expressed in Urdu, the synthesis of the finer points of the two religions were ultimately written down in the Adi Granth, the sacred bible of Sikhism.

Of the three religions, Sikhism was the strongest advocate of equality or equivalence among human beings. Anyone from any caste or class was welcome, and females came nearer to achieving religious and social equality through Sikhism than through the other vying religions of the region. This is especially amazing given that the ascetic Kabir, a low-caste Muslim weaver from Baharas, despised women and castigated sexual relations, and that Nanak subjugated his marriage and family to his growing religious beliefs. However, Nanak consistently praised women, denounced their oppression, strongly rejected suggestions made by his followers that women were evil or unworthy, and refused to make additions to the Adi Granth that would have reviled women.

Later, when the tenth guru, Gobind Singh, founded the Khalsa (the "pure"), the militant brotherhood of Sikhs to resist Muslim oppression in the seventeenth century, the company was open to both sexes and all classes. The sacrificial dedication was made to the goddess Durga (Kali); Gobind's wife, Jita, participated in the initiation ceremony; and the initiates, refuting caste taboos, all drank from the same container. Thus, women were initiated into the Khalsa taking the name Kaur, or princess (while the men became Singh, or lion) and were expected to perform the same duties as men. They could worship with men in temples and they were not expected to be veiled or secluded. But polygamy, concubinage, and suttee were prolonged well into the nineteenth century, in part because of the propensities of the Sikh ruler Ranjit Singh and in part because of northern Indian mythology. Kabir extolled the sacrifices made by Sur, the Rajput hero who died fighting, and Sati, his wife, who immolated herself to be reunited with him in the hereafter. To Kabir and his followers the actions of these two mythical figures expressed perfect loyalty and love to God, which real human beings should emulate.

These Hindu practices within Sikhism were condemned by most Sikhs; hence, by 1945 a Rehat Maryada, or guide to the Sikh way of life, was approved by the Sikh shrine committee.

---

*Guru Nanak lived during the fifteenth and sixteenth centuries.

Sikhs were told how to have nothing to do with caste, ideas of pollution, full-moon ceremonies, wearing sacred threads, or praying at tombs. Infanticide was condemned outright, as was child-marriage. Other men's wives should be respected as one's own mother, and their daughters as one's own. A man should enjoy his wife's company and women should be loyal to their husbands. Women should not be veiled and caste should have no place in marriage.[24]

While the social mingling of the sexes is somewhat restricted among all but the most Westernized Sikhs, including within their schools, marriages are less arranged than assisted to ensure the wife's compatability with the family. Moreover, the marriage ceremony, which is a combination of a religious one before the scripture (Guru Granth Sahib) and a civil service, recognizes women's rights and attempts to protect them. This recognition of women's value and equality continues to be evinced in the open pride and self-confidence with which most Sikh women conduct themselves in public—at their temples, or gurudwaras, in the marketplace, among the men, and in private within their homes.

By the end of the eighteenth century, India's culture and Hinduism's spirituality were at their nadir, their strength and creativity sapped by the lengthy Muslim domination. Likewise, the changes introduced by the Portuguese (fourteenth century), the French (seventeenth century), and the British (eighteenth century) were too many and too quixotic for easy absorption by a beleaguered religion. Yet, foreign influence and domination cannot be entirely blamed for the lackluster performance of Hinduism.

Hinduism's later leaders must shoulder much of the responsibility for its decline and lethargic state. Their obsession for ritual and the multiple subcaste system became increasingly burdensome to society. Many customs, once created with the highest spiritual motives and for the greatest social benefit, became petrified with time. As they became more imbued with religiosity, they became more entrenched and disastrous for society. Wretched practices like suttee, which the Muslims tried but failed to eliminate and which the British eventually eradicated; child marriage and infibulation; caste excesses and ritualistic aberrations became coated in holiness and were allowed to continue unabated. Such practices in the name of religion or its counterpart, social convention, parasitically drained the intellectual growth and moral conscience of India's leaders and people, diminished interest in learning, and lowered the already low status of Hindu women.

Hinduism's leaders, often of the upper castes, had become obsessed with achieving and communicating "higher" religious/spiritual experiences. Consequently, they neglected the masses and their need for not only religious and spiritual sustenance but also material and social guidance. They ignored Hinduism's historic perspective and avoided its pragmatic aspects. By preserving outmoded conventions for power's sake, they inadvertently undermined the foundations of Hinduism and left it too weak to support the overwhelming flood of changes.

Although Western influence has been (and continues to be) severely castigated by nationalists, it was Western Christian missionaries who provided the impetus to certain Hindu religious leaders to effect both religious and social reforms. Through their efforts, including some of the first translations of Hinduism's holy scriptures into readable form for the masses, they helped to infuse Hinduism with a new vitality.

Catholic missions and British administrators alike were as reluctant in the 1600s as development planners are today to interfere with the status quo of religion or culture in India. They generally avoided influencing or upsetting local customs and religion and declined to recommend or implement reforms. In fact, British political domination and Western religious tradition had surprisingly little impact on either the public's religion or its customs. Not surprisingly they were subsequently roundly criticized for not attempting to effect reforms that might have eased or eliminated some of the more debilitating quasi-religious practices.

Eventually, however, the repugnancy of practices like suttee and female infanticide or mutilation did motivate some missionaries, such as the Protestant William Carey (1761-1834), to advocate specific reforms: the elimination of suttee, the prohibition of child marriage, and the allowance of widow remarriage, among others, that, as it happened, most benefited females. Nevertheless, some of the strongest proponents of reform were an educated minority of Indians.

Those Indians,* knowledgeable about the rationalism and positivism of Western secular culture and the inherent social concerns of Christianity and of the world's other major religions, felt that one of Hinduism's main weaknesses was its lack of humanitarianism, social concern, and involvement. They also believed that India and Hinduism had jointly embarked upon misguided paths. They were highly

---

*Among them were Raja Ram Mohan Roy (1772-1833); Kesub Chunder Sen (1838-84); Dyanand Sarasvati (1824-83); Sri Ramakrishna (1836-86) and his disciple Swami Vivekananda (1863-1902), founders of the Ramakrishna movement; Rabindranath Tagore (1861-1941); Aurobindo Ghose (1872-1950); Mahatma Gandhi (1869-1948); and Jawaharlal Nehru (1889-1964).

conscious that "many of these [Indian] customs derived from very
noble religious intentions and were, undoubtedly, from a religious
point of view, extremely meritorious for those performing them.
But India, with its tendency to press things to their extremes, whether
speculative or practical, had entered into extremes that needed cor-
rection."[25]

From Roy to Nehru, these reformers sought a broad reformation of Hinduism and its inherent social systems, for they abhorred
the many social and religious abuses committed in the guise of Hinduism. Therefore, they sought not the abandonment of Hinduism but
its transformation and renewal by infusing it with a new spiritual zeal,
a greater social awareness. However, unlike their predecessors, the
reform efforts of Tagore, Gandhi,* and Nehru were assisted by the
impact of industrialism, communications, education, movies, transportation, socialism, and secularism on India's social fabric. Yet
they, too, did not produce enduring reforms in the areas of caste,
women's isolation and emancipation, and priestly control, in the main
because they would not—or could not—frontally confront and dissemble
those institutions.

For a while these visionaries managed to redirect Hinduism.
In some instances they did infuse it with a new spiritual vision, a
vision often retrieved from the earlier, less-mangled Vedas. In
other instances they infused it with a social pragmatism and made the
religion a servant of the people in their daily social and political lives.
Sometimes they managed to banish injurious customs. Since many
of the reforms advocated directly benefited females, the reformers
encountered frequent resistance if not outright hostile opposition
to their proposals. As a consequence of this hostility and because
of their own ambivalence toward female emancipation, various reforms were either dropped or watered down into uselessness. If
these visionaries had developed a greater consciousness of women's
worth and women's need, they might have better resisted social pressure to renege on reforms that would have helped women and their
development. The ambivalence toward women is clearly seen in the
writings and past actions of such luminaries as Tagore, Gandhi, and
Swami Prabhupada.

---

*Gandhi and his Nationalist movement tried to reform caste from
within Hinduism. His efforts were enhanced by the British alleviating
the worse abuses of caste and providing the Outcastes with equality
before the law and access to British-controlled schools. Gandhi's
persistence resulted in India's 1948 Constituent Assembly passing
legislation abolishing untouchability in any form and a legacy of legislation moderating caste thereafter.

Linked with their social and religious reforms, certain reformers used Hinduism as a political rallying point for creating a nationalist resurgence of pride to overthrow colonialism. For that specific purpose they encouraged Hindu women to break the bonds of tradition and purdah and to embark upon a course of political action for "God and country." This participation in the struggle for national independence as much as any social or religious reforms helped for a while to improve women's position and status in India. Yet in a sense women were used, as they have been in other liberationist struggles. Once colonialism was overthrown, women were urged or compelled back into their homes. Their usefulness was over.

Undoubtedly, the nineteenth-century and twentieth-century reformers tried to alter the depressed condition of their people. Directly and indirectly they affected women's status and position. They tried to give Indians access to those economic, cultural, and spiritual benefits traditionally experienced by India's upper social and economic groups. And in part they succeeded. But the momentum they launched appears to be wavering. Historically, this is not unusual. As Hume noted, "During more than half of its entire history Hinduism has had conscious protests and endeavours for improvement. But for the most part these have been ineffective."[26] The low status of women, caste, and priestly control have prevailed despite the onslaughts of new religions, sects, and reformers. Inexorably, Hinduism has absorbed to near annihilation the diverse rebellious elements. Buddhism became reduced to minuscule numbers. Jainism, founded by Mahavira in 557 B.C. in protest against inequality and the exclusivity of the Brahmin priests, declined to a stable, fairly prosperous following of six million to ten million adherents. Sikhism became largely confined to the Punjab.

Individual reformers and their attempts at reform have fared equally badly.* Where they preached religious tolerance and established new sects to practice that dictum, their adherents converted the sects into yet other subcastes. Where they preached sexual equality, their followers eschewed their wisdom and practiced sexual excesses in the worship of Vishnu or some other deity. And where they urged caste equality, their followers became undisciplined and divisive. As might be expected, women were buffeted by the winds of these reform movements but eventually gained little from them as both they and the reforms subsided into the morass of tradition.

---

*Ramanuja (twelfth century A.D.) preached freely to all to overcome caste exclusiveness and women's separation. Madhva (A.D. 1119-99) created a new sect. Ramananda (fourteenth to fifteenth century A.D.) preached religious tolerance for all. Chaitanya (A.D. 1485-1527) urged equality of castes and individuals.

Today Hinduism seems to be drifting backward into a spiritual and social void. It lacks outstanding leaders to expand its horizons and to make it a socially effective force. Its myriad movements—the Brahma Samaj (society of God),* Arya Samaj (society of noble persons), Ramakrishna,† and various ashrams—have faded in any real significance. Their numbers are relatively few, their organizations splintered, their social and religious messages diffuse. Except to their inward-looking followers—a scant few in the sea of millions—their impact is negligible. For the moment Hinduism lacks a leader of vision and stature who can propel Hinduism into becoming an effective force for social development and the positive spiritual revival necessary to such development.

Palpably, Hinduism pervades every corner of Indian society. It is religion, culture, and social mores. It is economics and politics, and it is more. It is intangible but real; diffuse but solid. If it is ignored by development planners and policy makers, it is ignored at the peril of development and change. "Despite India's claim to being a secular state, religion's involvement in politics is a central aspect of Indian national life, and it appears to some observers to be an increasing rather than a diminishing factor at both the local and national level."[27] This sentiment is echoed by K. P. Karunakaran, who is adamant that "no one who knows anything about the political developments of modern India can minimize the importance of the study of the interrelation between religion and politics in the country."[28] A case in point is the present Sikh desire for autonomy within India, a campaign that is not merely motivated by nationalism or politics but equally by religion. As the most militant of the Sikh fundamentalist leaders of the Akali Dal party of the Punjab, Jarnail Singh Bhindranwale, said, "Politics and religion are inseparable to the Sikhs but religion is more important than politics."[29]

Increasingly, political and economic demands are being couched in religious terms, often of the most fundamentalist variety, by various Hindu sects or religious minorities. What will be the ultimate consequences for women? Will the economic, social, and political gains they have made once again be usurped by religion's power bro-

---

*Founded by Ram Mohan Roy during the 1820s to undo the injustices perpetrated on females and by caste rigidities, it became reduced to a handful of thousands.

†Founded by Sri Ramakrishna and continued by his disciple in the mid-1800s as a social betterment movement, eventually it became a vehicle for the deification and worship of Ramakrishna, a source of dubious Eastern wisdom for discontented Western youth, and a reinforcement of sexual inequality and female passivity.

ers? It follows that sensible answers can only be given if studies of the interrelationships of religion's politics and economics are undertaken and implications for women's future in that context are well considered.

NOTES

1. Rigveda 10:90:12, in Robert E. Hume, The World's Living Religions, rev. ed. (New York: Charles Scribner's Sons), 1959.

2. F. Max Müller, ed., The Laws of Manu, The Sacred Books of the East, vol. 25 (Delhi: Motilal Banarsidass, 1967), 9:1-220.

3. Manmohan Kaur, The Role of Women in the Freedom Movement (1857-1947) (Delhi: Sterling, n.d.), p. 1.

4. Hume, The World's Living Religions, p. 25.

5. Will Durant, Our Oriental Heritage, The Story of Civilization, vol. 1 (New York: Simon & Schuster, 1954), p. 401.

6. Müller, The Laws of Manu, 9:2-11.

7. Ibid., 9:12-16, 77-80.

8. Ibid., 9:80-83.

9. Ibid., 9:74-76.

10. Ibid., 9:104-219.

11. Ibid.

12. Ibid., 10:1.

13. Ibid., 10:3.

14. Ibid., 10:6.

15. Ibid., 12:1-68.

16. Ibid., 12:69.

17. Rabindranath Tagore, Chitra: A Play in One Act (New York: Macmillan, 1916).

18. A. C. Bhaktivedanta Swami Prabhupada, Bhagavad-Gita as It Is (Los Angeles: Bhaktivedanta Book Trust, 1972), pp. 14, 128.

19. Philip H. Ashby, Modern Trends in Hinduism (New York: Columbia University Press, 1974), p. 128.

20. Ibid., pp. 62-63. See also G. Morris Carstairs, The Twice Born: A Study of a Community of High Caste Hindus (London: Hogarth Press, 1961).

21. Ashby, Modern Trends, p. 61.

22. Ibid., p. 70.

23. John B. Noss, Man's Religions (New York: Macmillan, 1974), p. 227.

24. Geoffrey Parrinder, Sex in the World's Religions (Don Mills, Ontario: General, 1980), p. 69.

25. Thomas Berry, Religions of India: Hinduism, Yoga, Buddhism (New York: Bruce, 1971), p. 66.

26. Hume, The World's Living Religions, p. 34.

27. Ashby, Modern Trends in Hinduism, p. 92.
28. Ibid., quoting K. P. Karunakaran.
29. V. G. Kulkarni, "The Sword of Separatism, Far Eastern and Economic Review, December 10–16, 1982, p. 26.

3

HINDUISM
AND
EDUCATION

Education in India might be said to be "integrally connected
with the 'dharma' of a community,"[1] a connection extending back to
Vedic times and accounting for the innate respect and tolerance Hindus have for learning, especially of a spiritual nature.

The beginnings of education commenced at least 3,500 years
ago in the forest schools, or tapovanas, of Vedic India, where gurus
orally taught the Vedas to successive generations of disciples and expected phenomenal feats of memorization. Before writing committed
the Vedas and other Hindu scriptures to paper, Hindu education could
be traced through the sruti and smitri literary traditions first initiated
by those forest rishis trying to amalgamate Aryan and non-Aryan concepts. The tapovanas, despite being secluded from urban influences
and primarily devoted to spiritual learning, also encouraged cultural
and practical knowledge.

A host of art forms multiplied from the early Vedic gatherings
around ubiquitous sacrificial altars.* A truly educated and therefore
cultured Aryan was expected to be completely familiar with these.
Similarly, since each tapovana had to be economically self-sufficient,
every dedicated student was expected to acquire practical skills by
helping his teacher and the guru's family with their agricultural and
household chores.

A student's education varied considerably, being determined by
his access to gurus, his affluence, and his Aryan or non-Aryan affilia-
tion. As with early Muslim education, the first Hindu students traveled widely seeking highly esteemed teachers. Completing studies on

---

*These included lyrics, legends, music, drama, poetry, history,
and recitals.

one topic with an esteemed guru, they would move on to another teacher
and another subject. A set curriculum, or universal education, was
unheard of. But the tapovanas came close to providing both to wide-
spread Indian students seeking a broad-based curriculum and, as a
consequence, flourished. Moreover, they flourished because they
were also conservers and propagators of Hindu culture.

Before the Upanishadic period, when princely courts stimulated
education and when only a limited intermingling of Aryan and non-
Aryan values, customs, and education occurred, Aryan and non-Aryan
education were essentially different and apart. Aryan educational
centers actually originated on their sacrificial grounds, while non-
Aryan places of learning arose at their holy spots, or tirthas, with
Varanasi on the holy Ganges being the most famous. There non-Vedic
philosophies like yoga or Jainism prevailed, and great conferences for
the spiritually minded were convened.

Different values and attitudes that eventually led to separate educational systems also arose from diametrically opposed practices.
The non-Vedic, indigenous cultures emphasized moksha, mukti and
nirvana, nonviolence (ahimsa), nonslaying of cows, vegetarianism,
and ancestral worship. The Vedic peoples emphasized sacrifices and
offerings, nonvegetarianism, and cow slaying in honor of guests or
for spirit propitiation. And the Aryans, long before caste became
entrenched, excluded India's indigenous inhabitants and even the original Aryan settlers from their rituals and centers of learning. The
submersion of non-Aryan or non-Vedic values by Aryan values and
the domination of non-Aryan attitudes by Aryan were eventually to
have repercussions on female education.

During the early Vedic and Upanishadic times, girls were given
some access to education and occasionally figured among the students
in the tapovanas. Because of the ambivalence shown toward women
by custom and the scriptures, female students typically came from
unusual or powerful families unfettered by social convention or pressure or were of exceptional brilliance and determination. Apologists
regularly single out Maitreyi, wife of the philosopher Yajnavalkya,
or the philosopher Gargi Vacaknavi to demonstrate that women did
participate in ancient educational gatherings.

Notwithstanding their paucity of numbers, during the Upanishadic
period, when the Kshatriyas began to regain power from the Brahmins,
women began to enjoy, for a short while, an equal eminence with men.
However, once the Vedic sacrifices became monopolized by the Brahmins, women were virtually excluded from all ceremonialism. The
Brahmins, intent upon inspiring awe and dominance, had forbidden
all castes but themselves to teach the Vedas and had prohibited the
Sudras, the Untouchables, and all women, including their own wives,
from studying the holy scriptures. With religion, ceremonialism, and

learning being totally intertwined, such exclusion automatically con-
ferred an inferior status on these groups. The prohibition was disastrous for female education and intellectual development. Its rever-
berations have been felt to the present, as witnessed by the existing
low female literacy rates in India and the resistance to the education
of girls and women.

In the four stages (ashramas) of an ideal Hindu life, the first
stage is the brahmacharya, or active student period of education,
hard work, and discipline. Hindus have, theoretically at least, "always expected that disciplined education should be considered the
prime religious duty of youth"[2] and have accordingly believed that a
sound education should embrace knowledge (jnana), physical and mental discipline (yoga), and religious and spiritual development. Therefore, religious people, including the Brahmins but not them exclu-
sively, also taught literature, medicine, agriculture, grammar, logic,
mathematics, culture, and practical skills. Females were, however,
rarely the recipients of such knowledge, since the four ashramas
were construed as affecting males, not females.

The brahmacharya stage was thus directed at male youth, who
in order to concentrate mightily on their work, were expected to maintain celibacy until they were entitled to enter the married householder,
or grihastha, stage. The introduction of girls into the tapovanas was
therefore strongly opposed on the basis that they would upset the discipline imposed on boys to ensure the preservation of that state of
celibacy and purity deemed necessary for the male students' knowledge
and enlightenment. In this way male celibacy and tapovana discipline,
along with brahminical aversion to instructing women and the exclusion of women from religious (and hence educating) duties, were invoked as further reasons to deny education to females.

Women's modest educational and intellectual gains during the
Upanishadic period and Buddhist era did not last long. Once brahminical power was regained, the more liberal-minded Kshatriyas weakened, and Buddhism's influence lessened. A major contributor to this
demise was the Code of Manu, which so decisively affected every facet
(spiritual, ceremonial, dietary, customary, family, burial, inheritance, and caste among other things) of each individual's daily life.

The Laws of Manu fully detailed the relationship of a student
with his teacher; his acts of duty and devotion; the ritualistic forms
of greeting, cleansing, and addressing before studying the Vedas; and
the method of controlling senses and organs during Vedic studies.[3] It
specifically, if not conveniently, enjoined Brahmins to teach the Vedas,
and Kshatriyas and Vaisyas to study them. However, it denied hope
to anyone, no matter how learned in the Vedas, of becoming equivalent
to a Brahmin in stature, respect, or influence. A 10-year-old Brahmin, unschooled and untutored, was deemed to have precedence over

a 90-year-old Kshatriya or Vaisya. A Sudra could anticipate only a grain of the respect accorded to the upper castes by dint of reaching the age of 100, not by mental, spiritual, or physical exertions. Since women were equated with Sudras, they could not anticipate being accorded much respect unless they lived to a ripe old age, had borne numerous children, and were not widowed.

The Code of Manu also carefully delineated the gradations of respect. [4] Kshatriyas might receive some respect for valor and Vaisyas because of wealth or commercial gain, but Brahmins acquired their venerableness, power, and seniority from the acquisition of sacred knowledge. An acharya, or Brahmin who teaches the Vedas, was to be given the highest regard, superior to that given to a student's natural father. A student's mother, deemed to gain stature from motherhood and the concept of the bountiful mother earth, was surprisingly, to be treated by the pupil as a thousand times more venerable than the father but as an unworthy compared with a teacher of the Vedas.

The Laws of Manu further dictated the behavior of pupils in the presence of their teachers, and even in the presence of their teachers' wives, who by osmosis acquired a semblance of the status and regard accorded to the Vedic teachers. [5] Otherwise, Manu cautioned against the untrustworthy nature of women and their propensity to seduce or lead astray fools and learned men alike. By urging the avoidance of women's company, including that of a student's own mother, sister, or daughter, the Code served to stop females, including the near relations of teachers, from entering the Vedic school system or being taught by their brothers, sons, and fathers.

Nevertheless, the Laws recognized the different aptitudes of individuals for studying and recommended varying lengths of study accordingly. At one extreme, truly dedicated students could spend their lifetimes in the service of a qualified teacher. Other students, seeking to fulfill the next three stages of life, could limit their studies to 36, 18, or 9 years, or even less if they had perfectly learned the Vedas. Since child marriage and early motherhood were the customary norm, even if females had been permitted to study the Vedas, the time and opportunity available to them for education would have been extremely limited. Is the situation much different in India today with the lack of universal, compulsory education beyond the age of 11, child marriages, and the poor enforcement of dowry or school-attendance laws?

Gradually the law givers, with Manu being the first and foremost, eroded what little position women had. They categorically stated that only men had a right to "higher" (eventually interpreted to mean "any") learning. Men then became defined to include only the Brahmins, Kshatriyas, and Vaisyas. However, with the development of the bhakti, or devotional cults; the replacement of the older Vedic teachers, or acharyas, with a new class of guru; and the democratization of centers of learning by removing them from the sacrificial ground to public bathing and pilgrimage places, women were allowed minimal participation in educational and religious pursuits. But tradition dies hard. Since religion and education were mutually inclusive, the basic exclusion of women from the religious sphere essentially meant rejection from, or diminution in, the other.

The rising and falling fortunes of women during the evolution of Hinduism can be traced through the copious Hindu literature (surpassing Buddhism's Pali Canon of 136 volumes). Unfortunately, relatively few Indians, including university graduates, have been able to read the literature for themselves. They therefore have not been able to see how Hinduism has evolved or changed or to understand what considerable influences have emanated from the literature for the good or ill of the general public. As noted before, much of the entrenched resistance to women's development or education can be traced through the literature to the sources that either proclaimed women's limited rights and extensive duties or declaimed against their worth, their spirituality, or their need for education and freedom.

Education in Indian terms, until very recent times, essentially consisted of being familiar with Hinduism's far-reaching canonical literature. Whether in the oral or written tradition, the opportunity to acquire that knowledge was mainly confined to the few—the Brahmins, the aristocratic Kshatriyas, and a handful of inquisitive Vaisyas. However, some pre-Vedic and early Vedic women were thought to have participated in early discussions with the rishis and to have been a vital vehicle for carrying on the oral tradition of Hindu literature from one generation to another. However, their role, like that of the Sudras, even the rishis themselves, was gradually circumscribed and eroded as the priests extended their power and skillfully removed competition from their orbit. Women have still been the main instruments for conveying orally the values, culture, and history of their people from generation to generation, but having been excluded from the fonts of knowledge, their oral tradition took on a mythical, superstitious quality. Manipulated and turned back on itself, this served to mire women in the prejudices and antipathies of the ages.

The first sruti (infallible, divine revelations) of the rishis ("forest-dwelling, saintly seers of the early Vedic period") were the Vedas. These were followed by the Brahmanas (ritual books or priestly writings) and Aranyakas (forest meditations), the Upanishads (Hinduism's highest form of intuitive visions), and the later Vedanta. *

---

*Various dates have been ascribed to the origins of the Vedas: between 1500 and 1200 B.C. or between 900 and 700 B.C.

Of the four collections of Vedic hymns, the Rigveda was probably the most important, being a virtual synthesis of the other three and a repository of Vedic Hinduism's most imaginative, profound thought and religious speculation.* It vividly depicts Hinduism's early mythology, its rituals and original deities. Altogether, it is an invaluable document for showing the evolution and flux of Hinduism through the centuries.

The Vedas graphically chart the fortunes of Hinduism's female and male deities, who emerge, gain public prominence, and decline. A local tribal god, Krishna, emerges as Vishnu's avatar, or human manifestation. Vishnu, once a nondescript Vedic god, arises from obscurity and becomes the Supreme Deity in Hinduism—until, that is, Hinduism split into two sects: Vishnu and Shiva. The destructive Shiva, an emanation of another fierce, pre-Aryan god, Rudra, thus escapes the oblivion that overwhelmed other equally prominent deities. Varuna, once the most highly regarded, omnipotent god, becomes merged with Brahman, the nameless and formless Supreme Reality, and practically disappears. And a lesser deity absorbs Indra, the upholder of human order. But goddesses especially suffer obscurity in extremis.

The importance of women in a society can almost be measured by the prominence of goddesses in the religious lexicon. A correlation seems to exist between the value attached to females and the number and influence of female deities. In pre-Vedic times, goddesses, including Prithivi, representing the earth, and Sita, the "furrow-in-the-field" who helps all growth, were well represented in religious thought. Gradually, their importance was diminished and they were relegated to a secondary role, with one unique exception, Kali. And that ferocious but occasionally benevolent goddess attained such prominence that a new sect was created and temples raised in her honor.

The Vedas also illustrate how totemism and animism became transformed into philosophic pantheism and transmigration.† Thus,

---

*Rigveda, Atharvaveda, Samaveda, and Yajurveda. Atharvaveda, or book of magic, was a collection of Aryan and non-Aryan traditions: home rituals, good and evil spells, popular prayer and worship procedures, and some speculative thought. Samaveda and Yajurveda were essentially collections of ritual hymns to be recited by priests at complicated public sacrifices (such as the soma) or by the public at their simpler, private sacrifices.

†Reverence for the cow and cow worship are thought to have arisen directly from totemism, or the adoption of a natural object or animal as a symbol of a tribe or clan, which is then often worshipped or propitiated.

over time the Vedas prescribed ever more new altars and complex
sacrificial rituals to invoke or propitiate a proliferating number of
spirits. However, the sacrifices were basically symbolic or magical, achieving spirit propitiation with goats and sheep; sacred fire;
soma; or, for very special occasions, a horse, rather than human
sacrifices in the style of Zoroastrian Persia.

As the complexity of rituals grew, so did the priests grow more
essential, more expensive, and more demanding. Ever quick to enhance their power, mystery, and prestige, they departed from the
oral tradition and wrote the Brahmanas, which established the regulations for the minutiae of daily life, the proper ceremonies and ritualistic usages, and a schedule of priestly fees and rights. The departure from the oral tradition was one more nail in the coffin of women's
inclusion in religious learning and the acquisition of knowledge.

Until this period—circa 900-800 B. C.—writing was rare.
Knowledge of early India was transmitted orally, either by scholars
in Sanskrit or by ordinary people in their local dialect (rather as they
still do today). When writing was introduced by either the Dravidian
or Hindu traders, bringing a Semitic script (akin to Phoenician) from
western Asia, it was quickly adopted by the Brahmin priests and used
as another device for keeping the populace in not-so-blissful ignorance.
With the Brahmanas becoming virtually the first sruti to be transmitted by script, the priests increased their dominance. And "slowly the
Brahmans became a privileged hereditary caste, holding the mental
and spiritual life of India under a control that threatened to stifle all
thought and change."[6] A stranglehold on education was thus maintained, and men as well as women were to be hindered in learning to
read the scriptures or to write.

While the Brahmanas have been regarded as a regressive step
for Hinduism, overlapping with that period was the beginning of the
Upanishadic era.* Many scholars believe that Hinduism achieved its
highest pinnacles of speculative thought and philosophy then. Like
other Hindu literature and even Hinduism itself, the Upanishads represented to seekers of knowledge a banquet of different philosophies,
answers, and interpretations. But basic to all was the central idea
of the Upanishads, Tat tvam asi, or "thou art that": the fusion of
subjective, personal Atman, or true Self, with the objective, impersonal Brahman, or Absolute, with both becoming One. Thus, the ultimate source of creativity is within one's self and vice versa. In
this it can be seen that Brahman is as central to Upanishadic litera-

_____

*This can probably be divided into three periods: the early Upani-
shads, 800-500 B. C.; the later Upanishads, after 500 B. C.; and the
Upanishads as reorganized by Shankara, eighth century A. D.

ture and Hinduism as God is central to Christian or Muslim thought. Consequently, Hindu scholars maintain that Hinduism, despite its pantheon of deities, is a monotheistic rather than polytheistic religion, and that the gods—not the priests—merely represent an intermediary path to Brahman and ultimate salvation.

The intellectual probings of the Upanishads combined with the rampant sacerdotalism and excessive ritualism to inspire disparate groups—skeptics, materialists, sophists, atheists, and nihilists—to rebel against the priests and their power. But these rebels also denied the sacredness of the Vedas and the Upanishads, so they developed contrary philosophies and godless religions. They reacted against the prevailing, priest-ridden theology for ethical reasons. To them the prevalent morality was mere social convention, not divine ordination, and the existing religion was a supreme convention to fool fools with. They despised the corruption, the discrimination, the abuse of power, and the denigration of men and women. They sought a freedom or openness in the flow of knowledge and resented the priests' strictures that prevented women and youth from engaging in philosophical deliberations. And they sought a new morality: good works, respect for all life (male or female, human or animal), and renunciation to achieve salvation.

The dissenters temporarily caused a decline of brahminical Hinduism, especially during 500 and 300 B.C., but few made a substantial dent in Hinduism. The others were soon obliterated by their mightier, more numerous enemies, the priests. In fact, the Upanishads had inadvertently hindered reform attempts and had sanctified the caste system and the priests' power by declaring that the caste system was a direct emanation of Brahman. Furthermore, attempts at institutional reform were nullified by the Laws of Manu. Nevertheless, a most influential revolutionary movement arose out of the Charvakas and other materialists. It caused the birth of two new religions—Buddhism and Jainism*—and strengthened a third, Zoroastrianism. Both Buddhism and Jainism were of the Nastika, or nihilistic, school, being ascetic and pessimistic, atheistic, and devotional but without a god. It is not wholly surprising that the founders of the two new religions should have been of the Kshatriya class, which had consistently rebelled against the prevailing sacerdotal ceremonialism, theology, and religious power of the priests. In essence the struggle between the Kshatriyas and Brahmins was a struggle for the minds of the people and control over their mental and spiritual knowledge and education. In reality the revolutionary philosophy of the Charvakas ended the Vedic and Upanishadic era; weakened the Brahmins' hold on

---

*See Chapter 3.

the mind of India; and left a temporary vacuum into which new religions could be insinuated, until Hinduism reasserted itself and effortlessly assimilated them.

The end of the Upanishadic period presaged the beginnings of the reaction and renaissance period (600 B.C. to A.D. 300) with its new religious and philosophical doctrines. Hinduism began to evolve away from pure ritualism toward bhakti as the supreme course of salvation.* As a consequence of the trend toward bhakti, with its inherent sense of personal involvement in one's own religious devotions, and the more egalitarian concepts contained within Buddhism, more opportunities became available to women to participate fully in their chosen religion without priestly intervention or domination. They and the general populace, having been relentlessly ignored, became primary targets for the priests seeking to recapture their preeminence. To reach and cajole them, the sacred teachings were expanded, and the popular Epics,† the Ramayana and the Mahabharata, were written. To this day town and village audiences assiduously follow the adventures of their heroes and heroines of these smitri Epics and listen spellbound to the Bhagavad Gita, the glorious sacred poem within the Mahabharata. In this way the masses were educated in the mores and values of their religion and culture, and heroines were given public prominence. In fact the Epics have been recognized by a few reformers or development planners as an excellent educational vehicle. Thus, a stage play in India, the ramwong dance in Thailand, and the wayang-kulit in Java and Singapore, each interpreting the Epics according to the tradition of the country, are used to convey new ideas about women, family planning, nutrition, and agriculture to spellbound audiences.

The affection of the masses for the Gita, which has virtually attained sruti status, largely springs from the poem's offering of universal salvation, opportunity, and hope to all, including Sudras and women. It was exceptional among Hindu scriptures for acknowledging that women had traditionally been equated with lower birth. It was unique in recognizing that women could have the attributes of memory, speech, intelligence, fame, and fortune (apart from the conventionally prescribed virtues of faithfulness and patience). It eased the masses' thralldom to the priests by granting that women and the lower classes, through devotional service, could have the same rights and privileges of access to the ultimate Supreme Being

---

*Bhakti implies devotion to a personal deity and through that intermediary ultimately to the Supreme Being.

†The Ramayana is the story of Rama's fight against the demon-king. The Mahabharata is the epic of India's creation.

as the "twice-born": "They who take refuge with Me, though of the womb of six—women, vaisyas, even sudras, they also tread the Highest Path."[7]

The Gita thus not only opened the way to spiritual salvation hitherto denied to women, but it opened up the way for women to acquire learning and to become educated. Unfortunately, it fell short by failing to exhort the specific better treatment of women and the lower classes. Hence, its actual effect on improving their status was minuscule. Even latter-day pundits, such as Swami Prabhupada, have conveniently ignored the Gita's assertion of equality in their determination to use the ancient Laws of Manu to restrict modern women's freedom and to deny them education or equality.

The Bhagavad Gita complemented the Upanishads by expanding Hinduism's four main doctrines of theism, devotionalism, avatars, and salvation through divine grace into seven concepts. Dharma, or a person's basic duties in life, emerged as Hinduism's most important concept and word, while nonattachment or self-detachment became the prerequisite for fulfilling that dharma; and the remaining five concepts eased life's burden of duties. Implicit within these concepts was the promise of a better life. Yet the Bhagavad Gita kept the spiritual (and social) gates closed to the lower castes and women by first reaffirming the words of Manu about the "inherent, unchangeable nature and function of the four castes" and then by attributing caste creation to the new avatar, Krishna. Women, equated with the lower-caste Sudras and therefore deemed to be possessed of an inherent, unchangeable nature and function, were again inhibited from striving upward to reach their spiritual or intellectual potential. Once again they were mired down by theological ambivalence and convention.

During the renaissance period,* new concepts, philosophies, religions, and literature vigorously intermingled and flourished. Although dates are vague and imprecise, "During this period almost all the main concepts and practices of orthodox Hinduism were developed."[8] Hinduism was in a constant state of flux. It gave birth to new religions and to six separate philosophical systems. In return it was influenced by its progeny.

Hinduism moved closer to the masses while moderating the power of the Brahmin class. It attracted disparate groups responsive to varied ways of approaching God and Salvation. It developed greater flexibility in the higher realms of speculative thought and simultaneously greater rigidity in the lower reaches of daily ritual and religiosity. It synthesized Aryan and non-Aryan cultures and produced bhakti cults, Saivism, Vaishnavism and Shakti sects, avatars and trimurti. It

---

*This was approximately 600 B.C. to A.D. 300.

widened its appeal, especially through personal devotionalism, and attracted multitudes of the ignored and the forgotten. Not least among these were women who saw an opportunity to assume responsibility for their spiritual life and to attain a semblance of personal freedom. By having greater access to spiritual enrichment, the doors to mental learning opened a fraction for women before being slammed tight once again.

The fluidity of Hinduism and the quest for personal control were effectively halted by the priests' forceful implementation of the Manu-Samhita,* massive treatises on the rituals and codes of conduct to be observed by all good-living Hindus. Of all Hinduism's religious or quasi-religious documents, the Laws of Manu have especially been responsible for entrenching prejudicial attitudes about females and caste in the Indian people.† The Laws' multitudinous rules have removed most motivation from women or men to question their position in society or within the family or to remove discrimination, prejudices, and myths.

When modern religious leaders continue to use the Code of Manu as justification for restricting women's evolution and education on the basis that women should not be given freedom,[9] then it is little wonder that the masses cannot be persuaded to discard myths and prejudices about females, menstruation and pregnancy, caste, dietary habits, or contraception. Laws of recent vintage will not easily dethrone laws of ancient vintage, especially when the priesthood or the ultraorthodox are obdurately reluctant to accede to changes likely to damage their status or power. Modern laws will have only superficial impact unless they are vigorously implemented; unless the masses, especially women, are sufficiently educated to understand the benefits of the new laws; and unless religious leaders are persuaded of the need for change.

Through the legalistic and ritualistic devices of the Code of Manu, the brahminical priest class cleverly shunted aside the Kshatriyas, manipulated the masses into unthinking fear and automatic response, and rendered females helpless and hopeless. This was in contrast with pre-Manu India, where women had relative equality with men in Vedic sacrificial ceremonies and could even become priests. The Laws of Manu effectively removed any semblance of independence

---

*Manu-Samhita prescribes duties and rituals for every phase of human life, including dharmasutras, the methods by which social duties prescribed in the Manu-Samhita were to be performed, and grihyasutras, the regulations determining Hindu living patterns and home rituals.

†Varying dates for these have been given: circa 1200 B.C., 250 B.C., or first century A.D.

and made females totally dependent upon the males of their family—
father, husband, and son.

To further ensure women's dependency, the Code barred women
from learning the Vedas, other sacred texts, or sacramental rites.
In fact, the Code draws upon Vedic texts to demonstrate that women's
"incapacity" was a historic, immutable rule and that, accordingly,
they were incapable of independence and learning.[10] The Code managed to twist its property inheritance rules to include the inheritance
and transmission of learning and so ensured Brahmin superiority over
all and the increased depreciation of women, since "a Brahmana, be
he ignorant or learned, is a great divinity."[11] The attitude that the
Code thus engendered toward female education contributed to the violent opposition to teaching girls and women in the eighteenth and nineteenth centuries. And it is still reflected in India's present education
and literacy statistics, which show that female education at all levels
is less highly regarded than male.

The Laws developed a peculiar dual status for women. As unmarried females or their husbands' sexual partners, they were accorded low esteem but were redeemed if they succumbed to social pressures to commit suttee upon their husbands' deaths. But as the
mothers of their husbands' sons (girls were of little importance),
they were given worth.

The historical ambivalence shown toward females by Hindus was
firmly rooted in the Laws of Manu, but it is little different from the
traditional attitudes or uncreative prejudice displayed toward females
in the literature of most other religions. As individuals and as human
beings, females have customarily been denied by their respective religions status, equality, and respect. But, as mothers or breeders
of cannon fodder, farm workers, or money earners, they have been
catapulted into a superficially exalted state.

The Puranic period continued the massive spiritual and cultural
movement of the Epic era.* As the people moved toward a more de-
votional-theistic tradition, religion became more personal and less
priest directed. Puja and bhakti emerged as the preeminent forms of
Hindu worship, and new scriptures that could appeal to the masses
and incorporate all interests were composed.

The Puranas became the first basic scriptures of the new bhakti
Hinduism.† Essentially, they were a compendium of all Hinduism's
historical and doctrinal developments and thereby depicted Hinduism
as a "diversified unity," composed of deities, caste duties, festivals
and rituals, sectarian beliefs, and bhakti worship of Vishnu, Shiva,
Brahma, and their Shaktis. They amply demonstrate Hinduism's age-

---

*Circa A.D. 200 to A.D. 1200.
†Circa A.D. 400 to A.D. 1200.

old characteristic of absorption, not conversion, and portrayal of a truth as a dual-faced if not multifaceted entity rather than unidimensional.

The Puranas were remarkable in admitting the hitherto inadmissible—women and Sudras—into education in and guidance through the scriptures. Thus, in the eyes of the ultraorthodox, the new sectarian Hinduism committed a major heresy by welcoming in those formerly ostracized groups and giving them opportunities to study the scriptures.

The Agamas,* given full canonical authority, provided the guidelines for the worship and rituals essential to the Shiva and Vishnu sects within the new Hinduism and provided for fuller participation by women, who attracted by the greater freedom of the sects, had become major adherents. The Tantras,† complex and voluminous, became virtually a new sruti. Tantric writings, in their seeking of the Inner, Eternal Truth, touched on all facets of the human experience and placed man at the sacred center of the cosmos. They were unusual in emphasizing the female side of nature and of man as essential to the search for the truth. Accordingly, Tantric adherents appear to have exhibited more tolerance toward females than was customary. The Tantric school of Hinduism greatly influenced certain schools of Mahayana Buddhism and may have contributed toward the tolerance accorded Buddhist women in Mahayana Buddhist countries.

But it was the Hymns that best represented the genuine day-to-day religious feelings and experiences of the average Indian and, moreover, showed the enormous latent creativity, in song and writing, of women, Sudras, and Outcastes. The Hymns originated in the Tamil region of southern India, where people were little concerned with the history, doctrine, and rituals of orthodox, sectarian Hinduism and felt free to vent their devotion.‡ Eventually, this medium of expression became popular in the north, where other women, such as the fourteenth-century-poet-saint Lalla, composed poetic songs to Shiva and Vishnu. The Hymns helped women to demonstrate in a vivid public form their ability to read and write, to learn and teach, and to reach the heights of mental and spiritual creativity.

The Puranic period closed with the composition of the six collections of Vedanta Sutras,# with southern Indian theologians again demonstrating their creativity by amalgamating Vedic and Upanishadic

---

*Circa A.D. 500 to A.D. 1000.

†Circa A.D. 400 to A.D. 1000.

‡These originated in southern India, A.D. 600 to A.D. 900, and moved northward during A.D. 1500 to A.D. 1900. In a major departure from tradition, the Hymns were written in the local vernacular rather than in Sanskrit.

#This was circa A.D. 800 to A.D. 1100.

concepts with the new Hinduism.* Of particular importance, they hu-
manized Hinduism by bringing it to the masses, especially to the excluded groups of women, Sudras, and Outcastes. However, despite
their creative thrusts, they could not counteract the burgeoning impact of Islam and the resistance of the ultraorthodox. So Hinduism
entered into a decline, or at least a quiescent state, which evaded revival until the nineteenth century, and women lost what few gains they
had made in acquiring some knowledge and liberty. While Buddhism
and Islam altered the Hindu perception of women and their inclusion
in educational and spiritual matters,† they tended to take Hinduism
in diametrically opposed directions, with Islam eventually exerting
the most significant pull.

The advent of Western thought and Christianity in India in the
eighteenth and nineteenth centuries considerably influenced Hinduism
and its approach to education, social welfare, and women. Hindu
doctrines were less changed than viewed in a new light by Hinduism's
revivalist reformers. One of the foremost of these was Raja Ram
Mohan Roy. Roy agitated for the abolition of suttee; he questioned
the need for purdah; and he urged a broadening of education to include
the Western sciences. His successors similarly tried to reinterpret
Hinduism in the light of changing modern conditions. In addition,
they engaged in comprehensive social work and attempted to spread
education among the most socially depressed classes.

Since the majority of women were perceived to be among the
lowest of the lowly, it was inevitable that many Hindu reformers
should turn their attention to the needs of women and to advocate female education. Through their efforts the status of women improved
and education was opened to all females. But the weight of tradition
and religiosity hampered their efforts then and continues to undermine the efforts of their successors now. The power of 5,000 years
of tradition is evidenced by the continuing discrepancy between the
education levels of males and females, a discrepancy that appears to
be increasing. In 1951, 20 percent more Indian women than men were
illiterate; 30 years later, 37 million more women or 28 percent more
were illiterate. [12]

Girls constituted 39 percent of all primary level pupils in 1974,
which amounted to only a 2 percent increase over the 1964 level. Yet
this increase is expected to drop. The percentage of all girls between
the ages of five and 10 enrolled in primary school was 52 percent in
1975, up from 48 percent in 1970 and 27 percent in 1960. [13] As admirable as these increases are, the fact remains that only 38 percent

---

*Two of the most outstanding were Shankara (eighth century) and
Ramanuja (A.D. 1050–1137).
†See chapters on Buddhism and Islam.

of the pupils enrolled in primary grades are little girls. Girls still only comprise 31 percent of the secondary level students—up 8 percent since 1960—and 25 percent of the tertiary level students. At the third level their numbers had increased only slightly (2 percent) between 1965 and 1977, and most were concentrated in the humanities. [14]

In Asia the percentage rate of increase of girls enrolled in all three levels of education increased substantially during 1960-65, but slowed down appreciably and even declined during 1975-80. [15] If India follows Asia's pattern, at a time when the gap between male and female education is still very wide, the outlook for the expanded education of its girls and women is not especially good. Undoubtedly, India's burgeoning population and the enormity of educating vast numbers of children are preventing a rapid increase of female education at all levels. But those problems are exacerbated by the weight of custom and religious tradition, which counteracts educational measures to reduce female illiteracy and ignorance.

The potential for an increasing population of female illiterates is already firmly established. Moreover, it will ripen into full fruition if steps are not taken to enlist the support of customary religious teachers for the expansion of knowledge among the masses, female and male. As long as only 16 percent of India's young girls between 10 and 15 enter secondary school and at least 40 percent actually receive no primary education at all, [16] India's problems of population, economic growth, and social development will continue to worsen.

Religion has historically been and continues to be one of the main inhibitors of the education of females. It could be a major positive factor if the aid of its religious leaders could be enlisted to reinterpret its doctrine and traditions to accommodate modern trends. It could be a creative force, as it was during the Puranic and twentieth-century reform periods, if Hinduism's high-minded activist and intellectual qualities were revived and if the degenerative aspects of Hinduism, which have prevented the improvement of women's (and the lower castes') lot, were modified or eliminated.

Whether such a reform could be accomplished without the existence of a centralized religious authority guiding religious instructors throughout the country is another matter. Centralization in itself can be a barrier to social and educational reform. Centralized religious reform movements have been known to fall prey to a dampening combination of orthodoxy, conservatism, and apathy born out of a self-indulgent, smug religiosity that contemptuously dismisses the need to reform regressive practices and attitudes. Hinduism's diversified, unwieldy form does not easily lend itself to centralization and centrally directed reform. Nor does it presently have a charismatic leader who can persuasively nudge India's innumerable local spiritual

leaders toward reform and revised attitudes. Without either centralized authority or a charismatic leader, or without a concerted effort
to enlist the active support of religious leaders, the prognostication
for the rapid improvement of total female education, employing Hinduism as an agent of change, is poor.

NOTES

1. K. M. Sen, Hinduism (Middlesex: Penguin Books, 1961),
p. 52.

2. Ibid., p. 22.

3. F. Max Müller, The Laws of Manu, The Sacred Books of
the East, vol. 25 (Delhi: Motilal Banarsidass, 1967), 2:70-249;
3:1-4.

4. Ibid.

5. Ibid.

6. Will Durant, Our Oriental Heritage, The Story of Civilization, vol. 1 (New York: Simon & Schuster, 1954), p. 407.

7. Annie Besant, trans., The Bhagavad Gita: The Lord's Song,
9th ed. (Madras: Theosophical, 1955), p. 137.

8. Sir Norman Anderson, ed., The World's Religions (Grand
Rapids, Mich.: W. B. Eerdman, 1976), p. 157.

9. Swami Prabhupada, Bhagavad-Gita as It Is (New York:
Collier, 1972), pp. 731-32.

10. Müller, The Laws of Manu, 9:3, 9:18.

11. Ibid., 9:317.

12. United Nations Educational, Scientific and Cultural Organization, Statistical Yearbook—UNESCO, 1982 (Paris: UNESCO, 1983),
table 1.3, p. I-21.

13. Statistical Yearbook—UNESCO, 1976, p. 172.

14. Ibid., 1982, pp. III-109, III-204, III-311.

15. Ibid., table 2.4, p. II-16.

16. Ibid., pp. III-51-58.

4

HINDUISM
AND
POPULATION

The tenor of Hinduism is one of pronatalism; not in the organized sense of Catholicism nor in the scriptural sense of the Koran, but rather, in its loose, free-flowing concepts of reincarnation and birth-upon-birth, the ashrama stages of life, the need for sons to perform ancestral and ritualistic worship and of children to justify women's existence. The emphasis on natality arises indirectly from custom, reinforced by Hinduism's treasured scriptures, rather than from specific edicts of "be fruitful and multiply" emanating from a centralized authority.

In the Bhagavad Gita, Arjuna discourses with Lord Krishna about successive births and deaths. He comes to understand that many births of the Lord are necessary to counter the "decay of righteousness" (dharma) and the evolution of adharma (the opposite of dharma). As Krishna proclaims, "For the protection of the good, for the destruction of evil-doers, for the sake of firmly establishing righteousness (dharma) I am born from age to age."[1] From this, Hindus envisage not only that their Lord, the Almighty and All Mystical, should be reborn, but also that they themselves should be reborn to higher (or lower) orders depending upon their past good (or evil) actions. For them to hinder rebirth through the prevention of births would be detrimental to their spiritual evolution and consequently distasteful to them as practicing, devout Hindus.

However, within the Bhagavad Gita and other equally important Hindu texts, ample flexibility exists to counter heedless actions that arise out of Inertia (such as indiscriminate, energy-sapping procreation) and are therefore incompatible with Hindu concepts of Harmony and Motion (or balanced population and ecology).

Birth is accepted as a regular part of life and, more important, of the Infinity. Accompanying and of essence to each birth are Har-

mony, Motion, and Inertia, with the prevailing feature determining
the characteristics of the human body. This arises from the Krishna's
proclamation that "my womb is the great Eternal; in that I place the
germ, thence cometh the birth of all beings. . . . In whatsoever
wombs mortals are produced, . . . the great Eternal is their womb."[2]

The most desirable characteristic is conceived to be wisdom
(and hence, good action) born of Harmony. Motion is seen as producing "greed, outgoing energy, undertaking of actions, restlessness,
desire," and ultimately, pain, while Inertia is seen as breeding "dark-
ness, stagnation, and heedlessness and also delusion,"[3] a state of
senselessness, unwisdom. The Eternal Being, Krishna, is as definite
about seeking and performing actions leading to wisdom as he is adamant about avoiding bodily and spiritually destructive Inertia.

In a formal sense, Hinduism is not actually opposed to family
planning and birth control. Certainly by extrapolating to modern circumstances, Krishna's admonitions could be applied to the inertia that
afflicts India and threatens to undermine population and economic development programs. Nonetheless, informal prevailing customary
traditions reposing in history and now entrenched in Hinduism do act
as inhibitors. On the most fundamental level, Indian traditions are
very pronatalist and as such counteract population policies. A Hindu
woman's daily life abounds with religious significance, which in turn,
redounds with fertility symbolism. The prayers and blessings intoned
by priests at Hindu weddings are redolent with phrases promoting procreation and fertility. The worst curses harangued down upon the
heads of enemies are those of infertility. A major virtue sought is
philoprogenitiveness—but not at the risk of being adulterous, inces-
tuous, or premaritally sexually indulgent.

Generations have worshiped the sacred fertile cow; the lingam,
the phallic symbol ubiquitous to the temples and courtyards of Hinduism; and the yoni, the female sex organ. Fertility cults, descendants
of pre-Aryan times, have thrived and survived. Gods and goddesses
have been imbued with extraordinarily prolific sexuality and fertility,
Shaktis and matajis with great bountifulness. For such reasons, basic
attitudes toward fertility and procreation will not be readily changed.
Nor will change occur unless and until women are accorded greater
status, not only by their religion and its priests but by development
planners, who will need to be convinced that women are central to
good development rather than secondary or peripheral. Indeed, change
will not be easily effected, because Hinduism is an amalgam of formal
religion and informal customs; because it is many pronged, multi-
tiered, and diffuse; and because it defies easy analysis. Since Hinduism means something different to everyone and lacks centralized
structure or leadership, the task of altering its adherents' attitudes
toward sex, fertility, and contraception is rendered even more diffi-

cult than within the relatively unified structures of Islam and Christianity.

It is often contended that priests of Hindu and Muslim persuasion rarely oppose family planning on religious grounds. But mutual distrust, even in communities such as Ballabgarh where Hindus and Muslims have traditionally lived side by side,[4] has frequently led to opposition. Religious animosities, which caused bloodshed in the past, become mixed up with political grievances. Since neither faith wishes to be submerged or subjugated by the other, religious fears are deftly manipulated by religious and political leaders. Consequently, family-planning programs and women become victims as local priests encourage zealotry and promote procreation to counteract the other competitive faith.

In many areas priests have overtly opposed family planning and contraception on specific, though irrational, religious grounds. The extent of their opposition has varied, however, according to the prevailing cult and caste; the educational level of priests and public; and the degree of priestly influence over villagers. It has also depended upon the dynamism of and the community's confidence in local social workers and government representatives; the impact of clinics and educational programs on the villagers; the frequency of outside contacts; and the degree of family limitation sought by local women as a result of mutual support and exchanges of information. An inverse relationship seems to exist between the educational level of women and the strength of their networks and the actual influence of the local priests—the greater the women's education and networks, the less the influence of the priests.

Religious traditions pervade the life of Hindus of all castes and at all levels. Undoubtedly, "traditions are the hardest of all windmills to tilt at: They aren't solid; they are not only in the blood but in earth and rock and wind, an invisible essence of all."[5] They may be seen in superstitious beliefs in ghosts and witches and in the universal acceptance of begging, or sannyasi.* They may be seen in the Hindu tolerance and acceptance of the contradictions of life—optimism and pessimism, negativism and positivism—and in the Hindu insecurity with the outside world and within themselves. It would be presumptuous, however, to attribute mainly to women these superstitious beliefs and traditional attitudes. They are an all-embracing feature of the lives of the Hindus and are by no means limited to the uneducated and illiterate.

---

*Sannyasi is the vocation and dedication of ascetics who have renounced the material life and turned themselves toward the spiritual, sometimes as genuine saddhus, or holy men, sometimes as charlatans.

Religious traditions are shown in the ubiquitous beliefs in astrology and horoscopes, omens that demonstrate God's presence in or withdrawal from a venture, and charms designed to rout evil. Ultimately, these traditions can develop among Hindu devotees a preoccupation with their atman, or spark of God-life, which they believe will, if properly tended, merge with the divine soul (Parmatma).

Religious traditions intrude upon Hindus in other ways. Most Hindus will claim to be Dev-gun by birth, rather than Rakshasgun (the only type of person who, having been born under an evil star, can theoretically see ghosts). Nonetheless, the majority will readily admit the existence of ghosts, their power and presence, and even profess to seeing them. Infertile women will blame their condition on seeing ghosts or, contrarily, will invoke ghosts to rid their barrenness.

Anxious women and men rely upon the local bhopa and his prophecies to cure their troubles (spiritual, mental, and physical), believing the bhopa to be imbued with the immanence of a divine power. Despite the masculinization of Hinduism's pantheon of deities, most bhopas maintain that their power is mainly derived from a supreme goddess or the mother goddess of the local shrine and only occasionally from a male deity. Whatever their complaint—pain, impotency, or infertility—supplicants will importune the bhopa to intervene on their behalf with the appropriate deities or spirits. Only extreme anxiety induces them to importune the deities directly. Since their imprecations often result in success, the supplicants remain convinced about the efficacy of bhopa and deity and see little sense in attending newfangled, unproved medical or family-planning clinics, often run by unsympathetic strangers, using strange potions and instruments.

Most Hindus admire and respect and often anticipate emulating the religious self-dedication of the sannyasi. They admire the sannyasi's inner calmness and steadfastness, so often lacking in their own daily, burdensome lives, caught up in poverty and turmoil. They believe that the sannyasi's renunciation of personal and material ties and sensual appetites leads to a clarity of inner vision. This, in turn, allows the sannyasi to foresee the future and to help the less fortunate achieve difficult goals. Interestingly, the desire to be sannyasi is a considerable antidote to the built-in fertility bias of Hinduism, since it encourages men in particular to relinquish sexuality after the householder stage of life and, through celibacy and abstinence, to aspire toward spirituality.

As discussed in Chapter 2, caste interrelationships provide stability to Hindu village social life and security to individuals. But religion and caste are inextricably intertwined. It is almost impossible to determine where one begins and the other leaves off since

the caste into which one was born was determined by the
accumulated sins and virtues shown in one's previous
existence, that was one's "karma"; and one of the aspects
of Hindu "dharm" (right behaviour) consisted in the acceptance of one's lot, and the observance both of the restrictions and the prerogatives peculiar to one's caste.[6]

Part of the acceptance of one's lot was the reproduction of children,
not only to serve as workers and parents' old-age security but also
to perpetuate lineage, to perform rituals, and to expand caste. Children were expected to be part of the impersonal, universal obligations performed by individuals for society's benefit. Their procreation was an assurance of the continuity and strengthening of caste,
without which Hindu society would be unstable and insecure. The
only honorable escape from performing one's reproductive duties was
to turn sannyasi, a difficult step for the average man beset with innumerable burdens and virtually impossible for the average woman.
Generally, a woman would be contravening convention if she turned
sannyasi herself, although she could follow her husband and renounce
the world if he wanted her to accompany him into his isolation.

While homosexuality is considered a shameful aberration by
Hindus, it is relatively common and reasonably tolerated as long as
it is practiced in secret. Lesbianism seems to be less prevalent,
but that could be more a function of the lack of data on women (partly
because of their shroud of privacy and seclusion) than an actual fact.
Male transvestites (hinjras) are regarded as being among the lowliest
of mendicants and often use public occasions, such as weddings, to
embarrass and provoke guests into giving alms. Becoming hinjras
is another way of escaping the all-inhibiting, suffocating caste strictures. Any Hindu blatantly adopting such a way of life is automatically outcasted and no longer bound by caste rules. Others achieve
the same freedom from caste restraints by becoming saddhus, or
"arrived ones."[7]

Ironically, despite their holy aura, saddhus are treated little
differently from hinjras, for neither is bound by caste rules nor acceptable to their community. Nevertheless, people believe in the saddhus' mystical state and inherent power and expect them to reap their
just reward in the next life. Accordingly, if the saddhus inveigh
against birth control measures or women using contraceptives, they
can severely jeopardize local family-planning initiatives. Thus, their
otherworldliness does not hinder them from influencing people and
programs.

A form of birth control long observed in India has been that of
abstinence for some months after an infant is born. In theory Hindu
parents are supposed to avoid intercourse for as long as a child

suckles. While some may resume relations within one month of birth or as long as two years after, most on average resume sexual activities within six months. Unlike Islam, which enjoins parents to refrain from intercourse for two years to enable both child and mother to gain strength, Hinduism is not so specific. In fact Hindu tradition dictates that the mother must stop suckling her infant and feed it on asses' milk (or other substitutes) upon becoming pregnant again to prevent weakening the new fetus.

Immediately after birth the mother and child remain secluded, for the mother is regarded ritually impure as during menstruation. She must avoid all contact with other family members and especially be kept away from kitchen, hearth, and cooking utensils. She remains in a state of ritual impurity for 40 days after the birth of a boy (longer upon the birth of a daughter) and cannot resume household activities or associations until she has undergone various ritualistic ceremonies. A local Brahmin priest performs a naming ceremony, a cleansing ritual when the house is cleaned out and contaminated materials are discarded or washed, and a worshipping of the water at the well. Only then is the mother restored to a state of purity and allowed to mingle freely with other household members.

Because of religious traditions, considerable ambivalence toward women reigns. On the one hand, a woman is in and out of ritualistic states of impurity, being regularly shunned and treated as a pariah and as regularly reinstalled to grace. On the other hand, as mata ("mother") she is imbued with some of the sacred qualities that attach to the sacred cow (gau-mata) and its veneration. For the Hindu, mataji fondly conjures up helpful mother goddesses. Shrines to matajis proliferate throughout the countryside and are consulted by conscientious devotees or the less devout, desperate to eliminate barrenness or to control fecundity.

Despite the veneration of matajis, the seal on female subjection, degradation, and ignorance was set for untold centuries by legalistic treatises on social and individual behavior. Of these dharmashastras, the Laws of Manu held the greatest sway. Where woman was concerned, "The Code of Manu set the tone against her in phrases reminiscent of an early stage in Christian theology."[8] The Code of Manu clearly and specifically outlines the duties of women and the protection that they as dependents must be given.[9] From the outset a woman's independence was proscribed. Whether a girl, a young matron, or an old woman, she must do nothing independently, even in her own house.[10] In childhood a female must be subject to her father; in youth, to her husband; and in widowhood, to her sons.[11] Should she exhibit independence and separate herself from her father, husband, or sons, she is threatened with the degradation of their families and hers.[12] The unquestioning attitude, passivity, and utter dependence even now evinced in most Indian women directly stems from this constant reiteration of dependency and threat of social disfavor. Bound tightly to the family, few would want or dare to being social odium upon it or themselves by taking independent action, including in matters of procreation and child care.

The Code, going beyond spiritual concerns, is a remarkably practical treatise. It advises wives on household matters—to be clever in home management, economical in expenditure, and careful in maintaining utensils. [13] And it assuages husbands by giving them the more esoteric duty of providing happiness to their wives "both in and out of season, in this world and in the next."[14]

Apart from being cheerful,[15] a wife is enjoined to control her emotions regardless of how erratic her husband is, how lacking in the very qualities she is expected to possess. Not only must she obey her husband (or brother) as long as he lives and not insult his memory when he is dead,[16] as a faithful wife she must also worship her husband as a god even if he is devoid of virtue, faithfulness, and other admirable qualities.[17] She must do nothing to displease him when alive or dead,[18] enduring hardships, being self-controlled, and staying chaste.[19] In other words, she had to be a paragon of virtue. The double standard prevailed with a vengeance—the woman alone had to possess the qualities of chasteness and faithfulness in addition to bearing all the other virtues deemed beneficial in a wife. Not least of these were to service her husband's sexual needs and to bear many sons. Her promised reward if she did her duty, slight though it was, kept her in thrall: the promise of heavenly recompense, including the dubious reward of being reunited with her unchaste, unfaithful, tyrannical husband.

The double standard prevailed even after death. A widower was encouraged to remarry and "again kindle (the fires),"[20] but a widow was threatened with disgrace in this world and, furthermore, in the next, where she would be ensconced in a jackal's womb and plagued by diseases.[21] Widows were discouraged from having acquaintance with other men or mentioning other men's names after their husbands died. Preferably they would emaciate their bodies by subsisting on flowers and roots rather than commit such heinous acts.[22]

Widows were strongly enjoined not to remarry (not even to men of higher caste than their departed husbands), not to beget offspring, and not to relinquish their newly acquired chasteness.[23] Constantly, they were reminded of their heavenly reward for virtuous conduct.[24] In the past, widowhood was even stipulated for young girls if their fiancés died before the exchange of marriage vows. Regardless of age, they were prohibited from all future engagements or marriage, subjected to all the rigors and iniquities of widowhood, and then denied married respectability and status leading to heavenly recompense.

In a sense, the old practices surrounding widowhood, which possibly affected between 500,000 and 2 million widows a year, many of whom were young with long years of fertility ahead of them, were a form of birth control. Widower remarriage, concubinage, and polygamy, however, would have likely counteracted the results of widow seclusion, suttee, and female infanticide. Consequently, when these undesirable practices became prohibited, their removal may have been a contributory factor to India's population explosion, thus demonstrating one of Hinduism's main tenets, causality. Every action has its reaction, its unforeseeable consequence.

With time widows became progressively subjected to harsher disabilities. Not only could they not remarry, they were forced into extreme isolation, cut off from all social contact, and treated as objects of charity in their home. Their heads were shaven, often forcibly. They were cast scanty leftovers of meals and clothes. They lived in paltry surroundings and were compelled to perform the most menial tasks for the household. They had absolutely no status in anyone's eyes, including their children's. They were the Cinderellas of Indian society. Rather than live out their lives in sheer desolation and abjection, many preferred to commit sati.

Sati, or suttee, meaning "devoted wife," was originally imported into India by the Thracians and Scythians, who carried a man's right of property in his wives, concubines, and slaves to the ultimate extreme—the burning of enough females on his funeral pyre to satisfy his eternal needs. The rich mainly perpetuated this custom, since the poor could ill afford such wanton waste of "property."

Both the Atharvaveda and Rigveda note suttee as an ancient custom, but the Vedic era of relative freedom for women saw it virtually extinguished. Unfortunately, it was restored in the Epic period, as the Mahabharata showed. Initially, the Brahmins opposed the practice as being barbaric, but upon failing to eliminate suttee, they subsequently gave it religious sanction by equating it with the eternity of marriage. And so it became religiously entrenched.

The Rajputs of Rajasthan expanded suttee on a major scale by creating johur, the remarkable custom whereby a Rajput faced with unacceptable defeat would immolate all his possessions—wives, the lot—before killing himself. The Muslims, especially Akbar, tried to curtail these practices, but with little success. Not until the British enforced a nationwide network of law was suttee virtually wiped out and widowhood given a modicum of protection and respectability. Even today the occasional self-immolation occurs, as do other outlawed practices, when certain groups band together away from the eye of the law. And widow remarriage is still deprecated, despite the active participation of such outstanding widows as Pandit Nehru and Indira Gandhi in social and political affairs.

Allegedly, widows were reconciled to suttee. But in fact they underwent the anguish of burning because of public pressure and religious coercion. This is graphically portrayed in the Padmapurana, wherein a wife's exacting duties to her husband included the duty of self-immolation. Specifically, "She must on the death of her husband allow herself to be burnt alive on the same funeral pyre; then everybody will praise her virtue" (emphasis added). [25] Not only did unctuous priests and morbid relatives exert moral pressure on widows, many barely in their teens, they applied physical pressure—forcible immersion in the flames, roping to the funeral pyre, and induced compliance through drugs and drink (notably soma). A widow's burning thus assured society of its virtue and was a cause for festivity.

Single women were little better treated than widows. Under the Code of Manu, marriage was regarded as essential—for men as well as for women—if not compulsory. Prolonged virginity was designated a social disgrace, but premarital sex to remedy that condition was tantamount to evil. Consequently, child marriage became crucial. And while unmarried men could be outcasted without social status or consideration, at least they, unlike young girls, could defer marriage to acquire some learning before entering the householder stage of life. Implicitly throughout the Code procreation was the destiny of all Hindus.

Once singleness was overcome and marriage achieved, the Laws of Manu laid down numerous duties to be performed by the spouses to ensure the continuity of the marriage. Without a doubt the heaviest onus was placed on the female partner, but the male was not entirely bereft of obligation in return.

The Code again reiterates the dependency of females on males[26] and specifies the duties of the three dominant males in an Indian woman's life,[27] duties that have been little changed by the incursions of modern developments. The father must arrange for the daughter's marriage, the husband must have regular sexual intercourse with the wife, and the son must protect the mother after the father's death. All must keep evil influences—liquor, traveling, wicked people—away from women,[28] since females are deemed too weak and feebleminded to withstand external influences. Husbands are enjoined to keep guard over their wives not so much by force as by keeping them occupied with housekeeping, food preparation, religious duties, collecting and spending the husbands' wealth, and (impliedly) bearing numerous children. [29]

The Laws of Manu are indisputably derogatory about women's characteristics: "their passion of men, through their mutable temper, through their natural heartlessness,"[30] which presumably render them disloyal to their husbands, and "(love of their) bed, (of their) seat, and (of) ornament, impure desires, wrath, dishonesty, malice

and bad conduct."[31] Like so many other religious edicts and interpretations about women, the Laws have perpetuated stereotypes of,
myths about, and injustices toward women.

The Code's assignment of religious and financial responsibilities to the household women may account for why the home role of
Indian women is actually stronger than is explicit within the Laws.
Certainly, the Indian mother-in-law is renowned for her dictatorial
and tyrannical hold over her menage, especially over her daughters-
in-law. It is she who is often accused of being the most resistant to
change, opposing family planning because it will deprive her of grandsons and stature and opposing female education because it will undermine her position as the transmitter of oral traditions. Most Indian
women, anticipating or achieving mother-in-law status, are unlikely
to reduce their lifetime's main chance for acquiring prestige, power,
and respectability by upsetting the Code or any other equivalent
treatise. Not unless they are guaranteed at least an equal return.

The presence of grandparents in the joint family deeply affects
the behavior and attitudes of couples. By custom the daughter-in-
law must defer in all things, even the handling and upbringing of her
own children, to her mother-in-law. Considerable tension inevitably
arises and is further exacerbated by the traditional tight emotional
ties between mother-in-law and son. The son dares not displease
his mother, and his lack of communication and companionship with
his wife further prevents him from breaking the apron string. Nowhere is this more apparent than in the daughter-in-law's attempt
to practice birth control. The lack of household privacy, the close
sleeping arrangements, the nonexistence of personal storage space
hamper young couples' attempts to practice family limitation.

Not only mothers-in-law but other family members interfere
with and blatantly intrude upon couples' personal decisions. The
brunt of abuse is heaped upon the head of the daughter-in-law for actually or potentially depriving the family of many grandsons. A
thwarted mother-in-law may ultimately call in the family priest to
invoke religious imprecations against the daughter-in-law's interference with God's will and the natural process of conception and
pregnancy or to brandish omens and signs prophesying disaster if
contraception is used. It would take a very determined and dedicated
daughter-in-law, backed up by a genuinely supportive husband, to
withstand such an onslaught and continue with family planning.

Even in the realm where women are presumed to garner some
respect and stature—childbirth and child care—the doctrinaire Code
of Manu strove to denigrate women and downplay their role. Conception was touted as the "husband's rebirth,"[32] not the woman's. But
the woman, not the man, was expected to ensure that rebirth by deco-
rous behavior. Consequently, a wife's fidelity, obviously more easily

discernible than her husband's, was exacted on pain of death, severe
religious sanction, or extreme punishment. The husband's faithfulness, by contrast, was subject merely to a caution to be faithful, primarily to keep his offspring pure, tainted by neither venereal disease
nor intercaste mixing. Both concepts—the husband's rebirth and
the double standard of fidelity—are hardly conducive to birth control.

Women are granted their essentiality through the production
and nurture of offspring, the performance of religious rites, and
their contribution toward their husbands' (and ancestors') conjugal
happiness and heavenly bliss.[33] Yet Manu, the advocate of procreation, has been responsible for depreciating women's childbearing
role. The Code has accorded greater importance to the male's seed
than to the female receptacle (womb) "for the offspring of all created
beings is marked by the characteristics of the seed."[34] This belief
and attitude have little altered among the rural majority of India. Accordingly, it has been difficult to develop respect for women's child-
conceiving role, respect necessary for the acceptance of family planning and birth control.

Moreover, the limitation of population was (and is) unlikely to
be favored by a populace that regarded children as an economic aid
to parents, old-age insurance, and the source of a husband's rebirth
and the perpetuation of his characteristics. The difficulty of implementing family-planning measures has typically been aggravated by
the people's need to have children to propitiate the manes and ancestral spirits upon the father's demise. With few exceptions, children
was interpreted to mean male. Thus, society and the Code thrust
upon women yet another burden: propagating children until enough
sons had been produced. And population was thereby given yet another
expansionary thrust.

If women did not produce male offspring they were deemed unfortunate. Hence, in times of their misfortune, a brother-in-law or
other Sapinda could be appointed by the husband (or by his relatives,
if he was dead) to have authorized intercourse with the "unfortunate"
woman for the purpose of producing male heirs.[35] The usual rules
against adultery and infidelity were apparently suspended to allow the
unfortunate woman's predicament to be remedied, while the otherwise
adulterous and incentuous parties were neither outcasted nor severely
punished.

As a corollary to the desire for boys, female children were
largely unwanted. While one or two to help the mother with household
chores were acceptable, others in the wrong proportion or sequence
of girls to boys were disfavored. Female children were regarded as
unable to fulfill the economic and spiritual functions deemed necessary
by society and religion and costly in terms of dowry and arranged
marriage fees. Consequently, female infanticide by starvation, poi-

sons, or sand burial became a regular, socially acceptable practice of the past and an occasional episode of the present. Ironically, abortion was roundly condemned, in all probability because of the fear of aborting a son and heir.

Today, female infanticide has virtually disappeared but unfavorable attitudes toward female offspring have not. Laws limiting dowries have had some impact in reducing the family's potential financial burden of a daughter's betrothal and marriage. Education has enabled daughters to be gainfully employed and therefore to become economically valuable to their families. And educated young men seeking educated young women for their wives have indirectly increased the value and worth of daughters. Nevertheless, the birth of a daughter is still less welcome than a son's in most poorer, less-educated homes where entrenched custom and attitude die hard.

With the deliberate flouting of the dowry law in all quarters, the prestige of large dowries on the increase, and marriage expenditures once again rising, the unfavorable perception of daughters as an economic burden might be resurrected. Deliberate infanticide may have been eliminated but a modern form exists, that of marasmus and other malnutrition-related diseases. Because of the age-old preference for boys, the priority in feeding given to males over females, and the better food and medical treatment boys receive compared with girls, the infant mortality of daughters from marasmus alone in 1973 was ten times higher than the infant mortality of sons.[36] And that nutritional gap between girl and boy babies has hardly narrowed.

Father-son relationships are circumscribed by the strict obligations imposed by tradition, the Laws of Manu and other Hindu law givers, and a customary reticence of affection between parent and child. A son is essential to a father to "rescue him from hell" by placating the manes and helping him attain nirvana by performing the appropriate funeral rites.

Eldest sons are expected to assure their sisters of adequate dowries, to act in locis parentis to their younger siblings, and perform afterdeath and ancestral rituals for their parents. Since only sons can release fathers from their debts to the dark-spirited manes and properly perform afterdeath rituals, the need for a son is an all-consuming desire of Indian men. Correspondingly, the need to bear a son is an equally urgent matter for Indian women, who are subject to the fears of social disapprobation and the application of the Code's remedies for the failure to produce male progeny.

Apart from economic concerns, the men's fear of the afterworld and the women's fear of the here-and-now have been at the root of large families. Yet a daughter, under provisions of the Code, could attain almost equal importance with a son and be practically a substitute if her father undertook to appoint her putrika. This would let her eldest son be designated the heir to perform the family's rituals and to inherit from his grandfather.[37] Although the application of this law could ease some of the pressure on Indian women to bear children indefinitely until a living male heir results, men have been customarily reticent about invoking this passage of Manu or have simply not known of it.

For the son's part, the obligations he feels toward his father and his father-substitutes (his elder brother, senior uncle if his father died, or guru) tend to create in him "an unqualified self-abasement, a willingness to accept what he is told as being infallible, and a confidence that by thus subordinating his will to that of the father-figure, he will be set on the true path."[38] Disapproval by these authority figures reinforced by custom, holy laws, and scriptures and backed up by mother-in-law diatribes still deter sons from pursuing their own courses of action, especially in relation to private family matters such as family planning and contraception.

Another major impediment to effective contraceptive measures is the belief arising from customary Hinduism that a woman's sexual appetite is more intense than a man's. Consequently, in order to prevent dissatisfaction, adultery, and other sexual aberrations on the woman's part, a husband is urged to satisfy his wife with due regularity. The more energetic profess at least twice a night; the more lethargic or devout, once a month. Since in many areas of India condoms, IUDs, diaphragms, and coitus interruptus are variously regarded as impeding a woman's satisfaction, they are avoided or discarded—with the inevitable results.

The lack of companionship and communication between husband and wife likewise deters their ability to discuss such intimate matters as contraception and family planning. Usually, as a result of protracted marriage negotiations in which the couple hardly participate, a man's wife comes to him as a stranger—unformed, uneducated, and unaware. Over time, in the more successful marriages, personal compatibility may develop and the couple may be able to discuss intimate matters like birth control. But by that time it is often too late, for they have become inundated with more children than they can economically or physically afford.

In part the difficulty a Hindu wife has in establishing a genuine personal relationship with her husband arises from Hinduism's holy books and sacred laws. As personal housekeeper and mother, who embodies the virtues of self-sacrifice, submission, and patience, she is expected to perform the duty of serving her husband as a god. Because woman is portrayed as a seductress and temptress, inducing good men to indulge in carnality, a good Hindu wife is everlastingly enjoined to be virtuous and dutiful. She must never oppose or interfere with her husband's wants or needs, whether food or sex.

The virtuous wife must not take initiatives that would contravene custom, the sacred scriptures and laws, her husband's rights, or her in-laws' perceived dues. Throughout her life she is subjected to a confusing compendium of religious beliefs, attitudes, laws, and customs, all of which dictate her obligations to and relationships with others in terms of passivity, submissiveness, and patience. As a consequence, only the most unique type of woman, possessed of confidence and self-assertiveness, is able to extricate herself from this welter of duties and to undertake a truly companionable relationship with her husband while also exercising control over her own fertility.

In part difficulties arise because many wives are but children when they come to marriage. The first child marriages, instituted to stop intercaste liaisons, can be traced back to a fifth century B. C. family law that specified that all young girls were to be married before puberty. Fathers, anxious for a good caste marriage, betrothed their young infants and later married them off at seven or eight years of age. The custom became more instilled when sanctified by the Laws of Manu and when Muslim invasions threatened India's unmarried female population with abduction and sale into slavery. Distraught parents used child marriage to protect their offspring and to seclude them from the marauders. This had the eventual effect, once Islam was finally imposed, of establishing a rigid system of purdah. Poorer families with an excess of daughters used child marriage as a means of survival. If they could not sell their daughters to widowers or elderly men, they would marry the youngsters to temples, where they became devadasis or nautch girls, used in their youth as prostitutes by the temples' priests or clientele and cast aside when haggard and wrinkled.

To avoid upsetting the unity of marriage or the fidelity between spouses, the Code placed an exacting duty on fathers to seek fitting matches for their children in caste and rank.[39] Eight types of marriage were allowed, with marriage by purchase the most highly esteemed, since it was based on sound economics and therefore the most viable. The recommended ages for marriage were 30 for a male and 12 for a female, although 24 and 8 years of age, respectively —or even younger—were permissible if the studentship phase for a male had ended early enough to allow him to progress into his next phase of life, the householder stage.[40] And, while the Code virtually ensured the completion of a young male's studentship phase before embarking upon the more arduous responsibilities of householding, it simultaneously denied, by its very insistence upon extremely young marriage ages for females, young girls the opportunity of attaining maturity without being thrust into the demands of matrimony and pregnancy.

Early puberty was, and still is, an excuse for early marriage in India. Early liaisons were made to check love matches, premarital sex, or undesirable attachments to persons of the wrong caste, background, or character. Child brides were considered more malleable and more easily indoctrinated into the way of the husband's (and mother-in-law's) home than older females with more dogmatic attitudes. Usually a child bride remained with her own family, even after the marriage, until puberty, whereupon she was whisked away from a friendly environment into an unfamiliar if not hostile one. This practice was especially representative of an extremely authoritarian, patriarchal family system and was no less assiduously practiced under Islam as under Hinduism.

Child marriages had disastrous consequences for youthful brides, contributing to early deaths, complicated pregnancies, and high infant mortality. They also caused young girls severe physical pain and deformities through the inability of their fragile, unformed bodies to cope with the physical demands of their older and larger husbands. In reality child marriages were a socially accepted form of child abuse, not least of the child brides' problems being premature pregnancies, premature births, and premature deaths.

Since under the Code and traditional social conventions widowers were allowed to remarry but widows were not, widowers could rarely find partners of equal age, circumstance, or physique. Besides, widowers evinced a predeliction for acquiring youthful, untarnished brides replete with substantial dowries. Hence, the disparity of age and maturity between bride and bridegroom became greater and more commonplace until reformers finally compelled the Indian Parliament in 1929 to prohibit child marriage.

Although child marriage was theoretically abolished—the legislation stipulating the marriageable age for females and males to be 14 and 18, respectively[41]—what marriage at the age of 14 constituted is open to question. Katherine Mayo's comments on child marriage and its horrific effects on youngsters' bodies, especially those already handicapped by malnutrition and undernourishment, are as relevant today as when she was writing. [12] Teenagers, whether 14, 15, or 16 (16 being the latest age recommended by the Child Marriage Restraint Act), are physically and emotionally not equipped to bear the turmoil of incessant pregnancies, the demands of husbands, and the burdens of raising children. Early puberty is completely irrelevant to their ability to cope. While Western industrialized countries are regularly castigated by such Third World countries as India for being too materialistic, decadent or unspiritual, or sexually permissive, at least every effort is made to protect children from sexual assaults. Child marriage is little more than sanctified or legitimized sexual assault.

Statistically, whether in India or in the wealthier Western countries where poverty is less rife and medical aid more available, teenagers are more prone to physical disorders and complications in their pregnancies than older women, whose bodies have been allowed to mature fully and properly. Teenage brides and their infants are more prone to early death and more susceptible to disease. Both are liable to be physically and mentally below average, ever contributing to the degeneration of society. India is by no means unique in having an abundance of teenage marriages and pregnancies. Trudging the streets of Adibjan, Jakarta, or Caracas are young, listless-eyed girls with swollen bellies carrying malnourished, disease-ridden babies and followed by equally malnourished toddlers. Yet legislation curtailing teenage marriages is nonexistent and the enforcement of what legislation there is is feeble. Neither the improvement of the physical condition of India's women and children—and, by extrapolation, Indian society as a whole—nor the amelioration of India's burgeoning population rate will be aided by the continued tradition of early marriages.

But the belief in early marriage is as hard to alter as beliefs in the supernatural, which are professed by others than the uneducated, poorer classes. Even the better educated, though declaiming otherwise, take an animistic view of life, especially of health and illness. This view becomes reflected in their attitudes toward sex, women, and childbirth, which are seen as imbued with variegated spirits and with great potential for defilement.

Most Hindus are highly conscious of the prospects for bodily defilement emanating from bodily secretions or excretions and go to great lengths to avoid their own contamination. Infinitely definitive caste rules and scriptural proscriptions ensure that they minimize defilement by observing meticulous washing and cleansing, purification rituals, and strict adherence to specific customs. For most Hindu women life is bound by hundreds of fine strictures, with the most obvious ones being the use of the right hand for eating, the left for hygiene; avoidance of showing the soles of one's feet to others except in disparagement; avoidance of touching other people's feet except as a sign of obeisance; avoidance of leftover food and Outcaste contact; and the prevention of cups, cigarettes, or pipes from touching lips.

Defilement can occur at any time and at any place. Accordingly, Hindus must constantly exercise precautions against it. Individually, they can remove minor defilement using specific purification rites. Apart from Outcaste contact, the most serious contamination is associated with women's functions—sex, menstruation, and childbirth. Because of the serious nature of defilement from these causes, the aid of a Brahmin priest must be sought for absolution. Similarly, because they imagine illness to arise from the invasion of the body by evil spirits and things such as bad air, priestly services are sought to exorcise the evil, by a summons or, for especially recalcitrant spirits, with threats and briberies.

The concern with bodily defilement has especially impinged upon sex and sexual relations. The belief prevails that in semen reposes strength; hence, its expulsion is regarded as energy sapping, weakening, and defiling. This arises from the belief that because 40 days and 40 drops of blood are needed to form but one particle of semen it must not be profligately dissipated. Because women are inevitably regarded as the cause of this energy dissipation, they are once again castigated for entrapping men, undermining their strength, and defiling them. Only the birth of sons can really absolve women from the sin of such actions. But meanwhile, semen conservation must be effected and the potential for bodily defilement minimized by strict adherence to customary and religious rules. These specify the occasions for sexual indulgence and the appropriate "hot" and "cool" foods to consume to aid semen development. Despite semen conservation being strongly advocated, through abstinence or celibacy and by avoiding sexual overindulgence or unacceptable sexual practices, the two duties of procreating sons and satisfying one's wife must be upheld.

The attempt to adhere to numerous, uncompromisingly strict rules has led to several interesting conflicts for Hindu men. Failure to abide wholly by the rules has led to feelings of guilt accompanied by jiryan (real or imagined spermatorrhea) and sensations of wasting away. The duty to procreate conflicts with the perceived need to conserve semen. The prevention of bodily defilement through using contraceptives, especially condoms, conflicts with the duty to satisfy one's wife.

> Celibacy was the first requirement of true fitness [physical and spiritual]. . . . [Yet] here was another inescapable dilemma, because one's sons must be procreated, one's wife satisfied—hence the need to compromise, to restrict sex to a defined number of occasions. In order to make good the depredations of sex life, certain rules must be obeyed. . . . It was not considered sufficient, however, merely to eat the appropriate diet in order to restore one's semen; nor was the sexual act regarded as the only way of losing it. [43]

It could be lost through badparhez ("eating wrong things") and also through badpheli ("doing what is wrong"). The latter

> included not only sexual promiscuity but every sort of violation of Hindu "dharm", such as, mixing and eating

with people of inferior caste; acting disrespectfully towards one's elders; drinking to excess; giving way to anger
or to lustful thoughts, to fear or to excessive worrying.
Consequently, any purulent discharge . . . from inside the
body was held to be "spoiled semen."[44]

Only unworldly religious devotees are perceived by the masses
as capable of indifferently coping with all physical privations and of
thereby attaining spiritual and physical perfection. Through meditation and relinquishment of material ties, the yogi is seen as acquiring
magical powers that let him transcend physical bonds. In the eyes of
the masses he attains godlike qualities, supernatural powers, and "an
intact store of rich, uncurdled semen in his head."[45] Perhaps this
perceived abundance is the reason why holy men, like young children,
escape from the vehement condemnation heaped on adults who masturbate.
    Since the ordinary man does not expect to aspire to such physi-
cal and spiritual achievement, unless perhaps in old age when he has
discharged all his earthly and household duties, he must compromise
by exercising moderation, performing acts of piety, and maintaining
strict voluntary control over his sexual appetites. He recognizes that
his frailty will regularly let him down, but this does not hinder him
from aspiring to attain a modicum of the spiritual perfection of the
holy man.
    By contrast, the average woman is not even expected to attempt
to attain physical or spiritual perfection through abnegation, deprivation, or abstinence. She is just not regarded as a suitable candidate
for aspiring to the highest levels of spiritual achievement. She is not
expected to become sannyasi, saddhu, or yogi. If she does, blatantly
and in contravention of all social norms, she is deemed irresponsible
or, worse, crazed. Not only is she then ostracized but she is deprived of all the respect accorded to her male counterpart. The road
to perfection and spiritual achievement for any woman must be solely
through her children or her husband; that is, sex and pregnancy.
    While a woman would be condemned for practicing abstinence
within marriage except while suckling a child, the ordinary man may
practice abstinence at any time in the belief that infrequency of intercourse and conservation of semen will produce robust children. In
this way he can act out one of Hinduism's venerable mythologies, that
of Hanuman's father, who allegedly slept with his wife but once in his
lifetime yet produced the mighty, the robust Hanuman. In Hindu mythology, many such fables abound about gods and goddesses who,
though sensuous and fecund, exercised sexual reproductive restraint.
But replication of godlike restraint is only tolerated in a man, not in
a woman, who would be deemed to be acting against the interests of
the gods, her family, and her husband.

Thus, concern with bodily defilement and its concomitants of semen conservation, production of robust children, and the attainment of physical and spiritual perfection through abstinence and celibacy could help to counterbalance Hinduism's pronatalism tendencies. Indeed, Hinduism's rich mythology provides enough vital examples of reticence in sex and procreation to offset certain fertility biases of Hinduism, as does Hinduism's four classical stages of life, the varnashrama.

Most Hindus subscribe to, even if they cannot fulfill, the varnashrama. With the exception of the householder stage (grihastha), the other three stages essentially require celibacy or abstinence. During grihastha—commonly designated to be between the ages of 25 and 40—a man is expected to marry, found a household, and raise a family. Having fulfilled the basic social and economic conditions expected of him (producing enough living children for old-age security and immediate labor, religious and social rituals, and social prestige, and providing adequately for wife, children, and other household inmates), he may partially retire, into vanaprastha, a semicelibate state. In this way some pressure is taken off the wife and she may expect to continue living with her husband for the balance of her fertile years without necessarily being in a state of unending pregnancies.

Population, sexuality, and women's fertility are variously handled by Hinduism's three levels of religious belief. The first, the formal and classical level of Hinduism, encompasses orthodox religious teachings, rituals, a knowledge of Hindu scriptures, laws and mythology, and adherence to defined paths leading to release from all material and human existence. This insistence upon the spiritual life, its practical application through varnashrama, and its mythology constitute Hinduism's greatest rebuttal to population proliferation.

The second and third levels of Hinduism, being very fertility oriented however, run counter to its classical level. The second level consists of minor deities that are publicly worshipped by lower-caste Hindus and, surprisingly often, privately accepted by high-caste Hindus. These deities, heavily imbued with fertility symbolism and the ability to converse with supplicants through the local bhopa, are frequently enlisted to help with sexual problems. The third level is rampant with good and bad supernatural or magical powers that either exist in vacuuo or within certain individuals. Ascribed with talents that affect the fertility of plants, animals, and humans, they too must be appropriately propitiated.

Within Hinduism but outside its formal classicism various secret religious cults exist to worship sexuality and to use the sex act as an act of worship. These cults, Laja-Dharm, are theoretically banned by civil law, but like the bhakti forms of worship, they attract a disproportionate number of women and Sudras. Whereas the more orthodox Hinduism shuns or minimizes the religious participation of women, Sudras, and Untouchables and denies them relatively equal treatment, these other cults encourage their participation and, indirectly, their fertility. Cultic celebrants tend to resist contraception, since its practice is considered a hindrance to devout worship and rituals and spontaneous, emotional outpourings.

Throughout India various tribes and groups of people still exist who continue to practice a mixture of pre-Aryan primitivism or animism and formalistic Hinduism. They more reflect the rambunctious, spontaneous nature of the former than the conservative, restrained form of the latter. Within these less-priest-dominated, lower-class, and lower-caste groups, men and women are basically equal; men's and women's work is essentially parallel and complementary; and marriage is freer and more companionable. Religious rituals are more extroverted and include blood sacrifices and demon worship—practices repugnant to devout Hindus—while love and sex are less inhibited by religious strictures.

Overall, the religion of these groups is less inward looking, duty bound, or guilt ridden. Consequently, their reaction to outside influences, including modernization, contraception, and family planning, cannot be expected to be the same as the reaction of adherents to a more formalistic Hinduism. They might be more receptive to drastic changes. Equally, they might be more resistant.

Weaving backward and forward through people's lives and beliefs—whether orthodox Hindus, cultic and bhakti worshippers, or tribal peoples—"there is an inextricable confusion of Brahminical Hinduism and primitive animism, of magical phantasy and superstition."[46] This welter of confusion infuses sex, intercourse, birth, and females with a mystique, an intrigue, and an incomprehensibility that reduce population policies to a quivering heap of irrelevancies when they ignore the existence of religion's all-pervasiveness in its many guises.

Although Hinduism is undoubtedly a pronatalistic religion, it contains many features that help to control fertility and natality. The desire for a life of spiritual perfection and contemplation, the seeking of a path to oneness with God and a removal from things material, the pursuit and harmony of the varnashrama, and the practice of asceticism contribute to a relatively tolerant acceptance of fertility control. A sense of moderation and tolerance in daily living; the recognition of fulfilling duties to and properly providing for wife and children; a lack of religious proscriptions against contraception; and the existence of a traditional pharmacopoeia of Ayurvedic medicines, treatments, and even abortifacients also expand the public's tolerance of contraception and family planning.

The fullsome acceptance of sexuality in life, as evidenced by India's literature and architecture, may contribute to a pronatalistic atmosphere and operate against changing attitudes toward fertility. Nevertheless, appreciation of the contemplative life, respect for sannyasis and saddhus, and acceptance of abstinence and celibacy help to create a not-totally-unfavorable attitude toward family planning and contraception. These features have, in effect, moderated the fertility bent in Hinduism to the extent that Hindus average smaller families than Muslims of comparable status and background.

Hinduism may well promote fertility, but it also proclaims moderation. Within Hinduism there lies considerable potential receptivity to family planning and birth control, provided its restraining influences on fertility are properly understood within the context of each region and religious group and provided its forces are properly garnered to convince Hindus that they are doing nothing contrary to their dharma.

A major hindrance to the revamping of attitudes and beliefs is the lack of a centralized religious authority that could work conjunctively with secular organizations to educate and reform traditionally held religious and fertility attitudes. For the moment, the burden is solely on secular efforts to provide economic and social development, change long-held beliefs and attitudes, and install nationally accepted population control programs before India is irretrievably swamped by human numbers.

NOTES

1. Annie Besant, trans., The Bhagavad Gita: The Lord's Song, 9th ed. (Madras: Theosophical, 1955), p. 64.

2. Ibid., p. 197.

3. Ibid., pp. 199, 200.

4. Dom Moraes, A Matter of People (New York: Praeger, 1974), pp. 9-10.

5. Ibid., p. 10.

6. G. Morris Carstairs, The Twice-Born: A Study of a Community of High Caste Hindus (London: Hogarth, 1961), p. 57.

7. Ibid., p. 61.

8. Will Durant, Our Oriental Heritage, The Story of Civilization, vol. 1 (New York: Simon & Schuster, 1954), p. 493.

9. F. Max Müller, ed., The Laws of Manu, The Sacred Books of the East, vol. 25 (Delhi: Motilal Banarsidass, 1967), 25:5:146-69.

10. Ibid., 5:147.

11. Ibid., 5:148.

12. Ibid., 5:149.

13. Ibid., 5:150.

14. Ibid., 5:153.

15. Ibid., 5:150.

16. Ibid., 5:151.

17. Ibid., 5:154.

18. Ibid., 5:156.

19. Ibid., 5:158.

20. Ibid., 5:168.

21. Ibid., 5:164.

22. Ibid., 5:157.

23. Ibid., 5:160-63, 165-66.

24. Ibid., 5:155.

25. John B. Noss, Man's Religions (New York: Macmillan, 1974), p. 173. See also Thomas Berry, Religions of India (New York: Bruce, 1971).

26. Müller, The Laws of Manu, 9:2-3.

27. Ibid., 9:4.

28. Ibid., 9:5-7, 13.

29. Ibid., 9:10-13, 16.

30. Ibid., 9:15.

31. Ibid., 9:17.

32. Ibid., 9:8.

33. Ibid., 9:27-28.

34. Ibid., 9:35-37.

35. Ibid., 9:56-62.

36. "Equal Rights Must Start in the Cradle," UNICEF News—Third World Women, no. 76(3) (July 1973), p. 17.

37. Müller, The Laws of Manu, 9:127.

38. Carstairs, The Twice-Born, pp. 71-72.

39. Müller, The Laws of Manu, 9:87-94.

40. Ibid., 9:94.

41. Child Marriage Restraint Act, Government of India, 1929, amended 1949 and 1956.

42. Katherine Mayo, Mother India (New York: Harcourt-Brace, 1927).

43. Carstairs, The Twice-Born, p. 84.

44. Ibid., p. 85.

45. Ibid., p. 86.

46. Ibid., p. 89.

5

OVERVIEW OF BUDDHISM
AND ITS IMPACT
ON WOMEN

All that exists is impermanent. All elements are self-
less. "Nirvana" is serenity, peace.

Samyutta-Nikaya

I, the individual, am the owner of action, the heir of
action, the birthplace of action, the relation of action
and the pathway of action.

Khantipalo Bhikku

By the seventh century B. C. the old Vedic society of the Aryans had dissolved, sacerdotalism had emerged, and the Brahmin
priests were firmly ensconced as the dominant class. The stage
was set for the development of a new social system based upon new
values and philosophical concepts. Malaise reigned as spiritual and
philosophical thought tried to break priestly fetters. A revulsion
arose against the wasteful sacrifices and interminable, self-indulgent
rituals of the Brahmana. Direct, individualistic ways to the sacred
Supreme Truth were sought. And as brahminical control tightened
around women's access to the Truth, women became restless and
sought new religious vehicles through which to express themselves.

At the time of Buddha's entry onto the stage, three basic forms
of religious ideology existed in India. Dominating was that of the
Brahmin priests. The second most pervasive was the animistic and
superstitious folk religion of the villagers. The third was that practiced by the shramanas, or nonbrahminical teachers, who opposed
the Brahmins and their self-serving sacrificial rituals. Sacrifices
had become debased, moving from being deity propitiation to becoming ends in themselves, and repugnance had followed.

The shramanas, of whom Buddha initially was one, disputed
the Brahmin's claims that the sacrifice had mystical supremacy over

deities and all other spiritual concepts and that they, as practitioners of the sacrificial arts, had preeminence. It had become apparent that the burgeoning industry of brahminically controlled sacrifices was economically wasteful; caused cruelty to animals and people, especially women and the Untouchables; and financially oppressed the masses. Besides, the results hardly justified the expenditures or oppression. Buddha, recognizing the need of the masses to cling to old traditions, did not totally discard the concept of sacrifice. Rather, he urged an unusual sacrificial approach that entailed a firm dedication to ideals and goals and the capitulation of self to the Doctrine of Dhamma and the Sangha.

Lacking money for elaborate sacrifices, the common folk relied upon age-old, pre-Aryan practices of magic, spells, incantations, taboos, charms, palmistry, and astrology. Despite professing to despise these practices, some shramanas and Brahmins, ever ready to expand their influence and wealth, embraced those "arts" (and the fees and authority that came with performing magical/mystical services).

Buddha recognized the need of villagers and town dwellers alike for security and succor in magic and mysticism. Hence he did not condemn folkloric religious practices, the popular belief in Brahma, * or the veneration of supernatural beings. He exhibited a gentle tolerance toward folk beliefs, using them as a vehicle for conveying the rather more-difficult-to-comprehend, abstract Buddhist ideas and employing them to illustrate Buddhist discourses. "In such a way. . . the original folk-beliefs were, over a long period, imperceptibly transformed and made to nourish Buddhist attitudes and to serve Buddhist religious goals."[1] For example, various evil spirits and demons were fused together to produce Mara, the Evil One, who came to represent the totality and root of evil in human experience. Buddha used Mara and other spiritual entities as a bridge between folkloric beliefs and abstract thought. He hoped to moderate fear-producing beliefs and practices with tolerance and dispassionate analysis. But Buddhism's tolerant incorporation of other beliefs eventually paved the way for its ultimate demise in India as its unique concepts became watered down and its control passed into brahminical hands. Its demise was also in part due to the low educational levels of the masses, especially women, who needed a fairly high degree of literacy to understand the abstractions of Buddhist thought and who, lacking the requisite education, lost interest in the ungraspable.

The main common ground that Buddha shared with other shramanas, who were both non-Brahmins and Brahmins by birth, was

---

*Brahma is the Supreme Creator deity of the Hindu triad of Vishnu-Brahma-Shiva.

opposition to the Brahmins' sacrificial system and caste. These
shramanas, with their disciples, formed many different sects with a
plethora of beliefs ranging from atheism to mysticism, polytheism
to materialism. Not a few of them became ajivikas, or homeless,
ascetic nomads who had symbolically immolated all their worldly possessions and external signs of rank, caste, and kinship to demonstrate
their disavowal of the old Vedic social and religious systems. Because
of the prevailing traditional attitude toward women seeking spirituality
on their own or turning sannyasi, few women actually became the
disciples of shramanas or became Ajivikas; that is, until Buddha's
time.

Initially the Ajivikas movement was individualistic, even anarchic. These very characteristics would have mitigated against women
participating in the movement, since their Hindu upbringing would
have trained them to be patient, submissive, and enduring, the opposite of individualistic or anarchic. But eventually two compelling
needs forced the Ajivikas to adopt a modicum of cohesive organization.
First, India's harsh monsoons compelled them to relinquish alms
collecting during the monsoon season and to coalesce for mutual survival. Second, the increasing power and control of certain monarchies
necessitated the organization of Ajivikas into viable, respected groups,
which worked to convince the kings that they could usefully contribute
to the public good and were not mere trouble-making anarchists.
Gradually these "men of the alternative life" developed numerous,
distinct philosophical schools whose views differed radically from
the existing Vedic beliefs and the hereditary priesthood. However,
over time they disagreed fundamentally among themselves and with
evolving Buddhist principles.

Merely a consideration of the concept of karma reveals great
differences of thought between the more prominent schools. The
group that inherited the name of Ajivikas, led by Gosala, rejected
the principle of karma. They believed that man has no real choice
of action in life, since everything is predetermined in a totally closed
causal system. A murderer to them is no more likely to acquire
blame for his deeds than a moral person is likely to acquire merit
for good deeds. To the average woman or man raised on a long tradition of karma, this would have been unthinkable. The Jains, led by
Mahavira, an associate of Gosala, contended however that a person
could ultimately wear out the bad karma. Release from the mortal
state of existence could be achieved by exercising free will and selecting moral actions over a period of transmigrations. Both sects practiced extreme asceticism, but the practice was immutable and predetermined for the Ajivikas while it was a matter of free choice for
the Jains in order to neutralize bad karma.

In contrast, the Materialist (Lokayatas) and the Skeptic, or
agnostic, schools adopted freer, less-painful approaches to

karma.* The Materialists maintained that man had complete freedom of choice and self-determination to take any action without fear
of the consequences, provided always that human pleasure was fully
enhanced. The Sceptics urged cultivation of peace of mind and friend-
ship by avoiding argument-inducing, peace-destroying religious concepts or association with priests and teachers. For this stance they
were called eel-wrigglers.

The Buddhists firmly rejected all four views and many others
besides. To a Buddhist, the doctrine of karma or moral causation
implies that persons can determine their destinies by making moral
or immoral choices and by performing moral or immoral acts that
produce different consequences. Life was generally dukkha—that is,
sorrowful, painful, and difficult—but could be tolerated by following
the Middle Way. To women, borne down by early marriage, seclusion,
ritual impurity because of female functions, painful miscarriages,
and childbirths, this concept made considerable sense and touched
a sensitive nerve. As a consequence, Buddhism attracted many
women in its early stages. Despite Buddhist doctrine disagreeing
with the other doctrines, they were unified in their opposition to the
prevailing system and in providing a viable environment for dissenting
ideas. However, the continuing success of Buddha's philosophy in
comparison with that of other sects, some of which disappeared long
ago, was as much a fact of intelligent organization as of Buddhism's
innate force.

Correctly speaking, Buddha did not become the Buddha until
his Enlightenment at Bodh-Gaya. Before that he was a Bodhisattva,
or a person with the potential for enlightenment and hence for Buddha-
hood. Born as Prince Siddhartha of clan Gotama of the Shakyan tribe
into a Kshatriya household, the young princeling led an uneventful,
protected life until almost his thirtieth year. His birthplace,
Kailavastu, was a busy trading town at the foot of the Himalayas,
north of Banaras and near Nepal. Two features of his birthplace
were to influence him throughout his life: its urban milieu and the
independent mindedness of the Shakyas, who were a republican-ori-
ented but not classless Himalayan tribe/people. Buddha's opposition
to the Brahmins may have been fostered by his birth into the Kshatriyas and the adamant refusal of the Shakyas to be intimidated by the
Brahmins. The Shakyan urban milieu also made Buddha aware of
the need for the smooth functioning of society, the creation of religious machinery, and concern for human welfare. And it influenced

----

*Loka means the common, natural, material world. Lokayatas
originally meant "nature lore" and was actually a branch of Brahmin
learning.

him to concentrate on towns rather than on rural areas for the dissemination of his teachings and the development of a following.

The earliest stories about Buddha's birth were quite straight-
forward. But over time legends developed a more miraculous, ascetic, or even antisexual line. Dreams of a white elephant entering
his mother's, Queen Maya's, womb signified the birth of a Buddha or
universal monarch. Stories evolved that a birth (not unlike the Virgin
Birth in Christianity) occurred when the Buddha-to-be entered the
Queen, who later bore him standing up. The baby was said to have been
born unstained with blood or other materials. Other stories professed
that Buddha's mother died a week after the birth to avoid further
sexual intercourse with her husband, King Suddhodana, for such an
act would be deemed unfitting for a woman who had borne a Peerless
One. Thus, despite Buddha's own attempts to tread the Middle Path
and to discourage bias against caste, gender, or sex, monkish
writers of Buddha stories gradually introduced an antisexual feeling
that later became translated into a negative attitude toward women.

When Gotama was 29, certain events occurred that led him to
contemplate life's sorrowful condition, to discard all personal fetters,
and to become a wandering ascetic in search of spiritual peace. The
picturesque Buddhist story portrays Gotama being confronted successively with a decrepit old man, a very sick man, a begging monk,
and a corpse. These occurrences raised issues never before contemplated by him. When he was next confronted with a holy man,
Prince Siddhartha was inspired to emulate the sage by striving for
spiritual enlightenment. Upon returning home after the four encoun-
ters, the Boddhisattva received the news of the birth of his son whom
he immediately called Rahula, or "fetter." For him the birth fettered
him to the troubles and temptations of family life and thereby denied
him the freedom to seek and attain enlightenment.

His sixth and last encounter was with the Shakyan maiden
Kisagotami, who inadvertently taught him to equate happiness with
the extinguishment of lust and passion. This led him to renounce his
home, his son, his wife, the beautiful princess Yasodhara, his possessions, and all sensual pleasures. The renunciation of his wife,
family, and pleasures was very much in the tradition of the Hindu
sannyasi, which was to be accepted and tolerated by those left behind.
In particular the wife, whether Buddha's or any other sannyasi's,
bore the brunt of the renunciation decision. In the abstract sense,
Gotama was emboldened to seek spiritual enlightenment by the sorrow
of life that he perceived around him and by the awareness that the
unending search by individuals for the satisfaction of their desires
only leads to a despairing sense of loss.

In his search for spiritual peace, Gotama followed the traditional paths of the ascetics of his day: celibacy, starvation, hal-

lucinations, filth, and self-mortification. But to no avail; enlightenment was not forthcoming. Then, deciding that extreme asceticism
was as much a form of vanity as self-indulgence, he embarked upon
another course of action; that of moderation, or the Middle Way.
And thus, meditating under the bodhi, or sacred tree of India, at
Bodh-Gaya, the Boddhisattva became the Buddha, the Awakened or
Enlightened One. Unlike other prophets, he did not profess to have
received a vision, heard voices, experienced a divine ecstasy, or
encountered thundering angels. In fact, within the generally accepted
definition, he did not undergo a religious experience or a divine revelation. Rather, he entered into a formidable intellectual penetration
of the human condition, a dispassionate analysis of its causes, and
the formulation of a doctrine to cure that condition to cope with life's
difficulties. From the outset Buddha did not try to found a religion.
That was to come later through Buddhism's adherents, who could
not for long tolerate pure abstract thought without the crutches of
religious symbols.

The truth of human existence is the foundation of Buddhist doctrine. Buddha analyzed it in various ways as a twelvefold causal
chain of causes and effects, as the Three Marks of Existence, and
as the Four Noble Truths. Each was developed by Buddha in a logical,
sequential way for the use of anybody, regardless of their class level,
their sex, and their previously held beliefs. The Three Marks of
Existence were based upon dukkha, anicca, and anatta (suffering,
impermanence, and ego-fiction). * When Buddha analyzed the human
condition from the point of view of the Four Noble Truths, he again
started from the premise of dukkha. The second truth maintained
that suffering is perpetuated by craving, desire, and greed. But the
cessation of suffering can be effected by the cessation of craving.
Cessation, or narodha,† thus became the third truth, while the

---

*Dukkha is the suffering and sorrow that arises out of all life's ex-
periences whether of the obviously distressful kind, such as death and
illness, or out of the apparently pleasurable sort, such as birth and
sensuality. Dukkha is a condition of and subject of anicca, or impermanence. And the suffering arising out of the impermanence of things
is due to anatta, or the fiction that an individual's ego is a permanent,
stable feature that must be sustained through time immemorial when in
reality ego is a changing, impermanent, nonindividualistic feature.

† Cessation of craving produced the consequence of cessation of
suffering and thus allowed the individual to attain nibbana (or nirvana
in Sanskrit), which might be equated with the recovery of health, the
cooling down of evil passion and egoistic fever. "Narodha" was employed as a synonym for nibbana, but it does not mean exactly the
same thing.

fourth, nirvana, was conceived as a way of attaining that cessation.
The fourth truth, or Buddha's way of achieving narodha, consisted
of morality, meditation, and the attainment of wisdom, with morality
being as important as the other two aspects of the Way. Pain would
end by overcoming craving, which in turn would come about by following the eightfold path of moral spiritual discipline. Morality was expanded to encompass right speech, including not speaking falsely;
right bodily action, including abstaining from killing, unlawful sexual
intercourse, and the use of drugs and alcohol; and right means of
livelihood, which obviated against stealing and other forms of corruption.

In essence Buddha was enunciating the doctrine of a world-renouncing life, which only a few could wholly follow because of the burdensome responsibilities placed by life on the shoulders of most individuals. Buddhism accordingly appeared to be "primarily for monks,
and it was said that the monk was the only true Buddhist. There
were lay followers from an early date, men and women, but there
was no doubt of monkish and male superiority."[2] Lay people might
work toward attaining nirvana or that state of wisdom by seeking rebirth as a monk in their next life or by striving to eliminate the notion
of a permanent individual ego and to develop impersonality and objectivity. This was especially difficult for women to do, as they were
essentially deemed to have no real spirit or soul and no real need for
spirituality or rebirth within the Hindu context. Hence generations
of convention had to be counteracted by Buddhism to allow women the
opportunity to work toward rebirth and nirvana.

Ultimately the new doctrine of wisdom was converted into a religion. Over the centuries, Buddha became endowed with supernatural
powers and divine qualities and then endured the ultimate metamor-
phosis: deification. Despite the impact of Buddhism's logic and
rationalism on Indian thought, both its demise in India and its subsequent survival in disparate Asian countries were ensured by its
conversion into another religious system. Implicitly Buddha and his
followers recognized the inherent difficulties of trying to change human
attitudes and values overnight, including their religiosity, and therefore avoided confronting or frightening the common people with radical views. Yet Buddhism did not offer the ordinary person, especially
the average woman charged with household rituals and excluded from
most spiritual pursuits, the warmth and security of innumerable
rules for daily living or a plethora of comforting deities. For the
majority it was a cold, passionless system that placed on them alone,
without the strength and mediation of priests, the intolerable burden
of seeking their own salvation and controlling their own destiny.
Again, for the average woman this was an anathema. Moreover, because Buddhism tolerated many practices and beliefs, such as mys-

ticism, polytheism, and astrology, that were in the main inconsistent with its central concepts, the conviction of its laity and the authority of the monks became too weakened to withstand the inroads of first the Brahmins and then the Muslims several centuries later.

However, long before that weakening occurred, Buddhism's first adherents, Buddha's five ascetic friends who had attained release from human bondage and achieved nirvana, were soon followed by other Banaras citizens. The first was a young man, Yasa, whose father became Buddhism's first lay follower, or upasaka. And, as with other reformist religions, women were numbered among the first adherents. Yasa's mother and another woman, upon hearing Buddha's words, became the first female lay disciple, or upasika, while others, notably Ambapali, a renowned courtesan, were among his followers. Their support of Buddhism went far beyond being passive initiates. They contributed funds, jewelry, and property for the upkeep of the disciples and the Sangha and actively encouraged others to join the movement. However, traditional male dominance prevailed and it was some years later before the women were formally admitted into the Sangha, or monastic order.

Although Buddhism gave more freedom to women, women were generally regarded as the inferiors and the possessions of men. This is portrayed by the Vinaya, which lists ten kinds of wives, including those bought for money, those used or enjoyed occasionally, those living together voluntarily or sharing homes woefully with other wives (as in polygamy), and those who are temporary wives. It also lists wives who are given certain things, such as cloth, or who perform certain functions (slaves, artisans, or water carriers).[3] In this way an aura of respectability was cast around prostitutes and concubines and a degree of worth normally associated with permanent, dowried wives attached to them.

This reluctance to give women equal standing with men can be seen in Buddha's ambivalence toward admitting women into the Buddhist Order, despite their great moral and financial support. In the first year of his Enlightenment, Gotama returned home and ordained his young son, Rahula, as a novice. Thirteen years later, when Prince Rahula asked, Buddha gave him his inheritance—upasampada, or higher ordination into his father's order. Once again Princess Yasodhara, whom Buddha had won in a contest of arms at the age of 16 and renounced in his quest for enlightenment, requested "her share of the treasure that the Buddha had acquired." Whereupon Buddha's foremost disciple, Ananda, asked, "Master, could women be accepted into the Holy Order?" And the Buddha, recognizing that suffering hurts all humans equally, replied, "Do not the woes of mankind afflict women as well as men?"[4] Finally after a wait of many years, Princess Yasodhara was allowed to enter the Holy Order and so became its first nun.

The acceptance of women into the Sangha was neither immediate nor automatic, Princess Yasodhara's ordination notwithstanding. * Buddha's reluctance to admit women into the newly established order was based on his fear that their presence would disturb the internal equilibrium and harmony of the Sangha. Some notable exceptions were Yasa's mother and her friend. Another was Visakha, the wife of a guild master of Savatthi, who was converted to the Dhamma as a girl and gave her jeweled headdress to the Order to provide funds for another retreat. Ambapali, the beautiful and intelligent courtesan, being treated with the same respect as kings and being invited to dine with Buddha, could not be intimidated or bribed by men of authority to yield her place at Buddha's side and she thereafter presented the Sangha with her park and mansion. And Mahaprajapati, Buddha's stepmother who sheared her hair after her husband's death, donned the saffron robes of the Order and repeatedly asked for admission.

Women were seen as a danger to the monks. Their proximity and sexual attraction were envisaged as distractions from vows of chastity and the search for spiritual freedom. Sexual intercourse was likely to produce children and the fetters of attachment and family life. Thus, the conduct of the monkish life, or brahmacharya, would be jeopardized. This, Buddha warned, could cause Buddhism to decline in only 500 years instead of the 1,000 years he originally predicted. As it has happened, the survival of Buddhism has far outlasted Buddha's dire predictions.

Buddha also feared that, traveling as teaching preachers, they would be subject to the dangers of banditry and assault that plagued the roads of ancient India. Besides, being women in a patriarchal society where women were of little account and were seldom engaged in outside philosophical debates, they would be personally subjected to abuse and harassment. Inadvertently they would thus be the cause of damage to their image as teachers and, by extension, to the substance of the new Order. In effect, Buddha's reluctance to admit women was based on the social conditions of a time when it was highly unusual for women to be taught, let alone to teach. Regardless of Buddha's reluctance, large numbers of women sought out Buddhism and its Order: nunswomen from wealthy, educated, noble families and outcasted women, single, unfertile, and orphaned. Buddhism's egalitarianism and its eventual acceptance of women's ordination encouraged many women to pursue spiritual and intellectual enlightenment untrammeled by prevailing antagonistic social conventions. Some women thus became renowned preachers, sages, speakers, poets, and writers.

---

*The Sangha was known as the Third Jewel of Buddhism, the other two being Buddha himself and the Dhamma, or doctrine.

Entrenched Vedic and brahminical attitudes that severely mitigated against change, especially where women were concerned, also influenced Buddha's willingness to allow women into the Sangha. Consequently, time and again Buddha refused to admit women. Eventually however, he was persuaded by the reasoning of his trusted disciple Ananda and the persistence of his stepmother, Mahaprajapati, to admit women into the Order. Whereupon Mahaprajapati and the women from the Shakyan clan went forth to teach the wisdom of the Shakiyamuni.* But even then the female order of Bhikkunis was founded upon a less-than-equal basis, with the women being subject to strict and humiliating rules that were administered not by themselves but by the Buddhist monks. A bhikkunis, or sister, regardless of having seniority of service or a brother, must always pay obeisance to the lowliest novitiate or the highest bhikku. She must wait for the order of brothers to appoint the sabbath and to preach the sermon; she must do penance for any wrongdoing to both orders; and she must ask for full instructions or orders, upon completion of the appropriate procedures, from both orders. A brother need only be subject to his own order. The double standard further prevailed in that a sister must not abuse or censure a brother, nor must she speak among bhikkus, although they may speak among bhikkunis.5 Yet it is not to be thought that the monks were not subjected to rules. Detailed regulations controlled a monk's behavior toward the nuns he taught and the women he met, including alms givers. The sexual instincts of monks and nuns were subject to the 227 disciplinary rules of the Vinaya Pitaka, which outlined the rules governing the Sangha. Among these, a monk could not sit alone with a woman, act as an intermediary, or touch or look at a woman, let alone masturbate or have sexual intercourse. Since contravention of the rules and breaches of chastity could result in expulsion from the Order, monks and nuns alike were carefully monitored for their own protection as well as for the Sangha's.

Mahaprajapati was the first woman to undertake the Eight Important Rules laid down by Buddha before she or any woman could be accepted into the Order as a fully ordained sister. Having established the ground rules whereby women could be admitted into the Order, Buddha continued to express his uneasiness at such a step: "But now, Ananda, since women have been permitted to go forth from the home unto the homeless life . . . not for long will righteous life prevail. . . . Now just as, Ananda, a man should cautiously build an embankment to a great waterwork, to prevent the water from flowing out, —

---

*Shakiyamuni, or "sage of the Shakyan tribe," was yet another title for Buddha.

even so, Ananda, have I cautiously proclaimed these Eight Important Rules."[6] Even on his deathbed, Buddha's lifelong ambivalence can be seen in his humorous answers to Ananda's questions concerning women.

> How are to conduct ourselves, Lord, with regard
> to women?
> Do not see them, Ananda!
> But if we should see them, what are we to do?
> Abstain from speech.
> But if they speak to us, Lord, what are we to do?
> Keep wide awake, Ananda! [7]

Whether Buddha's unease about women's full admission into the Buddhist Order was due to an unconscious bias against women formed by existing social attitudes or a distrust of women's ability to preach and resist temptation, it is difficult to say. What is obvious, however, is that the equal treatment of women was not a pressing issue with Buddha; his female relatives and Ananda persistently pushed for their inclusion. Ananda was to suffer the consequences of espousing the cause of women, for after Buddha's death, he was charged by the Order with introducing women into the Order and causing its decay.

Despite historical unease or ambivalence, Buddhism's inherent egalitarian strain has directly and indirectly benefited women in countries adopting Buddhism. Buddha abhorred the dogmatic, inegalitarian practices of the Brahmin priests. He believed that all persons suffer equally in striving through their own efforts to reach nirvana, that state of freedom from the horrors of the earthly world. For Buddhists, nirvana is "the summum bonum of Buddhism. A state of supreme Enlightenment beyond the conception of the intellect. Annihilation of all we know as the personal, separative, self."[8] It was a major departure from Hinduism to proclaim that any person, regardless of sex or caste, could aspire to that ultimate condition that is "permanent, stable, imperishable, immovable, ageless, deathless, unborn, and unbecome; that is power, bliss, and happiness, and the secure refuge, the shelter, and the place of unassailable safety; that it is the 'Good,' the supreme goal and the one only consummation of life, the eternal, hidden and incomprehensible Peace."[9]

Buddhism, as the world's first humanitarian religion, was founded less upon hard and fast doctrines than upon individuals finding their own enlightenment through their own endeavors, with assistance from the teachings of monks and lay priests. Therefore, over 2,500 years ago, the Order was established so that Buddha's disciples could spread His Teaching "for the welfare of the world, for the happiness of gods and men.' Both He and they taught, and between them they dispensed the Teaching to Kings and courtesans, to brahmins and beggars, to high and low alike according to their various powers of understanding."[10]

Being politically and socially aware, Buddha understood the need for creating a disciplined organization to ensure the perpetuation of his teaching and the continuation of the Buddhist way of life. He constantly reiterated this fact to members of the Sangha to whom he had entrusted the responsibility of faithfully keeping the Dhamma and acting as exemplars of a democratic, communal system of living. The Sangha itself had been modeled on the Vajjian republican sangha of the tribal assembly, which emphasized consensus and communality over individuality. However, the members of the community, the bhikkus,* were expected to avoid emulating the holy men of other religious sects who isolated themselves from or were parasitical upon society. As "sharesmen" they were expected to share their wisdom with the public, which in return would share with the bhikkus their food, clothing, shelter, and affection.

Contrary to the tradition of the Brahmin priests, the bhikkus had specific reciprocal duties toward householders. They were enjoined to share their knowledge and education with the public regardless of sex or class, to provide advice and affection, deterrence from bad actions, and spiritual guidance. Moreover, they were to enable householders of both sexes to become lay preachers, the consequence of Buddha's positive encouragement of women to act as lay preachers, a role they have effectively performed in Theravadin Buddhist countries to the present. As such the bhikkunis have provided role models for young girls in terms of learning, teaching, and acquiring a certain stature in the public domain that is not specifically tied to wifely duties or motherhood.†

Although the Sangha might have been a model for the whole of society, the masses were too steeped in ignorance and superstition to adopt a new philosophy that demanded a radical readjustment of their ideas and values. Buddha and the early Buddhists recognized this fact and attempted to draw the populace gently into an understand-

---

*Bhikkus literally means "sharesmen" rather than priests, monks, or mendicants. Therefore they are not beggars, nor are they begging for food when they go their early morning rounds, as is commonly thought by Westerners. There is a duality of sharing between them and the householders that obviates any semblance of begging.

†Members of the female order.

ing of Buddhism's meaning through the complementary and reciprocal relationship between the Sangha and the laity. This relationship was epitomized by the Sigala-vada Sutta, * which sets forth a householder's moral duties, domestic and social, [11] and Buddha's definement of reciprocal moral duties between six groups: parents and children, pupils and teachers, husbands and wives, friends and companions, masters and servants, and householders and Sangha members.

Buddhist scriptures differ considerably from Hindu scriptures in that mutual and equal duties are imposed on both marriage partners rather than mainly on the wife alone. [12] A husband was expected to behave as faithfully and as chastely as his wife, to treat her with respect and courtesy, and to adorn her and allow her authority in the household. Thus, the double standard of behavior that prevailed under the Laws of Manu was virtually obliterated by Buddhism. Although polygamy still existed, it was primarily among the wealthy and powerful; even then emphasis was placed on virtuous and faithful treatment of wives. And the practice of arranged marriages, typical of the Vedic epoch, became less rigid. Women under Buddhism were somewhat more independent than under Hinduism and were allowed some voice in selecting a marriage partner or requesting a "self-choice" assembly to choose a husband. While fathers provided dowries specifically for the daughter's benefit, bride prices were also paid. Hence daughters were not quite as unwelcome as in other societies; child marriage was relatively infrequent and was, in fact, rarely mentioned in Buddhist texts; and female infanticide was almost unknown. Buddha is alleged to have said to a king who complained about his daughter's birth that a girl might prove an even better offspring than a son, thus setting the tone for the acceptance of girls.

Buddhism also specified that master-servant relationships should be based on fairness and kindness. The Sigala was one of the first treatises to advocate a master's consideration of his employees in terms of their respective capacities and abilities, good food and pay, sick care, regular time off, and the sharing of "delicacies." Since so many women were in a state of servitude or bondage, the Sigala exhortation was bound to help the lot of those women in service to Hindus who had converted to Buddhism.

In addition to his other concerns, Buddha early recognized the need for a stable society unmarred by constant conflict if the Sangha

---

*Informally termed the Sigala homily, the Sigala-vada Sutta is one of both the best known and the finest pieces of Buddhist literature in Sri Lanka and Southeast Asia. Sangha members adhered to a more detailed code of discipline, the Vinaya, which might be regarded as an elaboration of the Sigala.

was to be an effective medium for conveying the Buddhist moral code to the public. Being a pragmatist as well as a social and political theorist, Buddha understood full well that such security was dependent upon strong but benevolent and enlightened monarchs. Hence he closely associated himself with the influential courts of his day and obtained lifelong support for his mission from contemporary monarchs. In effect he became one of the earliest proponents of development, for he proposed to existing rulers that they should adopt positive measures that would benefit society overall. By doing this he helped women's social and economic position as he encouraged the rulers to extend a wide range of benefits—social, educational, and economic—to their populaces. This was a major departure from the brahminical approach, which emphasized that rulers should work out their personal dharma and seek personal righteousness irrespective of the needs of their people.

Buddha did not deny monarchs their right to perform their personal dharma, but he envisaged for them a broader role that went beyond working toward personal moksha, or salvation by adhering to narrowly defined duties. He envisaged monarchs providing employment rather than sacrifices for their subjects; political stability rather than inglorious battles; and economic security rather than ineffectual ritualistic gestures. Thus, Buddhist theory made the king subject and instrument of the all-subordinating Dhamma, which ultimately should benefit the whole of society.

Whereas the brahminical concept of a ruler might be summed up as "might is right," the Buddhist concept adheres more closely to the view that might and righteousness are interdependent. Not only should the monarch derive his power from the people to be exercised on behalf of the people, his power should be tempered by a sense of harmony and world consciousness derived from adherence to the Dhamma and association with the Sangha. But not until Ashoka's reign did any monarch, regardless of personal acceptance of Buddhism, attempt to implement Buddhist concepts statewide. The result was Buddhism's growth and acceptance.

Gotama, the Buddha, died in 543 B.C. at the age of 80 after more than 40 years of ministry. Unfortunately, thereafter Buddhism did not last long as a flexible reform movement. It stagnated under the burden of social stratification, priestly edicts and aloofness from the laity, its followers' rigid interpretations, and its adjustment to peasant superstitions. It also splintered into numerous sects. In so doing, it became less rational and more reliant upon dogma and sectarian ritual. In India, Brahminism regained domination, with a return to rigid dogma, caste, and refutation of popular education. By contrast, in other countries where Buddhism was launched by Buddhist missionaries both during and after Buddha's lifetime, it became established with little hindrance from such politically motivated structures as the Brahmin priesthood. As a consequence, it retained relatively more of its inherent flexibility, its egalitarian qualities, and its veneration of universal education and teaching.

Soon after the Buddha's death, a council of Sangha was convened to determine the contents of the Pitakas, or the three main divisions of the Pali Canon. * A hundred years later a second council was held. At that time a minority of the Sangha protested the rigidity of the rules of the Pitakas and seceded when the majority refused to relax the rules. The minority were the forbears of today's Mahayanans, while the majority became the Theravadins. This split led to the numerous sects into which Buddhism splintered within a hundred years of its founding. However, until the reign of Ashoka Maurya, commencing in 270 B.C., Buddhism only grew slowly albeit steadily. For Buddhism to be totally accepted by the public, it required a ruler to adopt it. This Ashoka did.

While Ashoka's conversion might be said to have been a direct result of his revulsion for the wanton slaughter at the battle of Kalinga, it could equally be said that his womenfolk introduced him to Buddhism and influenced his conversion. His mother was a Buddhist; his first wife, Devi, was a lay supporter of the Sangha; and his son and daughter were respectively bhikku and bhikkuni, who traveled widely teaching the new wisdom. Thus during Ashoka's time, women were strong proponents of Buddhism.

As Ashoka's conviction about Buddhism and his reverence for Buddha grew, his disillusionment with brahminical greed increased, and he determined to apply the Dhamma throughout his empire. Eventually he became a upasaka, and although he passed legislation, he preferred to exercise persuasion through his ubiquitous Rock Edicts. These imperial edicts written on stone pillars exhorted his citizens to moral effort and proclaimed measures meant to improve the quality of life through the adherence to Buddhist principles. He clearly expected both bhikkus and bhikkunis, laymen and laywomen, to gain knowledge and wisdom from Buddha's sermons and to implement their message by concrete action. Ashoka, by his insistence upon nonviolence, tolerance, and generosity as the keystones to the practice of Dhamma, effectively developed Dhamma into an ethical sys-

---

*The three Pitakas consisted of the Sutta Pitaka, or sermons; the Vinaya Pitaka, or rules of the Sangha; and the Abhidhamma Pitaka, which is a compilation of metaphysics, psychology, and philosophy and contains a comprehensive system of mind training. Most of the Abhidhamma is regarded as later commentary or addition to the Pitakas.

tem that could be practiced by laity and the Sangha alike. To a large extent he was responsible for initiating a way of life that has been followed by the majority of Buddhists to the present.

Ashoka himself tried to rule as a genuine Buddhist ruler. He followed the Dhamma, adhered to the same social responsibilities he set down for his people, and maintained his ethical obligations. He was unique among rulers in refraining from hunting and similar useless monarchical pleasures and in strongly promoting the welfare or development of his people. He banned the unscrupulous killing of animals, urged the adoption of vegetarianism, and halted the indiscriminate burning of forests. He established numerous public works, including hospitals and medical services for people and animals; accessible wells; roadside shade trees; and the planting of new food crops and fruit trees. He appointed welfare officers to look to the needs of the old and young, the sick and poor, the rich and powerful. He anticipated that it would become easier for people to conform to the Dhamma if their lot was improved.

While Ashoka did not promote Buddhism as an official religion, during his reign Buddhism nevertheless made the transition from a philosophy to a religion. Like Buddha, Ashoka strongly disapproved of sacrifices. Similarly, he was mildly opposed to popular beliefs and superstitious rites, but he tolerated them. He was particularly scathing of the trivial, useless ceremonies that women traditionally and automatically performed (as much to preserve their meager social prestige as to propitiate spirits). Unlike Buddha, he had certain cosmological beliefs in common with his other contemporaries. He believed that through the vigorous practice of Dhamma the substrata of hell could be avoided; the improved moral condition on earth would attract the devas, or good spirits; and every person could then aspire to a higher, more rarefied existence. Despite his own views, he allowed a diversity of sectarian beliefs, provided they did not impinge upon or denigrate others. Among these were the veneration of stupas and the emergence of bhakti cults, which led to the worship of Buddha Gotama and innumerable other Bodhisattvas. * Thus the founder of Buddhism became the object of veneration. He who had repudiated worship as essential to attaining enlightenment ascribed only aesthetic qualities to stupas, and forbidden deification became deified.

Toward the end of Ashoka's reign, Buddhism had assumed many of the characteristics of a popular religion. This occurred despite

---

*Stupas were cairns containing the relics of heroes and important men. Ten stupas were immediately set up after Buddha's death, and others containing a relic or relics of the Buddha subsequently became shrines of worship. Bhakti denotes devotional worship.

Ashoka himself being predominantly a social reformer concerned with implementing a social philosophy that would help restructure society. As a reformer, Ashoka sent missionaries, including his son and daughter, far afield to establish the Buddhist Order. If he had not exhibited such missionary zeal (rather in the manner of Paul) it is likely that Buddhism, as with early Christianity, would have retrenched into a mere bhagavata cult, which would have worshipped Buddha's graven image and done little else. As it was, Ashoka's best reformist efforts in India were not enough to withstand brahminical pressures and popular beliefs.

Ashoka had demonstrated that a state could be ruled in accordance with the Buddhist system of ethics and morals. He had shown that social and political reform was fully compatible with Buddhism and had demonstrated that Buddhism could be an effective tool of development. As a consequence he had one of the finest and best-run, if not the most human, empires in India's history. But such progress could not and did not last.

Tolerance was met with intolerance, philosophy with superstition. Irrationality replaced logic. Reactionary Brahmin forces reversed the reforms initiated by Buddha and the Sangha and promulgated by Ashoka. "Buddhism, from its outset fatally tolerant of all other teachings, even when antithetical to its own, made little effort to stem the process, and soon a number of sects were exhibiting Brahman doctrines which were unknown in the earlier Teaching."[13]

In an effort to correct misconceptions about Buddha and Buddhism, a school for bhikkus composed the Kathavathu. * Through this they managed to preserve the original intent of Buddha and to preserve the true Buddha Way. Buddhism in its original form and concept would have vanished upon the collapse of Ashoka's empire 100 years after his death if that school, the School of Theravadins or elders, had not conscientiously attempted to preserve Buddha's earliest teachings. Once the bhagavata cult had become part of the Indian cultural scene, the Buddha became just one of the great spiritual beings worshiped in the Indian pantheon.

It is possible that it was the development of Buddhism from a socio-political philosophy to a popularly based religious cult which was one of the chief causes of its eventual decline and virtual disappearance from India. Once it had come to be regarded as a religious system

---

*This is one of the seven books of the Abhidhamma-Pitaka of the Pali Canon. As with most Buddhist and Hindu scriptures, its exact date of composition is unknown.

> it could be thought of . . . as a rival by those who adhered
> to, and whose interests were vested in, another religious
> ideology, notably the Brahmans.[14]

Ashoka's deep association with Buddhism would have also led
to considerable resentment. Indeed, a Brahmin state was established
under the new regime only 50 years after Ashoka's decease. The
Brahmins reintroduced the concept of the ruler fulfilling his personal
dharma rather than the more universal Buddhist Dhamma, and they
assumed strong advisory roles to the prevailing rulers, thereby ensuring that Buddhist influences were kept out of affairs of state. As
discussed extensively in Chapter 2, among the consequences of the
Brahmin priests regaining control were detrimental ramifications for
the position of women, their freedom and development, and their education and status.

Although Buddhism reached a nadir in India, it did survive in
basically three forms: first as part of the Indian pantheon; second as
the essential doctrine of Buddha within the School of Theravadins,
mentioned earlier, who maintained the Sangha in its purest state; and
third as the expanded philosophy of the original dissenting minority,
which became Mahayana Buddhism. Considerable speculation, which
cannot be dealt with in this space, exists as to how and why Buddhism
became divided over the centuries into the two main streams of Mahayana and Hinayana (Theravadin) Buddhism.* Suffice it to say that
if those two strong schools of thought had not developed, Buddhism,
the Sangha, and the Buddhist state would have petered out. Instead,
through Ashoka's missionary efforts and the persuasiveness of Mahinda, his son, and Sanghamitta, his daughter, the Hinayana became
thoroughly established in Sri Lanka. From there it filtered out to the
countries of Thailand, Burma, and Cambodia.

----

*Maha-Yana means literally the "great vehicle" (of salvation).
This northern school of Buddhism originated with the dissenting minority of the second council, but its syncretistic features and worship
of gods attracted to it a greater number of adherents than the Hinan-
yana school. It is generally practiced in Japan, Tibet, Nepal, and
Korea, and has been practiced in China.

Hina-Yana means the "lesser vehicle" (of salvation). The
Hinayana school was the earliest form of Buddhism, with the Thera-
vada being the sole surviving sect of the southern school of Buddhism.
It emphasized the doctrine or teaching of the Thera, or elders of the
Sangha, and hence was regarded as more conservative and rule bound
than the Mahayana. Now it is mainly found in Thailand, Burma, and
Sri Lanka.

Those three countries were originally influenced by Mahayana Buddhism, which in turn was modified by indigenous worship rituals. Subsequently however, those countries adopted and became the leading proponents of Hinayana Buddhism. Today, with the violent elimination of religion in Cambodia and the curtailment of freedom of thought in Burma, only Thailand and Sri Lanka retain a semblance of the original Buddhist state based upon a strong code of ethics and morality, democratic thought, and consensual action.

The Mahayana school rebelled against the more rigid, colder doctrine of Hinayana Buddhism taught by the Thera, or elders. The Theravadins wanted to adhere strictly to Buddha's original teachings and would recognize only sutras composed during Buddha's lifetime and up to the first council, held in 480 B. C.* By contrast, the Mahayanists attributed all sutras to Buddha, even those composed two or three centuries after his death. From the outset, disputes arose over the authorship and dates of sutras. At the first council, the Hinayanists attempted to confine attributions to Buddha to his actual sermons by drawing upon the memories of his most devoted disciples. But over 400 years their efforts were undermined by the tradition of oral transmission by schools of reciters who ascribed sutras and shastras alike to Buddha. Since only a few of the oldest documents remain, it is difficult to separate the two.

The Mahayana school attempted to reconcile the difficulties arising from combining the sutras and shastras by expanding the then-extant Buddhism into a more publicly acceptable philosophy. This meant making it less ascetic and esoteric and more positive, catholic, and emotionally satisfying. Accuracy of dates was immaterial, as was strict authorship. In sum,

> the Mahayana refused to be inhibited; the Hinayana was
> bound by the (Pali) Canon. The former were speculative,
> metaphysical; the latter rational and authoritarian. The
> Mahayana was fearless in its logic and mystical flights;
> the Theravada was content to be the guardian of the
> Dhamma as handed down. The closed circle of intense
> self-development (of the Theravadins) became a religion
> for all (in the Mahayana context), and a formula of salva-
> tion branched out into a heterogeneous mixture of appar-
> ently opposed and incompatible teaching.[15]

---

*The sutras were Buddha's sayings or sermons, although literally they meant "the threads" on which his teachings were strung. Shastras were treatises that cited the sutras as authorities and were written by specific authors.

As might be expected, such "opposed and incompatible teaching" was bound to affect women, their role in Buddhism and the Sangha, and the overall perception of women. An example of this was the decision of the Theravadin school to abolish the female order. For all that, the Mahayana school has never rejected Hinayana Buddhism but has merely regarded itself as a natural extension of central-core Theravadin concepts. As missionaries took Mahayana Buddhism to Tibet, China, Korea, and Japan, its doctrine continued to unfold in many diverse ways in accord with each country's particular values and characteristics. However, space does not permit a discussion here of the impact of Buddhism on those countries or the influence of Confucianism, Shintoism, or the imperial courts on Buddhism.

Central to both the Hinayanists and Mahayanists is Buddha's teaching, which urges self-reliance, flexibility, and action while subjugating individualism. The teaching anticipates that the individual will exercise free consciousness, taking into account past experiences and conditioning. Inherent in it is the philosophy that "I, the individual, am the owner of action, the heir of action, the birthplace of action, the relation of action and the pathway of action. Whatever action I have done, good or evil, that I shall be heir to (receive)."[16] On this basis priests who are skilled in morality, meditation, and wisdom are (theoretically, at least) free of past conditioning and therefore capable of exercising greater freedom of choice than ordinary human beings unversed or only partially versed in Buddhism's wisdom. Freedom from past conditioning, such as prejudice and antipathy, should render them more tolerant and understanding of their society caught in a conflict between old and new values. Likewise, it should enable them to guide their followers through the labyrinth of conflicts raised by traditional beliefs locking with modern needs.

Unfortunately, in the clash of old with new values, priests and laity alike have been unable to discard their past conditioning. Priests over time have railed against general education, female education, and coeducation; family planning, birth control, and contraceptives; and films, medicine, and modernization in general. The laity have followed suit or, where they have disagreed with the priests and hence by extension with their religion, they have withdrawn from their religion and its moderating values. The sad consequence of this is the negativism exerted by religion on modern society. Instead of being a constructive, dynamic force, it has been negative or at best inert.

Nothing in Buddha's teaching mitigates against reform, change, or development. Buddha himself was one of the world's first and greatest reformers, not only in the spiritual and philosophical realm but in the economic and social areas. His Buddhist Order was established to implement reformist ideas and to develop a new society, a society that Ashoka successfully implemented. Yet Buddhism has not been a major force for change and reform in recent decades. This could be because the preservation of Buddha's sutras and the Sangha's rules have been ritualized, and ritualization and hierarchy have taken precedence over action and flexibility. It could be because the Sangha has fallen into the trap of empty ritual and meditation, with the concept of a Buddhist state devoted to improving its society's quality of life forgotten. Irrational, deterministic fatalism instead of self-reliance and action may have caused Buddishm to falter in creating new Dhammic directions for adherents; its adherents became mired in apathy and rigidity. Nevertheless, even if Buddhism has not lived up to its original design of being a positive influence for social change, neither has it been a total hindrance. Likewise, neither has its priesthood been totally obstructionist.

While many priests have contented themselves with the mere form of Buddhism and some have reacted negatively to proposed social changes, many others have contributed positively to their respective societies. They have encouraged the secular and religious education of both males and females, social work and family planning, and political reason in difficult circumstances. If they have not actively participated in change, they have positively contributed by not indulging in the type of antichange histrionics favored by priests of other religions. Though some Buddhist priests may have been against concepts like birth control, as were the village priests of Sri Lanka, rarely have they incited their followers to hostility or social violence against new developments.

On the whole the Buddhist priesthood—especially the better-educated at the upper echelons—has been moderate in view and action and tolerant of the forces of change. Accordingly, in line with Buddhism's insistence upon consensus, the moderate majority have been able to curtail excesses by their more regressive or violence-prone colleagues. While they have not been prepared to go so far as to reconstitute the female order of bhikkunis, which was allowed to decline out of existence after Ashoka's reign, they have not generally hindered female education or women's progress. Perhaps this was due to the persistence and dedication of many women who, undeterred by the unwillingness of the Sangha in the Theravada Buddhist countries to reestablish the female order, became Sila-Upasika. These laywomen disciples closely observed the Sangha's rules and devoted themselves to charitable works. In fact, many of the Sila-Upasika became the first formal social workers of the Theravadin countries, where they are well respected by the community.

The lack of priestly opposition to female education and development may have been occasioned by the essential egalitarianism of Buddhism. What inequality can be discerned between Buddhist men and women might have even worked to women's advantage, commercially and professionally, in the early stages of modernization. Since women had traditionally been excluded from direct merit-earning activities in the Theravadin countries and since men traditionally would only undertake enterprises that produced spiritual recompense, the women actively filled the void. As a consequence they became respected and influential forces in their countries' development. However, that might now be changing as men devote themselves more vigorously to business and professional enterprises and less to merit-earning meditation and spiritual activities. Women will need to guard against a backlash being whipped up against their development and their full participation in society by either religious leaders or politicians using religion for their own ends. However, education, family planning, political emancipation, and work-force participation should help to guarantee women's relatively high standing in Buddhist countries.

As a social philosophy and a religion, Buddhism could be a major positive factor in providing the bridge between the old, traditional ways and the new. But it will not be if its authorities, intent upon preserving form and power, compress it and its adherents into a rigid, stultified mold. Were Buddhism to return to "its original concern with the public dimension of life as distinct from only the private world of soul-salvation,"[17]—the emphasis given to it by those uneasy with a philosophical Buddhism—it could become a vital factor in reform and development pointing to the true Middle Way.

NOTES

1. Reprinted with permission from Trevor Ling, The Buddha (Middlesex: Penguin Books, 1976), p. 91. First published in Great Britain by Maurice Temple Smith, London, 1973.

2. Geoffrey Parrinder, Sex in the World's Religions (Don Mills, Ontario: General, 1980), p. 44.

3. Ibid., p. 55.

4. Joseph Gaer, How the Great Religions Began (New York: American Library, Signet Key Books, 1958), p. 40.

5. F. L. Woodward, trans., Some Sayings of the Buddha according to the Pali Cannon (Oxford: Oxford University Press, 1973), p. 81.

6. Ibid., p. 82, quoting the Vinaya, 2:10.

7. Christmas Humphreys, Buddhism (Middlesex: Penguin Books, 1962), pp. 38-39.

8. Ibid., p. 244.

9. Edward Conze, Buddhism: Its Essence and Development (New York: Harper & Row, 1959), p. 40.

10. Khantipalo Bhikku, What Is Buddhism? (Bangkok: Social Science Association Press of Thailand, 1965), p. 17.

11. Ling, The Buddha, pp. 166–67.

12. Parrinder, Sex in the World's Religions, p. 55, citing the Digha Nikaya, the Jataka, and the Vinaya.

13. Humphreys, Buddhism, p. 47.

14. Ling, The Buddha, pp. 166–67.

15. Humphreys, Buddhism, p. 50.

16. Khantipalo, What Is Buddhism?, p. 33.

17. Ling, The Buddha, p. 294.

6

BUDDHISM
AND
EDUCATION

Undoubtedly, "Buddhism has its own long and noble tradition of scholarship, and of education of the young, with the result that some of the traditionally Buddhist countries of South-East Asia have an unusually high rate of literacy for Asia. It has encouraged equality of social opportunity."[1] Yet even Buddhism, relatively tolerant of women, initially limited female participation in its schools, a consequence of Buddha's own ambivalence toward women and his failure to specify their inclusion when he talked about teachers and students.

As Tathagata,* or Teacher, Buddha embarked upon the third definitive stage of his life. Convinced that he should communicate his discovery of truth and the Dhamma to others, he went to Banaras, the religious, philosophical, and intellectual center of ancient India where seekers-of-truth inevitably gathered. There he conducted a teaching session with five ascetics, friends he knew to be receptive to new ideas. As a consequence of understanding Buddha's discovered truth and acquiring a state of wisdom and dispassion, these five achieved a state of release from the bonds of human existence, or arahantship. With the excitement they generated by coming to the end of the Fourfold Way and attaining nirvana, many others, men and women, were attracted to the Tathagata's teaching.

From the outset Buddha inculcated in his followers a reverence for learning and a reverence for teachers. At his teaching sessions in Banaras in an organized, systematic way, he conveyed the Dhamma,

---

*Tathagata (Sanskrit) was one of Buddha's titles and literally meant "he who follows in the footsteps of his predecessors." Buddha believed himself to be merely one of a succession of teachers, or buddhas.

or Truth, to his first disciples, who were to become the first members of the Sangha. There, too, he gained his first upasika, or lay-followers, two of whom were women. However, because of his initial reluctance to incorporate women into the Sangha and thereby give them the same learning opportunities as men, he inadvertently gave validity to the actions of his subsequent followers, who neglected or deprecated female education.

While young boys were encouraged from the early stages of Buddhism to enter monastic schools of education run by Buddhist monks and to participate in religious-based tutorials, girls were mainly ignored. The education of the young, until its eventual secularization, was essentially the education of boys. This tendency was reinforced by various of Buddha's sayings that explicitly or impliedly stressed the importance of educating the male without specifically mentioning the equivalent for the female. In his injunction to his followers about the relationship of the teacher to the pupil he stipulated that "the teacher, brethren, should regard the pupil as his son. The pupil should regard the teacher as his father" (emphasis added). [2] The automatic assumption that males were to be both teacher and student was undoubtedly a throwback to Hinduism, the main difference being that Buddhism had removed the caste distinctions and educational monopoly established by the Brahmin priests. Despite the strength and intelligence shown by his wife, stepmother, and close female relatives, in the historical context it would have been unusual if he had envisaged women as teachers or girls as students. Or if he had envisaged that they could develop between them the close relationships equivalent to the father-son relationship of male teachers and pupils. Nevertheless, he set the tone for extended and universal education by enjoining his followers to immerse themselves in education for at least ten years under the charge of a teacher. Although he thereby set the stage for and the eventual acceptance of extended education among Buddhists, he in fact, was emulating Hinduism and the Code of Manu, which also had prescribed various long periods of study.

Further, when Buddha detailed to his young follower, the house-holder Sigala, the mutually reciprocal duties of teachers and pupils, he nowhere alluded to the possibility of pupils being both male and female. [3] He did, however, set basic ground rules for behavior and responsibility that were to have a continuing positive impact on Buddhist attitudes toward education in general. He did not restrict duties or responsibilities to students as Hindu treatises tended to do. In this Buddha was unusual, for apart from the onus he placed on pupils to respect their teachers and to show diligence in learning, he likewise placed an onus on teachers. Through the Sigala-vada Sutta, teachers were enjoined to inculcate in their pupils a sense of moral duty, a love of learning, and a knowledge of the teacher's every subject.

Using the parables of the good herdsman and of the ferryman guiding his ship, Buddha explained how and why wise teachers could guide others through a labyrinth of ignorance and unwisdom to the Norm or Truth, and how they could light a fire of truth seeking in others.[4] Buddha believed that seven factors led to wisdom: Inner Mindfulness, Searching of the Norm, Energy, Zest, Serenity, Concentration, and Mental Balance.[5] While these thoughts were conscientiously instilled in young Buddhist males seeking wisdom and merit, in no instance did Buddha address himself similarly to the sisters of the Sangha or the female laity. Nor did he ascribe learning possibilities and capabilities to women. As a consequence, for a long time women were assumed excluded from Buddha's plans for the general education of the populace. Eventually, orthodox or misogynist monks used this omission for their own purposes, including hampering female education.

Nevertheless, Buddhism's inherent tolerance, sense of equality, rationalism, and reverence for learning have helped to counteract such biases and barriers as might have negated female education or unduly deferred its inception. It is probably these qualities that have inspired Buddhist countries to develop comprehensive coeducation, to install women as teachers and administrators at all levels, and to encourage girls to pursue higher education in greater numbers than Hindu India, Muslim countries, or many Latin American countries. Traditionally, Buddhist populations have certainly had high levels of literacy—in some areas even attaining 100 percent—reflecting the high educational levels of females. No doubt the personification of the Perfection of Wisdom, the essence of all teaching, as the mother of all the buddhas, including Gotama the Supreme Teacher,[6] helped to inject a female component into Buddhism and its concepts of education. It came to be accepted that if the Perfection of Wisdom was the mother of all buddhas, by extrapolation women and girls could or should not be deprived of either learning or teachers.

Contrary to popular notion, the Buddha's teachings were neither negative nor fatalistic. Rather, they insisted upon a real choice of action for people through the practice of the Middle Way. And while people generally meant "men," nonetheless women were given more choice than before. Buddha did not subscribe to the Ajivikas' view of no freedom of choice. Nor did he subscribe to the Ajivikas' or Jainas' asceticism and the Materialists' hedonism as ways of attaining spiritual freedom. At one and the same time he rejected all traditional orthodox doctrines and formulated radical new concepts that incurred the resistance and displeasure of other antibrahminical sects.

Buddha's teachings, being dynamically intellectual, were not religious or spiritual in the commonly accepted sense of being dependent upon supernatural guidance, divine revelation, or theistic beliefs.

Throughout he emphasized education, self-determination, and learning, and teacher guidance rather than dictatorship. Accordingly, his teachings were more philosophical/ideological than religious, more rationalistic than spiritual. Buddha's first followers never regarded him as a divine figure endowed with supernatural powers. To them he was superb teacher with whom they could discuss, debate, and analyze life's idiosyncrasies with great seriousness and with humor.

Buddha had no religious role and he was never regarded ab initio as a savior. He labeled himself and was accepted by the first Buddhists simply as a Tathagata, whose duty as a teacher was to direct their attention to human matters but not to provide them with deliverance or to do their work for them. This attitude was to pose problems for numerous women and finally for Buddhism itself, since its emphasis on self-deliverance and strong intellectualism tended to remove from women the spiritual comforts and guidance of traditional or folkloric religions. It forced them back on to their own inner resources and often made them reassess themselves and their beliefs. Many could not handle that challenge and reverted to the old ways.

Nevertheless, within Buddhism there is considerable scope for analyzing a condition or exploring a situation. Since Buddha saw himself as an analyst rather than a dogmatist and insisted that all propositions, even his own, should be tested and scrutinized,[7] he instilled in Buddhism and its advocates a flexibility of action and thought that would permit the system to adapt to changing circumstances, not least of which were the evolving needs and demands of women.

Throughout its history Buddhism has evolved from a psychosocial philosophy into a religion replete with deities and spirits. Yet Buddhism's humanitarian social base, its rationalism, and its lack of dogmatism have afforded its adherents an opportunity to bring about reforms without upsetting popular beliefs and without being assailed by religious doubts or priestly interdicts. Thus, reforms affecting women, their education, their participation in public life, and the control of their own bodies and lives rarely evoked the religious fury and chastisement that similar reforms provoked in Catholic and Muslim countries. Indeed,

> one of the most important characteristics of the Buddha's teaching . . . the attitude of nonacceptance of traditional orthodoxy of any kind and, instead, a very marked "intellectualism" [combined with] the Buddha's insistence on the real possibility of human choice and freedom of action, and his opposition to fatalism. . . .[8]

have provided a latitude of thought. Indirectly, Buddha's nonacceptance of traditional orthodoxy and his concept of freedom of choice and action have formed substantial resistance to efforts to curtail the expansion of women's horizons through education and other means.

Likewise, the influence of the bhikkunis contributed to staving off efforts to restrict women's education. When the bhikkus became integrated into the Sangha, they with the bhikkus were as much educators of adults and children as they were proselytizers and advisers. To facilitate the propagationof knowledge, the bhikkus set up in their monasteries the first systematic schools for male children in India and then in Southeast Asia. With time, these attracted adults, usually men. Later, education was introduced for females so that they could also be helped to acquire the knowledge that would lead them to a fuller life, if not enlightenment. Although the bhikkus were enjoined to instruct all, they were also under injunction not to sit close to women, be in the same room as women, or look at women. This made the teaching of women awkward; hence, the bhikkunis had a vital role to play in educating women and were in a very real sense important role models.

Where opposition to female education and related reforms continues, it continues less because of Buddhism's basic concepts, whether taken as religious or as philosophical, than because of individuals determined to mutilate Buddhism for their own ends. The evocation of Buddhism's overwhelming positive characteristics by leaders would go a long way toward alleviating any doubts about the desirability of treating women on an equal basis and allowing them to become fullfledged human beings.

The acceptance of female education, the ability and wisdom exhibited by the bhikkunis, and the essential egalitarianism of Buddhism combined to facilitate female education in predominantly Buddhist countries. By contrast, in India the demise of Buddhism and the Sangha rang down the curtain on female education and spiritual teaching for many generations and made their belated revival more difficult. The veneration accorded to bhikkus and bhikkunis (or abbots and abbesses in the case of Japan) as teachers of knowledge and wisdom was transferred in the Southeast Asian countries to their successors, the secular teachers. When education reforms were subsequently introduced, this veneration was transformed into a fairly universal public acceptance of education for all. Hence, relatively high literacy rates, even among women, were quickly attainable.

It is sometimes contended that Buddhism inhibits the various aspects of development or modernization because of its fatalism, negativism, and merit-earning attributes. Yet, as pointed out, the basic tenets of Buddhism as enunciated by Buddha and practiced by Ashoka are dynamic, positive, and geared not just to the individual but also to society. Unfortunately, various Westerners, in analyzing Theravada Buddhism, have failed to differentiate between its basic tenets or doc-

trine, its religiosity or religious practices, and its political use.
They tend to see Buddhism's doctrine as deleterious to modernization,
devoid of the modernizing elements such as the Puritan work ethic allegedly inherent in Protestant Christianity, and inimical to economic
development. [9]

In reality it is more likely the religious attitudes, values, and
practices at the popular or folkloric level of Buddhism that inhibit
development. It is typically more at this level that opposition to female education has been raised than at the upper levels. Political
activists and scholars alike have managed to translate Buddhist doctrine to fit virtually any economic (including educational development)
or political situation. For instance, "U Nu found the bases of Burmese
socialism in the foundations of Buddhism, and Thai politicians have
employed Buddhism to support a form of free enterprise."[10] In essence, the basic tenets of Buddhism are so all-encompassing and
flexible that they can be fitted to a variety of needs and circumstances.
Thus, when politicians have wished to, they have managed to manipulate Buddhist doctrine in favor of or against modernization. By and
large, they have opted to interpret Buddhism favorably insofar as female education has been concerned.

Where problems concerning the education of girls and women
have occurred, the problems have tended to have a more general application to the populace as a whole than to females specifically. The
problems have encompassed the failure to set development and education priorities and adequate budgets for educational purposes, the
tendency to promote an education more relevant to a bygone colonial
era than the twentieth century, and a concentration on classicism and
rote learning rather than on employment-related training and logic.

Where education in Theravada Buddhist countries is still carried
out in religious schools, problems arise less because some students
are girls than because the teachers, being of the religious orders,
concentrate on traditional methods of teaching and religious subjects
to the virtual exclusion of modern subjects. The failure to educate
girls and boys in agricultural, vocational, or technological subjects
has mitigated against them gaining employment in the modern sector
or developing improved skills for the traditional sectors of agriculture and marketing.

However, gradually changes have occurred. Students have been
attracted either to secular schools or to those religious schools that
have included modern subjects. Yet, these very changes have created a concern for some religious leaders, the bulwarks of traditional religious values, that they and their faith would be undermined
by modern trends. And they have on occasion reacted to halt those
trends that they perceived could lead to a decline in their authority,
a disbelief in their faith, a diminution in the central role of religion,

and damage to the family structure. They have seen how "the penetration of western education not only reduced the attractiveness of religious schooling but often led to the substitution by Christian missionary education, thus undermining their occupations and values."[11]

For females the substitution of a Christian mission education in many countries of Southeast Asia was often a mixed blessing. On the one hand, it opened the doors of learning more widely to all females. It thereby influenced some religious leaders to accommodate females more wholeheartedly in their school system and various policy makers to agitate for a more comprehensive coeducational system.

On the other hand, the missionary-introduced education brought in values and attitudes that actually reduced the status and role of local Buddhist women, based as it was on the upper-class public school system of England, because it failed to take account of their local needs, values, and desires. Too often it trained them inappropriately in the "ladylike" pursuits of embroidery, music, and the arts, but failed to prepare them for the reality of their lives in Sri Lanka, Thailand, or Burma. At a later date, many nongovernmental organizations, legacies of the missionary era, would repeat the same error—training young women in home economics or providing them with sewing machines but failing to train them in the technicalities of machine maintenance, to provide spare parts, or to teach them marketing so that they might actually earn some income for their endeavors.

To alter this missionary legacy, educational policy makers have vacillated between reorienting their education systems to the traditional and nationalist (which means reviving their own culture, religion, and languages) or to the hard-core modern with its vocational and technological emphasis. In Sri Lanka, for example, the planners tried to give education a more Sri Lankan quality, but the subjects introduced were hardly relevant to the twentieth century. Trevor Ling has noted that Sri Lankan education remained highly academic rather than practical or vocational. This appears to be in keeping with the particular emphasis of the Buddhist monastery schools of the villages. The nonpractical nature of traditional Buddhist education is imparted mainly by the bhikkus, who are essentially prohibited by their religious rules from practical occupations, especially the cultivation of the soil.[12]

The ramifications of such traditional attitudes and practices combined with the legacy of colonial education and inappropriate Western education are several. Agricultural development becomes inhibited, new agricultural enterprises are less than successful, and domestic production becomes inadequate to feed the growing population. This in turn inhibits overall economic development and contributes to a worsening employment situation. Even though the trend is to educate females better than before and despite women generally having equal access to education (in Sri Lanka more girls are enrolled in secondary schools than boys, and in Thailand increasingly large numbers are attending the university), women are by no means protected from the ravages of unemployment.

Apart from employers' views that females are the weaker sex and need more protection but less pay and fewer job opportunities, women are disadvantaged by the lack of vocational and technical education. Typically, what vocational training exists—and that is often inadequate to meet the needs of graduates—is geared to young men to the virtual exclusion of women. Since employers, some educators, and a surprising number of ambivalent women regard a woman's work as relatively unimportant and secondary to the male breadwinner's, women tend to be excluded from courses that could lead to jobs or relegated to unremunerative domestic classes. In this way artificial barriers or divisions are created between the sexes. Worse, a vicious circle for women evolves, whether in Sri Lanka or other countries, for "women are regarded as not useful because they are untrained and are left untrained because they are not useful."[13]

Time and modernization are beginning to erode regressive attitudes about women, at least among many of the educated urban elite. Politicians and policy makers are increasingly recognizing that women cannot be left off the train of development. Not only could that be bad for their country, it could jeopardize their chances of reelection. But how long can the women and their nations afford to wait? Will women gain enough confidence through education and work to cast off old, inhibiting conventions and to compel the revision of attitudes? It could be an inordinately long time, if a country like Sri Lanka with high educational levels is anything to go by. There, where the women "are far better educated than the women of other Asian countries . . . the superstitions, taboos, and customs passed along from ancient feudal times continue to persist regardless of ethnic or religious origin."[14] These may possibly be counteracted by education, but that will depend in part on the extent to which development and education planners finally recognize the significance of religiosity in people's lives. Will they be prepared in their educational schemes to educate those people away from the devils, taboos, and negative attitudes of folkloric Buddhism to the positive ("I am the owner of action") tenets of Buddha's Buddhism? And will they be able to enlist the positive educational help of the spiritual leaders of the community?

NOTES

1. Reprinted with permission from Trevor Ling, The Buddha (Middlesex: Penguin Books, 1976), p. 15. First published in Great Britain by Maurice Temple Smith, London, 1973.

2. F. L. Woodward, trans., Some Sayings of the Buddha (Oxford: Oxford University Press, 1973), p. 46.

3. Ibid., p. 110.

4. Ibid., pp. 170–72, 207–8.

5. Ibid., pp. 54–55.

6. Khantipalo Bhikku, What Is Buddhism? (Bangkok: Social Science Association Press of Thailand, 1965), p. 7.

7. Ling, The Buddha, p. 140.

8. Ibid., pp. 14–41.

9. Reprinted with permission from Fred R. Von der Mehden, "Religion and Development in South-East Asia: A Comparative Study," World Development (Oxford) 8, no. 7–8 (July–August 1980): 545–53.

10. Ibid., p. 547.

11. Ibid., p. 549.

12. Reprinted with permission from Trevor Ling, "Buddhist Values and Development Problems: A Case Study of Sri Lanka," World Development (Oxford): 8, no. 7–8 (July–August 1980): 582.

13. Antony Brook, "A UNESCO Inquiry on Women's Status in Five Countries," UNESCO Courier, August–September 1975, p. 40.

14. Perdita Huston, Message from the Village (New York: Epoch B. Foundation, 1978), p. 63.

7

BUDDHISM
AND
POPULATION

Buddhism reflects many of the characteristics and attitudes endemic to Hinduism. Among these are striving for spiritual perfection; the eschewing of material ties or emotional bonds; a respect for moderation, abstinence, and celibacy; and an apparent tolerance for fertility limitation through its lack of formal religious proscriptions against contraception. Buddhism's concentration on the Middle Path, or moderation, and its innate tolerance basically contribute to a reasonable approach to the population issue, thereby avoiding much of the invective raised against population policies by religious authorities in other countries. However, popular beliefs in or misinterpretations of Buddhism's fundamental tenets have led women to believe just the opposite—that to be born a woman is a sin, a consequence of having done a thousand sins in a previous life. Therefore, to remedy that sin a woman must be submissive, bear children, and achieve merit through her male children.

Like Hinduism, Buddhism is disparate, diffuse, and uncentralized, particularly in the Theravada Buddhist countries. Accordingly, its religious structure is hardly effective in either conveying its reasonable approach to population issues or disseminating population and contraception information to the masses. The pronatalist image that has attached to Buddhism stems more from folkloric religion, cultural and traditional mores, or historical Hinduism than from Buddhism's teachings and scriptures. Buddha, while acknowledging the need and desire of the human race to indulge in sex and reproduction, advocated the Middle Way and the avoidance of extremes of indulgence, whether in drink, sex, emotions, pessimism, or optimism.

Because Buddhism expected all individuals to follow the Middle Path, to avoid extremes, to be self-reliant and controlled, to be compassionate and tolerant, and to exercise logic and objectivity, women

as well as men were accorded the respect due to intelligent human
beings striving for wisdom and enlightenment. As discussed before,
Buddhism on the whole has historically viewed women with a relatively
benevolent eye. It had eased the tentacles of a restricting Brahminism on Hindu women until the Brahmins reorganized and ousted the
reformist movement, and it had sufficiently influenced the lives of
the peoples of Southeast Asia (Java, Thailand, and Cambodia, for
example) and parts of India to ease the suffocating mantle of Islam.

The relative freedom and equality given to women by Buddhism,
the lack of continuous humiliation at the hands of priests, and the relative absence of inherent denigration of women within the religion itself have contributed to the average Buddhist woman's self-respect
and dignity. Exempt from religious and scriptural edicts condemning
her for her femaleness and sinfulness or urging her to justify her existence by procreating, she is largely free—in formal religious
terms—to direct her own destiny, reproductive or otherwise. But her
reproductive destiny is not just governed by Buddhist philosophy and
its application to fertility. It is dictated by her acceptance of custom
and fate, two aspects of life that Buddha himself strove against. A
woman in Sri Lanka, attaining puberty at age 12, is married off by her
parents because that is the custom and has her first baby at 13 years
of age. Another woman with nine children believes she will have no
more because her horoscope said she would have nine children and that
is preordained, fate.[1]

Buddhist philosophy is essentially based upon practical morality,
which in turn is based upon a threefold concept of morality. At the
lowest level, "selfish morality" pertains. That is, in order to fulfill
one's karma and be rewarded, one must be good. Buddhism does not
punish humans for their sins for it is anticipated they will reap their
own punishment, that they will be punished by their own sins. Yet
here again custom and religiosity operate in opposite directions to
formal Buddhism, with many Buddhist women, generally rural and
poorly educated, believing that the pain endured by women in pregnancy, miscarriage, and childbirth is a direct result of her sins
from a previous state of incarnation.

At the second level, Buddhism stipulates that a "rational morality" occurs whereby each individual's good or bad action causes
repercussions throughout humanity. Concentric circles of interacting
repercussions flow out from the center where the stone of the deed
has been cast. Awareness of action is thus born. The third level is
the achievement of the ideal, "motiveless morality," when virtue becomes its own reward.

For a Buddhist woman—or man—to achieve this ideal third
state, she should adhere to the Eightfold Path. Should, however, her
feet be distracted from the Path, all is not lost nor are recrimina-

tions many. Buddhism expects periodic deviation wrought by desire, hatred, delusion, or fear—the four motives of wrongdoing. And rather than condemn the deviation or inculcate brooding about sin, guilt, and forgiveness, it instead encourages the retracing of steps. It allows the Buddhist woman many chances to conquer the power of those motives by the practice of the simple but profound Eightfold Path, which is "a system of self-development according to law, a gradual process of moral evolution within the law of Karma. It is the Middle Way between the two extremes of unnatural asceticism and self-indulgence" (emphasis added).[2] Moreover, it opens the way to women to practice family planning and birth control without feeling guilty or sinful. But unfortunately, because most women are so poorly versed in Buddhism's tenets, they are prey to all the superstitions, pressures, and social conventions imposed on them by equally unversed and ignorant relatives, husbands, and neighbors.

Contrary to popular belief, Buddhism is more an action-oriented religion or philosophy than a belief-oriented one. Consequently the step Samma Kammanta, or Right Action, is of particular importance in following the Eightfold Path. The Five Precepts, or Pancha Sila, that qualify Samma Kammanta are killing, stealing, lust or sensuality, lying, and intoxicants. Thus, an individual is expected to personally vow (but not to God) to abstain from or, minimally, train to avoid these negative precepts. As such they lay on individuals the duty of mental and physical self-control and the use of common sense in Buddhist everyday life and thereby give women an opportunity to do what they think is right or appropriate in differing circumstances, provided they can extricate themselves from the weight of social disfavor.

The First Precept has particular relevance for family-planning practitioners, since it is a vow to oneself to avoid killing or injuring anyone or anything. But, while the Precept goes beyond the mere physical to thought, on the basis that evil thoughts give rise to evil actions, it does not preclude the use of common sense where conditions and needs dictate. For instance, in the matter of food and diet, Buddhism, unlike Hinduism or Islam, neither restricts diet to specific foods nor makes certain foods taboo. Rather, it accords with Buddha's teaching that diet is not a religious matter but a matter of need, individual preference, climate, geography, and occupation. And, insofar as Thai villagers are concerned, they are not morally accountable for slaughtering animals for food if a non-Buddhist does the killing and are therefore not precluded from eating meat. As their proverb goes, "If it weren't for bad people, good people couldn't eat chopped meat."[3] Ultimately Buddhism's main proscription is that neither evil desire nor greedy indulgence should motivate diet and consumption.

Theoretically Buddhism's First Precept should work against contraception and abortion specifically and family-planning programs generally. Writers such as Trevor Ling have noted that Buddhists in Sri Lanka and various parts of Southeast Asia have a potential opposition to all forms of contraception.[4] However, in practice that opposition has been applied with a certain degree of latitude that appears to vary from country to country according to the Buddhist doctrine adhered to, the overlay of religiosity, the amount of communal or sectarian differentials and animosities, the influence of the spiritual leaders, and the practical bent of the people.

The application of the First Precept thus varies according to whether the Buddhism practiced is Theravada (as in Thailand and Sri Lanka) or Mahayana (Korea and Japan) and whether it is strongly influenced by folkloric beliefs. In general the seriousness of taking life is related to the complexity, size, and sanctity of a being. Killing a bug is regarded as less serious than killing a snake, a snake less than a horse, and a horse less than a human. The seriousness of deliberately aborting a fetus therefore increases in direct proportion to its size and its increasing likelihood of becoming a living human being. However, as in most societies, irrespective of their religions, abortion merely for the sake of birth control or family limitation is strongly resisted.

The seriousness of abortion is further determined by prevailing popular folklore, which imposes rising degrees of hell on the woman involved and her "co-conspirator" in an act of abortion in proportion to the stage at which a fetus's existence is terminated. Thus, in Thailand and Sri Lanka where folkloric beliefs as powerful as Theravada Buddhism stipulate that aborters will be relegated to indeterminate suffering in hell, opposition to abortion is often stronger than in Korea or Japan and therefore much less socially accepted or practiced.

Yet contradictory beliefs or euphemisms for abortion can coexist in a society resulting in the acceptance of abortion in some quarters. For instance, in many Buddhist societies a human fetus is not deemed to be invested with life until actual birth or, as in Thailand, until three days after birth when the Khwan, or spirit, is regarded as having infused the baby with "human beingness." This partially explains why in certain Buddhist countries or communities abortion is not only not condemned for contravening the First Precept, but it is tolerated. Nonetheless, this does not mean that a woman undergoing an abortion could be particularly open about it, as she would still reap the disfavor of the community and perhaps even be ostracized. Family-planning clinics in Southeast Asian countries are therefore very wary about mentioning abortion in any guise.

Opposition to abortion and even contraception is often evoked in the name of Buddhist doctrine in those communities where it is feared that abortion and contraception will operate against the interests of the Buddhist community practicing it. For instance, in Thailand the traditional fear was that the minority Chinese would gain more commercial power at the expense of the Thai Buddhists, and in Sri Lanka the Sinhalese Buddhists feared that the Tamil Hindus and Roman Catholics, as they had in Vietnam, would wield power disproportionate to their numbers.

> It is this (persecution and social discrimination under
> European Christian rule) which more than any other
> single reason explains the conscious hostility of Budd-
> hists in Ceylon to population control. But in voicing
> their hostility they find it possible to argue not only on
> practical grounds but also on grounds of Buddhist doc-
> trine. [5]

Thus, religious doctrine may be used to serve political and racial needs.

In fact, "it is possible for the theorist to manipulate Buddhist doctrine in such a way as to enable him to view rapid population growth with approval."[6] For countries that had experienced growth rates between 2.2 percent and 3.2 percent per year, this could be disastrous in economic terms. For women, in both personal and economic terms, the pressure to keep producing large families would be injurious.

On one aspect of abortion the majority of Buddhists are in agreement, however, and that is the importance of the mother's life. Where medical needs dictate that abortion is essential to saving the life of the mother or to preventing further endangerment to her health, most Buddhists would exercise compassion and common sense. They would employ the grading inherent in determining the seriousness of taking life. Therefore they would give greater importance to saving the life of a woman in her prime who had contributed and was contributing substantially to her family and community over an undeveloped fetus that was unproved and unlikely to be a useful member of society for many years to come.

Since Buddhists do not believe in the existence of souls in the Christian, or more specifically the Catholic, sense, they do not become especially perturbed if contraception prevents the creation of potential souls. Similarly, Buddhists do not typically invest fetuses with souls from the outset of conception as Roman Catholics do or after 120 days as Islam hypothesizes. This lack of belief in souls may well encourage a positive attitude toward contraception, but the belief in the existence of an immutable number of sentient beings might well have the opposite effect. Birth control and family-planning measures could be hindered by the belief that all population action is futile,

since the total population of beings in the universe is immortally
fixed, can never be reduced by human action, and may only be altered
by beings reborn into different rank orders. A further impediment
to birth control could arise from the popular belief that it would be
unjust to deprive a sentient being from attaining its due reward of
improving its karma through rebirth into the highest rank order,
human. And insofar as women are concerned, if they believe that
being born a woman is a "sin" and inferior to being born a man, they
would not wish to deprive a human being a chance of gaining remission
for their sins by being born male and one step closer to nirvana.

To the Buddhist the total number of all sentient life remains
the same, since the combination of physical, mental, and spiritual
forces or energies that exist in the universe always remains constant.
Only the forms change. Only the forms are in a state of flux, mani-
festing their changes and the flow of energy forces by new forms of
existence or rebirth. Thus, "The notion that the total number of sentient beings can be increased or decreased by man's actions is completely contrary to the Buddhist concept of life and death."[7] Equally,
"For an increasing number to be achieving re-birth in the human
realm means that their 'karma' (or moral balance-sheet) must have
improved. An increase in human population is therefore something
to be welcomed as a sign of general improvement in the moral state
of the universe."[8]

Such pronatalist reasoning or belief has been reinforced by
Buddha's explanation of conception, requiring the simultaneous con-
fluxion of three elements. As the Lord Buddha said to his Buddhist
brethren:

> Now by the combining of three . . . the development
> of embryo is brought about. In this matter there is the
> coming together of parents: but if the mother is not
> pregnable and if no "gandharva" be at hand, then there
> is no development of an embryo. Again . . . if there
> be the coming together of parents, and the mother be
> pregnable, but no "gandharva" be at hand, . . . no . . .
> embryo. But when . . . there is the coming together
> of parents, and the mother is pregnable, and "gandharva"
> is at hand, then by the combining of these three there is
> development of an embryo. . . . At the end of nine or
> ten months she brings it forth, with great anxiety. [9]

Gandharva is interpreted not only to mean a class of devas that
preside over the conception processes but also a being waiting to be
reborn and

> the last moment of consciousness belonging to the "previous" birth. . . . Conception does not take place, despite the presence of the other factors, when there are no "aggregates" which have been "prepared" or "got up" for the physical heredity . . . pertaining to birth. . . . Between the cessation of the last moment of consciousness belonging to the last birth, and the arising of the first moment of consciousness of the present birth there is, according to the modern Theravada, no interval.[10]

The presence of both a spirit and a being awaiting rebirth tends to reinforce among Buddhists the outlook that conception will occur when the time is ripe. By extension, since puny human actions cannot circumvent dynamic universal forces, contraception was once regarded as being mere futility of action. Thus among the less educated, especially those women who had tried traditional methods and herbs to no avail, birth control was futile, pregnancy was inevitable.

In the last ten years considerable changes in popular attitude toward birth control and family planning have occurred. In large part this has been the result of government policy makers finally awakening to the fact that unbridled population growth was hampering their best developmental efforts, and that some form of population policy was in need of urgent implementation. Fortunately their efforts were not hampered by Buddhist theory. Since all living beings are temporary conjunctions of physical and psychic factors, if no conjunction of the factors occurs, conception does not take place and no being exists. Contraception thus becomes one of a series of factors. Accordingly it in no way contravenes Buddhist doctrine and its respect for life, because no living being has come into existence. However, a major educational effort is essential to convince Buddhist women that they are not contravening Buddhist doctrine and greater effort needs to be made to make women the central core of both family planning and development planning.

The belief in the presence of a being awaiting rebirth and in the need for karma to be worked out through rebirth has aroused active opposition to contraception in some quarters, such as among the Sinhalese Buddhist priests. Contraception to them becomes more than a futile action; it becomes a moral wrong to interfere with a being's karma and to suppress a being's rebirth and therefore life. Accordingly, depending upon the priesthood's influence over a community and its public expositions, contraception may be accepted or rejected. To a large extent the Thai Buddhist population has accepted family planning and birth control faster than the Sri Lankan. This is owing not only to the enormous innovative efforts of Khun Meechai Veeravaidhaya but also to the relatively nonpolitical profile of Thai monks, their noninterference, and the Thai belief that Buddhism does not mitigate against contraception. By contrast Sri Lankan priests have tended to be more political and influential and have condemned contraception as suppression of karmic rebirth. More telling, they feared that the Buddhist population would be outstripped by the other religious groups and tended to use religious doctrine to counteract what they perceived to be a threat to the Buddhist population and their power.

As Trevor Ling in his case study on Sri Lanka noted, during the 1950s and 1960s the Sinhalese resisted population control when it was observed that the other religious groupings seemed to be growing faster than the Sinhalese Buddhists. The Sri Lankan government's National Family Planning Program (1965) was strongly opposed by Sinhalese Buddhist monks of traditionalist outlook. Levels of family-planning acceptance among Sri Lankan women were low, and fertility rates were high. Then, after the Sinhalese percentage of the population had improved vis-à-vis the Tamils and Catholics, the Buddhist monks' propaganda against family planning eased off and women began to seek out traditional methods of contraception. By 1971 the program's methods were acceptable. As might be expected, contraceptive use was highest (53 percent) among urban, educated women (ten years or more of schooling) and among Buddhists (47 percent). The lowest acceptance rates were among the uneducated (29 percent) and the Muslims (26 percent).[11]

While priests themselves might contribute strongly to a pro-natalist stance, the Buddhist monkhood does so likewise, but indirectly. This occurs because of the merit that attaches to the son and his parents, especially to the mother, who have an ordained son in the Sangha. The acquisition of such merit is still especially important in the rural areas. Thus, sonless families striving to produce at least one son will mainly succeed in producing larger families than they originally intended. Childbearing and many children, being seen as signs of the Buddha's blessing, are highly regarded within Buddhist folk culture, which some view as a symptom of an earlier, pre-Buddhist belief and more endemic to rural, more primitive areas, such as northern Thailand, than in the urban, more populous areas like central Thailand.

Indirectly the monastic life for sons, if only for a short time during their youth, may have affected another determinant of fertility, the education of females. Because it was normal for sons rather than daughters to enter monasteries, boys, especially in rural areas, were inevitably better educated than girls, albeit their education was rather rudimentary. Therefore, while Buddhist religious theory does not differentiate between male and female except in the matter of admission to the Order, Buddhist educational practices had inadvertently created differences. These in turn could be said to have affected attitudes toward fertility and birth control if it is accepted that close correlations exist among education, modernization, and occupation on the one hand, and fertility on the other. For example, in Thailand wives of farm workers had 4.5 live births, wives of non-farm workers had 4.2, and wives of blue-collar workers had 3.9. Childbearing women with no education had 5.5 live births and with five years or more had 3.7. Urban women with over 11 years of education had 2.1 live births. [12]

Less attention has been paid to the possibility that religion can so inhibit modernization as to raise fertility and increase population growth. Nonetheless, in certain societies in such varied rural areas as Buddhist Thailand, Muslim Malaysia and Indonesia, and Hindu Bali, popular religion and daily religious activities involve so much of people's time, thoughts, and energy that they are minimally concerned with the more modernistic aspects of life. While

> Buddhist values [for example] are not directly inimical to industrialization; nevertheless, the practice of popular Buddhism in Southeast Asia tends not to encourage the growth of industry. This is mainly because the primary religious activity for the Buddhist lay population is "merit-making" [through alms-giving; gifts to monks; building, repairing, and furnishing temples; festivals; and lavish entertainment upon a son's ordination] ultimately for the purpose of obtaining a good re-birth. [13]

Traditionally in typical Buddhist cultures there has been little personal incentive to acquire the personal affluence that would enable individuals to embark upon and invest in those entrepreneurial activities that lead to nonagricultural occupations, modernization, and ultimately low fertility. Thus, while formal Buddhism as a religion and a philosophy has been neither especially pronatalistic nor anticontraception, the folkloric beliefs and practices of its adherents have often counteracted those attributes. In the formal Buddhist context marriage has not been regarded as a religious duty to be imposed on woman to save her from sin or on man to divert him from unnatural vices. Hence the beginning of married life was not to be marked by religious ceremony or blessing. In practice women are expected to marry early and men as soon as they can afford to, and wedding ceremonies are often lavish and costly.

The Third Precept of Buddhism's Middle Path calls for self-control in matters of sex, designated the most powerful of human instincts, lusts, and desires. To the Buddhist, sex is not a matter for recrimination, remorse, disgust, or guilt to be masochistically and sadistically suppressed. It is regarded as a natural, overpowering force that is a way of life, one's karma. A human's appetite for sex is believed to be as natural as the appetite for food, but the thoughtful Buddhist simultaneously recognizes that fleshly pleasures are inconsequential and temporal, that beauty and youth are fleeting, and that visual attractions are impermanent. Thus sex, though used to bolster man's vanity, should be controlled and gradually replaced by the pursuit of mental and spiritual perfection.

This acceptance of sex as a clean, creative, natural force has prevented most Buddhists from equating sex with uncleanliness, guilt, or contamination. By extrapolation women have accordingly not been imbued with the innumerable despicable traits as a result of their sexuality that other religions have thrown at them.

The average Buddhist woman has not had to live down a Puritan ethic, a guilty conscience arising from the first Fall, recriminations against sex and women by sexually thwarted patriarchs, and hysterical justifications for sexual activity. Instead, the Third Precept encourages Buddhists to aim at the control and sublimation of desires by rerouting creative energies from the purely physical to the emotional, mental, and spiritual channels. Such control is achieved not by castigation by external forces but through a gradual, inward, evolutionary process. This is not to say, however, that Buddhism has totally escaped the asceticism and misogynism that has afflicted other religions and caused their priests to label women, sex, and bodily functions as unclean, foul, and filthy.

Though Buddhist society generally accords to the poor, celibate monk the greatest social prestige, blatant and publicly proclaimed celibacy or abstinence is an anathema to the Buddhist if it is accompanied by the wrong state of mind. In other words, the attitude engendered by the Christian church through the ages would be unacceptable, since "mere physical control with foul thoughts in the mind is a greater defilement than a natural physical outlet with a wholesome, clean mentality behind. For as man thinks, so he is."[14] This attitude therefore helped to modify attitudes toward women or sex that might otherwise have veered to extremes of revulsion and denigration.

Another major reason for Buddhists not being violently opposed to population measures has been the restraint exhibited by the Sangha. On the whole the Sangha has refrained from commenting negatively on birth control or family limitation. In Sri Lanka and the Theravada countries of Southeast Asia, the Sangha's essential position and role —to perpetuate Buddha's teachings and wisdom and, so, Buddhist civilization—have been preserved. Three factors have contributed to this preservation: the political, whereby rulers were friendly toward and receptive to the Sangha and its teachings; the social, or the absence of social classes such as the Brahmins or priestly groups, who were fearful of the Sangha's influence and hence antagonistic toward its members; and the economic, which determined the ability of a country's economy in terms of wealth and agriculture to support the Sangha, its monasteries, and its bhikkus and bhikkunis either through patronage by the wealthy or local village support.

In India the above three factors worked in the opposite direction and brought about the demise of the Sangha. Rulers other than Ashoka were not generally receptive to Buddhist philosophy; the Brahmins were hostile; and the population growth so absorbed agricultural surpluses, especially rice, that popular support of the Sanghas could not be maintained.

While the Sangha, as the main transmitter of Buddhist values, has gradually adapted itself to being a professional bearer of a religion rather than a purveyor of philosophy, it has generally not become embroiled in everyday political or social problems. The exigencies of the Vietnam War led a number of Vietnamese Buddhist monks to express publicly their political opposition and to denounce the machinations of war promulgators. Fears of being politically overpowered by other religions led Sinhalese Buddhist monks to object to the establishment of family-planning clinics. Otherwise the Order has rarely intruded its own opinion about population concerns on the public.

On occasion politicians have sought to pull religious leaders onto the political scene or to use them for political purposes. Under Prime Minister U Nu (1947-62), "Buddhism and socialism formed the basis for economic and social development. . . . [He] believed that not only were religion and development compatible, but each was an essential ingredient necessary for the success of the other. . . . In Thailand, Buddhism, along with King and Country, became the tripod upon which the country's policies [theoretically] rested,"[15] but in practice religion was not really used to promote modernization. However, some bureaucrats and politicians have used religious leaders as allies to promote their causes or development projects and have thereby persuaded villagers to participate in schemes on the basis that their participation would earn them merit. By contrast, the Khmer Rouge so attacked religion and so depleted the ranks of Buddhist priests in Cambodia through murder and torture that they eliminated a key source of support for essential education and development programs and further contributed to their country's violent disintegration. However religion has been used, inevitably politicians and bureaucrats have ignored two essential ingredients of the religion-development equation—women and population. In the past these have been deemed inconsequential; in the present they are being given lip service; in the future they must receive full weight.

It is conceivable that if Southeast Asian Sanghas do not give more weight to the importance of women in development and to population problems they could be emulating the example of Buddhism in

India by hastening their own demise and the diminution of Buddhist values. Once major exporters of rice, the Southeast Asian countries and Sri Lanka have experienced difficulties in keeping their agricultural production "level-pegging" with their population increases. The lack of surplus will inhibit the laity's ability to support the Sangha as fulsomely as in the past despite the desire of the laity to acquire merit by doing so.

The lack of success of Sri Lanka's and Burma's agricultural policies—and to a lesser extent Thailand's—may be attributed partly to the education system, which is influenced by the impractical tradition of education encouraged by Buddhist culture. Because bhikkus are prohibited from practical occupations like cultivating the soil, they do not encourage their students toward agricultural development. But the problem becomes compounded when it is realized that women, as the "invisible cultivators" constituting between 30 percent and 50 percent of the agricultural labor force, are unlikely to receive appropriate training from traditional sources or from modern agricultural experts. Thus,

> Whether or not the increase in population in the Theravada countries is now running at such a rate that, before long, it will exceed the optimum size which allows an agricultural surplus to exist, sufficiently great to support both the non-agriculturally productive sectors of the national economy and the Sangha as well, is an open question. . . . [Their] economies . . . could be so adversely affected by the present rate of population increase that a situation could be reached in which it would be difficult to maintain the Sangha at its present size and, therefore, its present level of effectiveness. [16]

On that premise, it would be theoretically in the Sangha's best interests to involve itself more positively in economic and social reforms, including population restraint.

It is unlikely, however, that the Sanghas will want to become so immersed in social and economic problems. Even though

> Buddhism began as a theory of human existence with implications for human social structure, a philosophy not dependent in any way on theistic belief or theistic sanctions, not having any divine revelation as its starting-point, and yet tolerant of the theistic beliefs current in the [then] contemporary society, and capable of providing a transition from irrational to rational attitudes, [17]

it eventually became popularized and religionized. As the center of popularized Buddhism, the Sangha is expected to preserve Buddhist values and its own status as the embodiment of Buddhist wisdom and morality. Were it to deviate from this role and engage in social and economic matters, including population measures, female education, development, emancipation, and rural development, the Sangha could well lose its status and credibility within the Buddhist community and even weaken Buddhism itself. For the Sangha it becomes a catch-22 situation. It is damned if it does take action and damned if it does not.

While the Sangha as a whole may not oppose population measures, equally it is unlikely that the Order will strongly support them. Even if the Order wished to, its decentralized, diffuse nature mitigates against mustering the necessary cohesiveness to promulgate social reforms among its far-flung communities. Some knowledgeable and aware bhikkus and bhikkunis may be prepared to support measures to enhance women's status and to promote population restraint, but overall it will be incumbent upon an educated and aware Buddhist laity to take action on population questions in the knowledge that it will encounter little doctrinal opposition from the repositories of Buddhism.

The laity would also find that the other two gems of Buddhism —Buddha and his teachings, or Dhamma—do not necessarily contribute to the pronatalistic attitudes of Buddhist countries. Buddha himself certainly did not. He neither advocated procreation nor exhorted his followers to have many children. The fact that he regarded family as an impediment to spiritual growth and enlightenment is evidenced by his response upon the birth of his son: "A fetter [rahula] is come to me!"[18] He recognized the bonds that loved ones and dependents could exert on individuals. He therefore did not advocate adding material possessions, emotional ties, or children to life's difficulties.

Later in Buddha's teaching—the second gem of Buddhism—he taught that all life, all experience, is dukkha, a compendium of "grief, lamentation, physical pain, mental anguish, despair."[19] To the Buddha, among the various facets of life that were dukkha— illness, old age, death—the first was birth. When Buddha proclaimed that "birth is dukkha," he meant for both the mother suffering the trauma of numerous pregnancies and childbirths, and anteceding modern scientific knowledge, for the child undergoing the trauma of being forced from a tranquil deep into an inhospitable, cold world.

Buddha also saw birth as a repeat of an infinite series of births, with each being a terrifying experience. How much worse or dukkha if the birth was the result of an unwanted pregnancy, without the compensation of a goal achieved. The Buddha did not glorify birth or urge its multiplicity. Nor did he regard birth as due punishment for Original Sin or for being a woman. And he did not attempt to use birth as a justification for sexual relations and marriage. To him birth was yet another condition of life to be coped with by humans. Therefore human reproduction was never encouraged to satisfy either religious dogma or folkloric conventions.

High population growth rates in Theravada Buddhist countries have frequently been attributed to fatalism allegedly inherent in Buddhism. However, classical Buddhism basically was not a fatalistic religion, although some of the attitudes and values that subsequently evolved may have developed a sense of fatalism among its adherents. Buddhists essentially believe that past experiences shape the present choices of individuals and that those can lead to future repercussions; hence, everyone is capable of making good or bad decisions.

Classical Buddhism does not admit of sheer passivity or inactivity, for Buddha discounted the thesis that people are subject to fate, destiny, or doom. Freedom from past conditioning can occur with diligent effort and control and freedom of choice can become available. On this basis human beings need not be inhibited by past restrictions or prohibitions from exercising their will to restrict fertility. They need not rely upon God's will, or fate, to help or hinder their birthrate—only upon themselves. But most women, even relatively well-educated women, still believe themselves bound to fate. As a Thai teacher said, "No matter what women would like to have or demand, we cannot get away from the fact that we are women; we are weaker, have to bear and rear children. We are tied down in many ways in which men are not."[20] Humankind has the power of decision and for that reason "occupies a very important place in the Buddhist cosmos, not indeed because he is 'created in the image of God' according to Christianity."[21] In population terms, neither family nor society need be overpowered by a flood of humanity if people are prepared to exercise control over their own reproductive destiny.

Another Buddhist concept that can affect population growth is that every action produces an appropriate result. Action breeds reaction. But whereas Christianity would attribute "good" or "evil" motives or intentions to actions, thereby causing appropriately good or bad results, Buddhism prefers to avoid such attribution. Rather, it prefers to state that certain "skillful" or "unskillful" actions achieve specific ends. As Khantipalo Bhikku points out, [22] few people understand the future consequences of their present actions or the effect of past conditioning on their present actions (nor, he might have added, do they particularly want to make the effort to do so). Cause and effect of some actions may be readily discernible: sexual relations, then pregnancy. Others may require an intermediate lapse of time: successive births, expanding family, gradually growing economic and emotional pressures and burdens. And still others may cause events far in the future, unforeseeable to the average person:

excessive population growth, social congestion and violence, disruptive pressures on individual families, economic and environmental collapse.

Despite the interrelatedness of past, present, and future, Buddhism nevertheless places full responsibility for one's own actions into one's own lap. The most descriptive passage in Buddhist teaching on this particular moral responsibility commences, "I am the owner of action."[23] This imposition of initiative upon the individual opens the way to all forms of action, not the least of which is social reform and population restraint.

Buddhist women practicing contraception are in the fortunate position of not having to worry about committing a mortal sin in the Roman Catholic sense, since sin generically or specifically is a concept alien to Buddhist thought. If Buddhists break their Precepts, they know the consequences will vary according to the magnitude of their actions and intentions involved. Guilt is not imposed on a Buddhist woman, nor judgment, from some higher clerical order. What guilt exists is obliterated by striving to fulfill the Five Precepts, or the Buddha's Way.

The moral code of Buddhism is not an end in itself but a stepping-stone toward enlightenment. The Third Precept followed by laymen and laywomen is "I undertake the step of training to refrain from immoral sexual behavior." This commonly refers to adultery, a practice seen as hurting children, as well as both the innocent and unfaithful parties. The Precept also refers to the restraint that should be exercised by young unmarried people less because premarital sex is sinful than because it can produce unanticipated bondage in the form of emotional pressures, premature marriage, and unwanted children. The restraint advocated is not merely physical but mental as well, and it is reinforced by the expectation that girls will exercise the traditional virtues—virginity until marriage, fidelity, gentle manners and speech, politeness, domesticity, forbearance, and respect and obedience to one's husband—so prized in Southeast Asian countries and Sri Lanka. Breaking this Precept, however, does not result in the hell-and-damnation invective produced by other religions or in torturous physical and mental punishments.

To a large extent Buddhists have escaped fire-and-brimstone judgments and guilt-ridden consciences arising from "sinful" practices, especially in the realm of sex, procreation, and contraception, by adhering to three overriding ethics in their daily lives. First is their principle of nonharming (ahimsa), which prevents them from persecuting others for their beliefs (religious) or actions (adulterous or otherwise). Second is their principle of compassion (karuna), which not only ensures their tolerance of and sympathy for the shortcomings of others but also activates them to help others remove those sufferings. Buddhist compassion combined with nonharming has, generally speaking, prevented that awful religious perversion, so endemic in other religions, of hurting or destroying others (physically, mentally, or emotionally) to justify one's own sanctimoniousness or to "reform" others for their theoretical salvation.

Third, Buddhists believe that the vital first step on the way to enlightenment is the practice of morality in speech, thought, action, and livelihood. As a consequence of trying themselves to practice these principles in daily life and knowing that backsliding is all too easy, Buddhists are relatively uncondemnatory of other people's actions and are remarkably tolerant of their idiosyncrasies. For them, "morality is not a species of repressive observance from which to open the malodorous flowers of self-righteousness."[24] Thus their attitudes toward sex, contraception, and family planning have been relatively sanguine and free of religious inhibitions. Even their cultural milieu has reinforced this nonjudgmental and guilt-free attitude.

While certain barriers to population policies do exist in Buddhism, these are more likely to have been occasioned by cultural mores antedating Buddhism, by other less-tolerant religious influences, or by political leaders manipulating religion for their own biased reasons. Moreover, as Kumari Jayawardene noted: These barriers may arise from the way "superstition and religion are commonly, though not overtly, used by men to continue to dominate and control women's lives." Men consciously use superstition and religion to keep women down even though they do not believe these things themselves, and women perpetuate it among their children.[25] Generally, however, Buddhism's lack of religious barriers and inhibitions may account, in part, for the receptiveness accorded family planning and birth control by the populace and the steady decline in birthrates and population growth rates in most Buddhist countries over the last decade.

More research needs to be undertaken to ascertain the direct correlation between inherent religious values, attitudes, and inhibitions, on the one hand, and attitudes toward sex, family planning, birth control, and population restraint, on the other. Obviously, religion is hardly the sole determining factor as to why people accept or reject population policies. Indeed, it may not even be the key factor in some societies, particularly the more educated and affluent ones. Economic and education factors, including technological transfers, may well be the greatest determinants of reduced fertility. Yet it would be extremely shortsighted, if not foolhardy, given the increasingly short time allotted to countries before their populations double, to ignore social and cultural factors that subtly and unobtrusively insinuate themselves into society's lifeblood.

Of those social and cultural factors, religion's influence is one of the most pervasive and the most elusive. As such its impact should not be minimized, especially in those countries where economic advance and education among the masses have been too minimal to counter religion's influence. Those who have immersed themselves for any length of time in developing countries are only too aware of the average woman's dependence upon religion, her reluctance to run counter to her religious upbringing, and her fear of contradicting her religious leaders. Unfortunately, because of the difficulty of quantifying religion's impact with acceptable modern techniques, the observations or analyses of old-timers or empirical developmentalists are discounted by econometricians (today's gurus), who often rely less on actual country experience than on econometric modeling, based on the premise that what is nonquantifiable is discountable.

Religion, or more accurately religiosity, should be acknowledged as a salient characteristic of the social and cultural scene of most countries. Therefore it should be acknowledged as a factor to be contended with in any development program. Irrespective of the strides made by education, technology, and modernization, religion is still an essential, pervasive element of the everyday, routine living of the majority of people in developing countries. It is intimately tied up with population and women's status. As Perdita Huston discovered in her interviews of rural women in six countries,

> Their perceptions of "women's status" were still affected
> by numerous practices—often based on taboos, supersti-
> tions, religious beliefs, or even misinterpretations of
> religious tenets—that continue to have a stunting effect
> on their personal development. . . . Ranging in serious-
> ness from relatively harmless folk beliefs . . . to food
> taboos that harm health, to the physically violent prac-
> tice of female circumcision, such customs of course
> vary greatly in their psychological and physical effects
> on women.[26]

Ultimately, these perceptions will affect various aspects of population control. Therefore, as a palpable, tangible force religion should be understood and, although largely nonquantifiable, its potential for negative or positive impact on development schemes and population programs should be fully recognized.

Religion has always been a larger component of social and economic reform than has been given official credence by planners and policy makers. In the past it has been hidden or ignored. This situation is unlikely to prevail in the future. In fact, given the recent religious trends and upheavals in various prominent countries, religion can no longer be hidden or ignored without serious consequences for social and economic development; population growth;

political stability; and women's personal, social, and economic evolution.

NOTES

1. Perdita Huston, Message from the Village (New York: Epoch B. Foundation, 1978), pp. 70, 81.

2. Christmas Humphreys, Buddhism (Middlesex: Penguin Books, 1962), p. 109. The Eightfold Path or Eight Steps to Self-Enlightenment consists of Right (meaning the most perfect form) Understanding (Samma Ditthi); Right Thoughts or Motives (Samma Sankappa); Right Speech (Samma Vacha); and Right Action (Samma Kammanta), the keynote of the Eightfold Path and of Buddhism. The Path also includes Right Means of Livelihood, Effort, Concentration, and Meditation (Samma Ajiva, Samma Vayama, Samma Sati, and Samma Samadhi).

3. Sulamith Heins Potter, Family Life in a Northern Thai Village: A Study in the Structural Significance of Women (Berkeley: University of California Press, 1977), p. 73.

4. Reprinted with permission from Trevor Ling, "Buddhist Values and Development Problems," World Development (Oxford) 8, no. 7-8 (July-August 1980): 581.

5. T. O. Ling, "Buddhist Factors in Population Growth and Control," Population Studies—A Journal of Demography 23, no. 1 (March 1969): 60.

6. Ibid., p. 57.

7. A. A. Wichmann, "Burma: Agriculture, Population and Buddhism," American Journal of Economics and Sociology 24, no. 1 (January 1965): 76.

8. Ling, "Buddhist Factors in Population Growth," p. 54.

9. F. L. Woodward, trans., Some Sayings of the Buddha (Oxford: Oxford University Press, 1973), pp. 28-29.

10. Wichmann, "Burma," p. 78.

11. Ling, "Buddhist Values," p. 581.

12. Ling, "Buddhist Factors in Population Growth," p. 55.

13. Ibid.

14. Humphreys, Buddhism, p. 113.

15. Reprinted with permission from Fred R. Von der Mehden, "Religion and Development in South-East Asia: A Comparative Study," World Development (Oxford) 8, no. 7-8 (July-August 1980): 550.

16. Reprinted with permission from Trevor Ling, The Buddha (Middlesex: Penguin Books, 1976), p. 292. First published in Great Britain by Maurice Temple Smith, London, 1973.

17. Ibid., p. 296.

18. Khantipalo Bhikku, What Is Buddhism? (Bangkok: Social Science Press of Thailand, 1965), p. 10.

19. Ibid., p. 20.

20. Sumalee Viravaidja, "A Woman's Place in Thailand," UNICEF News—Third World Woman, no. 76(3) (July 1973), p. 25.

21. Khantipalo, What Is Buddhism? p. 48

22. Ibid., pp. 30-32.

23. Ibid., p. 33.

24. Ibid., p. 119.

25. Perdita Huston, Third World Women Speak Out (New York: Praeger, 1979), p. 49.

26. Ibid., p. 47.

8

OVERVIEW OF CHRISTIANITY
AND ITS IMPACT
ON WOMEN

I would educate women _more_ than men. Women bear
and raise the children—so women prepare the future.
How can the future be good if women are ignorant?

Maria Luisa

Education that conditions people to accept things as
they are . . . does not welcome those who criticize
and disturb it. It wants consenting individuals who accept its rules, its values, and its demands. And the
consent of women to this state of affairs is essential,
since they provide a vast number of free "services."
Women who rebel against being a marginal and exploited caste are a threat to the masculine role and all
its privileges.

Elena Gianini Belotti

When discussing the development of Third World countries,
planners of various persuasions will occasionally comment upon the
regressive tendencies of local religions that impede change in society.
Typically, however, they avoid comment about religion's impact on
development. To them it is an irrelevancy, a taboo, or an emotionally charged issue, best to be left alone. Should they consider religion a potential force, they tend to concentrate on the backwardness
of Islam, animism, Hinduism, and to a lesser extent, Buddhism.
They discuss the hold of Brahmin priests over Hindus and the sway
of imams over Muslims. They profess that beneficial progress is
hampered by priests who, rather than engaging in public works and
social reforms, confound their charges with dire predictions of untold degradation and corruption if they participate in modern changes.

Quote by Maria Luisa taken from Perdita Huston, Third World
Women Speak Out (New York: Praeger, 1979), p. 98.

Unfortunately, they seldom ascribe to Christianity the same development-hampering impediments suffered by other religions. Yet it, too, has provided some of the most severe constraints for improving conditions, especially among females within the fast-growing populations of developing Catholic countries. Many of society's denigrating myths about women have arisen directly out of religion. As a main source of undevelopment for women, religion must be recognized and challenged as wanting if women's potential is to be increased and poverty of development decreased. Narrow thought in Christianity, as much as in any other religion, has restricted the acceptance of women as full human beings with the capacity to expand their potential beyond restricted stereotyped roles. Archaism, assimilated unconsciously from the past, clouded Christian planners' attitudes toward women and their full integration into development as detrimentally as it troubled the visions of planners of other faiths. Only recently has it been reluctantly acknowledged in some quarters that various traditionally held Christian myths have permeated the thinking of development experts with consequent adverse effects on women's traditional and modern roles.

Perhaps the consequences of such attitudes were neither deliberately nor directly promulgated. Nevertheless, they have been detrimental to the women concerned and to their society. Even today, confronted with innumerable fact-finding studies and analytical briefs showing the benefits that accrue by fully incorporating women into development at all levels, the majority of planners still avoid righting this omission. Too many development experts within national aid agencies, international institutions, and nongovernment organizations alike trot out the old argument that where issues involving women and religion are concerned new attitudes or ideas should not be imposed on other peoples. But have they not already done so in a myriad of ways? Vaccinations, flouridation, irrigation, sewage disposal, pesticides, new hybrid seeds and different foods, television and radio, cars and superhighways, and secular education have all at one time or another run counter to existing mores, priestly arguments, and entrenched conservatism. What is more, they have drastically upset the traditional social balance, leaving those untrained and unprepared for the onslaught of changes worse off than before. Inevitably, these have been women.

Time and again, when new concepts have been introduced, traditional ways and ideas have altered, affecting personal lives and relationships, values, and the social fabric of a nation. More particularly, the changes effected by men for men have seriously jeopardized women's position in the home, in agriculture, in marketing and finance, and in the community unless special provisions were made to ensure the preservation or expansion of women's rights. It is therefore nonsensical to say that economic and social policies should not intrude upon religion or women because such action would interfere with a society's personal and cultural mores. Economic and social policies have already intruded! Rather than feigning a coy reluctance to interfere, it would be more to the credit of development planners to intrude into the domain of women by ascertaining their genuine needs and helping them undo the ills of religiosity and poorly conceived policies. By remaining inactive on the sidelines, they in effect allow economic policies to combine with religious archaisms to further downgrade women economically and socially.

The patronizing or neglectful attitude toward women held by most development specialists who are Christian may be unconscious or inadvertent. Whichever, the consequences are the same: neglect and disregard. The consequences are intensified by a peculiar ambivalence developed by those specialists. They have, on the one hand, incorporated into their essence the Christian concepts of humanity, individual dignity, and self-worth. On the other, they have incorporated some of the patriarchal attitudes of the church, among which is the concept of woman as a mystical half-person. As such, depending upon their particular biases and upbringing, they set her below, beyond, or above the same basic considerations of humanity and dignity as her male counterparts.

For many, reconciling these conflicting concepts is as difficult as it was for their predecessors to square the concept of human dignity with serfdom and slavery, which the church in the past condoned. The church has been notorious for leading from behind, but nowhere was this more reprehensible than where serfdom and slavery prevailed. There, the laity initiated the necessary social and legislative changes to eliminate those dual scourges and gradually pressured the churches to revise their attitudes toward serfdom and slavery. Eventually, the churches supported the laity-inspired reforms. On matters of humanity and decency, the laity has customarily expected the churches to fulfill their trust by exhibiting positive, humane, and visionary leadership. Undoubtedly, many individual clergy have fulfilled that expectation by resolutely confronting the same problems as their parishioners and working toward substantive reforms in keeping with the times and conditions of their society.

The official or institutional church, by contrast, has all too often failed the trust reposed in it by the laity. A distinct lack of leadership based upon humanity and compassion has prevailed. A clear propensity for politicking, quibbling over semantic theological differences, and bureaucracy has been exhibited. For example, the Vatican failed to condemn the treatment of both Jews and opponents of Hitler during the height of Nazism in Germany before and during World War II. It congratulated and waved its blessings over the countries of Cape Verde and Angola upon their newly gained independence but did little of substance to ameliorate the poverty there or to reduce the bloodshed between the opposing factions. It only weakly deplored the violence of the Irish Republican Army (IRA) but strongly abused advocates of contraception and divorce. It condemns abortion but provides no viable alternatives to millions of desperate women resorting to it. It opposes a married priesthood but assigns priests with little understanding of marital, sexual, and family problems to the confessional and counseling positions. And it continues to deny women's full participation in the church, while seeking to influence other denominations similarly. But the Catholic church has not been the only culprit. In its many debates on women's position, the Church of England could not finally divest itself of its ancient, monolithic attitudes that bar women from full membership in that church.

Proponents of general change and reform are often surprisingly passive about the improvement of women's lot. Too often they contend that, since the home is "woman's natural and right place," development directed at the menfolk will eventually percolate down to the women. However, they forget that in most nonmodern societies, including the Christian, women have had positive, substantive roles outside the home. Hence, policies failing to take account of their external roles undermine women's total social and economic position. But policy changes predicate attitude changes. These, in turn, require a reevaluation of attitudes traceable back to religious dogma and interpretations rooted in the rituals and cultural practices of pagan, pre-Israelite times.

Many of the entrenched, preconceived attitudes about women date back at least to the writings of Genesis. Regardless of modern communications and messages, Genesis still exerts a strong influence on people's minds. It is one of the first and most dramatic biblical passages taught in early childhood and it is one of the most frequently cited sagas in adults' sermons. It is little wonder that the most commonly held view of women's position among Christians springs from this first scriptural account.

Advocates of female subordination and inferiority—or mere non-thinkers—usually begin by invoking that part of Genesis wherein God is depicted as creating woman from Adam's rib during his sleep. [1] They staunchly maintain that woman has an inferior status because she was derived from Adam and not created as a whole entity by God. * They conveniently disregard Adam's own acceptance of her as a complete entity replete with a distinct and unique personality. The idea

---

*In Hebrew Adam means "man," hence modern exegists have interpreted Adam to mean "men" collectively or generically.

of woman's wholeness is amplified, however, by Genesis: "Therefore shall a man leave his father and his mother, and shall cleave unto his wife, and they shall be one flesh."[2] Inherent throughout the saga of man's creation is a sense of wholeness and oneness. Implied is the unreasonableness that Adam would wish to acknowledge as part of his bone and flesh an inferior being any more than a parent would normally wish to acknowledge the inferiority of his or her offspring. Equally unreasonable is the view that a person would want to leave the security and strength of a family, of mother and father, for a lesser, subordinated creature, an incomplete being. The concept of man and woman within Genesis is that of a melding of equal parts that fuse together to become companions and sharers-of-life, with neither being subordinate to nor dominant over the other.

Dishonest exegists, for their own motives and ends, have delighted in citing Genesis 1:26-27 to show that God regarded woman as secondary to man. They have deliberately obfuscated the verse "And God said, Let us make man in our image, after your likeness. . . . So God created man in his own image, in the image of God created him."[3] They have typically taken these words out of written context, ignored the social and historical milieu, failed to incorporate recent understandings from archaeological finds, and misrepresented the total meaning since time immemorial to their more gullible, less-educated congregations.

Rarely have exegists or priests continued the sentence in Genesis 1:26 with "and let them have dominion over the fish of the sea, and over the fowl of the air, and over the cattle, and over all the earth, and over every creeping thing that creepeth upon the earth" (emphasis added).[4] The pivotal word is them, not him, and though this would seem to be playing with semantics, it has been the core of misinterpretations of Genesis where women have been concerned. Even as Adam was used to mean "everyman" in Hebrew, so was the word man used generically to designate the whole human race.* Genesis says nothing about man as male having dominion over the earth. Rather, it specifies them to indicate that humans of both genders were in equal juxtaposition to each other.

Genesis further reinforces this state of equivalence when it continues, "Male and female created He them" (emphasis added)[5] and

---

*The use of gender-exclusionary language such as man, mankind, chairman, and so forth rather than gender-inclusionary language (human, humanity, president) has worked to the detriment of females by rendering them invisible in people's thoughts and imagination. This has resulted in their omission from the activities or action provoked by those thoughts. Their invisibility in development, politics, and society thus becomes complete and total.

"God blessed them, and said unto them, Be fruitful; and multiply, and replenish the earth" (emphasis added).[6]* Yet how often, in order to demonstrate that woman was created inferior to man, have these later sentences and pronouns been eliminated from explanations about the meaning and latitude of the text. Genesis neither shows man having dominion over woman nor God dividing other living creatures into dominant male and subordinate female. Since the division of other creatures into dominant and subordinate roles did not occur within Genesis, an inconsistency arises if it is maintained that the human species was so split. As it was, human male and female were portrayed in Genesis as creations with equal and joint dominion over other earthly living things. (Not that this has achieved particularly beneficial results, given the destruction that humanity has wrought on earth and its failure to exercise its stewardship responsibly.)

Another aspect of Genesis to be noted when considering its influence on woman's position is its authorship. Chapters 1 and 2 of Genesis were written by two different entities, P and J,† coming from two different eras. Each was trying to explain the creation of life, earth, and the universe in faithlike terms appropriate to their respective situations. Both were essentially reflecting the customs and conditions of their milieu in their writings. Accordingly, it is necessary to look at the social and historical context within which those authors lived if their meaning is to be fully discerned. Archaeological discoveries have provided a vivid picture of the type of life that existed before and during the emergence of the nation of Israel and the Hebrew culture and before and after the writings of Genesis. These findings have shown that when the Israelites entered Canaan they discovered settlements traceable to around 7000 B.C. Those ancient configurations considerably influenced the Israelites' culture, history, and eventually, their writings.

The writings of Genesis dramatically resurrect the lives of Abraham, Isaac, Jacob, and innumerable other patriarchal ancestors of the Hebrews. Archaeological findings and skillful interpretations have shown that those writings portrayed remarkably accurately the ancient patriarchal traditions that existed in the early settlements, traditions later incorporated into Hebrew and subsequently Christian tradition, thought, and custom. Many of the patriarchal traditions and

---

*This particular verse has also provoked further difficulties for women, population growth, and family planning.

†P (for Priestly Source) has been determined to be the author of Chapter 1, which was scribed around the fifth century B.C. J, or Jahwist (from Jahweh, the Lord), is thought to have written Chapter 2 sometime during the ninth or tenth century B.C.

attitudes elucidated in both the Old and New Testaments and in the Pauline epistles date back long before the authorship of Genesis— to the pre-Israelite settlements of 7000 B.C. Genesis authors reflected the faith, knowledge, and social conditioning of their times, even as today's writers reflect theirs. Therefore, the continued invocation of Genesis to substantiate and maintain woman's apparent inferiority is both ludicrous and damaging.

For eons woman's lowly position has been condoned because of the Adam-and-Eve narrative. Diatribes against women have been justified because of Eve's historicity as the originator of original sin, the capitulator to the serpent of evil, and the deceiver who induced Adam to disobey God's orders. Strong doubt has been cast on whether the original narrators intended to portray so narrowly in one man and one woman the dubious sin of sex, with the corresponding enticement of man into wayward patterns and disobedience. If they had, then their social and historical milieu must be recalled. In those ancient times, humans were settled in a harsh land, enduring incredible hardships, anticipating truncated lives, and bearing great pain with fortitude. Polytheism and paganism abounded. Matriarchy was displaced by patriarchal traditions, theoretically to provide cohesion and continuity. Mysticism attached to sex and childbirth, for anatomical and medical knowledge were nonexistent, and woman's sexuality, vividly depicted by her menses, became confounding.

If Adam and Eve storytellers had intended to write in broader terms, then their account becomes an all-encompassing work, an all-encircling contemplation of the human condition, travail, and experience in the world and in the universe. The narrative no longer remains narrow and restricted but becomes an enveloping view of God's original design for human beings (and other earthly creatures). Today's less doctrinaire and more visionary theologians and scholars believe that the Genesis authors described Adam to mean "collectively man" or "men collectively and generically" and Eve to mean "life"; hence, "Mr. and Mrs. Everyman."[7] Unfortunately, the meanly limited view of the Adam and Eve story by past (and some present) theologians, showing the universe's creator preoccupied with sex as the original sin and bent upon crushing down woman with unadulterated pain and hopelessness, has seriously jeopardized woman's position through the ages. Today, that tunnel vision is still apparent in papal encyclicals and media statements concerning contraception, divorce, ordination, and other issues directly affecting women.

Scholars now acknowledge that in its most comprehensive sense the concept of original sin meant an awareness of good and evil, with knowledge that there was freedom of choice between adhering to God's authority or flouting it. The biblical authors nicely illustrated the usual human frailty of blaming others: man blames woman, woman blames snake, snake blames God, but all avoid shouldering the blame for their own actions. Male theologians inadvertently reinforced this frailty by continually heaping blame for the wrongs of society on woman and her introduction of "original sin." Their denigrating attitudes subtly—and not so subtly—insinuated themselves into the minds of illiterate, gullible publics of the past. Today, denigration continues. Many modern theologians or their counterparts in unions, business, and government still exhibit a proclivity for blaming society's ills on women. But, since most of their public is too well educated to be intimidated by the specter of original sin, they employ euphemisms—working mother, career woman, self-seeker—to achieve the same denigrating result. Before attitudes detrimental to women can be overcome, Christians will need to understand the original social and cultural context of biblical writings and to be given access to honest and comprehensive biblical scholarship.

Literalism and twisted reasoning based on Genesis have also made women's lot more difficult. Fundamentally, Genesis is a dynamic description of the evolution of life, thought, and human consciousness. It symbolizes the human struggle to use knowledge to distinguish between good and bad. It does not depict the human condition as unending but, rather, holds out hope for regaining the old status given by God at creation. [8] Through the perverse interpretations of the ages, it has been given the dynamism of a stone, weighting down potential evolutionary thought toward all humans, particularly women. Literalism has destroyed the scope of the symbolism, of the inherent soaring philosophy. The letter of the writing has been adhered to, but its spirit has been denied. Likewise, convoluted reasoning based on the theological contradiction that woman is the weaker or inferior sex because she first bit the apple but man is the stronger or superior sex because he was persuasively induced to follow suit has also warped Genesis's original depiction of woman's role. [9] Such contradictory assumptions are no more reasonable than theological arguments that the subordination of a woman to her husband is an immutable fact arising from nature rather than a sociological fact arising from cultural conditioning and theological concepts of original sin. [10]

Genesis symbolically depicts the change of status for both woman and man: [11] for the woman, the loss of equal dominion over the earth as given in the beginning; for the man, despite being given a helpmeet* in his work, the loss of pleasure in his exertions. Sadly, it has been the woman's loss rather than the man's that has been emphasized. This rigid and misogynous rather than symbolic interpretation of

---

*Linguistically meaning "a suitable helper, partner, or coworker," and hence signifying equal status.

Genesis has greatly contributed to most women blindly accepting their indoctrinated role of passivity and subordination and most men dogmatically asserting the irrefutability of that role.

Nowhere in the New Testament did Jesus make statements demeaning of women. In fact, his very actions toward them, in a time when women were normally treated ignominiously, surprised both his disciples and the public. He treated them as real persons and as friends, to be listened to and helped. He addressed himself to their problems and, in consequence, reaped the vituperation of the powerful Pharisees. Yet, from the beginnings of Christianity, preachers and followers alike have ignored Jesus' basic tenets for the treatment of all humans and have not followed his exemplary actions toward women. Conceivably because Jesus did not specifically articulate women's need for equivalence or entitlement to equal treatment, future church patriarchs and clergy could justify to themselves their wanton disregard or denigration of women. Lacking exhortations or commandments to do otherwise, for those set in their ways and attitudes, Jesus' example was not enough.

At a time when women could be readily disposed of by their husbands, Jesus eschewed a double standard when he commanded all and sundry, men and women, not to commit adultery. [12] Being a Jew and knowing Hebraic law, Jesus was acutely aware that women could be beaten and stoned to death for unfaithfulness, proved or alleged, while having no control over their husbands' dalliances. He knew that women had no protection from or recourse against the Hebrew custom of being discarded by their husbands casually and without cause. He therefore undertook to give them protection against their spouses' actual and mental straying. [13] Similarly, he tried to protect them against casual repudiation, except in the case of fornication. [14] In those times forni-cation meant not so much "sexual intercourse" as "marriage within proscribed lines."[15] He reiterated that divorce should only occur upon the commission of fornication, that is, marriage within the prohibited degrees of relationship as outlined by Moses, [16] which therefore would render marriage null and void. [17] This injunction was especially important in a small, closed society where such relationships could produce not only inbreeding but also extreme jealousy leading to internal and bloody conflicts.

Throughout the New Testament Jesus is depicted helping women: raising Peter's mother-in-law from a fever, [18] reviving a ruler's daughter from apparent death, [19] and curing a woman ridden with a disease of 12 years. [20] Often he endured the opposition of his own disciples, such as when he healed a Canaanite woman's daughter. [21] To a great extent the women Jesus encountered throughout his life exhibited a greater faith in him and in his powers than did most men, including his disciples, who usually had to be convinced by some form of revelation. Possibly their faith in him was in part engendered by the regard Jesus displayed for them as human beings and individuals and in part because of his championing their rights, at a time when they basically had none, in the face of the Pharisees' hostility. Naturally enough, when power mongers see their power base undermined and their corruption exposed, they resort to retaliation. So it was with the Pharisees, who regularly tried to trap Jesus into answering their devious questions along their own regimented lines.

Apart from being thoroughly corrupt, the Pharisees were hypocritical. They contended that it was lawful to dispose of a wife for every and any cause accepted as justified by her husband and his male cronies in synagogue and society. However, they could not countenance a woman leaving a tyrannical, abusive husband. In the course of one of their many heated discussions with Jesus, they asked, "Is it lawful for a man to put away his wife for <u>every</u> cause?"[22] Jesus' response was that male and female were equally created and, through marriage, joined together into one entity not to be severed.[23] Whereupon the Pharisees, facilely exhibiting public dismay at Jesus' apparent undermining of the Law of Moses but privately upset by his attack on their petty and power-ridden rules, asked, "Why did Moses then command to give a writing of divorcement, and to put her away?" To that Jesus replied, "Moses, because of the hardness of your hearts, suffered you to put away your wives: but from the beginning it was not always so."[24] Jesus thus pointedly indicated that under the leadership of the Pharisees, women's lot had worsened since Moses' time. Moses, unlike Jesus, imposed a double standard on women of his era, as was and indeed continues to be the prevailing custom. But he nevertheless recognized the severe abuses women were subjected to and attempted to mitigate them somewhat in a manner unusual for that period. Among his various measures, Moses tried to protect women by having them released from tyrannical husbands through a writing of divorcement and by giving them some rights and protection, as with property inheritance.[25] With time, as Jesus noted, the mitigating laws passed by Moses were corrupted by the religious leadership to the extreme detriment of women.

Marriage itself has been treated with ambivalence by the church's celibate forefathers and priests. Often visualized as a cross between woman's snare for unsuspecting man and a repeat of the Garden-of-Eden episode, marriage has been portrayed as an inferior state in comparison with an ascetic religious calling. Inevitably, this view has had adverse repercussions for women. It is unknown whether Jesus was ever married, a proposition that the church, given its emphasis on celibacy, has preferred to avoid contemplating. Nonetheless, unlike Paul and subsequent theologians, Jesus neither declaimed against marriage nor intimated that celibacy was a preferable goal.[26]

In his teaching on marriage,[27] Jesus went beyond Moses and the Law to the beginning, to creation, to establish that the Christian ethic in this matter as in other matters was for all people, not just the overtly religious or Christian. His parables were designed to teach people how to determine right from wrong by extrapolating from fundamental principles, rather than from a series of complicated canonic or Hebraic rules prescribing rigidly for every occasion regardless of appropriateness.

Muhammad, dealing with an equally rigid, rule-bound society in a later era, recognized the inherent goodness and flexibility of Jesus' teachings and incorporated much of their content into his own works. Buddha similarly exhorted his followers many centuries earlier to exercise their judgment, working from basic principles, in deciding what was right for a given situation.

Jesus' break with the Pharisees was undoubtedly partly owing to his revolutionary teaching that individuals must seek their own salvation internally rather than externally from the intervention of priests. He shunned a supranaturalist ethic that imposed absolute standards from external sources. He thus encouraged his followers, first, to question the intrinsic wrongness in any given situation and, second, to resolve it by applying the fundamental commandments. This flexibility, characterizing Jesus' approach to people and problems, did not endear him to the hide-bound religious hierarchy. Nor did this flexible concept of compassion and conscience over doctrinaire law and dogma become automatically an integral part of the institutionalized Christian church. If it had, the abuses of racism, serfdom, and slavery and the abuses afflicting women, including their exclusion from full church participation, would not have been tolerated, let alone committed.

It probably was inevitable that the church's original forefathers should have sidelined Jesus' humanity, individuality, and flexibility, given their own social and geographical backgrounds. Their social customs were little different from many contemporary customs in the Mediterranean region and the Middle East among present-day Orthodox and Hasidic Jews, who harken back to the Laws of Moses with little capitulation to changing times and conditions. The early church patriarchs were necessarily affected by the rigidity of their society, the unquestioning and unconscious acceptance of Moses' Laws, and the legal interpretations of the potent Pharisees, Sadducees, and other high priests. Although they acknowledged the uniqueness and new goodliness of Jesus' teachings, they could not easily cast off the suffocating cloak of tradition. Incredibly, much of the Christian church's hierarchy, notably within the Roman Catholic church, still cannot shed those antiquated habits, which date back to ancient Middle Eastern times.

Women were among Jesus' helpers, followers, and disciples,[28] and they played a major role at his birth, death, and resurrection. But their roles in the new church decreased because of prevailing social conditions and because of Paul's monumental efforts to establish securely the young church and to implement his revolutionary program of action over severe opposition. Known variously as the original patriarch of the Christian church, rabbi, persecutor, Roman citizen, Hellenistic Jew, visionary, married man, celibate priest, compassionate prelate, and misogynist, Paul is often deemed responsible for placing women in lowly esteem and lowly position within the church and Christianity.

Being intent upon establishing the church and being without the full tolerance and vision of Jesus,[29] Paul had to compromise with the original church supporters, who lacking tolerance and compassion to an even greater degree, were shocked when human need was put above supposed sacrosanct regulations. Robinson explains their dismay by pointing out that an ethic based on conscience instead of regulation is "highly dangerous, and representatives of supranaturalist legalism will, like the Pharisees, always fear it. Yet I believe it is the only ethic for 'man of age.' To resist it in the name of religious sanctions will not stop it: it will only ensure that the form it takes will be anti-Christian."[30]

Talmudic law, based on Moses' Laws, Catholic canonic law, Protestant canons, and the numerous regulations of every other organized Christian church, reinforces Fletcher's statement that

> the old-fashioned casuists [and] Talmudists continually
> made rules for the breaking of rules. They were turning
> and twisting in their own trap to serve love as well as
> law, but unfortunately the only result is a never-ending
> tangle of legalism in any ethics which attempts to correct
> code law with loving kindness. The reverse of these roles
> is vitally necessary. It is love which is the constitutive
> principle—and law, at most, is only the regulative one,
> if it is even that.[31]

It could be argued that, if more compassion and conscience and less legalism and concern for precedent had guided church forefathers in the past (and many prelates in the present) in understanding the needs of the less fortunate, they might have sooner identified and undone the injustices and inequities meted out to women, minorities, and slaves in the guise of Christianity.

Paul, accepted as the church's first and foremost, if not greatest, theologian, achieved the spread of Christianity over a vast terrain, from Galilee to Rome. The difficulties he encountered—harsh weather, fragile transport, hostile mobs and politicians, persecution, imprisonment, and torture—were insurmountable, but he surmounted them. Without him this religion of a small Jewish sect could easily have been annihilated through persecution by the high priests and Pharisees, absorption by other sects, discouragement of Christ's disciples, and the general human tendency to forget or dismiss new ideas.

Because Jesus made such an overwhelming impact on people, it is easy to forget that he accomplished this in a place where "the atmosphere is Palestinian, the thought forms are entirely Jewish and derived from the Old Testament, [and] the scope is no larger than Galilee and Jerusalem."[32] This, combined with the Pharisees' hostility, their determination to eliminate Jesus, and the difficulties involved in spreading the Christian church throughout the Greek and Roman empires, must be kept in mind if Paul's ministry, teachings, and interpretations are to be understood. Likewise, if his relegation of women to a secondary and passive role is to be fully understood, it must be remembered that he was dealing with a polyglot of people, social attitudes, and customs. The role of women was not a burning issue. So, too, Paul's thoughts, words, and deeds often reflected his own varied background that unconsciously mitigated against the improvement of women's lot. It could be said that he had not achieved the state of being recommended by Buddhism: freedom from past conditioning so as to have more freedom for present choice.

Before Paul became a convert to Christianity and a predominant forefather of the church, he had been a staunch rabbi who had helped persecute the Christians. As Saul he had been well trained in the Torah and Judaic laws and customs. He had experienced Hellenistic influences, having been born in Tarsus, a Greek city in Cilicia, a province of Asia Minor. The son of a loyal Jew, he had the privilege of Roman citizenship, which he later claimed to save his life. He was a skilled tentmaker, who worked with Aquila and Priscilla, his lifetime loyal supporters and helpmates. He studied under the famous Gamaliel, the son of Hillel, the elder, who is regarded as the conveyor of the 631 laws of the Torah.

Paul was a religious zealot who tried to apply all the minuscule rules of the Torah to his private life, including marriage. As a rabbi who was very proud of his Israelite heritage and Jewish ancestry, he used his religious zeal to persecute the Christians and to be the instigator of and grand inquisitor at Stephen's death. This was his fanatical attempt to eradicate the new religion that appeared to challenge the Law of God as delivered through Moses, the ecclesiastical hierarchy of the synagogue, the interpretation of the scriptures, and the claim of the temple and synagogue to be the only access to God.

Paul was a man of many contradictions: patient and intolerant, humble and proud, zealous and doubting, fiery tempered and gently mediating. He appears to have been a person who mentally and spiritually towered over his physical size. Throughout history he has attracted both fanatical supporters and detractors, who each in their own way, have misunderstood his teachings, taken them out of context and twisted their meaning, or maligned him without regard for the social conditions in which he labored. This was true of the church fathers. It could become true of feminists and reformers unless they deliberately avoid repeating the same error when trying to combat the age-old pigeonholing of women (and men).

Undoubtedly, Paul did a great disservice to women through the ages by his comments and admonitions in Corinthians on public worship in the new church.[33] Daly is right when she says that "for 2,000 years women have endured sermons on the 'glory of man' theme and . . . a yearly harvest of theological essays and books dealing with the 'theology of feminity,' which rely heavily upon the 'symbolism' of the veil' and 'God's plan for women' as made known through Paul."[34] Paul's male interpreters failed to acknowledge either the prevailing social customs, similar to many Islamic customs today, or Paul's counteracting debates. For instance, his admonition that women should cover their heads in church reflected prevailing synagogal traditions, Old Testament interpretations, and first-century Middle Eastern customs.

Through gradual erosion and fashion changes, women's head coverings in most churches have all but disappeared today—without any apparent adverse spiritual effects. Yet many continuing church attitudes have an equally archaic background, especially in the areas of birth control and family planning, preaching and full membership in the church, divorce, and women's family and property rights. While some of today's fundamentalists or rigid opponents of women's development and emancipation would equally oppose adopting customs and attitudes from what they term backward parts of the world, they fail to see the rich irony that their own antiquated attitudes once emanated from precisely those parts.

Pauline injunctions have been used to "keep women in their place": within the confines of domesticity and outside the frontiers of education and professions. Most churches have used these to prevent women from teaching theology and catechism, taking theology degrees, becoming ordained, preaching, and playing a full role in the church. The failure to allow women full participation in the church's work has had its repercussions in the field of development. As long as male and female missionaries—the first development planners— accepted women in a church-prescribed secondary role, they could not possibly realize that many Third World women already had primary or equal roles in their own societies. Indeed, the missionaries apparently did not understand the need to help Third World women sustain those roles to prevent their status from being undermined. Nor did they understand the need to encourage those women to take a primary role in education and development if the goals of an educated, healthy community were to be achieved. The consequence was that females were herded into often inappropriate home economics and domestic science courses and precluded from agricultural, marketing, and economic development projects. This line of action was continued by colonial officers and, more recently, by international development planners, similarly imbued with the Christian notion of "woman's place."

Invokers of Pauline scripts cite such texts as Timothy as authority for keeping women silent and submissive,[35] on the basis that women are incapable of teaching or having authority over men. Yet biblical scholars do not believe that this text, owing to its phraseology, position, and timing, was written by Paul. Nonetheless, Paul has received the odium of an edict written by an author who bent the meanings of Genesis and Jesus' teachings to satisfy ancient social biases about women. Regressive attitudes toward women have also been justified by quoting Ephesians, which stipulates that wives should submit to their husbands as their head even as Jesus was the head of the church.[36] However, when this passage was written, Paul and his followers were living in a partly nomadic and partly paganistic agricultural society. There is no modern relevance in keeping woman in her place, listening but unlistened to, silent and unteaching,[37] when a modern, complex society inundated with the specters of overpopulation, stinking pollution, nuclear diffusion and disaster, and other horrific problems needs all hands on deck, and well-trained hands at that.

Paul had to walk an uneasy tightrope between the conservative Jewish Christians, Gentiles, and members of the Jerusalem church. The conservative Jewish Christians essentially adhered to Judaism in its entirety, differing only from the other Judaic sects in their belief in Jesus, the Messiah. Thus, they staunchly adhered to ceremonial and religious rituals, including dietary laws and circumcision. Various purposes have been ascribed to the practice of circumcision: a sacrifice to the goddess of fertility, preparation for sexual intercourse, a substitute for human sacrifice, or a health measure in a gritty and waterless environment. Although common to most Semitic peoples as well as Muslims, Egyptians, Christian Ethiopians, and many African tribes, within Judaism it was restricted to males. Female circumcision, or clitoridectomy, was not practiced, although it is still cruelly rampant in many parts of Africa and the Middle East. Circumcision in the Bible can be traced back to Moses, Abraham, and Ishmael and is thought to have been a symbol of the Jew's covenant with and offering to God.[38] Moses' wife, Zipporah, in order to save the uncircumcised Moses from the wrath of God, cut the foreskin off their uncircumcised son with a flint knife and threw it at God's feet. In this way she helped Moses to keep his covenant with God and not be "cut off from his people." From this it is believed mothers first performed circumcision before it was taken over by fathers and priests. Thereafter, all Jewish boys were expected to be circumcised eight days after birth and then named. However, many non-Jewish tribes of Africa and the Middle East continued to use, and still use, circumcision as one of the initiation rites youth must undergo to achieve manhood, while clitoridectomy and infibulation is used on girls for initiation into womanhood.

Overall the Jewish Christians wished to restrict membership in the new church to only those who conformed to those rituals and regulations. The Gentiles, on the other hand, while able to accept the ethos and montheism of Judaism, could not accept its rituals and regulations. The Gentiles, on the other hand, while able to accept the ethos and monotheism of Judaism, could not accept its rituals and regulations. Jerusalem church members, brought up in Judaic tradi-Orthodox group.

Throughout his missionary life, Paul fought this conflict between the Orthodox Jewish Christian view, which would have made Christianity a mere sect of Judaism and highly susceptible to being absorbed without a trace, and the more universal view, which sought to extend Christianity beyond Jerusalem to Jews, Gentiles, and others interested in the new faith. [39] The pressures and enmity he incurred when trying to break away from the trivial attitudes imposed on Judaism by the Pharisees and other religious leaders did not deter him from winning adherents to Christianity because of his conscientious and individualistic approach on such matters as circumcision[40] and segregation. [41] Paul did not feel that it was necessary to compel the Gentiles to undergo circumcision;[42] hence, he became known as promulgating "the gospel of uncircumcision."* Eventually, circumcision was abandoned when the Christian church became mainly Gentile. Further, Paul did not believe that it was necessary to separate men and women during worship, as was traditional in the synagogues; hence, women were allowed to mingle with men, an untoward action in those days.

Paul's actions can be seen to have been somewhat at variance with his words. Although his words, particularly when taken out of context, have created dissension among women and theologians, his actions and associations clearly show that he regarded women relatively positively, with a definite place in the church. For example,

---

*Peter, by contrast, was known as the trustee of "the gospel of circumcision."

he and his followers accepted the hospitality of Lydia, a Gentile businesswoman who later became a founding member of Paul's favorite church in Philippi.[43] He acknowledged "those women which laboured with me in the gospel" and urged his followers to help them.[44] As happens in so many religions, women were among the first converts and generous financial supporters of the new faith. Indeed, they were not just passive congregation members but were active preachers with Paul.

Paul relied heavily upon Priscilla and her husband, Aquila, who had been expelled from Rome for their Christian beliefs. They founded the local church in Ephesus and instructed Appollos, a Jewish Christian evangelist who preached a John-the-Baptist type of gospel.[45] Subsequently, "the brethren" wrote to Paul's followers asking them to accept Appollos.[46] Here the use of brethren is specifically generic, covering male and female, Priscilla and Aquila. Paul furthermore appears to have encouraged women to preach. Certainly, he took no umbrage at the evangelist Philip's four daughters "which did prophesy,"[47] that is, preached and taught. In fact, Paul, who had come from a violent background and been irregularly ordained,[48] recognized that for proclaiming the Gospel women "are given tongues," that is, the ability to preach. His actions should be equated with his words, especially when considering the ordination of women and their promotion within the church.

The restrictions imposed upon women from the past need replacing, for until they regain the vital role they originally had during the initial phase of the church, the attitude of congregations toward women will not fundamentally alter. As a minister in the Anglican Church of Canada recently admitted, "There are really no scriptural or theological barriers to incorporating women into all aspects of Church life, only social and conventional." But he further admitted that he found it difficult to promote women, especially the "more aggressive women's lib. types," as "they often upset the parishioners and their preconceptions."[49] This failure to give women greater visibility and responsibility within the church also eventually reflects on development programs and projects instituted by the church, for the tendency continues to be to exclude women from decision-making positions and to relegate them to secondary roles. Many projects have failed for less trenchant reasons than that.

Paul also endured the same enemies as Jesus, namely, those self-righteous Jews who engaged in continuous persecution and misrepresentation of the teachings of Jesus and, subsequently, of Paul. The Greeks and Romans initially had little to do with the calumny of persecution of the Christians. When they did, it was usually instigated by the elders of the synagogues, who feared having their authority eroded. Paul, having already tackled them about blindly adhering to

the Laws of Moses without the requisite faith, could well have deemed
it politick to avoid further confrontation over their social customs pertaining to their wives, concubines, and slaves. The viable establishment of the church was his main concern. Therefore, it is remarkable
that he gave as much thought to women in the young church as he did.

Paul distilled his 20 years of missionary experience and reflec-
tion and expounded his philosophy of Christianity in his Epistle to the
Romans. His basic theme is that the problem for every person is the
same: their own relationship with God. The passages in Romans[50]
depart from his earlier writings, which showed a preoccupation with
the minutiae of organization. To provide a balanced perspective of
Paul's attitudes toward women, Romans should be read in conjunction
with those earlier passages and, since they finally represent a distilla-
tion of his total philosophy, should be regarded as having paramountcy.
As Geoffrey Parrinder notes, "Paul has often been loosely accused of
inventing harsh teachings on sex and marriage [and, he might have
added, women], yet in some ways he was one of the most original and
enlightened of early Christian teachers. It was Paul who said that 'to
the pure all things are pure.'"[51] He resurrected the pagan symbol of
sacred marriage through the spiritual union of people with a divine
deity (God). By equating sacred, earthly union with divine redemption,
he greatly strengthened marriage, which was treated cavalierly by
men in those times. Likewise, he strengthened women's position in
marriage when he enjoined men to love their wives as their own bodies
and to avoid fornication.[52]

He recognized the importance of coitus in marriage and laid an
equal responsibility on husbands and wives[53] to respond and care for
each other.[54] He envisaged physical union as having a spiritual quality to it, as he saw the body being the temple of the Holy Spirit and a
member of Christ.[55] Overall, he approved of marriage and sexuality
in the Hebrew tradition and recommended that unmarried men and
women should marry. Yet Paul is often portrayed as being against
marriage and sex and therefore against women, because he practiced
asceticism and celibacy when he embarked upon his gospel mission,
leaving behind his wife. Moreover, his statement that "it is better
to marry than to burn" has given force to that portrayal. Unfortunately, the context in which he made that statement is typically ignored—
the imminent arrival of Judgement Day and the rebuking of immoral
elements in the Corinthian church who saw release from the Laws of
Moses as a license for promiscuity, idolatry, harlotry, and incest.
Conceivably within Paul's fundamental philosophy and overriding principles lies a powerful source of flexibility that could be used to undo
the wrongs perpetrated by the application of out-of-context Pauline
texts and to create an atmosphere in which unequal and unjust treatment of women is eliminated.

Paul wrote[56] that the Gospel is for all, regardless of faith, sex, or bondage,* "for it is the power of God unto Salvation every one that believeth."[57] He expanded by saying that "there is no respect of persons with God,"[58] and that God's rewards are to those "that worketh good."[59] He emphasized the need for inward faith and right thinking rather than a display of external religious trappings. His low esteem for those who professed a legalistic religion rather than a religion based on justice and compassion (and common sense) could be as applicable to much of the church's hierarchy today as it was to the synagogal elders then. He succinctly summed up their outlook when he said that God is against "all ungodliness and unrighteousness of men who hold the truth in unrighteousness . . . [and] became vain in their imaginations, and their foolish heart was darkened. Professing themselves to be wise, they became fools. And changed the glory of the uncorruptible God into an image made like to corruptible man."[60] His avowal of righteousness and justice could be aptly applied to the need for women's development within and outside the church.

In another area, Paul's interpretation of Genesis differed considerably from that of the church fathers, folklore, and even some modern clergy. To him Adam was a representative of pre-Gospel mankind and of the plight of the human race before the coming of Christ.[61] Although Eve is normally described as the transgressor and although Paul is usually imputed to have so treated her, he actually discusses the transgressions of Adam, whom he regarded in the generic and collective sense as being a person "held in thrall by pride and disobedience, [so that] mankind could expect no other fate than death, the symbol of corruption and failure."[62] He likewise saw the Law of Moses as being an interim measure to tide mankind over until, with the coming of Jesus, atonement would eliminate the transgressions of Adam; that is, mankind.[63] Unfortunately, the often-quoted but not Paul-authored Timothy[64] has undermined Paul's liberal interpretation of Genesis in Romans,[65] where he does not embark upon a Timothy-type diatribe against woman, Original Sin, and Eve's transgressions but, rather, reflects on humanity's propensity to disobey.

Overall, Paul believed that God's commandments through Jesus, with faith and conscience dictating just and right actions, overrode the Law of Moses and the morass of trivial rules set up by the synagogue elders. Pulled into a dispute over the observation of ascetic practices and holy days, he concluded that an element of individual discretion

---

*"There is neither Jew nor Greek [Gentile], there is neither bond [servant or slave] nor free, there is neither male nor female; for ye are all one in Christ Jesus."

and conscience should be allowed within Christian behavior, provided it did not hurt or jeopardize others. In accord with this, he urged that no one should stand in judgment of another and "that no man put a stumbling-block or an occasion to fall in his brother's way."[66] Paul's concluding greetings to his colleagues, including the women— Phebe, Priscilla, Mary, Junia, Trypena and Tryphosa, Rufus's mother and Paul's mother, Julia, and Nereus's sister[67]—indicate that Paul very much included women in the church's work. The rigidity that has surrounded women for centuries and caused their suppression, submission, and subordination largely emerged from the church patriarchs standing in judgment of woman, as symbolized by Eve, and condemning her. They have not harkened to Paul's admonition not to put either "stumbling-block or an occasion" in her way; hence, they must assume considerable responsibility for curtailing women's development within the church and outside it.

Corinthians contains some of the most extensive text about women, and it has been subsequently much used to damage women's position and image in society. But the writings were Paul's attempt to discipline the squabbling, licentious Corinthians by reprimand and reason. When dealing with matters raised by the Corinthians,[68] he carefully differentiated between Christ's teachings and God's commandments and his own opinions or concessions. For instance, he stated that separation, or divorce, was against God's command and therefore immutable, whereas his counsels on virginity and celibacy were his opinions and not permanent regulations. Evidently he did not intend to set himself up as an ultimate authority—a point not fully appreciated by some church leaders and feminist writers. His counsels were also predicated on a Second Coming with a new Resurrection and Redemption, which would transform human physical relationships into spiritual ones, and on the all-pervasive Jewish synagogue customs, first-century traditions, and obscure interpretations of the Old Testament.[69]

Paul commended celibacy over marriage or sex to ensure spiritual readiness for the imminent Second Coming.[70] For this he encouraged men and women alike to look beyond their physical attributes and needs to their spirituality and inner essence.[71] Accordingly, he has been attributed with developing the strong antipathy toward heterosexual relations and women's participating role especially, which has characterized the Christian church's guilt-ridden and hypocritical attitudes toward sex and women. Undoubtedly, Paul decried male and female homosexuality, as did the Hebrews. But St. Augustine and other patrists, including St. Thomas Aquinas, for their own warped reasons, perverted Paul's admonitions on celibacy, marriage, fornication, wifely submission, and duties into an unrecognizable mess—a mess that through the ages became messier with every Vatican pronouncement.

Contrary to the prevailing attitudes of his times, Paul accorded a fair degree of equivalence to women and expounded a basically egalitarian Christian theory. However, it ran into conflicts with Hellenistic philosophy, obsolete Roman law dragged out to satisfy dissidents (though Imperial Rome initially had a relatively egalitarian attitude toward women), pagan practices emanating from nomadic and agricultural life, and of course, firmly entrenched Jewish customs. [72] In trying to reconcile those conflicting views, Paul came up with some inconsistent policies that theologians and clergymen thereafter misused and misinterpreted.

One of these concerned the ritual of head covering—a custom of the Gentiles but not the Christian church. Gentile headgear was used to distinguish between the men and women in the congregation, while the Jews believed that covering the head would scare away the angels of destruction, Semjaza and Azazel. [73] Paul's initial argument in favor of women's head coverings [74] was summarily dismissed by him on the grounds that the Christian church had no such custom. [75] He obviously attached less importance to this ritual than subsequent theologians did. As William Neil says, "He does not appear to convince even himself with his reasoning, and concludes by justifying his position from the fact that it is generally 'the done thing.'" [76] Klausner additionally maintains that not only was Paul bowing to public opinion, [77] he was also exhibiting a form of opportunism and social conservatism.

Paul really put the cat among the pigeons with his statement that "the head of every man is Christ; and the head of the woman is man; and the head of Christ is God." [78] This has been perpetually used by priests and laity to push women into submission before men and husbands alike. It also caused unfortunate repercussions in some developing countries where women traditionally on a par with their menfolk were downgraded through the teaching of missionaries imbued with Pauline mythology.

Later beliefs and subconscious thought about women's secondary role also emanated from Paul's ill-conceived statement that "he [man] is the image and glory of God: but the woman is the glory of the man." [79] Despite Paul's subsequent modification of his fundamental Christian philosophy, [80] the damage to women was done. The church itself has done little to explain the difficult social and cultural milieu Paul was in or his overriding principles and egalitarian philosophy. Instead, the church has presented half-truths as whole truths and is now in the embarrassing position of having to extricate itself from its self-created muddle in the face of fast-evolving social and economic roles for men and women, increasing individual freedoms, changing values, the population explosion, and other upheavals. The first move toward eliminating erroneous and belittling impressions about women could be made by the church helping the public to under-

stand the distinction between Paul's Christian philosophy and his politically motivated pragmatism.

The church could likewise show that, insofar as women's ordination and preaching are concerned, Paul's injunctions against women
speaking in church[81] were based less on Christian religious ethics
than on Halakhah rules in the Talmud.* In fact, not even the Penta-
teuch† (the law), regarded as having precedence over the Halakhah,‡
says that women must keep a churchly silence.[82] Paul's invocation
of Jewish rules was a device to keep peace among the mixed, disor-
derly, and dissenting congregations and not a Christian religious
ethic.[83]

Paul's egalitarian, reformist texts directly contradicted his
more restrictive writings and paved the way for reformers to oppose
the misuse of the Bible by those attempting to justify their ignoble
stances on segregation, slavery, and the suppression of women's individual and general rights. Based on justice and compassion, these
reforms were often initiated by the less hierarchy-bound churches—
the Quaker, Unitarian, Evangelistic, and Wesleyan Methodist—in their
revivalist forms. John Wesley was particularly responsible for re-
interpreting women's role within the church on the basis that if both
sexes can receive an "apprehension of divine grace," both can be
capable of instructing. The determining criteria were the results attained. This attitude prevailed throughout the 1800s, as evinced by
W. B. Godbey, a scholarly Methodist evangelist who in 1891 wrote
that "the Pauline prohibitions about women's speaking in the church
were to maintain order and not to keep women from speaking. I don't
know a Scripture in all the Bible by whose perversion the devil has
dragged more souls in hell than this."[84]

The result of such attitudes was to involve women more deeply
in the church as ministers, preachers, and deacons and to give them
a greater sense of worth as persons. Churches that were more firmly
entrenched under overriding authorities, such as the National Council
of Churches (United States) or the Vatican and were more complacent
because of the size of their power base, were considerably more tardy
in recognizing and undoing age-old injustices. At one time the percentage of women preachers in the evangelistic churches was between 20
and 30 percent, but in recent years this has dropped owing to the social dominance of the established churches and accommodation to pub-

---

*Body of Jewish civil and ceremonial law and legend comprising
the Mishnah and the Gemara.

†First five books of the Old Testament, traditionally ascribed
to Moses.

‡Body of Jewish law in the Mishnah.

lic convention and conformity.[85] Notwithstanding, they still have
many more than the Catholic, Episcopalian, or Anglican churches.

Today, nearly 200 years after reformers like John Wesley, the
culture and attitudes of the established churches dominate, based
more upon Paul's Judaic assumptions and experience than on his
radically new theology. They seem to be in the same position as
Paul, who despite being a "genius, gifted visionary, theologian, teacher
and organizer, found it difficult to adapt his social thought to conform
with his radically new theology."[86] Constance Parvey points out that
"on the theological level, by envisioning the new interdependence of
men and women in Christ, Paul makes a fundamental breakthrough in
new images for women, but on the cultural, social level, he clearly
identifies himself as a first-century Jewish teacher for whom arguments from custom have authority and validity of their own."[87]

Perhaps initially Paul could not see the social and cultural implications of the new theology he was preaching, but careful reading
of Romans tends to bely that thought. Rather, as William Neil emphasizes, those writings show a man who has consolidated and reconciled
his years of teaching and preaching, his background, Judaic assumptions, and Christ's philosophy and then analyzed and interpreted the
significance of the new religion for the immediate social scene.[88]
One is left to wonder why the churches, particularly the Roman Catholic, have been incapable of following suit. As with petty bureaucracy,
so well depicted in Gian-Carlo Menotti's opera The Consul, it could
be because the churches have embraced trivial rules and age-worn
precedents that are irrelevant for today's problems instead of compassionate theology and just philosophy.

From the foregoing it is evident that the new religion of Christianity neither envisaged a subordinate role for women in theory nor
intended to relegate women to a subordinate role in practice. But
very quickly that is exactly what happened. Why was the promise of
the new theology—equivalence and equality between women and men—
so lost and corrupted? This entails examination of the original church
fathers, their concerns for the organization of the new church, their
social position, their influence on community attitudes toward women,
and their own biases.

It took almost 1,800 years before a conscious awareness grew
up among Christians that Christian doctrine was incompatible with
slavery and racism. Even then, it was only a very few years ago that
the final official vestiges of slavery in the United States were eliminated by the passing of civil rights bills and equal opportunities legislation.[89] The legal documents, though publicly altering a situation
that was incompatible with Christianity, still have not totally altered
the private and pervasive attitudes that hold that blacks, Chicanos,
nonwhites, and non-Christians are inferior and should be relegated to

subordinated positions. Such an attitude was exemplified by the comment of a well-to-do white woman to the author on the blacks' Resurrection City in Washington, D.C., in the 1960s when rains had poured down nonstop: "It's a sign from God. You know, forty days and nights of rain. . . . It's a sign that they should not be challenging the status quo, they should keep their place [under the whites]."

It has taken even longer merely to recognize that Christian theology is incompatible with sexism. Somehow the elimination of sexism by the church has been deemed of less importance than the curtailment of racism, even though sexism affects over 50 percent of the population. Yet sexism is no more than racism in different clothing. Certainly the elimination or moderation of sexism has not paralleled, publicly or privately, that of racism. And it is unlikely to unless and until the church fathers, indoctrinated with 2,000 years of Christian mythology about women, are willing to scrub the slate clean. They would have to dismantle their misinterpretations of the New Testament, their Old Testament ideas of woman's place, and their automatic acceptance of the misogynistic attitudes of their predecessors and the church. They would also need to reevaluate their own biases and recognize that their attitudes have been based upon the unjust principles and untenable premises of men from a different era, social milieu, and power-based authority.

Many of today's antediluvian attitudes reflect the paganistic views of Babylonian, Canaanite, Persian, Greek, Jewish, Roman, and pre-Christ times. They reflect the views of such philosophers as the Hellenistic Jew Philo and Paul's successors in the first century A.D. They reflect the attitudes of the greatly influential patrists Justin, Tertullian, Clement of Alexandria, and Irenaeus in the second century A.D.; Origen, the Greek theologian, in the third century; and Augustine, Jerome, Leander of Seville, and the Orthodox Greek theologian Gregory of Nyassa, in the fourth century. Their beliefs ranged from the naturalistic to the apocalyptic and from the dualistic to the monistic when considering the order of creation, God, spirituality, and man-woman relationships. Yet they had a common denominator: the difficulty of reconciling corporeality with spirituality. Tertullian was basically a rigorist, who shared the Gnostic antisex feelings and world-renouncing attitudes of the early church, but he did not condemn marriage or denounce it as a "polluted thing," since that would have amounted to disparagement of the Creator. But he believed that celibacy was preferable for those seeking perfection, spirituality, and sanctity. Tertullian's belief thus helped to reinforce the idea that sex and material comforts should be scorned and despised. The concomitant of this attitude was the downgrading of womanhood, which was reinforced by Tertullian ascribing the fall of man primarily to woman.

As Muhammad did, early Christian teachers opposed infanticide and supported the care of orphans, but unlike him, they held marriage and parenthood in little esteem. One exception was Clement of Alexandria, a mild man who praised the happiness of a Christian home, disagreed with Paul that man cannot serve both God and wife, and recommended marriage. Nevertheless, he too favored virginity over marriage and reiterated woman's role in the Fall. His follower, Origen, being more literal and rigid than Clement, castrated himself to maintain his virginity and save himself from temptation. It is said that he later had considerable cause to regret such drastic action.

An attempt was made by early liberal church writers to dispute the claim that virginity was better than marriage, citing Mary as an example of the worth of marriage or maintaining that a celibate priesthood was preferable to a married clergy. They maintained that "the single life was an evasion of responsibility" but "were viciously attacked by Jerome, one of the most learned and scurrilous patristic theologians, who advocated extreme asceticism."[90]

Clerical marriage (or concubinage) was rigorously opposed by the patrists up to and beyond the tenth century. Yet a form of cohabitation, theoretically based on sexual asceticism, between male and female hermits and between celibate clergy and "housekeepers," appears to have developed as compensation. After the Reformation, clerical marriage was reestablished in all but the Roman Catholic church, which is under increasing pressure to abandon universal and compulsory celibacy. It is thought by many observers of the Catholic scene that if the church wants to expand its shrinking priesthood, within 20 years married clergy will be the norm. Should this occur, it is likely to have a major impact on the role of women within the church and on the church's external activities that affect women. Moreover, it should help to develop a healthier attitude toward sex and sexuality, family planning and contraception, and women's need to have control over their own bodies. With the imposition of monasticism, celibacy, and the confessional, "not only the penitent but the priest [a single man] must have been affected by constant [and often prurient] inquiry into forbidden sexual behaviour, and beneath much of it lay the assumption that sex belonged to the lower nature, if it was not positively evil."[91]

Trying to outdo Jerome in scurrilous and disastrous edicts was Augustine, the bishop of Hippo. A lewd sex glutton who could not reconcile his sexual needs with his spiritual, Augustine wrought his distaste for himself on woman, "the Temptress." Conceding that the Fall only occurred because man (the spirit) yielded to temptation, he nonetheless threw the full weight of his fury and distaste on woman, assigning her to an even more debased position. He believed so strongly in Predestination and Original Sin that he maintained the whole human race was a mass of sin, destined for hell, including unbaptized babies. Sexual intercourse was bestial and inherently evil, hence all offspring were the result of the parents' "sin." Marriage and childbirth did not escape his rantings. Childbirth was the consequence of lust, while marriage was a useful vehicle for diverting the evil of coitus into a positive end, procreation. Disagreeing with Gregory, he believed that only nonsexual monism could exist in God and spirituality, whereas Gregory identified maleness with monism and the spirit. [92] His pronouncements have had disastrous consequences for traditional Christian ethics and for women and the population policies of nations.

Unlike the Buddhists, who believe that everything has two sides that are reconcilable, the original church fathers were emotionally and spiritually incapable of reconciling opposites. They became entangled in webbed skeins of reasoning because they could not accept the existence of apparent opposites: good and evil, corporal and spiritual, woman and man, sex and soul. They could not tolerate the idea of the creation of man (male) in God's image with the debasing act of sex necessary to produce offspring nor the idea of woman's spiritual equivalence with woman's socially determined position of subordination. They only seemed able to reconcile their own biases and peculiarities with Christian theology and thereby to secure for themselves redemption and a place in heaven by relegating their bodily needs, desires, and temptations (woman) to the dust heap of denigration and abuse.

Because of their inherent inability to reconcile opposites, including the two doctrines of creation with its Fall and ultimate redemption, and because they could not accept God and "he who was made in the image of God" as being anything but spiritual and noncorporeal (certainly not corporal and bisexual), they resorted to half-truths. One of the first half-truths propagated, starting with Philo and continuing down to the present day, was the presentation of Genesis as authority for the myth that only man was created in God's image and that woman was a secondary afterthought. The first century patrists through the fourth-century church fathers found it untenable to think of God, "man in God's image," or spiritual reason as being androgynous. They thought only in monistic, not dualistic, terms and consequently were unable to admit that Genesis actually treated male and female equally. They equated man, being first mentioned in Genesis, with spirituality and hence a primary position, and woman, appearing in the second paragraph of Genesis, with the nonspiritual and corporal and a secondary role. The result was a half-truth and myth to dog women's footsteps through the centuries to the present.

The patrists virtually eliminated any possibility of Christianity assigning duality and bisexuality to God as other religions have done

to their respective deities. Whatever twisted and warped routes
these and other patrists took, the results were essentially the same:
man is soul and spirit in a corporeal body, woman is merely body.
Therefore, since flesh must be subdued by the spirit, the body (that
is, woman) must be subdued and subordinated by man. And since
that sinful body caused man's downfall, subordination must be rigidly
enforced.

It is ridiculous that current attitudes about women should have
been determined some 1,500 to 2,000 years ago by men who were a
product of their times and location. It is even more ridiculous and sad
that such attitudes have been occasioned by those men's personal
problems and biases. As with Augustine, many of the other spiritual
leaders were possessed by a guilt and obsession arising out of their
youthful sexual indulgences and the prevailing religious atmosphere.
Unable to shoulder the blame themselves, they condemned women.
Thus, they used their religion to justify their excesses. Not satisfied
with this injustice, they used ever more convoluted reasoning to show
woman to be lowly and inferior in all respects, to ensure woman's
debasement, and to preserve an androcentric view of man. Augustine,
the highly acclaimed father of the church, has been particularly responsible for disseminating this view of women.[93] In fact, he and
the other spiritual leaders have undermined and denied the egalitarian
precepts of Christianity and its concept of equivalence of spirituality
in male and female. Is it not time for both church and laity to undo
this warped injustice?

NOTES

1. Gen. 2:21-24.
2. Gen. 2:24.
3. Gen. 1:26-27.
4. Gen. 1:26.
5. Gen. 1:27.
6. Gen. 1:28, 1:31.
7. William Neil, Harper's Bible Commentary (New York:
Harper & Row, 1975), pp. 17, 18.
8. Gen. 3:21-22.
9. Gen. 3:16.
10. Mary Daly, The Church and the Second Sex (New York:
Harper & Row, 1975), p. 4.
11. Gen. 1:28-29, 2:15; see also Neil, Harper's Bible Commentary, p. 21.
12. Matt. 5:27.
13. Matt. 5:27-28.

14. Matt. 5:31-32.
15. Neil, Harper's Bible Commentary, p. 344.
16. Lev. 18:6-23.
17. Neil, Harper's Bible Commentary, p. 344.
18. Matt. 8:14-15.
19. Matt. 9:18-25.
20. Matt. 15:22-28.
21. Matt. 19:3-12.
22. Matt. 19:3.
23. Matt. 19:4-6.
24. Matt. 19:8.
25. Num. 27:1-11.
26. Matt. 19:10-12.
27. Matt. 7:14; see also John A. T. Robinson, Honest to God
(Philadelphia: Westminster Press, 1963), p. 110.
28. Acts 9:36-41.
29. Matt. 12:1-14.
30. From Honest to God, by John A. T. Robinson. © SCM
Press Ltd. 1963. Published in the U.S.A. by The Westminster
Press, Philadelphia, Pa.
31. Fletcher, Harvard Divinity Bulletin, October 1959, pp. 7-18.
32. Neil, Harper's Bible Commentary, p. 415.
33. 1 Cor. 11:3-16.
34. Daly, The Church and the Second Sex, p. 81.
35. 1 Tim. 2:9-15.
36. Eph. 5:22-24.
37. Daly, The Church and the Second Sex, pp. 81-84.
38. Geoffrey Parrinder, Sex in the World's Religions (Don
Mills, Ontario: General, 1980), pp. 180-82.
39. Acts 15:1-33; see also Gal. 2:11-21.
40. Acts 16:14, 17:3; and Rom. 2:25-29.
41. Gal. 2:11-21.
42. Parrinder, Sex in the World's Religions, p. 183.
43. Acts 16:14-15, 40.
44. Phil. 4:3.
45. Acts 18:26-27.
46. Acts 18:24-27.
47. Acts 21:8-9.
48. J. B. Phillips, The Young Church in Action (London: Geoffrey Bles, 1955), pp. xiv-xv.
49. Personal conversation.
50. Rom. 1-3.
51. Parrinder, Sex in the World's Religions, p. 211.
52. 1 Cor. 7:2.
53. 1 Cor. 7.
54. 1 Cor. 7:3-5.
55. 1 Cor. 6.

56. Gal. 3:28.

57. Rom. 1:16.

58. Rom. 2:11.

59. Rom. 2:10.

60. Rom. 1:18-23.

61. Rom. 5:14-21.

62. Neil, Harper's Bible Commentary, p. 450.

63. Rom. 5:18-19.

64. 1 Tim. 2:9-15.

65. Rom. 5:19.

66. Rom. 14:12-13.

67. Rom. 16:1-23.

68. 1 Cor. 7:1-11:34.

69. Neil, Harper's Bible Commentary, p. 455.

70. 1 Cor. 7:1.

71. 1 Cor. 7:1-40.

72. Julia O'Faolain, Not in God's Image (London: Temple Smith, 1973), p. 128.

73. 1 Cor. 11:10.

74. 1 Cor. 11:5-6.

75. 1 Cor. 11:16.

76. Neil, Harper's Bible Commentary, p. 459.

77. Joseph Klausner, From Jesus to Paul (London: Allen & Unwin, 1943), pp. 567-68.

78. 1 Cor. 11:3.

79. 1 Cor. 11:7.

80. 1 Cor. 11-12; Gal. 3:28; and Acts 2:17-18.

81. 1 Cor. 14:4-35.

82. Klausner, From Jesus to Paul, p. 568, n. 32.

83. 1 Cor. 14:40.

84. Reprinted with permission from Donald W. Dayton and Lucille Sider Dayton, "Women as Preachers—Evangelical Precedents," Christianity Today, May 23, 1975, pp. 4-7. © 1975 by Christianity Today.

85. Ibid.

86. Constance Parvey, "Women in the New Testament," in Religion and Sexism, ed. Rosemary Radford Reuther (New York: Simon & Schuster, 1974), p. 123.

87. Ibid., pp. 127, 128.

88. Neil, Harper's Bible Commentary, pp. 447-48.

89. U.S., Civil Rights Act of 1964, Statutes at Large, vol. 78; idem, Civil Rights Act of 1968, Statutes at Large; and idem, Voting Rights Act, Statutes at Large, vol. 79.

90. Parrinder, Sex in the World's Religions, p. 220.

91. Ibid., p. 222.

92. Parvey, "Women in the New Testament," p. 154.

93. Ibid., p. 162.

9

CHRISTIANITY
AND
EDUCATION

Education historically was the preserve of the wealthy or the religious orders. To a large extent, priests dominated the transmission of knowledge and controlled access to institutions of learning. No education in the early days of a Christian country's history was immune from this monopoly exercised by the religious orders. The lack of modern technology and communications systems was not the main contributing factor to this monopoly; rather, the desire to exercise and retain power over the plebians was paramount. With the exercise of educational power went spiritual (and financial) power; and priests were not about to relinquish such temporality.

Irrespective of Christianity's purported egalitarianism, the misinterpretation of specific scriptural passages, particularly Pauline sayings, and the exclusion of women from full membership and participation in the church have rendered women nonequal in the eyes of governing priests (and, by their extrapolation, in the eyes of God). This diminution of women had the unfortunate result of erecting the time-worn myths that women were incapable of absorbing the same amount of education or the same in-depth knowledge as men. Further, the myths stipulated that women's minds, like their bodies, were weaker, punier, and therefore less fact absorbing or logical and that their intellectual needs were inconspicuous and did not need the same nourishment as their male counterparts. Attitudes and myths die hard, and none have died harder than those attributing to women weaker brains and weaker educational needs than men. In the so-called modern, liberated, twentieth century, those myths and attitudes are daily encountered by girls embarking upon education in the fields of science, mathematics, law, forestry, and economics and by women choosing careers in allegedly masculine fields.

The continuance of retrograde attitudes and myths is perpetuated by such biblical passages as the following:

> Let your women keep silence in the churches; for it is not
> permitted unto them to speak; but they are commanded to
> be under obedience, as also saith the law.
>
>   And if they will learn anything, let them ask their hus-
> bands at home; for it is a shame for women to speak in
> church. [1]

Not that these passages were specifically advocating the noneducation
of women. As discussed in Chapter 8, Paul was striving to keep order
and discipline among a very unruly congregation that was predisposed
toward excesses of immorality. He was not seeking to stop women
from being educated. But, as has always happened, is happening,
and will continue to happen, his words were taken out of context in
terms of subject, time, and situation, so that he and women were for-
ever burdened with the myths that women should be restrained from
speaking in church (preaching) and should be taught privately, if at
all, by their husbands (restricted learning). Pope after pope has invoked these and other similar passages, natural law, and ontology to
justify the stand, at one time or another, against women's equality,
coeducation, career women or working mothers, education, and work
for self-fulfillment over and above opposition to women's full participation in church matters, ordination, and preaching.

    Although Vatican II's Declaration on Christian Education was
not specifically against coeducation, it was regressive insofar as female education was concerned because of its emphasis on sex-role
differences that tangibly and subtly affect textbooks, curricula, teachers, and teaching. [2] Teachers were strongly admonished that "they
should pay due regard in every educational activity to sexual differences and to the special role which divine providence allots to each
sex in family life and in society." [3] In a sense the rigidity and opposition to equal education for women expressed by Pope Pius XI in 1929
was still being adhered to, albeit more subtly, by Vatical II during
the 1960s.

    Pius XI, as has been and still is the wont of the Roman Catholic
church, fell back upon spiritual symbolism, Original Sin, and natural
law to justify the denial of equal education. In his Encyclical Letter,
"Divini Illius Magistri," he stated: "Besides there is not in nature
itself, which fashions the two quite different [sexes] in organism, in
temperament, in abilities, anything to suggest that there can be or
ought to be promiscuity, and <u>much less equality, in the training of
the two sexes</u>" (emphasis added). [4] To women's ultimate detriment,
he equated promiscuity with equality, coeducational training, and equal
education. The hostility toward women's equal education evidenced
in papal writings appears to have sprung from a deep-rooted belief in
women's inferiority. The hostility appears to have been further rein-

forced by the fear that female emancipation, which could arise from education and the deployment of women's full potential, would upset the natural order between man and woman, woman and God, and woman and the church. Allusions are made to woman's innate modesty, her natural need to obey her husband, and her honor and dignity as reasons for not educating her as thoroughly as a man.

Pius XI regularly inveighed against female emancipation as being contrary to the natural condition of woman, which was deemed to be subjection and subordination to and linkage with her husband. Anything else was assumed to be "false liberty and unnatural equality." Women were expected to submerge their own rights and needs in the total service of the family. Moreover, they were expected to perform in accordance with the dictates of an external authority, the church. Although Pius XI recognized that most working mothers had to work for economic reasons, he effectively produced guilt in those who were gainfully employed outside the home. In essence, he harassed married working women by intoning, "It is doubtful that such a condition [entering the fields of work and public life] is the social ideal for the married woman."[5] He particularly aroused guilt in many educated women who, relatively well off, wished to work less for economic than for personal reasons. In this way he contributed to stifling their initiative to acquire and use a more-than-average or basic education and to a diminution of their self-worth and dignity. Needless to say, neither he nor subsequent popes objected to women voluntarily giving hours and years of their life to powerless and menial tasks, tasks generally avoided by men, within the church.

Pius XII reinforced this bias against working married women by subtly denigrating them through calling their "true womanhood" into question and by differentiating between the rewards men and women respectively should expect from work. He pronounced that men should expect public esteem and prestige among many other tangible rewards. Women, however, should only expect social esteem arising from their maternal, not their professional, role. He thus ingeniously reinforced the guilt in women for not pursuing strictly maternal goals, and thereby helped to reaffirm the pronatalism of Catholicism through the discouragement of equal education and career opportunities for women. Once again a church father was able to undermine the equality of women as established by God and Jesus. Women might be spiritually equal before God, but they could not be equal before or with men in daily, practical terms.

Double-think and double-talk about matters relating to women have for too long figured prominently in the Christian church. At last, some fresh thinking and compassionate understanding by some unique church figures in the last 20 years have been causing a reassessment of traditional, discriminatory stands. The Anglican and

Episcopalian churches in Canada and the United States, respectively, have taken considerable strides to overcome pervasive inequality and biased representation, but whether they will be able to take the ultimate step toward full equality for women will largely depend upon how firmly their leaders are committed to egalitarianism in view of the dogma and attitude of the Catholic church toward women. In striving for ecumenicity, those churches have tended to minimize women's issues, since those could be the major barrier to reaching accord with the Roman Catholic church.

The fresh winds of change that blew through the Vatican during Pope John XXIII's brief reign died to a whisper upon Pope Paul VI's ascension. Pope John was surprisingly cognizant of the fact that women are genuine human beings with aspirations and potential not far dissimilar from men's. In his "Pacem in Terris,"[6] he demonstrated a singular awareness of women as human beings, an awareness lacking in his predecessors' (and successors') pronouncements:

> Since women are becoming ever more conscious of their human dignity, they will not tolerate being treated as mere material instruments, but demand rights befitting a human person both in domestic and in public life. [7]

> Thus in very many human beings the inferiority complex which endures for hundreds and thousands of years is disappearing, while in others there is an attenuation and a gradual fading of the corresponding superiority complex which had its roots in social-economic privileges, sex, or political standing. [8]

> Human beings have the right to choose freely the state of life which they prefer . . . with equal rights and duties for man and woman . . . [including family and religious life]. [9]

Pope John was unusual in recognizing that an inferiority complex had been inculcated in women over the centuries, that women were striving to shake off the shackles of inferiority and to be recognized as dignified human beings, and that they had a right of choice comparable to men's. He was even more unusual in predicting that the male sense of superiority might moderate as men, too, were able to exercise greater freedom of choice.

Vatican II's Pastoral Constitution on the Church in the Modern World fully recognized that discrimination of every kind, including that based on sex, should be eradicated, being contrary to God's intent. [10] It recognized that fundamental personal rights were still not being universally honored, such as in the case of women who are "denied the right and freedom to choose a husband, to embrace a state of life, or to acquire an education or cultural benefits equal to those recognized for men" (emphasis added). [11] Despite declaiming that the church would unequivocally champion human rights, Vatican II nevertheless continued to express the church's ambivalence toward women assuming full adulthood in society. It persisted in assigning women to a traditional domestic role and in reiterating that their role arose from and was dependent upon nature and the church's concept of natural law. It could not finally cut its bondage to its Hebraic past.

Pope Paul VI was prepared to grant that women were scripturally given perfect equality in nature, dignity, and rights. But he constantly weakened that premise with ambivalent comments about equal education and equal work opportunities for women and with damning statements about divorce and birth control. This is exemplified by his evocation of woman as "the creature most docile for any formation" at the hands of husband or priest, rather than of a thinking, educated, independent person capable of rational decision and logic. Furthermore, he seemed intent on preserving her in that state of malleability by preventing her from practicing birth control, having access to contraception information, or obtaining divorce, even in the most dire of circumstances.

In a sense Pope Paul inherited Pope John's aggiornamento, or modernization movement, which resulted in a revolution larger than Pope John had foreseen. Traditional authority was challenged; values inside and outside the church were questioned; and reform was demanded in the face of conservative recalcitrance. Pope Paul has been viewed by many as having introduced more changes than any pope since the Council of Trent (sixteenth century), particularly a revision of the liturgy to make it more accessible to the masses, a streamlining of the Curia bureaucracy, and a genuine attempt to achieve ecumenicity. But he gave a firm no to reform in those areas that especially affected women: the ordination of women, artificial birth control, divorce, and married priests.

He brushed away the disciplines of many centuries: the tradition of not eating meat on Fridays, the Index of Forbidden Books, and charges of heresy and excommunication as a result of theological disputes. He pushed for religious liberty, with the result that the Catholic church finally affirmed that it respected the rights of conscience of other believers. And through his 1967 encyclical "Populorum Progressio" ("On the Development of Peoples") he pushed the church to become more sensitive to the social and economic distress of people not only in Italy and Europe but in the Third World. He warned that rich nations must share their wealth with poor ones or risk the wrath of both God and the poor. By internationalizing the Synod of Bishops, he gave a greater sounding board to many Third World prelates. But ultimately, he was not able to extend the universality of reform, liberty, or sensitivity to women. He was not prepared to develop a real working relationship with the synod to adopt the majority view on such issues as the religious education of youth, celibacy, and women's ordination. For whatever reason—his own asceticism and unawareness of women's needs, the tradition of patriarchal authority and paternalism within the church, a romanticized view of family and motherhood— Paul was unable to grant women the full worth of his proclamations on liberty, conscience, and economic and social improvement. Indirectly, he became responsible for hampering that very economic and social justice he wished for Third World peoples, for by failing to accord women full worth and emancipation, he contributed to their continued subjugation in macho-Catholic societies. Without the full liberation of women, the full education of children and development cannot be achieved.

In the summer of 1968 he wrote the controversial "Humanae Vitae" ("On Human Life"), which ignoring the advice of the special papal birth control commission to accept certain methods of contraception, totally rejected artificial birth control. He cited "natural law," the usual fallback position of conservative Catholic theologians, and warned that the use of birth control would lead easily toward conjugal infidelity and a general lowering of morality. Furthermore, he envisaged that society would move away from traditional family patterns toward greater self-indulgence and that the rise of militant feminism would "either masculinize or depersonalize women." Underlying his concern seemed to be a fear that if women became too highly educated outside the traditional parameters, they would become unsuitably aggressive, radical, or revolutionary.

Eight years later a ringing condemnation of premarital intercourse, masturbation, and active homosexuality was issued under a mandate from Pope Paul by the Congregation for the Doctrine of the Faith. This was an attempt to provide guidelines and clear up the confusion that had taken hold of Roman Catholic bishops, who found themselves confronted by progressive theologians giving support to local pastoral priests for their compassionate and conciliatory attitudes toward their parishioners and their sexual behavior. In the Vatican's view, homosexuality is "intrinsically disordered and can in no case be approved of"; premarital sex is wrong, for sex "must be within the framework of marriage" to provide stability and an ordered environment for children; and masturbation "is an intrinsically and seriously disordered act." This declaration, the Declaration on Certain Questions concerning Sexual Ethics (1976), never veered away from the traditionally held natural-law theory of the church, which states that the immutable laws written by God are part of human nature and are timeless and unchangeable. The church's duty, therefore, is to transmit these immutable laws "however much the opinions and morals of the world may have been opposed to them."[12] Since one of the immutable laws is "woman's nature" and given the Vatican's stance on timeless principles and immutability, it is difficult to see whether the Vatican can substantially alter its perception of women and cease circumscribing their potential as human beings with immutable-law proscriptions.

Pope Paul's human rights proclamations and instructions on women's issues thus contributed to keeping women in a state of dependence and subjugation through the repetition of ignorance and pregnancy and prevented them from becoming complete human beings. Undoubtedly, Paul was subject to the currents and vagaries of the powerful bureaucracy of the Roman Curia, and he was hard pressed to moderate the tensions between liberal and conservative clergy, tensions that threatened to create great schisms within the church. Pressed from all sides, he could not afford to make the equality of women a central issue, even if he wanted to. And little evidence exists to show that he wanted to. As so often happens in a political world, the women and their concerns were jettisoned for expediency's sake.

Pope John Paul I (Bishop Luciani of Venice) was pope for too short a time (barely a month) to have had much impact on women's and birth control issues. He exhibited flexibility, which boded well for the future, when he congratulated the English parents of the first test-tube baby (girl), despite other Catholic theologians condemning the experiment, and again when he said that "progress is a great thing, but not all progress is good for man." He also showed that he could alter course upon due deliberation when he decided, during the Second Vatican Council (1962–65), that perhaps he and others had been wrong in their teachings that only the true Roman Catholic religion had rights. He appeared to bring not only an element of moderation and compassion to issues and people, but a recognition that people were individuals capable of thinking for themselves and making their own decisions. "The individual conscience must always be followed, but the individual must make an effort to have a well-formed conscience, . . . in informing itself first on what the law of God dictates."[13]

What John Paul might have achieved for women can only be left to speculation, but the role his successor envisages for women is becoming increasingly clearer. In Septebmer 1981 Pope John Paul II reaffirmed that man has an intrinsic worth and dignity and that any system that degrades that worth or dignity is wrong.* Using his third

---

*It is interesting to note that the Roman Catholic church is increasingly attempting to "de-sex" the language of the Bible and liturgy to make women feel less invisible and more included.

encyclical, or formal policy-setting letter to the Roman Catholic church, "Laborem Exercens" ("On Working"), he reemphasized his "concern for the welfare of the individual, criticized the dehumanizing aspects of modern life and committed the Church to the cause of social justice."[14] While he asserted that labor has priority over capital, he nonetheless reaffirmed the church's belief in the right to private property, with everyone having the right to goods. He equally condemned laissez-faire capitalism and excessive bureaucratic centralization or socialism, since both tend to exploit the worker and to reduce "him" to a "cog in a huge machine." He has consistently shown much compassion over human rights issues and great concern for the rights of workers, including fair wages and medical benefits. It is implied that these concerns and rights are undoubtedly meant to extend to women. But do they in reality? As usual, the vexing question (for the church) of the role of women has created an ambivalence in the application of enunciated principles. On the one hand, John Paul has emphasized that women have the right "to fulfill their tasks in accordance with their own nature, without being discriminated against and without being excluded from jobs for which they are capable." Nevertheless, on the other hand, he has stated that "the true advancement for women requires that labour should be structured [so that] women do not have to pay for their advancement by abandoning what is specific to them, [their] irreplaceable role [as mothers]."[15]

Nevertheless, various Roman Catholic theologians have been fighting to moderate or reverse the Vatican's stand on women's concerns and related issues. And many priests and nuns "in the field and at the grass-roots" have worked practically to counter what they regard as the church's retrograde teaching. One of the most fiery and controversial of the theologians has been the Reverend Hans Kung of West Germany who has consistently challenged traditional Roman Catholic teachings on papal infallibility, priestly celibacy, the prohibition against women in the church, and birth control. Investigated, disciplined, and censured by the Vatican and threatened with removal from the Catholic faculty at Tubingen (the position is not controlled, however, by the German bishops, and so he was not removed), Kung has vowed to continue his struggle against the "increasing intolerance" within the worldwide church. "The Vatican's current drive for theological conformity has ushered in a new climate of fear for many progressive Catholics," he said. "Not since the time of (Martin) Luther have they fought so much against one person (Kung)."[16] Mary Daly, self-styled as a post-Christian feminist, likewise incurred the wrath of religious authority—in this case the Jesuit-run Boston College— for writing The Church and the Second Sex and was fired for expressing her views freely about the church's sorry treatment of women.

In Latin America, with little support from the majority of bishops and generally much opposition, priests and nuns working among the poor initiated one of the most influential movements among Latin America's 300 million devotees, the communidades de base, or base communities. From Mexico to Argentina, about 150,000 communidades exist to take care of "the needs and wishes of Latin America's largest class, the desperately poor, the uneducated, the politically unorganized."[17] They tend to spring up in the most destitute, slummiest areas—80,000 exist in the most poverty-stricken states of north and northeast Brazil alone. Again, the religious hierarchy has interfered with social and economic progress. Bishops have ordered priests and nuns to cease and desist in their communidades activities, including agitation for education, family planning, potable water, sanitation, political "conscienzation" (or the development of political awareness and action) and to leave their parish or the country for good. Whether because the religious hierarchy is hand-in-glove with the government or military dictatorship of such countries as Argentina, where the communidades were practically wiped out; whether it is inherently fearful of any change that might undermine its traditional paternalistic authority; or because it fears that women and the poor will threaten their own personal power and wealth, the communidades have had a long, difficult time in winning acceptance from Latin America's bishops. Finally, in February 1979 the Conference of Latin American Bishops (CELAM) acknowledged the potency of the communidades for evangelization, education, and liberation. But Pope John Paul II somewhat dampened this achievement by categorically stating that Latin American clergy should be "priests, not social workers or political leaders or functionaries of temporal power."[18] Despite his own high political profile and his distinctive political bias and style, the Pope seems to be intent on dragging the church's messengers back into isolation, away from uniting in common cause with the poor and disadvantaged against poverty, oppression, and suppression. Yet to these, especially women and men who are ill educated, never had anything, and never expected much, the communidades are the "schools where we learn to be somebody."

The ambiguity that exists between official church doctrine or attitude and church practice at the community level is similarly evinced in the Philippines, where the chasm between the have and have-nots is enormous. There the official church body, led by Cardinal Sin,* "is overwhelmingly conservative and refuses to confront the government openly. What is more, many of the conservative bishops have economic interests they do not wish to jeopardize by being openly critical of the government."[19] As a consequence of this conservatism, which identifies with President Marcos's government, two other political alignments have emerged, the Left (Marxist) and the Center. Both

---

*No pun intended.

of these progressive groups believe that the church needs restructuring; that past social justice, which consisted of establishing educational and medical charitable institutions to fill economic gaps, is inadequate and irrelevant; and that people must be educated to realize that the existing economic system is the root cause of their poverty and unjust treatment. Despite the need for reform, the agitation by these groups, and the sorrowful state of so many poor women, it is estimated that the majority of nuns still confine themselves apathetically or complacently to their convents rather than embark upon a teaching, politicization mission among the poor.

The Philippine church has adopted two pastoral approaches: the institutional, with its traditional support from the church and the lay and clerical elites; and the people approach. Popularly called the church of the poor, the people approach worries the church hierarchy because it may advocate armed revolt, and it worries the government because it is eroding government influence, especially in the rural areas. The Marcos government has countered the radicals and tamed the conservatives by closing down church-run publications and radio stations, raiding religious sanctuaries for dissidents, and threatening to legalize divorce and abortion. Thus, the dilemma for the church is still the choice between prayers and politics.

Apart from introducing the padrino system into the Philippine social structure and merging with non-Catholic or animistic traditions and beliefs to produce a distinct Filipino folk religion, Catholicism also developed an extensive education system. This emanated from the efforts of Spanish missionaries to educate children abandoned by Spanish soldiers and others. Educational institutions eventually encompassed parochial schools and tertiary colleges, universities for men and (unusually) universities for women, and a range of postgraduate courses run by Jesuits and Dominicans. By 1978, 173 of the 1,791 Catholic-run schools were colleges and universities. But many Filipino women feel that, despite Catholicism's positive educational and social legacy, it has harmed their status and their progress. Pope John Paul II's emphasis on the family continues to place a heavy burden on women to marry early and bear child after child and thereby curtail their education and work opportunities. They believe that the church's ban on divorce places them at an emotional, legal, and financial disadvantage vis-à-vis the men, and that the ban on birth control does likewise, quite apart from the disastrous effects the ban has on the rampant birthrate and malnutrition in the Philippines.

Undoubtedly, at the popular level Christian missionaries of all persuasions have been instrumental in establishing educational bases in countries where little or none had existed before. Through sheer dedication and hard work they created school systems and introduced both children and adults to hitherto unknown knowledge. Many instituted programs and the teaching of subjects that they thought were appropriate to the needs of the local people, even if such action directly contravened dictates from their superiors at home. Many others, blindly adhering to their hierarchy's prescriptions even if they were irrelevant for the country concerned, imbued their followers with concepts of Original Sin, temptation, and inequality where none had existed before. They perpetuated the myth of female inferiority by providing schools and curricula geared to the male. Because of their own preconceived ideas based upon certain Christian notions and papal pronouncements concerning females, they ignored (or condemned) a country's social customs that permitted a frankness of association and mutual cooperation between men and women.

In various societies, missionaries segregated boys and girls and differentiated the courses taught to the two sexes. The consequence was that the boys were taught the potentially more rewarding and useful subjects in the vocational, mechanical, and scientific spheres and the girls were taught domesticity in the Western vein, irrespective of its usefulness in their everyday lives. Historically, girls in Christian missionary institutions were not given equal education, not necessarily out of spite or a spirit of inegalitarianism but because the education or training of girls must be in accord with their "natural condition" or the "natural order of things." Today, they still lack the support necessary to acquire the same education as boys, education that could lead them to self-sustaining, income-producing opportunities. Before they can hope to achieve such full educational equality, school administrators and policy makers must look honestly at their biases, recognize that many are religiously based, and strive to alter the regressive religious thinking that has had a continuing detrimental impact on female education for far too long.

NOTES

1. 1 Cor. 14:34-35.
2. Mary Daly, The Church and the Second Sex (New York: Harper & Row, 1975), pp. 26, 44, 109.
3. Declaration on Christian Education [Gravissimum educationis], no. 8, cited in ibid., p. 121.
4. Pope Pius XI, "Divini Illius Magistri," Encyclical Letter, December 31, 1929.
5. Pope Pius XI, "Address to Married Couples," September 10, 1941.
6. Pope John XXIII, "Pacem in Terris," Encyclical Letter, April 11, 1963.

7. Ibid., n. 41.

8. Ibid., n. 43.

9. Ibid., n. 15.

10. Vatican II, "Pastoral Constitution on the Church in the Modern World" [Gaudium and Spes], in The Documents of Vatican II, ed. Walter M. Abbot, S. J.; trans., Joseph Gallagher (New York: American Press, 1966), p. 199.

11. Ibid., p. 228.

12. "Thou Shalt Not—And Shall," Time, January 26, 1976, p. 41.

13. "A Swift, Stunning Choice," Time, September 4, 1979, p. 71.

14. "Work Is for Man, Not Man for Work," Time, September 28, 1981, p. 58.

15. Ibid.

16. "Fiery RC Theologian Fights 'Intolerance,'" Ottawa Citizen, October 24, 1981.

17. "The Church of the Poor," Time, May 7, 1979, p. 71.

18. Ibid.

19. Sheilah Ocampo, "A Pope among Politicos," Far Eastern Economic Review 105, no. 8 (February 13, 1981): 16.

10

CHRISTIANITY
AND
POPULATION

Protestantism and Judaism both at the popular and official levels (fundamentalist and orthodox sects excepted) have endorsed the use of artificial contraception to prevent births and to regulate the size of families. Official Catholicism, by contrast, has continued to condemn all forms of contraception except the natural methods of abstinence and rhythm. But Roman Catholic fieldworkers have often disputed this policy and encouraged their followers to pursue their own consciences in deciding whether or not to use "unnatural" forms of birth control. Indeed, the Catholic laity has increasingly ignored hierarchal proclamations and practices birth control in accordance with its own specific needs. As one Catholic woman said, summing up the attitude of many others, "Any sane Catholic would!"

Leading Catholic theologians, such as Father O'Brien of Notre Dame University and former priest Ivan Illich, strongly criticized Pope Paul VI's 1968 encyclical, "Humanae Vitae," which even condemned coitus interruptus as an "unnatural" form of contraception. They criticized the encyclical for being repressive, for causing mental and psychological turmoil to devout Catholics, for contributing to the world's population explosion, and for exacerbating the physical suffering of innumerable women.

The official Catholic stance has hurt women other than just Catholics. By lobbying against UN and other international programs to curtail runaway population growth, whether in Catholic or non-Catholic countries, it has damaged the effectiveness of those programs and, coincidentally, has delayed economic and social development, especially as it pertains to women. It has hampered family-planning and population efforts by playing on the fears of national leaders of other faiths who imagine family planning and birth control to be forms of genocide, neocolonialism, exploitation, or external interference with internal religious and customary mores. It has indulged their fantasies that birth control leads to promiscuity and venereal disease or that more people equal more national power, expanded prestige, and greater development.

Many European and North American Catholics have, in recent years, disregarded papal edicts and official Roman Catholic pronouncements. They have followed their own consciences—perhaps not without some inner confusion, however—and practiced family planning to an impressively effective extent. This does not mean that they are no longer influenced by their religion, as a survey of 60,000 U.S. women showed.[1] Rather, they have acquired a greater knowledge and awareness of the issues involved than their predecessors had and, as a consequence, have attempted to reconcile the differences between reality and doctrine. Many of the newer views have risen from traditional sources: for example, from Quebecois, who can now claim to have one of the lowest Canadian birthrates, or from the devout Italian women who successfully pushed for divorce and abortion reform in Italy despite vehement Vatican opposition. Catholic biologist John H. Thomas cogently sums up their attitude.

> The [Catholic] Church must affirm that the birth rate
> must soon be brought in line with the death rate—that is
> a growth rate of zero. This is the responsibility of all
> people regardless of race or religion. The Church must
> recognize and state that all means of birth control are
> licit. . . . [It] must put its concern for people, their
> welfare, and their happiness above its concern for doc-
> trine, dogma, and canon law. . . . It is time that the
> Church stops being like a reluctant little child, always
> needing to be dragged into the present.[2]

Thomas's comment was in 1968. Today, the official Roman Catholic church is still mainly concerned "for doctrine, dogma and canon law," even though those were gleaned from other eras for other conditions. If the church were to give people's actual needs and quality of life priority over dogma, it could have a major impact on population-related problems. However, despite the church's considerable resources, dedicated people, and great organizational powers, that is highly unlikely in the near future, as long as the present Holy See emphasizes a return to conservatism, a withdrawal from direct social reform, and a denial of women's right to control their own bodies and their own lives.

The relatively liberal view of marriage, family planning, and birth control held by the Judaic and Protestant faiths is a fairly recent phenomenon, which just began to emerge after the Industrial Revolution. Nevertheless, inherent in their views and dominant in Catholicism is a pronatalism that is a testimonial to their common heritage, their common geographic background and social system, and their common scriptural writings.

Old Testament Jewish society lived a rugged, precarious existence perched on the edge of war, famine, and early death from disease and starvation. Life was short; mortality was high. High birthrates and numerous children offset disaster and ensured racial survival. Faith and fatalism were essential to emotional survival. Since lands were empty, overcrowding was not a major issue. Early Judaic-Christian theological doctrines reflected this struggle for survival by encouraging procreation, incorporating it into their body of doctrine, and condemning anything likely to reduce its preeminence. Before modern medicine, knowledge, and science, this earlier pronatalist, survivalist view was perfectly justified. Today, when mortality has been severely pruned and life expectancy greatly extended and when survival has become a consequence of overpopulation rather than of underprocreation, the continuance of another age's doctrine is no longer justified. But, within the context of religion, original need became converted to subsequent doctrine, which in turn, became unshakable dogma.

Judaism, Protestantism, and Catholicism have at one time or another all based their justifications for pronatalism on Genesis. They appear to have disregarded the fact that

> [those] writings . . . were addressed to an innumerous people struggling to establish themselves in a relatively infertile, arid land, bordered in several directions by belligerent tribes at a time when warfare involved hand-to-hand combat. Under such conditions, the relation between population size and survival was abundantly clear.[3]

Because survival then was a dubious proposition, the unquestioning attempt to emulate Adam and Eve by fulfilling God's original command to "be fruitful and multiply"[4] was not only justifiable but essential. Equally, given that Noah and his seven family members were presumed to be the only human survivors of the rampaging Flood,[5] attempts to emulate Noah's clan by obeying God's command to repopulate the empty earth with individuals willing to abide by God's Law were understandable. In both instances a heavy responsibility to perpetuate the survival of the human race and God's morality rested on their shoulders.

However, to build up a case based on Genesis for continuing unadulterated procreation in a world already suffering the consequences of almost four-and-a-half billion people is nothing short of irresponsible. But it continues unabated by religious officialdom, by conservative clerics, and by educated laity who despite their education adhere (albeit often unconsciously) to archaic myths of natalism. Politicians and businessmen, too, irrespective of unemployment and economic crises, unimaginatively and ignorantly counsel "more babies" as their antidote to declining material consumption, capital expansion, and productivity. Needless to say, these pronatalist attitudes place tremendous pressure on women to live up to their male-designed destiny and to produce more children than the world needs or they can cope with.

Catholicism, in particular, has substantially contributed to pronatalist tendencies by emphasizing the procreative side of marriage over the companionate side. Genesis with its "be fruitful" provisions has been invariably invoked as a primary reason for giving precedence to reproduction over affectionate companionship within marriage. And, it has only been in the recent past that church fathers have deemed companionship to be an important, essential element of marriage. As noted earlier, they deemed procreation as the justification for carnality-based marriage. Yet the Old Testament itself is replete with examples of warm marital companionship and conjugal devotion as ends in themselves, despite the prevailing patriarchal society and its social customs, which made wives their husbands' property and daughters their fathers'. The failure of the church to emphasize the companionate side of marriage has had particularly adverse repercussions on women in the macho societies of Latin America, where men primarily marry to affirm their masculinity and to father children—numerous children—to prove their virility. Marrying women for love and companionship is far down their list of goals. And women, taught by the church to be submissive and trained by society to be their husband's uncomplaining beast of burden, expect little but abuse, work, and babies. "'Machismo', the myth of the superiority and inborn authority of men over women, is not only part of the traditional customs and beliefs in Latin America, but is very much alive in modern stratified societies. . . . [It] has become an oppressive ideology expressed in many different attitudes and forms of behaviour, especially in economic life, employment and sexual life."[6] And it has been reinforced by the church's attitude toward women, their role in life, their sexuality, and their maternality. Much of the cause of women's suffering in Latin American countries is due to machismo, but little has been done by religious authorities to instruct the macho men in new attitudes and behavior and to untie the women's cords of macho bondage.

In a sense, the two meager "be fruitful" passages in the Old Testament have contributed to this state of being for women. Their emphasis on procreation was later inadvertently reinforced by a single

Old Testament passage: "And Onan knew that the seed should not be his; and it came to pass, when he went in unto his brother's wife [Tamar], that he spilled it on the ground, lest that he should give seed to his brother. And the thing which he did displeased the Lord; wherefore he slew him also."[7] Proponents of natalism have vociferously used this passage for support of their position against fertility control and for birth expansion. Objective religious scholars, having conducted exhaustive research into the social conditions and mores of Old Testament times, have pointed out that a completely different meaning can be attributed to the story of Onan. They maintain that the passage signifies disapproval of Onan's refusal to perform the ancient Jewish custom of levirate rather than disapproval of coitus interruptus (and, by extrapolation, other contraceptive methods).

In the Old Testament lands, as in the Indian subcontinent and various Middle Eastern countries, an acceptable social practice prevailed (and still does in some areas). This was the levirate system, whereby the brother of a childless dead man married the widow. The rationale behind this was to give her children (preferably male) so that they might perpetuate the deceased man's name and lineage and, additionally, assume ancestral and inheritance duties. Onan opposed this practice by refusing to give up what would have been effectively his children to his dead brother and the deceased's lineage. For Onan's disobedience and refusal to fulfill social obligations, and not for coitus interruptus, he suffered the ultimate consequence of death.

Historically, coitus interruptus was a socially acceptable contraceptive practice of ancient and primitive peoples. It only became unacceptable as celibate monasticism and asceticism took hold of the church, denigrating women, sexuality, and marriage; extolling virginity; and making reproduction the only reason for sex and marriage. The sequel to the Onan episode reinforces the levirate explanation.[8] In it the widow, Tamar, undertook specific action after Onan's death to ensure that her father-in-law, Judah, fulfilled his levirate duty to her by giving her his third son, Shelah, to carry on the tradition. Eventually she, the father, and the third son performed their respective duties to the deceased and thereby, coincidentally, to the widow, the family, and society.

Originally, the three Western faiths accepted the story of Onan as an indictment of contraception, in general, and coitus interruptus, in particular. Gradually, in light of scholarly revelations, Judaism and Protestantism (except for their more literal-minded sects) abandoned this interpretation. Catholicism continued to diverge from the other two faiths over the meaning of the Onan passage—as it did over the two "be fruitful and multiply" passages—and used it to illustrate its repugnancy for birth control and to bolster its scriptural and theological taboos against contraception. A side effect of the Catholic stand concerning onanism and coitus interruptus was to remove from men motivation or responsibility to not make women pregnant and to impose on women almost the sole responsibility for making family-planning decisions and taking birth control measures.

That some of the most influential Catholic theologians and laity—and some Protestants—can still raise the specter of onanism as support for their continuing vehement opposition to birth control is a paradox. A paradox because, while they would be thoroughly disinclined to subscribe to systems of non-Christian ethics that include such practices as levirate, purdah, puberty and circumcision rites, female bondage and servitude, they willingly incorporate other selectively chosen practices of a bygone era. Since these selectively chosen practices or tenets tend to have a particularly harsh impact on women and their lives, one is left wondering if the need to reinforce such arguments is less because of and in opposition to contraception per se than because of an entrenched historic bias against women and a fear that women's emancipation through contraception will release a force no longer easily subdued by male-dominated church authority.

Other Old Testament passages have, however, permitted some moderation of the stand that procreation should be the primary end of marriage and that contraception should be prohibited. These are the portrayals of marriage as an affectionate companionship and of children as individuals worthy of affection, esteem, and care. Using these, the three faiths have moved to an acceptance of a less-restrictive procreative role for women in marriage and a greater, all-inclusive, parental responsibility for the welfare of children. Such moderations in attitude and belief have been a harbinger for the acceptance of some form of family planning and a recognition that fathers as well as mothers have a responsibility to look after and raise their children.

The New Testament, through Jesus and Paul, expanded the precepts of marriage, the family, women, and divorce for better and for worse. The regard and respect Jesus had for women was demonstrated more by his actions toward them than by his words. His actions flew in the face of existing social mores, which relegated women to a secondary position. He raised them to a status of near equality in marriage and, contrary to the views of the Pharisees[9] and the Law of Moses, positively affirmed that the basic purpose of marriage was the lifelong companionship of one man with one woman. [10]

Yet Jesus also inadvertently contributed to a negative attitude toward marriage and family. As discussed in Chapter 8, the negative overtones toward family matters in Christianity arose from several sources: the Old Testament, the Laws of Moses, and the patriarchal system; from Paul's pronouncements; and especially from the early church patriarchs. With Jesus teaching that spirituality and obedience to him had precedence over the household, [11] the way was opened for future theologians to ascribe to him a preference for asceticism and celibacy over the married state. His words have been used to justify the negative attitudes and actions toward marriage and sex of the few who pursued spiritual and physical asceticism over the many who chose marriage. While the former were accorded disproportionate honor, respect, and prestige, the latter were accorded condescension. Even today this attitude carries over in the automatic respect and obeisance accorded to those in orders regardless of their secular and spiritual achievements. But it must be noted that the greater regard in orders is reserved for the man over the woman, who because of her less influential role, is less revered, unless she has attained the stature of a Mother Teresa of Calcutta.

Equally contrary to long-standing Jewish tradition, Jesus made the husband's obligation to preserve the unity of marriage as binding as the wife's. In one fell swoop Jesus demolished the right of (Jewish) husbands to unilateral divorce; established an equal duty on wife and husband to preserve the marriage; and laid the foundation for making divorce virtually unattainable (until many centuries later) under any circumstance. It was by making the companionship function of marriage as important as the procreative that Jesus effectively laid the base upon which Protestants eventually built a case for the acceptance of contraception as a valid part of marriage. His counsel even enabled some Catholic theologians to justify their support of abstinence or the rhythm method of contraception on the grounds that the prevention of unwanted pregnancies could strengthen marriage bonds.

Jesus' attitude toward and acceptance of children as individuals rather than as objects to be manipulated by adults also contributed to a revised view of marriage and parenthood. Eventually, this renewed recognition and assessment of what Jesus' actions and words could mean for the Christian community was to cause a reconsideration of women's role within marriage and parenthood. The Anglican bishops at the historic Lambeth Conference of 1958 succinctly summed up the newly emerging attitude.

> The Biblical revelation . . . does not limit the function of sexuality and the family to the reproductive purpose. Equally deep-rooted in Genesis is the reflection of a second factor—the need of men and women for each other, to complement and fulfill each other and to establish a durable partnership against the loneliness and rigour of life. [12]

Unfortunately, the apparent tolerance and understanding exhibited toward the function of marriage at Lambeth has not been completely extended to the related matter of divorce, where the total breakdown of marriage has occurred, and remarriage in church. Although sufficient consensus exists within the congregation of the Church of England and the General Synod's Marriage Commission, a liaison of Evangelical and Anglo-Catholic churchmen has prevented a consensus in the General Synod to allow the remarriage of divorced persons in church. [13] The conservative, traditionalist element, while carefully couching their opposition in theological and spiritual terms, appears bent upon penalizing divorced persons and rendering them guilt ridden for their failure to maintain the indissolubility of marriage. Not only have women suffered from this stance, since they are most often blamed for not holding a marriage together, but men and children have also suffered.

Gradually, the Protestant and Catholic faiths in North America have recognized that declaiming against divorce is not going to halt the soaring divorce rates. They have progressively turned greater attention toward marriage through marriage preparation and counseling. While it is perhaps premature to say that they subscribe to the attitude of divorce reformers that marriage should be made harder and divorce easier, they are beginning to recognize the realities of North American married life. However, in Latin America the same predeliction to recognize those realities seems to have materialized more slowly. Church weddings in countries like Venezuela are too costly for 30 to 50 percent of the rural or urban poor, so women find themselves pressured into common-law marriages, which are in turn condemned by the church. With time, as the men play marital hopscotch, the women find themselves locked into a series of common-law marriages and a string of children. Unable to extricate themselves from unending poverty and drudgery, some seek contraception, others seek abortion, and yet others abandon their children. Again they are condemned by macho society and the church. If they can afford to marry "properly" in church and are then abused or abandoned by their husbands, few are able to afford the financial or psychological consequences of seeking a divorce. Few are granted that escape, and those who are are inevitably criticized.

While the majority recognize that the church must adapt to change if it is to maintain leadership of its flock, a vocal and strong evangelistic and Catholic-oriented minority seeks refuge in "natural theology," the Law of Moses, and the indissolubility of marriage as reflected in the New Testament. Although this minority admits that Jesus did not see himself as a legislator, it is quite prepared to assign legislative force to all his teachings, over and above his commandments, and thereby impose a moral and physical onus on people where none was intended. But its members fail to recognize that women, especially as they become more educated and start to think for and about themselves, are increasingly less willing to be bound by archaic, unreasonable strictures or by meaningless theological verbiage and logic.

Undoubtedly, the majority of clergy is concerned with the church's caring ministry for people. But because of the minority's dogma-based opposition to more liberal grounds for divorce, remarriage in church, contraception, the ordination of women, and for other equally controversial social issues, the majority's position suffers. While women have always formed the bulk of the churches' followers and congregations, in increasing numbers, they are eschewing the church and are seeking other support systems to help them contend with modern-day problems. Many with internal reluctance and confusion, despite their belief that the church is irrelevant and unnecessary, nonetheless attempt to keep the faith by bringing their daughters and sons to church or quietly praying within the sanctuary of their own homes.

Sooner or later the churches will be overruled by secular authority if they do not help people to reconcile their needs with their faith in a reasonable, balanced way. In Italy in 1970, the Parliament handed the Roman Catholic church a major defeat when it passed its divorce law. And the people reaffirmed that defeat in a referendum endorsing that law. Eight years later, despite stiff opposition and vehemence from the Vatican, the church was handed another major defeat when abortion was legalized for the first time in Italy's history. [14] Women are seeking sustenance from other sources; hence, a revival of interest in goddesses and witch cults and a plethora of books on the female component of ancient religion are appearing in North America and Europe. Worldwide, a quiet rebellion against church authority (but not against religion and faith per se) is occurring as women especially attempt to rid themselves of religion's negative overtones, particularly where those pertain to personal and family matters. Pierre Trudeau, the prime minister of Canada, once said that the state has no place in the bedrooms of the people. Increasingly fewer people want the church there.

Unlike Buddhism, Hinduism, and Islam, which recognized marriage, household duties, and sex as a natural phase of life, early Christianity under its early progenitors inculcated in its clerics and congregation alike the distressing attitude that a monastic, virgin life devoted to God was far superior to a married life. Sex was seen as an unfortunate animalistic proclivity, redeemed by the production of children. By contrast, Islam condemned celibacy and the ascetic life as unnatural and contrary to both human nature and God's will. Hinduism and Buddhism perceived marriage and family as one stage en route to spiritual enlightenment and the release from worldly suffering.

The non-Christian religions have traditionally taken a more balanced view of the needs and urges of human beings than the Christian. The early church fathers railed against women, marriage, and sex. Augustine, the leader of vituperation and vilification, ranted against the concept of companionate marriage and used onanism to inveigh against contraception. For him, "Intercourse, even with one's legitimate wife, is unlawful and wicked where the conception of the offspring is prevented." [15] This did not deter him from validating prostitution—an essential means of taking care of men's urges—while condemning prostitutes as harlots. Jerome and Thomas Aquinas added the weight of their judgments that women were the source of evil and that conception occurred at the cost of "original" virtue and innocence. Insofar as they were concerned, contraception was sinful, against the Holy Scriptures, and contravened the only valid reason for marriage and sex. And since celibacy was akin to spirituality, spiritual attainment was unobtainable by those who did not follow an ascetic life. [16] Not only did they impose a heavy burden of guilt on themselves, but they imposed great guilt on women and contributed to the general Christian populace's sense of fear and revulsion.

Aquinas contributed to the ossification of Christian doctrine and canonical law for centuries to come by consolidating his views into his famous natural law. The offshoot has been that to this day, when questions are raised about the status and role of women, contraception, family planning, and marriage, there is an automatic invocation of Aquinas's natural-law formulations by Catholic clergy, Protestant conservatives, and fundamentalist laity. No matter that Aquinas write his natural law under his own peculiar stress, in a very different era, and without the benefit of scientific knowledge. His natural law, along with the early patriarchs' interpretations of the scriptures, was to form the rigid canonical law of the early Christian church and, later, Roman Catholicism. In essence it stipulated that the primary end of marriage was the procreation (and education) of children and that family limitation was a mortal sin. As might be expected, the guilt experienced was enormous and came to be recognized as a major stress factor in their daily lives.

The influence of Aquinas can be seen in the canonical law that impelled Pope Pius XI to state that the prevention of procreation was a "sin against nature . . . which is shameful and intrinsically vicious."[17] Many observers regarded that pronouncement as a slap against women (seeking control over their reproductive faculties) and against the Protestants, who were initiating fresh views about marriage and family limitation. Canonical law, like common law, is based upon chain-linked precedent. But unlike common law, which generally uses precedent as a stabilizing force in reconciling past conditions with present and future needs and even as a springboard to effect legal changes compatible with existing social change, canonical law tends to use precedent to entrench doctrine and dogma irrespective of new conditions and needs. Periodically, common law breaks the bonds of staleness and emerges with fresh attitudes. Canonical law by contrast appears to become more warped, restrictive, and entangled.

The canonical law invoked by Pope Pius XI was essentially based upon the two dominant propositions that man can find God's purpose by use of his reason, and that God makes this purpose known through the physical arrangements of nature.[18] Man is assumed to be contravening God's design and committing a mortal sin if he frustrates any physical arrangement of nature, such as by employing contraception. Ironically, man's highly touted mind, or ability to reason, is not expected to be used to prevent the catastrophe of overreproduction or in any area in which the teaching church assumes it has a monopoly of superior knowledge.

Gradually, pushed and shoved by laity, liberal clergy, overall conditions, and women determined to seek their own destiny, Catholic officialdom has somewhat abrogated Aquinas's natural law and past canonical pronouncements by granting that the companionate aspect of marriage might be a valid, but not primary, reason for justifying the use of abstinence or rhythm to limit family size.

Many liberal Catholics described this moderated stance as hypocritical, since whether natural or artificial contraceptive methods are used, the end result is the same: conception is prevented. They felt that another unnecessary emotional and psychological burden was being imposed upon couples, and particularly upon women. Women from uneducated backgrounds would be especially hard pressed to practice rhythm, owing to their lack of literacy or numeracy, or to persuade their husbands to abstain. How effectively can black or chicano women in U.S. ghettos or women from the barrios of Mexico, Peru, or Venezuela employ rhythm or abstinence when they are illiterate and their (common-law) husbands beat them up? Likewise, liberal Catholics regarded as hysterical or ill informed church pronouncements that birth control would produce "evil" consequences: promiscuity, free love, race suicide, economic stagnation, and social collapse. They justifiably argued that leaders of countries with pressing population problems would seize upon such contentions to bolster their own hard-line views against contraception and birth control policies. Such geographically disparate individuals as Uganda's deposed leader Idi Amin and former presidents Sukarno of Indonesia and Echeverria of Mexico, in company with other politicians too numerous to mention, managed to ignore the fact that even without the help of contraceptives their countries have experienced epidemics of sex-related diseases, promiscuity, consensual unions, economic collapse, or internecine extermination.

Sooner or later political leaders will need to recognize, notwithstanding the Catholic church's opposition, that contraception and solid population-growth policies are as essential to the well-being of their nations as economic, educational, and agricultural policies. Transmigration schemes (Indonesia), expulsion (Nigeria), or illegal migration (Mexico) will only be futile attempts to stem the tide of excessive procreation. But will women's leaders and organizations—and women themselves—recognize the need for sound population policies? Many see the need for contraception and family-planning programs for themselves and their immediate family. It is unlikely that many understand the need for a population policy for their own country or that they are each, individually, a part of the total population equation.

Another implicit belief that arose from early attitudes of the church and still holds currency today is that couples, especially women, should not be released from the painful, onerous consequences of their marital and sexual behavior. Contraception, therefore, being contrary to God's plan, is visualized as creating an inimical relationship with God. Hence, users should suffer the results. In some quarters the belief persists, moreover, that contraception ultimately deprives Catholicism of potential, immortal souls that could contribute to Catholicism's everlasting power and glory. This is not unlike Buddhism, Islam, and Hinduism, which equate births with an enhancement of their numbers for the glory of God and the strengthening of their faith.

The underlying influence of the ascetic and celibate tradition has had the unfortunate, albeit unconscious, effect of inhibiting frank, open, public discussions on all aspects of birth control, family limitation, and population restraint. It has hampered effective handling of national and international population questions and has made even the most committed birth control practitioner reluctant to confront population problems overtly and with immediate action. This is intensified when it is realized that the Catholic church will only permit natural birth control if it can be justified on moral grounds.

Pope Pius XI in 1951 allowed that medical, eugenic, economic, and social considerations might exempt couples from the "positive duty" of reproducing. It looked as though any one of these reasons would be sufficient justification to release women from the religious imperative to procreate. But subsequent interpretations of his statements produced doubt. A dichotomy arose between those Catholics who enthusiastically praised the parents of large families in overpopulated areas for ignoring such exemptions and those who, perhaps belatedly, acknowledged that excessive population growth would block orderly economic and social advancement and substantially reduce the quality of life. These latter also recognized that females would suffer the most if economic development were undermined by the failure to implement population and family-planning policies and programs.

Despite such inter-Catholic disagreements, which perhaps augur well for the future liberalization of birth control policies in general, inherently and fundamentally the Roman Catholic leadership is still firmly opposed to artificial fertility control. Pope Paul's pronouncements not long before his death in 1978 differed little from those of the U.S. Catholic bishops, who in 1959 avowed that U.S. Catholics would not support "any public assistance, either at home or abroad, to promote artificial birth prevention, abortion or sterilization, whether through direct aid or by means of international organizations" (emphasis added) and "that the promotion of artificial birth prevention is a morally, humanly, psychologically and politically disastrous approach to the population problem."[19] From an international development point of view, this dogmatic approach has serious consequences for countries whose employment, industrial, and agricultural strategies cannot contend with more babies; more youth; and the resultant need for more jobs, schools, health clinics, sewerage, clean water, and so forth. On a local level it has serious consequences, as millions of dollars of aid are channeled through Catholic nongovernmental organizations (NGOs) to local projects that are often undermined by the lack of a family-planning or birth control component.

The obduracy of the Roman Catholic hierarchy is reflected in the massive, costly lobbying and emotional vocal campaigning against the legalization of abortion in the United States, the U.S. Supreme Court's decision legalizing abortion, and the use of public monies to fund the abortions of indigent women. More important, viable alternatives to abortion have been eschewed. Antiabortion literature has been (and is) remarkable for its elusive nature and vituperation, its unpreparedness to supply alternative solutions, its unwillingness to propose other counseling and information sources, and its avoidance of discussion of the actual conditions that force women into taking drastic measures.*

Antiabortion forces, whether in the United States, Canada, or Europe, which are strongly church backed and financed, have shown a singular disregard for the desperate realities of life faced by many women. They have ignored the fact that in Latin America abortion has reached pandemic, not epidemic, proportions—not because women like abortion but because they are totally desperate. They have equally shown a remarkable tenacity and mental "single-trackedness" in condemning abortion while opposing (or at least not supporting) contraception. They have obstructed the work of other organizations com-

---

*An example of church-related pressure was the Roman Catholic boycott of Metres-for-Millions in Ottawa, Canada, in the early 1980s because a local family-planning association was allowed to participate.

mitted to educating the public about sex, marriage and marital relations, family planning, and birth control; counseling individuals of
both sexes about their choices and options; explaining family planning
and birth control; and supplying inexpensive, effective, and readily
available contraceptives. They have implanted in people's minds a
subconscious negativism toward birth control by inextricably mixing
the abortion issue with contraception, thereby preventing rational,
detached discussion. The immediate victim of antiabortion attacks
is the woman. The ultimate victim, however, is the quality of life.

As a consequence of their actions, antiabortionists, however
morally valid their stand, are as responsible as aborters for the very
fetal deaths they are committed to preventing. By failing, in collabor-
ation with birth control proponents, to provide the right climate for
contraception, antiabortionists and the church must assume substantial responsibility for contributing to a major increase in unwanted
pregnancies, illegal and botched abortions, and maternal morbidity
and mortality. As usual, the damage—mental, psychological, and
physical—is especially heaped on women. But, as Father William J.
Gibbons said, "There is no possibility the Church will change her
strong condemnation of this [artificial contraception, which vitiates
the God-given sex act], whatever the problem may be."[20]

This stance has profound implications for the economic and social development (and population restraint) of various regions of the
world. But no area will be more affected than fast-expanding Latin
America. In part it suits many Latin American leaders and politicians
to be (or appear to be) beholden to the church. For reasons of political patronage or personal conviction, they prefer not to offend the
church by pushing family planning clinics and contraception too hard.
Though consensual unions, illegitimate children, and abortions are
rampant facts of life in Latin American countries, Roman Catholic
doctrine on birth control will continue to dampen population policies
and to intimidate individuals trying to effect change. The resultant
future will encompass increased populations, rising abortion rates,
and more abandoned children apart from more urban congestion and
pollution and regardless of improving economic indicators.

The Protestants' relatively liberal attitude toward family planning, marriage, sex, birth control, and divorce has not long predated
the Catholics' reluctant acceptance of family planning through natural
methods. In the 1920s the Protestants were equally vehemently
against birth control. Then in the 1930s the Church of England—
ironically the church whose doctrines had been the closest to those of
Thomas Aquinas—reversed its anti-birth-control view and developed
a systematic approach to those issues. In 1958, at the historic Lambeth Conference, the Church of England emphasized the need for family planning, especially in those areas with fast-growing populations.

Its action was particularly amazing, given that then the full demographic implications of population growth anywhere were not wholly appreciated. It also strongly advocated the acceptance of appropriate family-planning methods, provided they were in accordance with Christian ethics and were motivated in the interests of the family and of society.[21] Its advocacy of family planning was also motivated by humanitarian concerns, not least of which was a growing awareness of women's humanity and needs in a modern society.

Irrespective of the lead of the Lambeth Conference, agreement among Protestants was by no means unanimous. Protestant attitudes and stands varied according to their beliefs: liberalism, conservatism, fundamentalism, or Anglo-Catholicism. Ultimately, the majority opted for responsible family planning and parenthood and, accordingly, accepted the use of contraception for those purposes. A minority turned back to literal interpretations of the Old Testament and its passages on procreation and onanism.

Irrespective of that minority, three basic, virtually irreconcilable differences still exist between the majority of Protestants and the Catholics. First, the morality of birth control is at issue. The Protestants claim that universal, objective criteria against contraception and family limitation do not exist. The Catholics counter this by claiming that scriptural edicts and canonical law establish criteria that entirely vitiate the use of birth control, recent modifications (abstinence and rhythm) notwithstanding. The Protestants further contend that the morality of fertility control is dependent upon a couple's motives and goals rather than on the methods employed. The Catholics dispute this, contending that the immutable natural law of the goal of marriage is procreation and that once broken, immorality enters the breach and grips the institution of marriage. Therefore, the natural law must not be broken nor subject to evolution and human logic whatever the needs.

The second major difference occurs over the definition of the primary goals of marriage. The Protestants have come to regard companionship as the primary end of marriage, with children as a satisfying and responsible adjunct. The Catholics have continued to claim procreation as its raison d'être.

The third area of substantive disagreement is the applicability of religious doctrines and their designated targets. The Protestants are concerned with the happiness and welfare of individuals, couples, families, and eventually society. They regard the use of birth control methods as a matter of individual motive and conscience and individual preference to be implemented in accordance with individual family needs. The Catholics, by contrast, restrict the exercise of individualism whether of conscience, goal, motive, or logic, since their dicta maintain that individuals and therefore couples must follow the directives of the church and its (celibate, non-family-oriented) clergy.

Although individuals of different faiths may not differ markedly from each other in their final completed size of family, nevertheless their respective religions do influence their attitudes toward conception, women, marriage, contraception, family planning, adherence to religious dogma and principle, church and clerical authority, expectation of family size, types of birth control, and world population growth. Religion, whether of the popular or official type, at the individual level does appear to affect the way people plan their families and their general outlook on related population matters. This, in turn, is bound to affect the policy behavior of politicians, planners, and civil servants.

Not enough full-scale demographic studies that specifically take account of religious differentials and their effect on natality and women's role have been undertaken. But those that have been conducted illustrate religion's influence on attitudes and behavior.[22] Such studies show that more Catholics than Jews or Protestants theoretically disapprove of family limitation and population restraint, in general, and restricted family size (such as the two-child families normally practiced by most Jews), specifically. Fewer Catholics than Protestants or Jews use contraception, including natural methods. Fewer plan their families, although in actuality most do not want sizably larger families than the other two faiths and ultimately do not have noticeably larger families.

Catholics, in comparison with either Jews or Protestants, tend to come belatedly to family planning, and then only after they have reached their emotional, physical, or financial tolerance level of x number of children. Even while acknowledging specific goals, such as university education for all their children, and recognizing the emotional and financial drain of a large family, Catholic couples are both reluctant to advocate birth control at the beginning of marriage and unwilling to admit or counsel contraceptive use publicly when they have reached their tolerance level of children.

Some Catholic women try to escape their emotional conundrum by resorting to medically recommended and, hence, socially approved hysterectomies. Although it could be contended that hysterectomies are the ultimate form of contraception, totally denying all future conception, it does not seem to have the religious stigma attached to it that other contraceptive methods have. But it is a costly price for women to pay to avoid condemnation. Others, out of desperation or defiance, request their obstetricians to perform tubal ligations, often without their husbands' knowledge, after what they regard as their last, unplanned, inadvertent pregnancy. The Jewish faith, except for its most fundamental or orthodox members (like the Hasidics), appears to practice the strictest degree of family limitation. In part this occurs because they greatly esteem a comprehensive and thorough education for their children, male or female.

Even among those Catholics who do practice birth control, methods differ markedly from those of Protestants and Jews. Unconsciously imbued with a distaste for sex that lacks procreation as its main goal or is not a spontaneous exhibition of intimacy, they are more likely to use family planning haphazardly or hesitatingly than the other faiths. Whether in North America or in Catholic European countries, where some of the world's lowest birthrates prevail, 50 percent and more of Catholic contraceptive users employ church-prescribed methods.

It has been commonly thought that urbanization, employment opportunities, education levels, and income differentials were the main determinants of the differences in birth control attitudes and practices between the three faiths. Religious ideology typically has been given little import. But those researchers who do incorporate religion into their analysis have found that in the United States it affects natality patterns, in Europe it affects methods used, and in Latin America it affects overall birthrates. It was noted, for example, that Catholic women who regularly attend church were more likely to be anticontraception and less avoiding of conception than Protestant women. By contrast, Protestant women attending church were more likely to be aware of the consequences of overpopulation and large families than their Catholic counterparts. In both instances their attitudes were influenced by the pro or con attitudes of their respective religious leaders toward population matters. [23]

Obviously, religious ideology is neither the only nor the main determinant, but it is a factor in population-related matters. It partly determines the pace of progress in liberalizing contraception information distribution and contraceptive use; in loosening attitudes toward homosexuality, abortion, and sterilization; and in developing enlightened policies of population restraint. Its influence is in inverse relation to modernization, education (particularly of females), and urbanization. Where the degree of modernization is low (for example, in most parts of Latin America and the Philippines), religion's influence is generally strong, attitudes toward family limitation are negative, and birthrates are high. Where the degree of modernization is high, religion's influence declines proportionately. Individuals tend to become more self-deterministic by exercising their own logic and refusing to abide by church dictates or clerical interference in private family matters. Individualism, especially as expressed by educated men and women, thus represents a challenge to the church's authority. How the church handles this will in part determine its continuing influences over public policy.

The obstacles raised by religion and religious leaders not only inhibit individual action but seriously retard policy makers' initiatives and effective public policy. These obstacles largely figure in the reluctance of most countries to designate the population question as a major or primary issue or to treat the women's issue seriously. Although these two issues are closely linked together and have a major bearing on the economic and social development of nations, they are normally treated as having only secondary or peripheral importance. Only a handful of countries—Singapore, Barbados, India, and China—have what could be termed nonpronatalist policies.

Religion has made the population question unduly emotional and politically sensitive. Public officials (former World Bank President Robert McNamara was a visible exception)[24] have typically shied away from recognizing or raising the question. But when they have, they have tended to minimize women's role in the whole population equation and to neglect consultation with women at all levels. The consequence is to deprive the public of knowledge and debate about population problems, to confuse or undermine women as to their role, and to render concerted action minimally effective. Even in the United States, "Fear of disturbing religious sensibilities confines the government's population research to those lower levels [below policy making] and limits its usefulness by the restrictions of extreme caution."[25] However, it is interesting to note that the U.S. administration, abandoning its religion-inspired caution, finally gave open recognition to the need for a public policy on population and regularly incorporated the research of the Population Council into the government's prognostications for the future of the United States. That caution prevails in countries more dominated by the church than North America and is extended to the fear of upsetting political balances of power if the church, as a major political force, is not handled with kid gloves by politicians.

While restrictive laws pertaining to population matters in some Christian countries were undoubtedly initiated by the Catholics, the Protestants also contributed to a restrictive climate. One of the most rigid of these was Thomas Comstock, who effectively campaigned in 1873 to have the U.S. Congress legislate contraception literature as obscene and to ban birth control information and devices from the mails. Over one hundred years passed before the Comstock laws were erased from all state law books. The perpetuation of these restrictive laws, despite their Protestant origin, was unfailingly owing to the massively organized and financed support of the Catholic hierarchy. In a sense the laissez-faire attitude of Protestantism; its reliance upon individualism; and the tentative, loosely organized approach of the non-Catholics created a void of influence. Being less dogmatic, the non-Catholics relinquished their political hold, which directly contributed to a general official neglect of the population question.[26]

Yielding the floor on population issues affected international as well as national policies. The failure of non-Catholics to mobilize and take a unified stand on the population issue—without neglecting obvious economic and social concerns—allowed the Roman Catholic position to be imposed on international organizations and developing countries, especially in Latin America. Quite apart from stifling debate or concrete action, it encouraged the Third World leaders to avoid facing up to the imminent consequences of continuing high birthrates.

Politicians and leaders have traditionally avoided confronting religion as an inhibitor of action on population matters. Instead, they have preferred to attribute their reluctance to get involved with religion or population to the public's opposition to governmental interference with private life, including the right of individuals to have as many children as they want irrespective of the needs of society or society's ability to cope with an expanding population. The fact remains that blatant governmental and religious interference has occurred in many other spheres of private life, not least of which has been interference with the right of individuals not to have children or to exercise a particular sexual orientation. Regardless of country, this interference has manifested itself in a variety of ways that have prevented women in particular from practicing birth control, using safe, reliable, inexpensive methods; limiting family size to avoid exhaustion of food, money, emotions, and physical strength; obtaining therapeutic abortions to save their health and their lives; and obtaining informed, nonintimidating family-planning and contraception counseling.

Scientific and technological advances combined with changes in social conditions and mores should have granted women freedom from frequent, debilitating pregnancies and couples freedom from the intolerable burdens of excessively large families. Unfortunately, such reproductive freedom, especially at the lower and poorer ends of society, has not occurred. Governmental interference, urged on by religious ideology, still exists in most countries in their restrictive civil and criminal laws against birth control, abortion, and sterilization and in their tax, housing, and social-welfare legislation, which penalizes the childless or small family in favor of the large. And in each instance of such governmental interference, who suffers the most? The women do. Slowly this situation is changing as more women make their needs strongly known throughout the political spectrum and as more women gain access to and control of political mechanisms within church and state. But progress is slow, as most hierarchies of government and church raise barriers against women's reproductive freedom and the restraint of population while condoning, through inaction, pornography, wife battering, sexual assault, demeaning advertising, sexism, and sex stereotyping in work and recreation.

Emotional reaction greets recommendations that governments more fully apprise themselves of the population issue at home and abroad; initiate positive, action-oriented policies reflecting that awareness; and encourage families through education and incentives or disincentives to limit their size (preferably to two or less children). That society should strive for zero or negative population growth is an anathema to most people raised in the belief of popular religion that the human race should "be fruitful and multiply" willy-nilly. Many women, spurred on by the illogical rhetoric of some politicians and a few feminists, are likely to fall into the trap of opposing population-growth policies on the basis that these are yet another colonial, male-inspired plot to keep women down. Yet support for a balanced, humane population policy could help to eliminate the present situation—government interference in fertility matters through retrograde laws and the intimidation of women through civil or criminal prosecution. The present system amounts to being one of persecution. A sound, compassionate population policy could give women the freedom they seek—from social pressures, religious edicts, government control, and physical constraints.

Undeniably, there are dangers inherent in trying to encourage or persuade the public to reduce family size or overall population size. India exemplifies a country where drastic measures—coercion, bribery, forced sterilizations—were employed to carry out its population policies. This unreasoned, fanatical approach eventually backfired and set back its family-planning program by five to ten years, an unfortunate occurrence given that its latest census (1981-82) showed that India had underestimated its population growth by over 17 million. The same possibilities for persecution, prosecution, and manipulation existed when humanity was urged to expand its numbers. However, there is no reason why that past should be emulated. If those dangers are recognized now while the population problem is still barely manageable, if sensitive, nonintimidating measures are established, and if a monitoring system is set up to counteract inhumane trends, the likelihood of draconianism taking over will be considerably lessened. Contrary to the Indian experience, Thailand, through the imaginative but sensitive efforts of Meechai Veeravaidhaya, has managed to avoid the pitfalls of implementing a comprehensive family-planning policy by recognizing the inherent dangers of imposing a population policy on the Thai without consulting them or seeking their advice. Women were key to the success of that policy and its implementation. The introduction of reasonable and sound population policy must occur, however, before governments become overwhelmed by unmanageable population size. At that point they are likely to become so desperate to solve population-related issues that their measures will be hardly recommendatory. Instances worldwide already serve to illustrate the desperate measures (bellicosity and war, tribal annihilation, torture of minorities, repression, expulsion, and intimidation) governments will take to cope with what are essentially population-oriented problems. Such governments will either then completely ignore religion or call upon religion to justify their draconian measures.

Twenty-two years ago, Pope John in his "Mater and Magister"[27] became the first pontiff to acknowledge that population in the developing countries was one of the world's most intractable problems. Circumscribed as he was by church dogma and precedent, he could not take the logical step of recommending direct action through family planning and birth control in conjunction with economic and social development. Instead, he recommended adaptation to (population) growth by urging countries to promulgate a more equitable distribution of the world's resources. Today his stand, reinforced by later pontifical statements, is still regularly bruited by the leaders of developing countries to justify their reluctance to implement population measures and their polemics against the West's inequitable sharing.

Certainly there could and should be a more equitable distribution of resources. However, the cause of economic and social development is not aided by the world's most prominent religious leader sidestepping the population issue and discouraging the use of a major component of the solution: population limitation. The world's people have already adapted as well as they can to their growing numbers. If they are to experience a reasonable life, with an adequacy of food, clothing, and shelter, how much further must they adapt, to what level of human degradation, in order to accommodate their exponentially increasing numbers? A further deterioration of their already impoverished condition is inevitable without numbers limitation, a situation that a country like China is only too aware of. And yet the Vatican is still congenitally unable to bring itself to take the initiative in recommending population-growth restraint, in conjunction with the many other economic and social reforms essential to the elimination of poverty, to its own Catholic organization, the various international bodies, or world leaders.

Since Pope John's acknowledgment, population and poverty have grown by leaps and bounds, superseding all development efforts. Undeterred, many influential Catholic leaders continue to ignore or dismiss the need for population measures, thereby perhaps unconsciously encouraging many national political leaders to ignore demographic problems and to puff and pontificate about the world's inequities. At what point will Christian and governmental leaders coalesce in their recognition of population as an explosive problem? When will they acknowledge religion to be an inhibiting factor in implementing population policies? At what point will Catholics abandon their age-old opposition to fertility control and population restraint and mobilize their enormous resources? And when will women recognize that the population problem is their problem too? Hopefully before the thirtieth day![28]

NOTES

1. "How 60,000 Women Feel about Religion and Morality," McCall's, May 1978, pp. 127-29, 209-12.

2. Paul R. Erlich and Anna H. Erlich, Population, Resources and Environment—Issues in Human Ecology, 2d ed. (San Francisco: W. H. Freeman, 1972), p. 350.

3. Alice Taylor Day and Lincoln H. Day, Too Many Americans (New York: Dell, 1965), p. 79.

4. Gen. 1:28-31.

5. Ibid., Gen. 6:8-8:20.

6. Herman San Martin, "Machismo—Latin America's Myth-Cult of Male Supremacy," UNESCO Courier, March 1975, p. 30.

7. Gen. 38:9-10.

8. Gen. 38:12-26.

9. Mark 10:6-9.

10. Deut. 24:1-4.

11. William Neil, Harper's Bible Commentary (New York: Harper & Row, 1975), p. 372.

12. The Lambeth Conference 1958: The Encyclical Letter from the Bishops Together with the Resolutions and Reports (London and Greenwich, Conn.: Society for Promoting Christian Knowledge and Seabury Press, 1958), pp. 143, 147.

13. London Times, May 19, 1978.

14. Ibid., p. 5.

15. Day and Day, Too Many Americans, p. 84.

16. Harold Cox, The Problem of Population (London: Jonathan Cape, n.d.), pp. 172-74.

17. Pope Pius XI, "Casti Connubii" [On Christian marriage], Encyclical Letter, December 31, 1930.

18. Day and Day, Too Many Americans, p. 86.

19. Ibid., p. 88.

20. William J. Gibbons, S.J., "Responsible Parenthood and the Population Problem," Paulist Fathers' News (n.d.), p. 27.

21. The Lambeth Conference, sec. 5.

22. Dudley Kirk, Recent Trends of Catholic Fertility in the U.S. (New York: Millbank Memorial Fund, 1955). See also "How 60,000 Women Feel."

23. Ronald Freedman, Pascal Whelpton, and Arthur A. Campbell, Family Planning, Sterility and Population Growth (New York: McGraw-Hill, 1959).

24. Robert S. McNamara, An Address on the Population Problem (Washington, D. C.: World Bank, 1977). See also World Bank, "Population Planning Sector Working Paper," 1972.

25. Day and Day, Too Many Americans, p. 97.

26. Richard M. Fagley, The Population Explosion and Christian Responsibility (New York: Oxford University Press, 1960).

27. Pope John XXIII, "Mater and Magister," July 1961.

28. If the leaves in a lily pond double every day, having started off with one leaf on day 1, and the pond is full by the thirtieth day, when is it half full? By the twenty-ninth day! See Lester Brown, The Twenty-ninth Day (New York: W. W. Norton, 1978), pp. 1-2.

11

OVERVIEW OF ISLAM
AND ITS IMPACT
ON WOMEN

Muslim women had a curious destiny: to be successively
sought after for their charms, despised for their impurity
and venerated for their fertility.

Jean Mathé

Men have authority over women because Allah has made
the one superior to the other, and because they spend
their wealth to maintain them.

Muhammad
The Koran

Supporters of Muhammad contend that he improved women's position in society immeasurably. Detractors hold that Muhammad actually denigrated women and point at his practice of polygamy as an
indication of his low esteem for women. His supporters counter
that, given pre-Islamic practices, he had no other recourse when he
was trying to bring about radical social changes. Moreover, he
handed down commandments that would have protected females, but
successive generations of followers variously interpreted them for
their own reasons, often to the detriment of women. Therefore, his
supporters say, his original intent was often corrupted by his successors. As with the other religions, it is necessary to go back into history, to pre-Islamic times, to see if Muhammad actually effected a
major evolution of attitudes and practices toward women over time.

Before the seventh century A.D., the life led by the majority of
the varied peoples of Arabia was seminomadic. Overall, they were
neither politically unified nor spiritually cohesive, for the main bond
of every group was the bond of the tribe.

The area, the cradle of three of the world's major religions,
was the Arabian peninsula, bounded by water (the Red Sea, the Indian

Ocean, and the Persian Gulf) on three sides and desert (the Syrian) on the fourth. The peninsula was a land of emigrants, for it was an inhospitable land that could not for long sustain large populations. Despite its size—over one million square miles—its topography could barely sustain ten million persons. Consequently, whenever the maximum, or even optimum, population was reached, its inhabitants would move forth to the north, south, east, and west. These migrations, usually at 500-year intervals, accounted for the rise of such civilizations as the Canaanites, the Phoenicians, the Amorites, the Hebrews (Habirus), the Akkadians, the Armaeans, the Nabataeans, the Ghassanids, and the Muslim Arabs.

Geography has played a major part in bringing about the considerable differences that have existed—and still exist—among the Arabs: the settled and the nomadic; the northerners (Qaysi) and the southerners (Yamani). Although the Arabs may be deemed to have mutual racial unity because the Bible and the Koran state they are descended from Shem, the eldest son of Noah, and hence are Shemites (Semites), in fact, anthropologically this is not so. But regionally, they do show certain common linguistic and cultural characteristics.

The north and south, with their different climates and topography, occasioned sharply contrasting ways of living. The southerner, the Yaman and the Tihamah in the southwest corner, because of accessible water and fertile lands, developed agricultural settlements that yielded the early Minaean, Sabaean, and Himyarite civilizations. Those early settlements thrived on agriculture and trade and established a form of theocratic and autocratic government, which the subsequent advent of Islam assimilated rather than altered.

The northerner, because of the hostility of the desert steppes of west central and northern Arabia, was essentially nomadic (semi-nomadic in thriving times) and neither able nor disposed to establish settlements. Yet it was among the Adnanis that Islam took the firmest root.* And it was their language, Arabic, which was to be the language of Muhammad, the Koran, and the new faith. The Yamanis (Qahtanis), equally proud of their heritage and similarly considering themselves as the true Arabs, dismissed the Adnanis as intruders and their representations as distasteful. Such differences were obviously destined to create friction between the groups. Islam eventually modified but never completely overcame this tension.

Many pre-Islamic traditions, arising from the differences between northerner and southerner, between urbanite and nomad, and

---

*The Admanis were northerners who believed themselves to be descended from a single source: Qahtan, or Adnan, from Ishmael, son of Abraham and Hagar.

among tribes were carried over into Islam. Many others were not. The matriarchal family system disappeared. Kinship stopped being reckoned through the women's side, and women were no longer controlled by their own families but, rather, by their husband's relatives. Nonslave women lost much of their independence and could not choose or refuse husbands, offer themselves in marriage as Khadija did to Muhammad, or easily return home if they were abused or if their husbands took another wife. Although not actually incorporated into the Koran or into the Hadith,* certain differences were, for political and social reasons, eventually incorporated into Muslim jurisprudence and moral codes and eventually given religious substantiation. The persistence of many pre-Islamic customs and values combined with recurring conservatism weakened what beneficial impact Islam, as originally conceived by Muhammad, might have had on women.

When Orthodox and not-so-Orthodox Muslims, justifying the lowly position and status of their women, maintain that their position is so designated by God, the Koran, or Muhammad, they are in reality attempting to provide religious justification for tribal practices predating Islam. Various factors influenced pre-Muslim Arab traditions: trade, contacts with Jewish and Christian settlements, customs, values, and religion. Many of the values were handed down from the quintessential nomadic Arab—the Arab who for survival led a lonely, seeking, uncluttered life, roaming from oasis to oasis, searching for water and grazing land, subsisting on the barest of food and resources, relying only upon self and clan, and leading a hard, austere existence. This nomad was mobile, highly individualistic, aggressive, loyal to a limited few, hospitable, and religious in an uncomplicated way.

Mobility was the key to survival and anything that hindered it was discarded. Mobility was also the key to the strong sense of individualism and inherent democracy that existed. Consequently, a tribe consisting of an elected sheikh and his family, other free families, slaves, and unrelated but accepted and protected strangers could not tolerate useless members, useless animals, or useless goods. Girls had limited usefulness because they could neither engage in raids against other tribes nor replace those males lost in such attacks. Bedouins, having few resources, could not afford to keep unnecessary, uneconomic people and frequently resorted to female infanticide to minimize their burdens. On the other hand, the tribe practiced a democracy whereby the sheikh, as the only elected official, had more duties than privileges and presided over a council composed of men, seers, priests, and even the occasional wise woman, who counseled

---

*A technical term for the tradition of what Muhammad said or did, or a body of traditions relating to the Prophet.

him on daily matters as equally as he gave them advice. Since custom rather than law provided the guidance for decisions, with the aggrieved party carrying out the verdict, the result was often harsh, if not bloody, for feuds among tribes and even family members frequently sprang into being.

Mobility also prevented the development of more sophisticated social institutions. Instead of law and political structures, the tribes used blood ties and kinship for social regulation and reinforcement of their tribal mores. Because kinship embraced the support and protection of the tribe, it was crucial that relationships within and without the tribe should not be weakened through ill-conceived alliances or marriages. Marriage, as an alliance, needed strict control. Women, despite relative independence in those pre-Islamic days, were used as tribal ties and were carefully controlled to ensure the efficacy of the marriage and the strengthening of tribal bonds. Too, the mobility demanded by the desert required endurance, tenacity, aggressiveness, egotisim, and self-reliance—or an abundance of qualities deemed manly—to the virtual exclusion of purported womanly virtues. Yet the tribeswomen themselves possessed those tough, resiliant characteristics basic to survival. Bedouin stories and poetry extol the bravery, nobility, and devotion of their women, who oftentimes ferociously defended their menfolk from the attacks of their enemies.

The cult of the desert not only affected the Bedouin, the roaming Arab (from its Semitic root meaning nomad), but also the townspeople of the Arabian peninsula. Its particular influence was felt along the trade routes, such as in Mecca in the Hijaz of west central Arabia, where Muhammad's family and nomadic kin group would periodically assume the trappings of desert life. Both depended on each other for support for raids and warfare or for negotiation, cooperation, and trading. Islam reduced tribal warfare but not the interdependency of the nomads and townspeople or their mutually supporting values.

Before the advent of Islam, the Arabian peoples practiced a polytheistic religion comprised of myriads of gods and goddesses and cultic rituals, animistic and daimonic worship, pilgrimages, blood sacrifices, prayers, and holy wells and stones. Within these early Semitic religions were the seeds of the monotheistic religions of Christianity, Judaism, and Islam; the solitary worship of such tribal gods as Jehovah and Allah; Bethel of the Old Testament and the black stone of the Kaaba in Mecca; and the elimination of the female aspects of religion. Nothing arises from nothing. Similarly, no great religion, monotheistic or otherwise, has arisen from nothing. It has emerged from preexisting beliefs, conditions, and faiths that in time, through circumstances, evolution, and the intercession of great leaders or prophets convert it into a sophisticated faith binding on the masses rather than on a tribal or cultic few.

The early Semitic roots should not be forgotten when considering the impact of the three monotheistic religions on women. Many present attitudes toward women, their roles, and their functions have their roots in a long-ago desert religion. A recognition of their source should make it easier to rearrange or discard those attitudes that, perhaps relevant to a camel age, are not appropriate to a rocket age.

Within the pantheon of deities, Allah, God of the Worlds (variously known as Ilah to the South Arabians, al-Ilah (the deity) to the Bedouins, Il (god) to the Babylonians, and El to the Canaanites and Israelites) was the top god of pagan Arabians. The other three most commonly resorted to by the Hijaz tribes were all female and were Allah's daughters: al-Huzzah (power), al-Lat (the goddess), and Manah (fate). Because of the high reliance placed on female goddesses, Muhammad, trying to wean the Arabians from idolatrous practices, recognized that then-extant attitudes toward women were hypocritical and wrong.[1] He observed that the people worshipped al-Huzzah, al-Lat, and Manah, female angels, and other goddesses of the pantheon and praised God for their existence yet decried the birth of their female children, bewailed their fate, and resorted to infanticide by burying their daughters alive in the desert sands.

Probably more than his Christian counterpart Paul, Muhammad was aware of the social ills around him: the inequality among different classes in Mecca, the great gap between the haves and have-nots, and the poor treatment of girls and women. He seemed strongly conscious that before fundamental social, economic, and religious reforms could take place, people's attitudes and beliefs needed changing. He consciously strived to change attitudes toward females by showing the people of the town and desert the inconsistencies among their beliefs and the hypocrisy of their actions. He particularly found distasteful the people's ascribing to God their own mean traits and attitudes, thereby indicting God as the liar and wrongdoer rather than themselves. He strongly advocated that women should be treated with kindness and respect and should not be whipped like slaves. Wives should be properly fed and clothed and not struck, reviled, or rejected and abandoned. And he managed to reduce female infanticide by showing the hypocrisy inherent in the people's ranking of their own women and daughters, their blaming of God for their own wrong judgments rather than themselves, and their feelings of disgrace at the birth of a girl, who emanates from an all-good, blameless god.[2]

Muhammad was born into a Meccan society in which changes were already occurring as a result of the dominant tribe, the Quraysh. Their forceful style of trading and developing an urban center eschewed tribal or kinship restraints in favor of legal and extrafamilial constraints. The wealth and power of the Qurayshites came not only from controlling the transit trade routes but also from controlling the holy Kaaba, the center of hundreds of pagan deities where Allah also reigned. To provide economic security and to minimize uneconomic, bloody feuding, the Quraysh declared the Kaaba and surrounding area, increasingly expanded, as haram ("forbidden area"). Warfare and bloodletting in tribal disputes became forbidden within this holy area. This provided inviolability and protection to transients and pilgrims and, in effect, exchanged kin-group dues for a form of social law.

Both to attract traders and pilgrims and to ensure the inviolability of the area, the shrewd Qurayshites concluded pacts with neighboring tribes and ringed the Kaaba with the representational deities of those tribes. Gradually, Mecca became the religious and social focal point for the Quraysh, the resident but non-Quraysh Arabs, and other Arab tribesmen. Local shrines were abandoned in favor of the jiwar ("protection") of the Kaaba's haram. Allah took precedence over all deities and reigned supreme. As more nonkin Arabs coalesced in the Meccan area for protection and extra privileges, local deities became ignored. Allah was endowed with their all-encompassing powers, responsibilities, and duties in addition to tribal and familial custodianships. Allah thus became the imposer of duties and responsibilities; the guarantor of rights and obligations; the central, paramount spiritual figure. In fact, Muhammad, arriving at a time when social and religious foment was already in evidence, was able to take advantage of the social and religious disruptions, disparities, and disturbances to propagate his new religious philosophy.

Simultaneously with this religious change a social and economic change was occurring. The Quraysh, as they developed trade routes and acquired greater power, also developed a different social structure, based more upon a composite of different tribes and an oligarchy of rich merchants than upon the homogeneity of kin groups and their mutual values and relationships. The outcome was that social distinctions evolved, levels of class appeared, gaps between the haves and have-nots became exacerbated, and the society became divided by class and ethnicity. Matriarchy was giving way to patriarchy, and polyandry was yielding to polygamy. Kinship only gave the appearance of uniformity and cohesion. In fact, the social constraints of the tribe were breaking down without real replacements, such as an effective legislative or legal system, owing to the actions of the Quraysh aristocracy and their council of oligarchs. Discrimination occurred, injustices were perpetuated, and the freedom of women became further eroded. One group (the inner Quraysh) exploited the other groups (the outer Quraysh). Social ferment, directed especially at the oligarchy that had instituted untenable and undemocratic practices, bubbled at all levels. The area, ripe for an upheaval, was ready for a religious and social reformer.

Muhammad, through meditation and divine revelation, was undoubtedly a true prophet, who revealed to his people God's word through the medium of the Koran, the holy book of Islam, the religion of submission. He was a zealous reformer, a consummate politician and statesman, an author (though many claim he was an illiterate), and an orator. He was also a product of his background, his times, and the social and religious agitation. He was in contact with many different ethnic groups, including Jewish settlements in the Hijaz, particularly Yathrib (later to be known as Medina) and certain Christian groups either in Mecca itself or along the trade routes. Directly or indirectly, he was influenced by the religious concepts of other prevailing religions through discussions with their leaders; by observing their various customs, such as alms giving, praying, and fasting; by noting the establishment of their church and school institutions; and by acquiring knowledge of their beliefs through intensive study of their scriptures.

As much as Muhammad appreciated Christianity and, through the Koran, spoke of the kindness and mercy of Jesus and his followers, he despised the celibacy and monasticism of Christianity. To him "the best thing in the world is a good woman," to be enjoyed through marriage and not avoided by celibacy. He personally did not equate women with evil and uncleanliness, nor was he fearful or despising of women's menstruation. Accordingly, he tried to set an example to his followers as to how women should be treated. While being a man of sexual experience, he was also a "man of deep religious feeling, firm principle. His family life has been taken as a model for successive generations . . . [and thus] as a married man and a father Muhammad was a more suitable pattern for ordinary believers than celibate or world renouncing religious leaders."[3]

Muhammad was born after the death of his father in A.D. 571, into the noble but impoverished house of Banu Hasm, one of the outside Quraysh clans. His mother died when he was six. As an orphan, he was first raised by his grandfather and then by his paternal uncle, Abu-Talib. Living in the straitened circumstances of an orphan considerably dictated his attitudes toward people less well off than the dominant merchant class. He inveighed against those who perpetuated social inequities. He objected to the maltreatment of women, especially widows and female orphan children, and especially condemned female infanticide. Muhammad declaimed against the rich exploiting the poor. He protested the injustices that were perpetuated as the wealthy became stronger and kin ties broke, leaving the less fortunate without recourse to kin conscience or institutional justice. Through his years of meditation, the Prophet became convinced of the need for social and religious reform that would give cohesion to a changing society. He saw the new religion as a springboard for equitable social and economic changes in a fomenting, fragmented society.

His marriage to the wealthy trader and businesswoman Kadijah gave him the opportunity to meditate and develop his ideas without fear of want or internal obstruction. Kadijah is known as the first Mother of the Faithful, who encouraged Muhammad in his prophetic and spiritual pursuits. It is likely that this influential Qurayshite widow, who was sufficiently impressed by Muhammad's ability as one of her caravan traders to offer him marriage in accordance with the practice of those times, had considerable bearing on his thoughts about women, widows, polygamy, and protective rights. After her death at 65, when he was 50, he took more than the four wives prescribed by the Koran. But during Kadijah's life Muhammad married no other woman, even though polygamy was endemic throughout the Arabian peninsula. It can be argued that his later marriages to nine wives and five concubines were prompted by his egalitarian, compassionate attitude and by his political sense. Each of those he married and gave his protection to were widows, deserted women, or orphans who would have been otherwise abandoned in accordance with existing social norms. The sole exception was Ayesha, the beautiful and witty daughter of his chief follower and the first caliph, Abu Bakr. In any case, the fact of his many marriages is less important than why Muhammad contracted them, his preaching of social justice and egalitarianism, and his attempts to improve the conditions of and attitudes toward the less fortunate in society, who so often were female.

Apart from Kadijah, his initial converts were mainly the poorest elements of the Meccan society. These were followed by Abu Bakr, the Meccan merchant and later the first caliph; Muhammad's cousin Ali, who later married the Prophet's daughter Fatima; and Muhammad's adopted son, Zayd ibn-Harith. Ali and Fatima thus effectively perpetuated the Muslim founder's line, as Muhammad was left with no male successors, since all his sons died in infancy, except his adopted son, Zayd ibn-Harith. They responded to his teaching about one God and submission (Islam) to God much as the baser elements of Corinth responded to Paul and disaffected Hindus responded to Buddha, not through fear of eternal damnation but because of his enunciation of egalitarian principles. And as with new religions or philosophies promising egalitarian treatment, women were attracted to Islam and became its steadfast supporters and strongest adherents. It might be asked whether the reformist, equality-promising religions have warranted the faithfulness and adherence women have shown through the centuries.

Because both religions, Islam and Christianity, attracted the lower strata of society, the founders of each encountered similar scorn and derision from the elite of their respective communities. But it was not long before such scoffing turned into worry and fear as society noted that the upstart social and religious reform movements were gaining momentum, converts, and impact. Their power, wealth, and status quo were being threatened, so they counterattacked. In Muhammad's case, the Qurayshite aristocracy and leadership took up a campaign of persecution and oppression against him and his followers in Mecca. This constant harassment eventually forced the Prophet and his supporters to abandon Mecca for Medina. Their departure, in A.D. 622, became known as the Hegira, or Hijrah: the first year of the Muslim calendar, the beginning of the new Islamic era, and the end of the old Jahiliyah, or age of ignorance.

In Muhammad's life there were two distinct phases: the Meccan and the Medinan. The Meccan phase saw the Prophet preaching monotheism, submission to one God, social justice, duties and equality, ethics and morals. It saw him trying to convince his Qurayshite kinsfolk of his divine revelations to act as the Prophet and to be a messenger of God's word. They, thinking him mad or power seeking, treated him to derision and persecution.

The Medinan phase saw Muhammad being sought out by the Yathrib tribes of the Khazraj and the Aws to settle their disputes and becoming an arbiter, organizer, statesman, law giver, soldier, and politician. Thus, the temporal Medinan period gave him the opportunity to be more than a Prophet. It gave him the chance to forge a unified society whose religious and social differences were subordinated to an overriding theme of Islam, to develop ethical and legal practices, and to counteract intolerance and resistance to change.

Despite religious differences among the Medinans, they were likely predisposed toward monotheism because of the large number of Jews (virtually 50 percent) among them. The original delegation seeking out Muhammad in Mecca to settle its disputes was composed mainly of Jews: 10 out of the 12. They and other religious groups readily accepted Islam because of its emphasis on ethics and its tolerance of other religions as then preached by Muhammad. Moreover, the patriarchal system and the patriarchal god of Islam would have paralleled those of the Hebrews, who would have felt comfortable with the new faith. Finally, they could accept Islam because of Muhammad's ability to bring about reconciliation among their own fractious groups and an effective guarantee of order. Medina, the city of the messenger (Madinat al-Rasul), symbolized the coalition of a new faith and social order.

These Meccan and Medinan periods are clearly reflected in the Koran, which is regarded as Muhammad's one and only miracle. Contrary to the miracle-worker image ascribed to him by his subsequent followers, Muhammad never regarded himself as a miracle worker. And, as much as he admired Jesus and his teachings, referred to frequently in the Koran, he abhorred stories of Jesus' miracles. His sole claim was that he had been chosen to be a Prophet, and as the last Prophet he envisaged himself as an instrument of Allah, whose voice was reflected through Muhammad onto the pages of the Koran.

The Koran clearly shows that Muhammad intended to effect not only theological but social and economic reforms. It likewise reveals that he was almost as much concerned for the well-being of females as for males. At the outset, when he is admonishing the Meccans to give up greed and covetousness for alms giving and charity, idolatry and lying for truth and Allah, he specifically pairs females with the opposite sex, categorically and without qualification, when he says, "By Him who made male and female."[4]

It is theologically significant that Muhammad did not represent Allah relegating females to a secondary or more lowly position than males. Naturally, it has been said that the Prophet through the medium of the Koran, did not go far enough in advocating greater equality for and better treatment of females. It also has been said that he was not consistent enough in applying his principles uniformly to men and women, being like Paul, a product of a traditionally conservative society and a man caught up in the political ramifications of establishing a new liberal religion. If he had been, he might not have encouraged patriarchy to supersede the existing matriarchy so totally, nor might he have instituted the veiling of women and the seclusion of wives and concubines. Nevertheless, considering the age in which he was preaching, his limited but concerned recognition of women and some of their specific problems was quite remarkable.

Although Paul and Muhammad both preached equality, Muhammad demonstrated a much greater consciousness of the lowly status of women, girl infants, female orphans, widows, and slaves. Moreover, he attempted to better their conditions by specifically referring to their wretched situations and by giving explicit commandments to improve their lot. Both religious leaders were intent upon building up, in the face of fierce opposition and persecution, a new faith, a religious organization, and a unified society. Of the two, Muhammad often seemed the more radical reformer, rooting out and overturning some of the worst aspects of then-existing community life. His refusal to maintain the status quo and to compromise with injustice, corruption, and turpitude often resulted in headlong and oftentimes ferocious conflicts, which Paul generally avoided. In time Islam was to gain a reputation of conquering by the sword rather than of conquest through compassion and submission.

Muhammad went to the heart of prevailing traditions, both among the settled and the roaming Arabians, when he condemned the custom of infanticide, among others, as being abhorrent and subject to severe judgment on the Day of Reckoning.[5] Whether over matters of female infanticide[6] or the Meccan hypocrisy of idolatrous worshippings of female deities while subjecting their own daughters to death or ostracism,[7] Muhammad did not hesitate to back up his rebukes with visions of Judgment Day reckonings and punishments. He enjoined the Meccans and his followers to observe certain decrees, such as looking after their own parents; giving charity and kindness to one's kin, the poor, and wayfarers; being kind to others; being honest in all dealings; and avoiding being vain or odiously proud.[8]

Besides advocating acts of compassion, very much drawn from the Christian ethic, in surah 17 of the Koran Muhammad laid down an all-encompassing code of conduct that gained him the enmity of many, including his own Quraysh kith and kin. He attacked the prevalent practices of his day in the following:

> Kill not your children for fear of want, for them and for you will we provide. Verily, the killing of them is a great wickedness.

> Have nought to do with adultery; for it is a foul thing and an evil way.

> Neither slay any one whom God hath forbidden you to slay, unless for a just cause.

> And touch not the substance [inheritance] of the orphan, unless in an upright way, till he attain the age of strength. And perform your covenant.

> And give full measure when you measure, and weigh with just balance.

> And follow not that of which thou hast no knowledge [sometimes translated as "accuse not any of a crime if thou art not sure of his guilt"]; because the hearing and the sight and the heart, each of these shall be enquired of [at the day of the resurrection].[9]

Obviously, a person who wanted to eliminate adultery and an existing double standard, infanticide, dishonesty, cheating and corruption, fraudulent use of orphans' inheritances and the breaking of contracts, false accusations, and irrational and unjust killing—when these practices were endemic throughout society—was bound to incur the displeasure, if not wrath, of his fellowmen.

Muhammad effectively replaced the practices of polyandry with polygamy but, at the same time, restricted polygamy to four wives, with the proviso that all were to be treated equally. It is thought that polygamy was instituted or strengthened because large surpluses of women prevailed after the men were killed in battle and because the paternity of children of polyandrous liaisons had become of little account. Polyandric women thus had to become monandric under Islam;

however, before doing so, they were first expected to obtain their families' permission and then their dowry to ensure future moral and financial support. Muhammad also extended earlier Arab prohibitions against marriage within specific blood-relationship degrees so that they were as equally applicable to the father's side as to the mother's.

Muhammad, not content with setting the bear at the bees' hive, stirred up the furor further by stressing the importance of women as wives and persons, by spurning the bias against childlessness and girl children, and by scorning fate or predetermination as a determinant of all of one's actions. He underscored the importance of women by symbolizing the Meccans' wives as one of God's boons, to be counted among the food and the supplies of life, for which men should be grateful and respectful.[10] He likewise showed concern for the underdog by emphasizing to the Meccans that they should give graditude to Allah by sharing their bountifulness with their slaves, of whom many were naturally women, "so that they may share alike."[11] And he further enhanced women's position by giving greater stability to marriage.

Before Muhammad, marriage in the Arabian peninsula, in accord with the chaos and disintegration of the times, was lax. Laws or restrictions governing the duties and responsibilities of either party in marriage—or out of marriage, as in divorce—were nonexistent. Muhammad, in trying to reform society and to establish Islam, had to suppress and replace two repressive and blood-letting allegiances: pagan and tribal. "The first was replaced by allegiance to Islam and the second by allegiance to the family as a social and primary group."[12] Muhammad then had to ensure that the father and the mother would not only be the nucleus of the family, but would be the repositories of trust, loyalty, obedience, and affection by the other near members of the family. In doing this he sought to break prescriptive ties with the clan or tribe and thereby to discourage the warring, jealousy, and rivalries that customarily dominated pre-Islam Arabian life. Not only did Islam enjoin obedience to parents but also "condemned conformity to [traditional] ancestral worship or ancient beliefs and customs of forefathers."[13]

Various Koranic injunctions are explicit in their prescription to obey and love one's parents but none more so than surah 17:23-24.

> Thy Lord hath ordained that ye worship none but him; and kindness to your parents, whether one or both of them attain to old age with thee: and say not to them "Fie!", neither reproach them; but speak to them with respectful speech; and defer humbly to them out of tenderness; and say, "Lord have compassion on them both, even as they reared me when I was little."

The dismay expressed by many Muslims at the breakdown of the Muslim family because of modernization thus has its roots not only in conservatism but in history. They fear that the breakdown of the Muslim family will cause the disintegration of the Islamic state and reversion to past splits. They fear that Muslim society will move away from its firm social foundation and will ignore the Prophet's injunctions that have molded Islamic thought and unity. In essence, they fear a void being created within themselves and their society, a void that cannot be filled by mere materialism. Yet they are caught in a "cleft-stick" between the past and the future. Nowhere is this more apparent than in the relationships between the sexes and the institutions that govern those relationships.

The institution of marriage and the family, as conceived by Muhammad, by no means existed solely for the reproduction of the species. It had a much broader social reason and base.

> Marriage in Islam is a social institution advocated by the Faith, the Holy Book and the Prophet's tradition. It is urged upon man[kind] because it constitutes the foundation upon which society can be built. Marriage rests upon a contractual arrangement entered into by a man and wife, not limited to a period of time, because it is meant to continue and endure. In Islam no group of people is debarred from matrimonial life—monastic celibacy does not exist in Islam. [14]

Muhammad tried to strengthen marriage by linking it to the will of God and invoking Judgment Day. As the new society emerged "from a background in which religious and sexual behaviour were not always related, into one in which the prophetic faith was applied to all elements of life,"[15] the Koran set forth injunctions that were to regulate behavior and change past practices. Women were not to be lightly discarded by their husbands. Although Islamic divorce essentially benefited men, stipulations were made that divorced women were to keep their dowries and were to be sent away with kindness and without loss of reputation. Other minimal duties were imposed on husbands, such as looking after their wives properly, not keeping them by compulsion, or vexing them.

When a man declared that he had divorced his wife, a three-to-four-month waiting or separation period was to follow before the final dissolution to give a woman the opportunity to return to her husband if she was pregnant or to allow for a resumption of sexual relations. However, if a woman was divorced by a man three times, she could not be remarried to him without an intervening marriage to and divorce from another man.

Irrespective of its social basis, leading Muslim jurists have disagreed about the Prophet's injunction that "everyone in the right conditions" should be settled in marriage. Some have interpreted the injunction to mean that marriage is permissible or preferable, that it is recommended, but not obligatory in such a way as to make the unmarried persons blamable within the context of the Koran. Others have envisaged marriage as a vicarious duty to family and society. Yet another group of jurists has regarded marriage as a duty decreed and binding upon everyone. A final set of jurists has laid down different rulings on marriage: voluntary or permissible, preferable, disliked or disfavored, forbidden, or obligatory in accordance with varying circumstances. But all base their theses on the Koranic verse, "And marry those among you who are single and your good servants, and the handmaidens."[16]

Muslim jurisprudence does not make marriage obligatory for all fully responsible people, nor does it treat healthy bachelors as sinful or punishable if they refrain from marriage, provided their delay is indefinite rather than permanent and for good cause. For instance, a man could delay marriage if he was a student or had few financial resources. If he wished to marry a "pagan" he had to wait until she was converted to the Muslim faith, although he could marry a Christian or a Jew. However, Muslim women could not marry men of other faiths until those men were converted to Islam. Muslim jurisprudence tends to stipulate that marriage is obligatory for the person who can cope with the financial and other burdens of marriage but cannot sustain celibacy (until marriage) and is likely to commit fornication or develop dissolute habits.[17] Homosexuality was forbidden by the Koran and the Hadith, but it tended to flourish because of the preponderance of eunuchs and male slaves. Transvestism also flourished. Since such conduct was regarded as highly indecent, it was punishable in various ways. But the severest punishment was reserved for adultery: for anyone caught in flagrante delicto, the Koran ordered that both the man and woman be scourged unpityingly with 100 stripes.

While women have especially suffered the consequences of adultery, being beaten or stoned to death, this extreme punishment actually did not originate with the Koran but from the Torah of the Jews and later from the multiplicity of traditions of differing authenticities. The Torah specified that married people should be stoned to death and that unmarried people should be lashed 100 times and then banished for a year. According to Ayesha, Muhammad's spirited and independent-minded wife, Muhammad tried to temper the Jewish law with mercy, urging leaders to let the accused go if possible on the basis that it is preferable "to make a mistake in forgiving than to make a mistake in punishing."[18] But strict Orthodox Muslims to this day appear to prefer to invoke the Hadith to justify hand lopping for stealing or death by stoning for adultery than to invoke the Koran or Muhammad's plea for mercy.

The provision for or advocacy of marriage was apparently made to ensure firm foundations for both family and society and to lessen social disintegration by reducing the opportunities for vice. Very few, with the exception of the crippled, mentally unstable, and financially indigent, can escape the marriage net laid down by Islam. This can be observed by how, in an attempt to avoid marital irresponsibility and instability, Islam provides specific legal safeguards to ensure family security, health, and enjoyment of life. Its social provisions could be said to have been the harbingers of family planning.

Muslim law categorically forbids anyone to marry if he is not capable—financially or otherwise—of shouldering marital responsibilities. An action to the contrary is regarded as an unlawful act punishable by God, since it undermines family security and structure. Islam seeks material safeguards for the family and expects a man to demonstrate his ability to support a family before and upon marriage by providing a premarriage dowry, contracting to maintain the wife in her accustomed style during the marriage, and ensuring that specific expenses would be paid if divorce occurs. A husband who cannot provide the dowry and the costs of marriage cannot expect to retain his wife or to cause her to live in poverty of his own making. Thus a wife would be entitled to leave her husband and to return to her own family. However, she would be subject to horrendous social pressures to remain with her husband, no matter how abusive. Hence, it is a matter of speculation how often such provisions—or modern legal provisions—are resorted to by women.

Indeed, modern Muslim apologists maintain that a man can marry only one woman at a time and cite the Koran as actually favoring monogamy. For historical and political reasons, the Koran first enjoined men to marry between one and four wives (the number of concubines were unspecified) if they feared that they could not act equitably toward their orphans (wards). The aftermath of wars and battles—surplus women and orphaned girls with and without dowries and inheritances— was in part responsible for this provision, for Muhammad saw men taking in and marrying girls in order to get their hands on the orphans' property. Polygamous marriage is said to have been encouraged because many women and children were left destitute when innumerable men were killed in battle; many of the orphans were girls who needed protection; the practice of many guardians was to refuse to marry off their orphaned wards so as to keep their property; and polygamy was as common in the Arab world as in the Chinese, Indian, and African ones. A maximum of four wives at any one time imposed a severe limitation on polygamy as then practiced. But the Koran further en-

joined that men should marry only one wife if they feared that they
could not treat each woman equally and fairly.

Unfortunately, popular and fatalistic misinterpretations of such
texts as "If they are poor, God of His bounty shall enrich them"[19] or
"For them and for you will we provide" have allowed impoverished
marriages to occur.[20] In fact, misinterpretations of texts and out-
of-context quotes have unfairly conspired to give Islam its reputation
of being a fatalistic, God-will-provide religion. Further, they have
undermined the security of the wife and the family—aggravated by the
social strictures against women being educated and employed outside
the home—and have implicitly condoned the irresponsibility or lax
work habits of many husbands.

Since Islam anticipates a healthy liaison between partners in
marriage, any health or physical defects discovered in either partner
before marriage justifies the termination of the engagement or marriage contract. If such defects are discovered after marriage, the
marriage may be annulled or separation or divorce granted. Muslim
law thereby attempts to ensure not only a healthy, enjoyable relationship between couples but also attempts to avoid the propagation of
defective children. Muhammad was conscious of the advantages of
building up a viable nation of strong, healthy people; hence, he advocated marriage only between mentally and physically healthy partners
and instituted strict prohibitions against intermarriage between cous-
ins and close relatives on both the mother's and father's sides. This
was a reversal of pre-Islamic practices that allowed men to marry
their father's wives or two sisters together.

Throughout the Koran, Muhammad combined a sense of predetermination with self-determination and used that combination to combat various injustices, including that of vehement bias against childlessness and daughters. While he allowed that God determines what
is to be on earth and in the afterlife, he nevertheless accepted that
within prescribed boundaries individuals could exercise to either their
benefit or detriment certain singular freedoms. He was not unlike
Buddha in urging people to take responsibility for their own actions.
The Prophet clearly showed his concept of predeterminism in his description of Allah as the creator of heaven and earth, the giver of
wives, the provider of male and female cattle, the gatherer of varied
people and creeds to form one religious nation, the provider of abundance and rain, and the invoker of wind and waves.[21] Yet he proclaimed that an individual can exert some influence over predestination, since "nor happeneth to you any mishap, but it is for [by] your
own hand-work" (emphasis added),[22] provided only Allah is worshipped
and certain conditions kept. The conditions to be kept were avoiding
crime and evil, observing prayer and charity, giving forgiveness and
alms, redressing wrongs, and undertaking reconciliation.[23]

Nevertheless, Muhammad appears not to have been adverse to invoking predestination to achieve a specific objective or to sway people's attitudes. When Muhammad tried to overcome traditional biases against childlessness and girl children (and therefore, indirectly, small families) he invoked predestination to compel the people to equate having children or not, having only boys, having just girls, or having both with awe and gratitude for God's gifts and works. He declared: "God's the Kingdom of the Heavens and of the Earth! He createth what He will! and He giveth daughters to whom He will, and sons to whom He will: Or He giveth them children of both sexes, and He maketh whom He will be childless; for He is Wise, Powerful!"[24] Unfortunately, the inherent promise of this declaration, which effectively gave equal status to children regardless of sex and to parents regardless of the sex or number of children produced, was not fulfilled, not in the seventh century and not in the twentieth. Attitudes were not greatly changed. Female children, childless couples, and small families were held and have continued to the present to be held in low esteem, and most women have continued to be relegated to a battery-farm chicken existence.

Muhammad's philosophy of balancing predestination with individualism had considerable potential, largely achieved during the golden age of Islam, for developing a society, a culture, and the individual. Eventually, the concept of individualism was knocked out of balance with predestination and was submerged with the aid of a rigid, rule-bound religious hierarchy that converted Muhammad's broad theology into ossified thought and extreme passivity. The potential inherent in the Prophet's commandments for helping the maligned and disadvantaged was accordingly diminished; fate had decreed their lot and little was done or was expected to be done to improve their conditions. And the fate of the female, the most nondescript of all, was sealed.

NOTES

1. Caesar E. Farah, Islam: Beliefs and Observances (Woodbury, N.Y.: Barron's Educational Services, 1968), pp. 16-35.
2. J. M. Rodwell, trans., The Koran (London: Everyman's Library, 1963), 16:59, 17:42, 37:150, 43:18, 53:28.
3. Geoffrey Parrinder, Sex in the World's Religions (Don Mills, Ont.: General, 1980), p. 155.
4. Koran 92:3.
5. Koran 81.
6. Koran 81:8-9, 16:61, 17:33.
7. Koran 16, 17:42.
8. Koran 17.

9. Koran 17:33–38.

10. Koran 16:73–74.

11. Ibid.

12. Hasan Sa'id Karni, "The Family as a Social Group," in Islam and Family Planning, Report of the proceedings of the International Islam Conference held in Morocco, December 1971 (Beirut: International Planned Parenthood Federation, 1974), 1:41.

13. Ibid., p. 52.

14. Zahia Qaddura, "Woman's Rights in Islam," in Islam and Family Planning, 1:69.

15. Parrinder, Sex in the World's Religions, p. 160.

16. Koran 24:32.

17. Muhammad el-Mekki el-Naciri, "Family Planning in Light of Muslim Legislation," in Islam and Family Planning, 2:36–41.

18. Parrinder, Sex in the World's Religions, p. 165.

19. Koran 24:32.

20. Koran 10:152.

21. Koran 42:6, 9, 26, 27, 31.

22. Koran 42:29.

23. Koran 42:35, 36, 38–42.

24. Koran 42:48, 49.

12

ISLAM
AND
EDUCATION

While reading and writing existed in a limited way in pre-
Islamic societies, the masses were virtually excluded from learning.
The few schools that existed in the Arabic countries were mainly restricted to the wealthy and their relatives. With the advent of Muhammad and Islam, public participation in education widened, for Muhammad decreed that education should be universal and that priests should
conduct literacy classes using the Koran.

In early Islam, Christians and Jews predominated as teachers
in the elementary places of instruction, the kuttab. Their main tools
of instruction were the Koran and the Prophet Muhammad's teaching.
Gradually, Muslims gained ascendancy as teachers, but controversy
soon broke out. Conservatives and reformists debated whether religious instruction based on the Koran could be properly combined with
more general, pragmatic education. Traditionally, the elementary
level was supposed to concentrate on religious learning, since the
three Rs were deemed to be subjects suitable only for higher-level
students under the tutelage of esteemed professional teachers. Education for the masses, the prerogative of the kuttab, accordingly became equated with religious training and little else. And female participation became severely restricted, despite Islam's theoretical
encouragement of both boys and girls to attend school. At the age of
six, little boys were typically sent to the Koranic schools, which
were often situated near the mosque in the old bazaar quarter. Since
little girls generally were less free to go running about, even if they
were not yet in purdah, and since women were less apt to attend
mosques for their prayers, the young girls, lacking chaperoning and
adult female example, infrequently participated in the lessons. However, if she were lucky enough to have a learned father who could accept girls being educated, she might have been able to join her brothers
in learning the Koran.

This way of using the sacred texts to teach reading and grammar to children is [and was] one of the countless examples of the deliberate and permanent confusion between religion and daily life. Through the most ordinary acts, Muslim life became an uninterrupted act of faith, impregnating the heart and mind of all concerned. [1]

Under the medieval education system, few links existed between the kuttabs, or Koranic schools, and higher education for the select few. Since narrow religious instruction was deemed inadequate for future rulers, a palace-school education emerged to give princes a broader knowledge base in preparation for ruling. Nevertheless, the kuttab, with its systematic approach to learning, the Koran, and the faith, was instrumental in developing a new concept—adult education for the masses. Adults embraced learning so enthusiastically that a recognition soon arose that adults as well as youngsters should be encouraged to seek education by giving them access to teachers and facilities. Further encouragement was given to those more able adults by promoting them to higher echelons of learning.

Legal, moral, and theological debates were vigorously pursued at the upper echelons. These occurred more often in private homes than in mosques under the patronage of such broad-minded, wisdom-seeking men as the caliphs Harun al-Rashid and all-Ma'mun in the eighth and ninth centuries A.D. A variety of views were both encouraged and tolerated; petrification and rigidity of outlook were absent. By the twelfth century, Arab intellectual excitement and practical application had devised a sophisticated and manageable system of mathematics including algebra, trigonometry, and a broadened application of geometry; applied sciences, with chemistry, optics, and mechanics leading the way to practical uses; and geography, minerology, geology, and zoology, opening the doors for scientists 500 years later. Their knowledge encompassed medicine, which actually used diagnosis, anatomical knowledge, and hygiene to further patients' remedial dentistry and a plethora of new medical instruments. [2] As the ulama (the learned clerical class with social and religious authority) attained dominance, this intellectual freedom became increasingly curtailed, so that by the fourteenth or fifteenth century a substantial decline in Muslim creativity had occurred from which it has not yet fully recovered.

Paralleling the growth of medieval education were the evolution of large, official mosques and semipublic libraries and the founding of private and public schools. Each mosque seemed to have its own library and some were enormous, with thousands of volumes. A passion for books had been fanned by Islam's "democratization of knowledge and the dissemination of a written works." [3]

Literature, poetry, music, philosophy, architecture, and ornamentation all flourished. It is said that the ordinary people might have been excluded from this intellectual excitement if it had not been for the numerous itinerant poets, storytellers, and philosophers discoursing wherever crowds would gather. Certainly, there is little doubt that one-half of the ordinary people were excluded, for women could not participate in the public gatherings or enter the men-only coffee houses where so much of the storytelling or philosophizing went on. And even among the wealthy or intellectual elite, women were not wholly included in the intellectual ferment. Undoubtedly, many of the female elite could read and had access to tutors and libraries, but they would generally have been excluded from the intellectual debates or pursuits carried on by their menfolk. And so their ability to benefit from the intellectual expansion of the Muslim world was restricted, as was their ability to pass on their knowledge to the less-well-off women.

Although other subjects were investigated, the mosques, kuttabs, and other institutions continued to emphasize religion and Islam's interaction with various academic topics. Their spread was owing in part to competition between the Shi'a and Sunni movements, which sought to develop separate ideologies and separate schools of learning. One outcome of their controversy was the establishment of the world-renowned Islamic University of al-Azhar in A.D. 972 in Cairo by the Shi'ite Fatimids.

Sunni leaders, encouraged by the public, took the unprecedented step of lending state support to and providing public funding for Sunni schools. Orthodox madrasahs, or theological schools, became progressively stronger as they attracted more scholars who, in turn, created new disciplines, new textbooks, and above all, new ulama. As the madrasahs became more tightly institutionalized, especially during the Ottoman Empire, the ulama became ever more castelike and hierarchal. They demonstrated a highly organized administrative capacity and established numerous higher seats of learning. But they also became influential repositories of orthodoxy and petrified conservatism, so that even today, institutions like Deoband in India have refused to accommodate modern conditions and expand their limited curricula. Even the esteemed University of al-Azhar required an act of parliament before it would institute faculties of practical science. And the idea of opening up such institutions to coeducation has caused considerable mental and spiritual angst, for it is still strongly felt in some quarters, and even growing in others, that "unrelated men and women should have little cause to meet,"[4] since the laws of nature and the human sexual urge, if given free course, can run wild and upset the ordered social system and family that are at the base of Islam.

Education in the Middle Ages basically emanated from individuals rather than from schools. The teacher was of central and pri-

mary importance; the school, secondary. Students traveled cease-
lessly to be with certain teachers for particular subjects, and teachers, rather than schools, issued the certificates that entitled students
to teach others. The most esteemed scholars tended to be the products
of individual teachers rather than of the collective madrasahs. But
few women figured among these, as the various prohibitions against
women traveling freely or associating with men other than their intimate family worked against women being educated to any great extent.
Only the privileged few acquired learning and became scholars. Of
these, many distinguished themselves in the fields of jurisprudence,
law, literature, and politics; their opinions were also sought, and a
few sects, like the Kharijites, even allowed women to perform the
duties of the prestigious job of judgeship. [5]

Gradually, as the madrasah system strengthened, original free
thought (ijtihad) weakened during the tenth and eleventh centuries.
The legal and intellectual sciences suffered accordingly. Stagnation
and ossification set in.

> The real reason for the decline of the quality of Islamic
> learning was the gradual starvation of the religious sciences
> through their isolation from the life of lay intellectualism
> which itself then decayed . . . [and] the "Ulama" had
> gained the experience of developing their own sciences and
> teaching them in such a way that a defence would be erected
> for this body of teaching. . . . Even more important . . .
> [they developed] the content of the orthodox sciences . . .
> so that they would be isolated from any possible challenge
> and opposition. [6]

The ulama and madrasahs effectively stifled creative thinking.
For them any challenge was unsupportable. Contrary views were
damnable. New knowledge was useless. They substituted dogmatic
theology for rational philosophy. Nothing could vie with or question
it. Pedantry prevailed. And fertile, imaginative Islamic thought became infertile, sterile. As with Catholicism, it became increasingly
more difficult to rejuvenate, to resurrect from its convoluted morass
of dogma. Not only did rational sciences languish, so did higher
theology. In the 1600s Katib Chelebi ascribed this stalemate to theological dogmaticians who were

> many unintelligent people . . . [who] remained as inert
> as rocks, frozen in blind imitation of the ancients. They
> passed for learned men, while all the time they were ig-
> noramuses, fond of disparaging what they called the "phil-
> osophical sciences", and knowing nothing of earth or sky.

> The admonition "Have they not contemplated the Kingdom
> of Heaven and Earth?" (Qur'an, VII, 184) made no impres-
> sion on them; they thought contemplating the world and the
> firmament meant staring at them like a cow. [7]

His comments are perhaps as relevant to theological dogmaticians of
whatever faith today as then.

As subjects of learning narrowed in scope and intensity, academic standards sank to a nadir. Greater emphasis was placed on
rote learning and creative thought was minimized. Subjects and books
were few, school years were few, and students had little chance to
mature intellectually so as to be able to grasp the complexities of
religious-philosophical thought at the highest levels. Not trained to
employ logic, they learned by rote. Instead of understanding the subject, they memorized the book. Few original works emerged, for intellectual effort was expended on writing commentaries on commentaries and ultimately trivial marginal notes. Dogmatic theology became more dogmatic and inert with each successive commentary.

The madrasah system fortunately did not constitute all Muslim
education. Islam's most famous savants often were educated privately at home in a very broad curriculum under specific teachers.
But they were usually an affluent minority who could afford the expense
of private tuition or scholastic travels. Also they had the position and
power to withstand the condemnation of the ulama for avoiding the
madrasah system.

The fundamental weakness of Muslim learning in the Middle
Ages—and one that partly remains today—was its concept of and attitude toward knowledge. Knowledge was something to be passively acquired. It was not an active pursuit based upon an individual's own
efforts—researching, discovering, speculating, analyzing. Knowledge
was through osmosis, transmitted by an indoctrinated few. It was not
to be rational, positive, or creative. If it were, it would upset the
orthodoxy and status quo; accordingly, "Orthodoxy, anxious to safe-
guard tradition, came out . . . heavily against reason, which it
wanted to keep in strict subordination to dogma."[8] For obvious reasons the reliquaries of dogmatic theology did not want their power
diminished.

Dogma, orthodoxy, skewed concepts of knowledge, reliance
upon historical social relics, the pervasiveness of the madrasahs, and
the unyielding power of the ulama have been perpetuated in modern
times. This condition is no more unique to Islam than it is to other
faiths. Most religious leaders appear to balk at fundamentally re-
thinking their religions in order to make them relevant to changed
conditions and rapidly evolving societies. Nowhere was this more evidenced than in their response to women's needs and women's position
in religion.

Law became rigid; certain provisions of the Qur'an were
interpreted in such a way as to relegate women to an inferior position. Their education was considered undesirable,
and women came gradually to be looked upon as objects of
ornament. They were secluded and were denied participation in public life. Later, women continued to share with
men the responsibilities of everyday life—raising children,
managing homes, taking care of the family, working in
outdoor or home industries—yet they were never allowed
to join in community affairs, although their activities affected those affairs directly or indirectly. [9]

But as Shwikar Elwan warns, foreigners should not therefore deduce
that bedouin or rural women automatically held an inferior position in
the family because of the lack of formal education or the existence of
seclusion. [10] Many, especially the matriarchs of large families of
sons, held a dominant position and greatly influenced their children.
Many others were little more than servants or beasts of burden, destined to do their husbands' bidding. As recent interviews with Muslim
women in various countries show, the women, especially the younger
ones, do not feel they have a dominant or influential role to play vis-
à-vis men. Rather, they feel inferior, unequal, submissive, subjugated—and that they attribute to their great ignorance and lack of education. But times and attitudes are changing. As a woman interviewed by Patricia Jeffrey said, "When I was married it was fine for
a girl to be stupid . . . because her in-laws could be sure of her innocence. But I'm not going to do that to my two daughters. My marriage has been spoilt by my own ignorance and embarrassment." [11]
Or, as another commented,

> It's not that our father is against education for girls . . .
> he wanted us educated but with "izzat" [honor] . . . [and]
> our grandmother [who] used to come . . . and make such
> a fuss about us big girls going to school. . . . But we all
> resent the way that she's interfered in our lives . . . we'll
> have to live our lives out lacking in education, and all be-
> cause of her. [12]

After the initial thrust of Muslim education, females were practically denied access to learning. Excluded from worshiping with the
men, they were excluded from the mosques where most education occurred, the kuttabs, and the madrasah system. Those who received
education usually came from affluent, prestigious families that could
afford to hire private tutors and could equally afford to ignore social
opprobrium cast at female education. Prevailing attitudes toward

womanhood and woman's place; the institutional practices of veiling, seclusion, and polygamy; the subordination of wives to husbands; prejudices about girls and their usefulness; and the lack of women teachers—all directly mitigated against the general education of females. Likewise but indirectly, the limited curriculum, the narrow scope of education, the subjugation of reason to custom and rote learning, the inflexible orthodoxy of the power-bent ulama, and the inflexibility of the madrasahs further worked against universal female education. Although the situation is gradually changing at varying paces within different Muslim countries and communities, a carry-over of these attitudes and practices still impinges on women's education and emancipation. Women's education is still predicated on the thought that the differences between the sexes justify the seclusion of women and the different treatment of education meted out to males and females. Influential commentaries by such men of the orthodox school as M. M. Siddiqi, Khurshid Ahmad, and Maulana Abul A'la Maududi attempt to vindicate the view that, since a woman's sphere of activity is basically domestic and maternal while man's is external, and since a Muslim woman normally need not earn a living or undertake hardships in the economic sphere, different types of education are appropriate and justifiable for men and women. [13] Essentially, women's training and education, they maintain, should be confined to their domestic and nuturant functions so as to make them more useful to their families and homes.

Despite Islam permitting men and women alike to acquire success, education, and honor, and despite Islam according women equal religious and spiritual rights with men (although not quite fully equal earthly rights), the orthodox maintain that such equality is specifically applicable to each sex's own natural sphere. Men's and women's roles are complementary, not competitive; therefore, education should be appropriate and confined to those roles. While in theory this isolation of women from broad-based learning may mean no disrespect of women, in practice women are disrespected and disregarded for their ignorance. As Jeffrey states: "Thus, sexual apartheid entails 'separate development' as well as segregation. [But] there is little evidence that separate ever is equal (whether in the field of sex or race) even when it is dressed up as functional interdependence."[14]

With the impact of Western influences on Islam and on Muslim culture between the eighteenth and twentieth centuries, various challenges arose and crises developed between the old and the new. Challenges arose from many directions: from new political processes, expanded communications and news media, external contacts, military involvements, revamped judicial machinery, and modern education. Some of the most destructive impacts emerged from early Christian missionaries who, without understanding Islam's historical background, condemned Islam for being heathen. Equally damaging was Western criticism that, based upon a concept of Christian moral superiority, was insensitive to Muslim society's needs and developments. Notwithstanding these external forces, the greatest challenges arose from within Muslim society itself.

Modernist reform movements emerged in an effort to meet the new challenges head on and to reconstitute Muslim society in accordance with modern changes. But the reformers, anxious to modernize Islam's prevailing social traditions, soon found themselves caught up in conflicts between reason and faith, modernism and fundamentalism. Conflicts that were quiescent for two or three decades again flared up. The root cause of much of the recent violence and rediscovered rigidity in Iran, Pakistan, Libya, Algeria, and other countries might be more ascribed to the eternal tug-of-war between fundamental traditionalists and reforming modernists than to political tensions among disparate elements.

The challenges to tradition have been especially acute for the institutions surrounding women. Early Muslim modernists strongly argued for the equality and education of women. The first major advocate of female emancipation and education was the Muslim reformer Jamal al-Din al-Afghani, who promoted the radically progressive idea that women had the same intellectual capacities as men. Qasim Amin, a liberal Egyptian, followed and wrote The Emancipation of Women and The New Woman, landmarks in the Arab woman's emancipation movement. A strong advocate of women's rights who recognized that women's emancipation was crucial for Egypt's social and political development, Amin encountered vehement opposition from conservative elements. Bahithat el-Badiyah, a woman writer who fought for compulsory education, also encountered great opposition and hostility. Basing their arguments upon the Koran and upon Islamic reasoning, these reformers effected substantive changes in the education of females. Their efforts led to legislation that de jure effected changes in women's education, political status, and various aspects (divorce, polygamy, inheritance) of their social status. "Governments became increasingly aware of the important relationship between the education of women and modernization."[15] Unfortunately, however, despite the reformers' good intentions and the legislation, women's position de facto was little altered. Weakly implemented legislation and unchanging attitudes encouraged reaction, which replaced modernism with conservative fundamentalism. The first to feel the backlash of change were inevitably the women, as old prohibitions were resurrected or new prohibitions were patented to hinder their progress. Comprehensive and universal female education inevitably becomes retarded unless political leaders are prepared to counteract regressive trends often instituted by religious leaders fearful of losing their power and influence. As the noted Algerian writer Assia Djebar observed, "Women in general . . . are conscious of the fact that the Muslim man, however revolutionary he may be within his own union or party or in discharging his civic responsibilities, all too often clings in his domestic life to the old ways."[16] This will affect the way he perceives women's role, their needs, their education, and their development. He will still expect his wife to tread the traditional paths and to submit passively to his "weakened and ineffective authoritarianism." In turn he will do relatively little to improve women's situation, and his wife's silence will aid and abet his inaction. "Indeed, Muslim women are all too often silent, and they appear to be so all the time," comments Djebar. "The assumption, sometimes overstated, that they exercise a measure of authority behind the scenes is small consolation and one which is generally offered to oppressed minorities."[17]

Fortunately, in some countries women have refused to remain silent and political leaders have been prepared to confront the opposition. Governments like those of Egypt, Iraq, Jordan, and Syria have made significant attempts to improve female education and participation. The wives of national leaders have spoken out, and certain political leaders have taken specific action to combat prejudice. In Jakarta, Governor Ali Sadikin was just such a political leader. When a new comprehensive school was built in the early 1970s in central Jakarta to meet the needs of a local kampong, or village, religious zealots opposed its construction because it was secular and coeducational. They feared that its existence would detract from the influence of the nearby Koranic school and that coeducation would contribute to social immorality. Urged on by the local mullah, fearful that his influence over the villagers would decrease and with that one of his sources of revenue, the zealots burned down the new school. They also intimidated and harassed the girls to prevent them from attending classes. Governor Sadikin was so appalled by this show of religious intolerance that he personally put up the funds for the reconstruction of the school, having reprimanded the religious leaders for their actions and warned them on pain of punishment against future vandalism. He further emphasized that the secular school was not attempting to undermine the Koranic school but was supplementing its teaching by preparing young Jakartan girls and boys for modern life. Once the villagers were assured that they and their children would not be subject to further intimidation, they sent their children not just to the secular school but also to the Koranic school for religious instruction.

Similarly, in the Delta area of Bangladesh in the mid-1970s, villagers were reluctant to send their children, especially their girls, to the new secular schools for fear of incurring the wrath of the local priests. In such a closed society, where women were shut away from all outside influences unless they were of the educated and Westernized elite, this fear of priests had an even more devastating effect on their children's education than in the more open Muslim society of Jakarta. Sons were sent mainly to Koranic schools, where they were imbued with traditional myths and prejudices along with genuine religious training. When sent to the less-preferred secular schools, it was on an ad hoc, indefinite basis. Daughters, being effectively barred from Koranic schools, rarely received any schooling. What schooling they received rarely exceeded a couple of years and was subject to segregated schoolrooms and the availability of female teachers.

Bangladeshi women were restricted from attending adult literacy classes by their husbands, their families, and the local priests. Gradually, education for women was allowed once it was publicly realized that the classes would be secluded, taught by women, and at hours that did not interfere with household tasks. Even then the task of obtaining their husbands' permissions was not always easy. Very often the husbands, backed by the local mullahs, objected to all female education whether for daughter or wife on social and religious grounds. Today, largely because of the upheavals caused by the 1971 civil war and its aftermath, Bangladesh's political leadership has reassessed the needs of its women and their potential contribution to economic and social development. More than most other regimes in the Islamic world, it is promoting female education at all levels and the participation of women in all phases of national life. The fact that attitudes toward female education are changing and becoming more positive is evidenced by King Fahd recently stating that Saudi Arabia should encourage more women to become educated, to proceed on to higher education, and even to enter the work force.

On the other side of the world, a not dissimilar situation existed in predominantly Catholic Quebec. In the early 1960s legislation was introduced there to loosen the priestly grasp on an educational system that was classical in format, religious in substance, and quite ill-equipped to prepare its students for other than the traditional jobs of priest, soldier, and lawyer. Legislation, forward-thinking provincial and federal leadership, and changed attitudes challenged the existing educational hierarchy and its priestly proponents. New educational systems and concepts that reduced the overwhelming religious content of curricula greatly aided French-Canadian graduates in being incorporated into the modern sector.

Unquestionably, those changes substantially affected both women and men. But because female education had been so shamefully neglected for so long, Quebec women had to climb much further up the educational ladder than men to gain even a semblance of parity. Nevertheless, irrespective of continuing disparities, they have experienced other benefits. They have gained freedom from familial and priestly restraints and the freedom to think for themselves, to pursue their own lives without imposed guilt, and to limit family size. Their education has helped them to withstand priestly condemnation for practicing contraception and thereby refusing to emulate their mothers' and grandmothers' lives of thralldom to unending pregnancies and large families. A publicly applauded but religiously criticized result of their education was the reduction of Quebec's birthrate to the lowest in Canada.

However, it will still be some time before universal (free and compulsory) education for Muslim girls after puberty obtains. In part this will be a direct function of purdah and an indirect result of Islam. In part it will emerge from attitudes, perceptions, and misconceptions. So long as purdah exists, the belief will prevail that girls do not need education at all or that they need only minimal education relevant to their restrictive functions and roles. Moreover, it will continue to require a costly duplication of facilities, which most governments cannot afford; accordingly, since the education of boys is invariably deemed the most essential, fewer or minimal expenditures will be made on the education of girls.

Considerable debate between modern Islamic reformers and the orthodox has been carried on about whether the Koran imposes seclusion and veiling on women for all time and all reasons as a result of the Prophet's edict that his female relatives should be veiled. Reformists believe that Muhammad urged veiling to protect his relatives from the prying eyes and gossip of the public. Orthodox Muslims believe that equality in Islam the religion did not alter the differences between the sexes, who should be kept apart and different. They worry that education could alter those differences and close the gap between the differences to the ultimate detriment of Islam's stability as a social and political force. And so the debate rages. What perhaps is more important is the perception Muslim women have of the relationship between Islam and purdah and education. Even though Islamic tenets do not necessarily impose an immutable state of purdah on women, most women, especially the rural and illiterate women, believe that it does. Because they believe it does, they find it hard to break the bonds of purdah and to demand equality beyond the veil. This then is often the crux of the problem surrounding the status of women: less what formal Islam stipulates for women than what women and men believe Islam stipulates. Misconceptions about Islam have transpired to keep women in their place and be-waquf, or ignorant. Much of this has been a result of the vital role women play in the socialization of girls (their impact on boys is fairly nominal) and the perpetuation of sexual ghettoization, which they attribute to Islamic doctrines.

Essentially, Muslim religious leaders have disregarded the dualism inherent in Muhammad's approach to situations: the legalistic, legislative act versus the idealistic, moralistic intent. Muhammad and through him the Koran, on the one hand, dealt pragmatically with existing conditions by first recognizing their existence. Second, they made specific legal prescriptions to ensure right treatment of the conditions and to achieve certain immediate social effects. On the other hand, Muhammad issued moral precepts designed to demonstrate how he would improve society when conditions and attitudes permitted.

Muhammad recognized that society could not be radically changed overnight, but he provided sufficient latitude in the Koran and his teachings to allow for substantive change: the elimination of slavery and polygamy, the improvement of women's lot, the use of contraception, the relative parity of the sexes, and the respectful treatment of females. He adopted (and this is evident throughout the Koran) a legal, for-immediate-use approach to daily problems and a moral, for-the-future implementation of Islam. Unfortunately, the majority of ulama have persisted in adhering to the legalistic, narrower approach rather than attempting to rethink the social ethics, justice, and institutions of Islam in light of the latter. Instead of adopting Muhammad's moral, for-the-future approach in considering (and possibly dismantling) the social institutions and mores of Islam that detrimentally touch women, the ulama and the madrasah system have retreated into a legalistic conservatism based upon historical layers of marginal interpretations and commentaries. They have continued to ignore the fact that Islam at its inception started from a clean slate or that social institutions of the past were specifically devised for the conditions of the past. They seem to prefer to cling tenaciously to past institutions that often are an anathema to the present, while evading Muhammad's broad-horizoned, moral approach to issues. As Fazlur Rahman observes, "In a sense, conservative 'Ulama of today are far more uncompromisingly and, indeed, unthinkingly conservative than were their predecessors."[18] And as Manning Nash discovered when studying in Iran, the clergy seem less interested in economic development or modernization that could benefit their people than in being vigorously opposed to, or nominally neutral toward, development. To him they appeared more capable of creating turmoil than of "sparking transformation" and "organizing society for transcendence."[19] They have been bent upon destruction and the routing out of modernism. And since the emancipation of women was seen as one of the worst evils of Westernization or modernization, female education, employment, and freedom were drastically curtailed and women were vigorously propelled back into seclusion. Many women, caught up in the spiritual and emotional outpouring, even encouraged and acceded to the dismemberment of their liberty and education. Then they knew not what they did. Now they do, but the fight to regain those rights they so precipitously and unthinkingly yielded will be difficult and long. The clergy—the mullahs, the mujtahids, the ayatollahs, and the ulama—will not easily relinquish their hold.

With the see-sawing between modernism and conservatism within Islam, apologists have largely replaced modernists. In their extreme defense of Islamic virtues, apologists have deliberately misinterpreted and misunderstood Western values and mores so as to justify the continuation or reinstitution of such practices as purdah, polygamy, and minimal education or noneducation of females. Apologists have deliberately equated coeducation, modern education, and the vaunted independence of Western women with prostitution, which they seem to believe can only be avoided by maintaining seclusion, dependence, and noneducation. Many young women and men who, as an elite, became accustomed to the privileges of education in the 1960s and early 1970s have already incurred a rude awakening. In their determination to reestablish fundamentalist values and to reject the Western, they supported the overthrow of regimes in countries such as Iran, Afghanistan, and Pakistan with little thought for or understanding of the possible ramifications of such actions. Many women have since become dismayed, if not shocked, to discover that the enthronement of conservative Muslim fundamentalists has meant an increased intolerance for emancipation and the education of women. Such fundamentalists, given political power, have contrived to deny and will continue to deny their own women their rightful place in society and the educational system.

If entrenched biases against women are to be altered, more needs to be done than establishing coeducational or girls-only primary and secondary schools and universities. The conservative ulama, the apologists and fundamentalists, and the madrasah system will require educating and convincing that modernism is reconcilable with tradition and can be beneficial to the community. This might be accomplished in part by incorporating into modern education Islamic subjects and research, handled by thoroughly trained and broad-minded staff. These teachers would be able to apply the moral intentions of the Prophet and the Koran to modern conditions rather than maintaining the status quo through the application of outdated legalisms. They could teach Islamic religious subjects dynamically and positively, with a view to demonstrating the relevancy of Islam to modern individuals and societies. A basic reformulation of Islam by the ulama, making Islam relevant to modern needs and acceptable by modern minds, could reduce the present conflicts between modern secularism and Islam. They could, in effect, strengthen Islam and make it a positive, dynamic force instead of a negative one. And they could disabuse critics of the belief that Islam is incompatible with development. As Saleem Qureshi points out, the Koran basically does not concern itself with specific political and economic schemes, except for some provisions concerning usury and inheritance. Rather, it emphasizes social justice and fairness and the duty of humans to God and to each other. However, he fears that Islamists, particularly in those states such as Pakistan where Islamists have linked cause with a religiously oriented military leadership, will use Islam to make fundamental and repressive changes in existing economic and political structures. He believes that Islam can provide the framework to meet the challenge of the twentieth century, but he fears that "it is the subversion of the spirit of Islam by forces which press Islam into their narrow parochial and personal interests that is debilitating Pakistan and exploiting Islam."[20] He is especially fearful of the danger of uniting military power with religious sanction, since numerous past calamities have occurred when the temporal has been tied to the spiritual.

A basic question to be addressed insofar as females are concerned is whether the ulama or madrasah system would be amenable to reforms that would give girls and women the benefit of Muhammad's intent rather than merely the letter of his law. At present it seems unlikely that they will be fully incorporated into Islamic studies and research or given religious voice. A social and religious base comparable to their legal status will in all probability continue to elude them. Yet change for society as a whole and for women specifically is inevitable, regardless of obstacles set up by religious institutions. According to Fazlur Rahman, should Muslim societies and their institutions fail to provide females with an adequate answer regarding the relevancy of Islam to them as modern, individualistic human beings, the only alternative left to them will be some form of secularism. Since this solution would be tantamount to changing the very nature of Islam, which could cause an extreme conservative backlash, Rahman advocates "a constructive and bold humanism that would restate Islamic social ideals" to back up necessary social reform and legislation.[21]

The relevancy of religion to the modern woman of whatever faith is at one and the same time a challenge and a crisis—a condition not yet fully recognized by most religious leaders. If institutionalized religions continue to thwart women from attaining full personhood by blocking their access to education, by interfering with their attempts to control their bodies and fertility, and by inhibiting their full religious participation, women will quietly but firmly remove themselves from the ambit and influence of their respective religions. Modern conditions are giving women alternatives to religion. Moreover, women are gaining sufficient confidence to extricate themselves from the tentacles of backward leaders and institutions. Ultimately, unless religions and their leaders respond constructively to women's needs, more women will avail themselves of alternatives to religion and, without fanfare, relegate institutionalized religion to the sidelines.

NOTES

1. Jean Mathé, The Civilization of Islam, trans. David Macrae (New York: Crescent Books, 1980), pp. 35-36.

2. Ibid., pp. 119-28.

3. Ibid., p. 129.

4. Patricia Jeffrey, Frogs in a Well: Indian Women in Purdah (London: Zed Press, 1979), p. 20.

5. Shwikar Elwan, The Status of Women in the Arab World (Ottawa: Arab League Information Centre, 1974), pp. 3-4.

6. Fazlur Rahman, Islam (New York: Doubleday, 1968), pp. 227-28.

7. Ibid., p. 229.

8. Ibid., p. 234.

9. Elwan, The Status of Women in the Arab World, p. 4.

10. Ibid.

11. Jeffrey, Frogs in a Well, p. 125.

12. Ibid., p. 127.

13. Khurshid Ahmad, Family Life in Islam (Leicester: Islamic Foundation, 1974); M. M. Siddiqi, Women in Islam (Lahore: Institute of Islamic Culture, 1952); and Maulana Abul A'la Maududi, Purdah and the Status of Women in Islam (Lahore: Islamic Publications, 1962).

14. Jeffrey, Frogs in a Well, pp. 21-22.

15. Elwan, The Status of Women in the Arab World, p. 5.

16. Assia Djebar, "A Noted Algerian Writer Presents Her Views of Muslim Women Today," UNESCO Courier, August-September 1975, p. 28.

17. Ibid.

18. Rahman, Islam, p. 314.

19. Manning Nash, "Islam in Iran: Turmoil, Transformation, or Transcendence?" World Development (Oxford) 8, no. 7-8 (July-August 1980): 555-61.

20. Saleem Qureshi, "Islam and Development: The Zia Regime in Pakistan," World Development (Oxford) 8, no. 7-8 (July-August 1980): 573.

21. Rahman, Islam, p. 289.

13

ISLAM
AND
POPULATION

The story of the fast-growing populations of most Muslim countries is told less by dry data than by the overcrowded cities, the illiteracy and ignorance, the malnutrition of children, the inadequacy of food crops, and the fatigued condition of women. The Muslim world no longer lags far behind the population growth of Latin America, the world's fastest-growing region, but is rapidly catching up. For some this may be a matter of pride. For others it has become an urgent, nagging worry. Many Sudanese, for example, still cling to the belief that the Sudan needs more, not less, people to populate its land. They fail to acknowledge that their desert land is already unable to support its present population of 23 million (increasing at about 3.3 percent a year) and its domestic animal population of 40 million to 50 million. They disregard the deforestation and denuding of the countryside. They discount that about 80 percent of the women are anemic, 87 percent of the children are undernourished, and 90 percent of Sudanese women are illiterate.[1] Changes of attitudes toward the Sudan's population situation are beginning to occur at the highest government echelons, but how long will it take before they are translated into new attitudes and practices at the grass roots, or for that matter, at the ambassadorial level? In essence, as recently as 1982 the ambassador to Ottawa reiterated the sentiment of the chief gynecologist of the hospital at Khartoum, who said: "But everyone . . . appreciates that the Sudan needs <u>more</u> population. Definitely we are aware that we haven't got a population <u>problem</u>."[2]

Linked in with the attitudes toward population growth and therefore family planning are the attitudes toward women and their role in the population equation. It is of relatively little importance if women are granted rights under a country's constitution or legal system or under Muslim law if they are illiterate and ignorant of those rights or how to use them. As a woman member of the regional parliament in Southern Sudan said: "Our constitution grants women equal rights in all walks of life, equal pay, equal job opportunity and so on, but there are times when people exploit the ignorance of our women. Not many of our women know what is in the Constitution."[3]

Rights are of little importance if men believe that women should produce many children to satisfy the male vision of a large, strong country or if women themselves pass on attitudes of ignorance from generation to generation, although they may be against the very attitudes or practices they transmit. Such an ambivalence is seen with respect to female circumcision, widely practiced in the Sudan and other African and Muslim countries. Despite women knowing that female circumcision causes pain, trauma, hemorrhage, infection, intercourse and childbirth difficulties, urine retention, and other complications, they—the mothers, aunts, grandmothers—still insist that young girls endure torture at the hands of quack midwives without the benefit of anesthetics, antibiotics, or antitetanus treatment. If the girl is lucky she will endure minor circumcision or ablation of the clitoris. If she is unlucky she will suffer the cutting off of the labia minora and majora, sometimes down to the bone; she will then be tightly sewn up, leaving the smallest hole for menstruation. At childbirth she will be cut open with an episiotomy and resewn afterward. It is not unusual for women to undergo this process eight or ten times or to get themselves "tightened up" for their husbands.

Why does female circumcision persist? The men claim that the women want it or because virginity must be preserved. The women claim that the men like it and it is done for men's pleasure. Also, they say that women are not expected to enjoy sex; if they do, they are castigated as being loose and could be discarded by their husbands. Circumcision thus is supposed to eliminate all feeling and desire. Many men and women claim that it is a tradition blessed by Allah that should be perpetuated in the name of Allah. Steeped in ignorance, it is difficult for them to go against social opinion, tradition, and religiosity.

Even in Egypt, the first Muslim country to launch a national population policy (in 1960), where concern about population matters is greater and education at all levels is higher and more universal than in most Muslim countries, attitudes and practices have been only gradually changed. Laws have been promulgated to eradicate female circumcision and to promote contraception and family planning. Female circumcision has become less frequent and then usually practiced only in a minor form. Women have become increasingly aware of the benefits of family planning and smaller families and are encountering less resistance from husbands and old-timers in using contraceptives—that is, if they tell them, which for discretion's sake they often do not. But apart from the lack of family-planning infrastructure and adequate medical and paramedical services to reach out to Egypt's 45 million people, population policy still runs into the barrier of religion. Educated Egyptian women interviewed by Perdita Huston said that "religious leaders confuse family-planning efforts with the overall emancipation of women, and 'though the religious leaders might accept the arguments for population control, they cannot for the life of them consent to the emancipation of women.'"[4] They frequently mentioned religion as a factor hindering progress.

When it comes to analyzing the causes of a Muslim's country's population growth rate, it becomes necessary to look beyond the hard demographic and economic data to the unquantifiables of religion, tradition, and attitudes toward women's emancipation. Women's emancipation is the sine qua non of population planning, but if it is resisted by religious leaders for religious reasons, then progress on the population front will be halted or severely retarded. The observable differences in population growth rates among the different Muslim countries are therefore in part attributable to the state of women's emancipation and the attitudes of religious leaders toward family planning and women's integration into development. Such differences are also dependent on the extent to which secular leaders manipulate religion and tradition for their own purposes. For instance, the lowest population growth rate (of 1.9 percent per annum) is that of the most Europeanized country, Turkey, where secularization and women's emancipation occurred at an early stage of modernization. The highest rate is Iraq's, at 3.4 percent. (Kuwait's 8.2 percent rate is heavily skewed by immigration.) Somewhere in between lie the population increase rates of the other countries, with a list to the higher side.[5] It will be interesting to observe Iran's population growth rate now that Iranian women are being sent back to the chador and away from emancipation and the emphasis is on women's breeding role for the glory of the Islamic state.

Overall, mortality rates are generally declining in the Muslim countries. The lows of 7 and 8 deaths per 1,000 for Kuwait and Malaysia demonstrate the efficacy of their public health schemes. Even a high of 26 per 1,000 for Afghanistan, with its general lack of medical facilities, its political chaos, and its primitive attitudes toward women and childcare,[6] is a substantial improvement over the mortality rates of two generations ago. Fertility rates, however, continue to be substantially higher than death rates, ranging from 37 per 1,000 for Malaysia to 52 per 1,000 for Morocco,[7] thereby accounting for the sudden upturn in population growth. Even though infant mortality rates are still high (appallingly high for countries like Niger at 200 per 1,000), overall mortality rates for some countries have already bottomed out at 7 or 8 deaths per 1,000, a normal level for Western industrialized countries.

In many Islamic countries, mortality rates still hold a great potential for sharp decreases through public health measures and economic development. Unfortunately, due to the inattention paid to family planning and contraception as essential features of public health programs, their fertility rates are hardly likely to show equivalent declines. The consequent widening gap between mortality and fertility rates presages one certainty for the future: a rapidly increasing and doubling population. Without population-restraint measures, Muslim countries on average can expect to double their populations in only 23 years. Kuwait will accomplish that feat in only 9 years, while Gambia, despite its adult and infant mortality rates approaching fertility rates, will take just 37 years.[8] While swiftly reducing mortality rates is a popularly accepted goal, a parallel reduction of fertility rates is less sanguinely regarded by most Muslim governments. It might well be asked why their timidity or reluctance to encourage fertility-rate reduction when research, increasingly undertaken among women by women, shows categorically that most women themselves on average want no more than between two and four children. They want good health and a good life for themselves and their children. They see the connection between fewer children and social and economic benefits. They want and are prepared to use family-planning devices. But will they be supported in those wants by the men—whether husbands or political leaders?

In addition to the problems arising from doubling, population shifts in age structure and distribution will create additional burdens on the economy. The dependency burdens that will arise from lower mortality rates and high birth rates will become accentuated. Already, most Muslim countries are experiencing the difficulties of coping with the consequences of a fast-growing population. The problem is exacerbated by the fact that a substantial part (on average 44 percent) of their population is under the age of 15, relatively unproductive, and unable to contribute taxes or capital to their countries' economies. Simultaneously, these under-15s require vast outlays of money and effort for their education, health, and welfare. With a few exceptions (Libya, Kuwait, Saudi Arabia), per capita income is low ($80 for Afghanistan to $330 for Malaysia).[9] Health services are generally poor, and illiteracy, particularly for females, is high. More unproductive children and youth, euphemistically termed an increased dependency burden, will merely intensify existing problems, put pressure on existing facilities, and stretch to a breaking point limited financial resources. Even the most finely tuned development plans will not be able to counteract that trend, except perhaps in those countries that are oil rich, unless population measures are taken to help extricate the majority of Muslims from a state of impoverishment, ill health, and illiteracy. Needless to say, there are those who claim that Islam will act as an effective block to any such action.

Non-Muslims typically perceive Islam as a strongly pronatalist faith and often contend, as Dudley Kirk did, that it "has been a more effective barrier to the diffusion of family planning than Catholicism."[10] While Islamic scholars might agree that Islam is inherently pronatalist, they strongly object to it being portrayed as a major barrier to family planning and the use of contraception. The truth probably lies somewhere in between the two views.

At Islam's formal level there is considerable flexibility that would allow the practice of family planning. Within the Koran, the Prophet's sayings (hadith) and traditions (sunna), the consensus of Islamic theologians (ulama), and the analogies (al-qiyas)—the four basic sources of formal Islamic jurisprudence—are directives on marriage, sex, procreation, celibacy, children, and family. On the whole they are not incompatible with family planning, population-growth limitation, and contraception. Even abortion and sterilization are treated with a fair amount of latitude and practicality.

The treatment of family planning and contraception at the folkloric level of Islam, where the evil eye, spirits, incantations, and mystical herbal brews still enfold the people, is quite another matter. There Islam, combined with rusticity and mysticism and manipulated by uneducated village priests and others with semblances of religious aura and authority, is probably a very effective barrier to change of any kind.

Most modern Islamic scholars would neither dispute the need for family planning in the Muslim world nor use religious injunctions against it. They would exercise the flexibility and practicality inherent within Islamic jurisprudence, which not only does not disfavor the dissemination of family planning and methods but permits it, subject to the interests of the joint couple, the family, and society. However, although neither Islamic theologians nor Islamic jurisprudence constitute effective barriers to family planning, they may inadvertently contribute to barriers by being out of touch with the masses and the village priests, or imams, who often exercise the most sway over the people.

Religious barriers need not be formal, written, doctrinaire. They can be folklore and customs held dear by the masses and transposed into tenacious religiosity. They can be misinterpretations of holy scriptures and theological doctrine by local priests. They can also be blind adherence to one or two notable passages that reinforce custom and customary attitudes because qualifying passages that would otherwise elucidate the chosen verses are excluded.

Barriers also arise from Islam's diffuse, unorganized nature, which mitigates against close communication between authoritative

Islamic scholars and the local, popular-level priests. This lack of contact consistently prevents new concepts and interpretations in light of changing conditions from filtering down to the masses. In that respect Islam is an effective and enduring barrier to family planning.

Muslim political leaders, whether former presidents Sukarno and Nasser, a present leader like Qaddafi, or a deposed dictator like Idi Amin, by their refusal to introduce population policies in other than the encouragement of breeding, lend credence to the accusation that Islam is a barrier to family planning. Their close association with Islam, the intertwining of political Islam with religious Islam, and leaders' invocations of religion as a reason for not instituting birth control programs reinforce that suspicion. They thereby do a disservice to their religion that becomes misunderstood abroad; to their religious scholars, whose opinions are disregarded or misinterpreted; and to their own people, who are left to suffer the consequences of archaic, half-understood beliefs. With their lead reinforced by ancient and modern scholars' interpretations, Islam in fact could be a very positive force in influencing fertility behavior, sending fertility rates down rather than traditionally up.

Many eminent Muslim savants recognize that modern conditions are drastically changed from Muhammad's day. Less hands are needed in the fields, in family businesses, and in households, while many mouths still remain to be fed, many minds to be educated, and many bodies to be clothed. The productivity of children is decreasing, while the costs of supporting and educating them is increasing. Parents are becoming caught in a squeeze between modern developments and age-old beliefs.

Most parents as yet emphasize the quantity of children rather than the quality and unwittingly contribute to their own and to society's problems. Women believe—and their local religious leaders reinforce that belief—that Islam directs them to procreate and multiply. Moreover, parents believe, exhibiting their customary stoic fatalism, that "Allah will provide" and that they will somehow manage, however tenuously. Besides, if they do reduce their fertility and have fewer children than their neighbors, they run the gamut of guilt feelings, public ridicule and scorn, religious taunting for interfering with God's plan, and sensations of debasement. Many women fear contravening the Koran by limiting their families and practicing birth control, unaware that neither the Koran nor Islam forbid family planning. When told that the Koran says it is better to have few children and to give them a proper life, women tend to respond that they wish they had know that earlier, before they had so many children.

As Omran points out, Islam is sufficiently practical and flexible to allow adjustments to changing conditions without detracting from its basic principles. "Since Islam is meant for all nations at all times, it must face up to changing social and environmental patterns over time, and it carries within its doctrine plans for such change." Further, "Islam anticipated problems arising from population pressure and its economic impact." This was demonstrated by the prophet Muhammad saying, "The Day of Judgment will not be until the child becomes a nuisance", "The most gruelling trial is to have plenty of children with no adequate means"; and "A mother shall not be pressed unfairly for her child, nor a father for his child."[11] If this understanding of Islam could be conveyed to women, much of the social and religious pressure to have children yearly would be lifted from women's backs. It would help to reinforce those development, education, and health measures that are perceived as crucial to bringing down fertility rates.

The success of family-planning programs in predominantly Muslim countries will largely depend upon how successfully religious and political leaders convince their constituents that by practicing birth control and restricting family size they will not be contravening Muhammad's teachings, the Koran, and Islamic jurisprudence. The masses will need to be reassured that they are not committing <u>haram</u> (that which is forbidden, wrong, or illegal). They (and particularly the least educated, the women) will need to be weaned away from the tightly held folk beliefs and religiosity that detract from Islam's inherent flexibility with education, information, and persuasion.

The stagnation or immobilization of Islamic societies faced with a difficult population situation arises from four strongly held precepts. First and foremost is the rule that marriage is for every person, man and woman. There are many sayings and traditions of the prophet Muhammad that support this and have in effect relegated singleness to social Coventry. Unlike Jesus, Paul, and the patriarchal fathers, who placed spirituality achieved through asceticism and celibacy above family and marriage, Muhammad said: "Marriage is my 'sunna' (way). He who ignores my 'sunna' is not my follower ('laisa minu')." "The evil-doers of my nation are the bachelors in it."[12]

Second, Islam frowns upon celibacy other than that before marriage and upon sexual activity outside marriage. However, within marriage, sexual gratification is deemed not only necessary but also highly desirable. Traditionally Islam has not deemed sexuality repugnant or debasing, as has Christianity, provided it was kept within the bounds of sacred marriage. In old Arabia before Islam, sexual relations were condemned as an evil necessity worthy only of contempt, and therefore women were treated as the instruments of debasement. "Against that [backdrop], Islam considered those relations as sacred and clean, and maintained that they must be practiced with care."[13]

Muhammad tried to rectify the social conditions surrounding marriage and to improve society's attitudes toward marriage and sex by inculcating in couples mutual love, tenderness, and respect within their marriages, their sexual relations, and the procreation of children. To a large extent he succeeded, but even today folkloric beliefs depicting sexual relations, menarche, and childbearing as unclean and contaminating activities requiring purification rituals still prevail and counteract the Prophet's teachings.

A third factor is that only a tiny proportion of Muslim women (somewhat under 3 percent) never marry during their reproductive lives. Most are married throughout the entirety of their reproductive lives, and many who are divorced or widowed remarry. Unlike in Hinduism or pre-Islamic society, divorcees and widows are not socially shunned or restricted from remarrying.

Last, Muslims have traditionally married at a young age. In the past, marriage for Arab Levant girls—and most young Muslim females everywhere—occurred soon after puberty. This in itself was regarded as an improvement over Ottoman law, which specified nine as the legal age of marriage for girls. Today the trend is toward later marriage—in the range of 17 to 22—especially among urban dwellers and the better educated. Early marriage of girls is still perpetuated in the rural agrarian societies because of parental conservatism and obsession with codes of modesty and honor; traditional concern with premarital chastity, which is automatically assumed to be tarnished the longer wedding arrangements are postponed; and familial preoccupation with suitable bride price or dowries from husbands' families. Rural parents are still more likely to exclude their daughters from discussions about their prospective husbands or marriage arrangements than urban parents. And prospective in-laws in the rural areas are inclined to want an unformed, malleable bride who can be easily incorporated into the joint household and trained in household duties. [14]

In the past, the gap in age between bride and bridegroom was considerable, the bride often just out of puberty and the bridegroom in his 20s or 30s. This gap was attributable to the father's (or male relative's) urgent duty to marry off the girl before any codes of modesty or honor were damaged and to Muhammad's injunctions to young men not to marry until they were sufficiently mature and financially able to support a wife and family. With the greater emphasis on female education and the recognition that education can often improve marriage chances, parents—urban more so than rural—are acquiescing to postponed marriages. Muslim girls are marrying later, and the age gap between males and females is closing.

By and large Muslims have not suffered the consequences of a preoccupation with celibacy, asceticism, and monasticism as Cath-

olics have. However, it might well be contended that excess concentration on modesty, chastity, and virginity, with their corollaries
of circumcision, seclusion, and segregation, has achieved the same
results: the relegation of women to strict domesticity, unending
pregnancies, and unceasing child rearing. It might be contended
that the main difference between the two faiths is that in Catholicism
sexual gratification must be denied except when justified by procreation, and in Islam sexual gratification must not be denied, hence procreation. Thus denial and gratification converge at the same apex:
procreation.

Islam, like Catholicism and Hinduism, has perpetuated a dual
notion of womanhood and a paradox. On the one hand, woman is
exalted and glorified as a wife, submissive to her husband and to male
domination, and as a mother of many children (preferably sons). On
the other hand, she is treated as an inferior human being whose sexuality is a source of evil, guilt, shame, and temptation and who must
be rigidly controlled by numerous social strictures. Either way she
is not seen as an integrated whole, a total human being with unfulfilled
potential and untapped resources.

Muhammad (and Islam) effectively set the stage for family
planning with his emphasis on financial and health considerations in
marriage. The prohibition of sexual intercourse during nursing
(ghail) arose from the fear of weakening the mother with another premature pregnancy and depriving the suckling child of its main source
of nutritious food during its most tenuous and most formative years.
Today, as in Muhammad's time, in tropical countries premature
weaning and the replacement of mother's milk by often contaminated
animal milk or baby formula in unsterilized receptacles and the premature introduction of unnourishing, starchy solids are among the
major causes of deadly infant gastroenteritis and other intestinal-
tract diseases. One of the most commonly quoted sunna of Muhammad,
which support ghail, is that attributed to Abu Dawud. "Do not kill
your children under false pretenses, for the suckling of the child
when the mother is pregnant has the same effect as when a horseman
is overtaken by an opponent and thrown off the horse."[15] Furthermore, the Koran explicitly recommends suckling for two years and,
impliedly, abstaining from sexual relations for that duration.
"Mothers, when divorced, shall give suck to their children two full
years, if their father desire that the suckling be completed."[16]

As Muhammed el-Mekki el-Naciri points out, Islamic scholars
are generally agreed that such directives have five main results:

Improved infant health and safety
Improved wife's health and safety
Respite and rest from pregnancy, and precautions against post-preg-
nancy complications

Sufficient parental time and devotion for the existing child, without
    further immediate distraction and hardships
Reasonable intervals between births and responsible spacing of
    children[17]

Prolonged lactation and abstinence were, therefore, both accorded
favor by Muhammad and his traditions, Koranic directives, and Muslim jurisprudence. In themselves they demonstrate that family planning was neither unknown 1,400 years ago nor inadmissible. Considerable awareness of the effect of frequent pregnancies on the health
of both mother and child was evinced. When allied with other Islamic
considerations of health, welfare, happiness, financial security, and
even national interest, it can be appreciated that neither Muhammad
nor Islam generally—except for the most conservative elements—condemned family-planning practices that were conducive to the stability
of the family, the cornerstone of Muslim society.

    The acknowledgment by Muhammad and eminent Muslim jurists
of the need to adopt measures that would stop pregnancy and cause
the temporary (sometimes interpreted as indefinite) cessation of procreation was further reinforced by the Prophet's apparent acceptance
of azl, or coitus interruptus. The main sunna attributed to Muhammad
to support his acceptance of azl, accepted by all Muslim scholars as
genuine, is that related by Jabir, one of his companions. "We used
to practice 'azl'; during the time of the Prophet while the Qur'an was
being revealed. The Prophet came to know about it but did not forbid us."[18]

    Azl has been opposed and even denounced by some Muslim
jurists on the grounds that it is a form of minor infanticide or is
equivalent to the burial of children alive. The majority of jurists,
however, counter this argument by maintaining that the prevention
of the start of life, which is not even stage one of the seven stages of
life formation, is not tantamount to infanticide. Life cannot be killed
if it has not been initiated. Additionally they contend that were azl
in disfavor or countenanced to be avoided by sunna, coitus interruptus
is neither specifically prohibited by Koranic texts or traditions nor
by analogical reasoning (qiyas) based on a precedent for which a text
is available. Therefore neither texts nor precedents disfavor azl.

    The early Muslims were obviously acquainted with a wide va-
riety of contraceptive methods, of which azl was the most customary
and the most reliable. Early Islamic medical textbooks both described
and prescribed birth control methods, including for example, azl;
abstinence; prolonged lactation; massage; suppositories concocted
from herbs, mud, and herbal (and sometimes poisonous) brews; and
other concoctions and abortifacients. Muhammad's apparent approach
was that if it did not work then it was God's will that a woman should

conceive, rather than the opposite approach adopted by the Catholics that it is God's will that women and men should not practice contraception.

For the most part, leading Muslim scholars have acknowledged the exigency of population pressures on the family and on society and have acceded to the use of traditional and modern birth control methods. The use of modern methods is seen as a mere transposition or extrapolation from azl. The majority would probably echo Muhammed el-Mekki el-Naciri's sentiment that "actually nothing justifies any hesitation in advocating the use of the other preventive methods of this age because they are substitutes for 'azl' and have identical aims."[19]

From Islam's sunna, which designated under what conditions azl could be practiced, analogies have been drawn to indicate when the newer birth control methods might be used. Past reasons for practicing azl were many and varied: avoidance of pregnancy during nursing; husbandly dissatisfaction with his wife and refusal to have children by her; and wartime practices of capture, ransoming, and slavery. Extreme financial necessity was regarded as a minor motivation. Whatever the reasons, they were regarded by the incomparable Islamic jurist al-Ghazzali as being perfectly sufficient and valid for past motives and future precedents. Drawing upon precedent and analogous reasoning and exhibiting considerable flexibility and practicality, he (and his successors) permitted azl to prevent a woman's life from being endangered by pregnancy, to protect her health, to preserve her beauty, and to ensure the health of her present and future children and, hence, the family's well-being. In essence he reduced the pressure on women to breed nonstop and he helped to remove the guilt or embarrassment so often endemic to women trying to control their fertility. Further, al-Ghazzali allowed that azl was permissible to limit the number of children if the family was in difficult financial straits and if additional offspring were liable to force the father into debt, dishonest living, or embarrassing situations. Thus men too could limit the size of their families without the fear of being thought unmanly.

From straitened family finances, successive jurists have been able to extrapolate to generally depressed economic and social conditions when work is unobtainable. The most enlightened jurists have then urged the reduction of family size to ease family burdens, recognizing that a strong Islamic society is not based upon a mere multiplicity of children. Their viewpoint has not been without opposition from conservative Muslims who still envisage women as fast breeder-reactors and still believe that numbers equal quality.

Contrary to popular myth, formal Islam advocates quality to the extent that, should quantity detract from quality, quality must prevail. Islam undoubtedly sees procreation as a way of expanding its constituency and finding more true believers for Allah. But Islam adds the caveat that those believers must be strong—physically, mentally, and spiritually—and not weak. Fewer strong followers are preferred to larger quantities of weaklings. This is again in contrast with formal Catholicism, which envisages procreation as a method of obtaining a prodigious number of souls for God and the faith, irrespective of quality.

If there is no outright Islamic prohibition of azl and other contraceptive practices; if there is legal, emotional, physical, and financial validity for restricting multitudes of children; and if there is considerable latitude to do so, why has Islam the reputation for being against family planning and birth control? As with Christianity, much of the blame can be laid on the excessive and simplistic use of two Islamic expressions about marriage and reproduction. Taken out of context, they have been used to justify indiscriminate and unreasoning procreation and pronatalism. Their inherent simplicity, without mentally confusing elaboration, has appealed to and been absorbed by people's basic instincts and motives.

The texts have been promulgated by local priests, who frequently have not the intelligence, education, or the willingness to understand them in their full contextual background of the Koran, past Arab social and demographic conditions, Muhammad's sayings and traditions, Islamic jurists' reasonings, and Muslim legislation. Public, priests, and politicians alike have limpetlike clung to the two traditions on marriage: "Marry and beget children" and "Marry so that you multiply because I will make display of you in front of the other nations on the Day of Judgment even I will make a display of those prematurely born (alsiqt)."[20] These texts, which have been quoted ad nauseum to support pronatalism and nonstop reproduction, have been supported by past social customs and economic conditions that have traditionally necessitated a multiplicity of children. Unless and until eminent Islamic jurists and scholars are better able to convey formal Islam's pro-family-planning view to the masses, local antibirth control forces will carry the day among the public. Fertility will continue to rise; ill-nourished children will continue to be produced; women, weakened by successive pregnancies, will perpetuate backwardness; and Islam will fail to live up to its potential.

In the more richly endowed countries—Saudi Arabia, Kuwait, the United Arab Emirates, Iran, Libya—where a major economic constraint against having ever more children has been removed or modified by oil wealth, pressure may be reexerted on women to produce more children than they either want or need. Muslim jurists there, being of a more conservative bent than their counterparts in such countries as Egypt, Malaysia, and Indonesia, might well use

Islam to reinforce their pronatalism bias. If they did, they could detrimentally affect population policies and advancement-of-women policies in other parts of the Muslim world besides their own. And Islam would continue to be labeled a barrier to family planning and development.

Theoretically Islam is opposed to abortion and sterilzation. But careful consideration of Islamic jurisprudence shows that the latitude that obtains for the implementation of family planning and birth control also prevails for abortion and sterilization. Whether Muslim or not, abortion already does exist and has existed since time immemorial in countries throughout the world. What is more, it will continue to exist if viable alternatives are not made readily available. Again, whether in Muslim countries or not, abortion is on the increase, both among those women who are motivated to adopt family planning and limit family size and among those who are less motivated but are finally driven to the wall, to abortion, by too many children.

Several factors have contributed to the increase of abortion. Those that have influenced the public to limit fertility and family size, comprise modernization and urbanization, nationalism and a consciousness of congestion and environmental degradation, and a general though vague awareness of the health hazards of excessive fertility for the individual and community. Some factors affecting private inclination and motivation toward smaller families include the increasing economic liability of children and their improved chances of survival; the emancipation of women; the declining influences of parents and relatives; and the perceived trend, through media and government, toward smaller families. Together these private and public motivations have helped to create an atmosphere in which contraception and family limitation are more tolerated.

The majority of women who resort to abortion to achieve those private and publicly supported goals do so reluctantly, when failure looms and desperation sets in. Failure to control fertility and to prevent a pregnancy is often owing to a woman having no access to family planning and counseling clinics, birth control information, and inexpensive contraceptives. She is often the subject of retrograde legislation and societal pressure while bearing the brunt of her husband's unwillingness to practice birth control or suffering the consequences of well-motivated but inexperienced contraception use. Only a tiny minority of women consciously and deliberately use abortion as a contraceptive when viable alternatives are available.

It is not only Muslim countries that have repressive legal codes that treat abortion as a criminal act and that severely punish the woman and, on occasion, the abortionist. And it is not only the ethical and cultural code of Muslim physicians, largely determined by their religious bias (as in non-Muslim countries) that mitigates against the proper counseling and treatment of women who seek birth control or ultimately abortion. Regardless of whether the codes are Muslim or not, the consequences for women are disastrous. If these codes continue, as Omran points out, "to push women with unwanted pregnancies into the squalor of shanties and the hands of butchers, the inevitable result will not only include unnecessary maternal mortality and morbidity but a deluge of complicated, septic abortion cases requiring extensive medical care and services."[21] Just as an example of the economic waste that prevails when viable alternatives to abortion and medically safe and monitored abortion facilities are not provided, Omran noted that 50 percent of the cost of maternity services in Cairo University Hospital alone was due to illegally performed abortions. This is neither atypical for other Muslim countries nor for countries as far removed as Argentina and Thailand. And anyone who has toiled in the emergency wards of Canadian or U.S. hospitals can see the awful aftermath of botched abortions. But the fact is typically suppressed. The waste of life, energy, and money is enormous and unnecessary. So too is the fear, pain, and guilt imposed on women.

Muslim politicians inevitably, like politicians worldwide, shy away from advocating the legalization of abortion on the grounds that it would be contrary to religious principles and would encourage permissiveness. They refuse to acknowledge the existing fact that abortion does exist and is assuming epidemic—some would say pandemic—proportions. They dismiss the fact that the repugnancy of abortion is not eliminated by illegalizing it on the one hand and by refusing to provide satisfactory alternatives to it on the other. They exhibit irresponsibility, if not cowardice, by attributing their refusal to liberalize family planning and to legalize abortion to religious principles when their religion in fact provides them with some latitude for reversing direction.

In the Koran itself there is no statement for or against abortion. Instead, there is an exposition on fetal development as it was understood in ancient times and on ensoulment, or the stage of fetal development at which the body is presumed to become imbued with soul. Modern Muslim scholars have used these expositions as the starting point for their discourses upon the permissible or forbidden nature of abortion.

First and foremost is the Koranic statement about fetal development. "Then we placed him, a moist germ in a safe abode; then made we the moist germ a clot of blood; then made the clotted blood into a piece of flesh into bones; and we clothed the bones with flesh; then brought forth man of yet another make."[22] Authoritative interpretations of this passage by such renowned scholars as Imam Ali, the fourth caliph; Umar; Ali; and others confirmed this concept of

fetal development. Furthermore, they affirmed that azl was not equivalent to minor wa'd (early infanticide, especially of females) because
the process of development of the fetus had not been started, let alone
arrested.

The next stage of determining whether abortion had occurred
was the stage at which ensoulment was presumed to happen. Islamic
scholars practically unanimously agree that a soul does not automatically and simultaneously occur with fertilization but rather enters
the body at a later stage of pregnancy. They turn for guidance on
this point to one especially relevant Hadith: "The germ of one of you
is concentrated in his mother's womb in the form of a drop for 40
days; then he becomes the clot of blood for the same period; then he
becomes a piece of flesh for the same period; then the angel is sent
to him to ensoul him."[23]

Religious literature, using this as authoritative precedent,
thereafter deemed that ensoulment occurs 120 days or three stages
after the initial conception. Therefore, the expulsion of a fetus before
it received its soul, up to 120 days after conception, was not deemed
wa'd, or infanticide, by the majority of ulama.

Interestingly most ulama, regardless of their religious pro-
clivities or attitudes toward abortion in general, favor induced abortion no matter what the gestation period if the mother's life is endangered by pregnancy. The reasoning for this is best summed up by a
fatwa of Sheikh Mahmud Shaltut.

> If the continuation of pregnancy endangers the mother's
> life and if the only way to save her life is by inducing
> abortion, it becomes mandatory that abortion should be
> induced because the mother's life is independent and
> she is the origin of the foetus and the support for the
> family, and it is not logical to sacrifice her life in
> order to save the foetus with a dependent life.[24]

Thus Islam not only allows abortion but requires it for a mother's
safety and health regardless of gestation period. Otherwise Islam
permits abortion for medical reasons up to 120 days after conception
and before ensoulment and then thereafter prohibits it.

Muslim theologians are no different from any other group of
theologians or laity in experiencing heated debate over whether abortion is allowable within the context of Islam or should be allowed for
other than medical reasons. Some (Zaidis, Hanafis and Shafi'is) condone abortion for any reason prior to the stage of ensoulment or the
120-day limit. Others (the more conservative group of Hanafis and
Shafi'is) have deemed it makruh, or disfavorable without sufficient
occasion to justify it. Yet others, notably the Maliki theologians

totally prohibit abortion, although a few of their number consider it mainly makruh.[25]

On the whole, however, formal Islam is remarkably tolerant of abortion in the early stages of pregnancy. While religious leaders and politicians alike might understandably deplore the use of abortion as a contraceptive, they have sufficient religious sanction to condone the legalization of abortion and thereby wipe out the miscreants who yearly perpetuate untold suffering on hundreds of thousands of women. As discussed earlier, they also have sufficient religious justification for the provision of an extensive family-planning and contraceptives program as a viable substitute for abortion. By using the sanctions granted to them, they could bring women, anxious to avoid untimely pregnancies and abortions, within the orbit of trained medical staff who could counsel them on family planning and the proper use of contraceptives and steer them away from the misery of further unwanted pregnancies and botched abortions. They could substantially contribute to the reduction of fertility and national population growth without jeopardizing their religious principles and strengthen Islam and their nations in accordance with Muhammad's teachings.

Theoretically, Islam is also against sterilization, but this opposition is based more upon inferences gleaned from Koranic passages than from direct religious interdictions against sterilization as such. Objections have grown out of Koranic passages that portray Satan's determination to alter God's creation[26] (sterilization is seen as both a Satanical act and an alteration) and from reported narratives and traditions prohibiting castration.[27]

Probably the most vehement objection to sterilization arises from ignorance and myth, which equate sterilization with castration. Not only do the uneducated masses suffer from this misapprehension, but so do better-educated religious and political leaders. Since it is equated with physical disfigurement, loss of virility, and emotional or psychological imbalances and since it allegedly contravenes the Prophet's specific prohibitions against celibacy and castration, sterilization has been subjected to a welter of emotionalism and irrationality. Sterilization is especially objected to when it is applicable to men. As in most non-Muslim countries, the onus of preventing births tends to fall on the woman. It is of less moment if a woman has a tubal ligation or a hysterectomy, even though those methods are more physically punishing to a woman than a vasectomy is to a man. Fear of vasectomies tends to be rooted in men's fear of dismemberment, whereas women's fear is rooted in the fear of God and in the myth that sterilization will kill someone. Thus folkloric mythology, which is still deeply engrained in the masses, has contributed to this lack of logical analysis by equating sterilization with the evil eye, demon spirits, and Satanic works.

Without specific Islamic prohibitions against sterilization, its lawfulness and permissibility may be assumed provided it is taken with the mutual consent of both spouses. The failure to obtain mutual consent can render the act of sterilization unlawful, since it would be considered an act of aggression against the right of procreation that is due to the nonconsenting spouse. Additionally, the Imam of the Muslims, as the head of the Muslim community, can prohibit it for secondary reasons or special circumstances, such as in the (temporary) interest of the nation or in the interest of one of the spouses, provided that such action is in accordance with general Koranic tenets and Prophetic traditions.

Nevertheless, to counteract the suspicions and misconceptions of the majority of people, considerably more than proclamations by enlightened and knowledgeable spiritual leaders will be needed. Concerted, broad-based leadership demonstrating its approval and acceptance of sterilization plus public education will be needed to convince the public that sterilization is not castration, not loss of virility, not contravention of spiritual directives, not social ostracization, and not against God's will.

Despite Muslim objections to Islam being labeled a barrier to family planning, nevertheless there seems to be little correlation between the consensus of Muslim theologians favoring family planning and its methods and the public maintaining their traditional high levels of fertility and large families. For people brought up in a tradition of many children, family limitation appears to contravene nature, custom, and religion. Their objections are sustained by Koranic statements treated simplistically and taken out of context by local priests unaware of the sophisticated reasoning and analogies of their superiors. Most village priests, through their own lack of education, are not able to convey to their followers new concepts that are extrapolated from historic principles to fit modern conditions. Nor are many of them willing to, because of their conservatism, which treats of any kind of change with suspicion and intolerance, and because of their fear that their local prestige and influence would be abrogated by change and individualism.

The anti-family-planning attitudes of the uneducated masses and the local priests are inevitably reinforced by a strong, vociferous minority of conservative Islamic theologians and scholars who depict family limitation, birth control, and the emancipation of women as evil, dangerous, and sinful. They connect modernization and materialism with the disintegration of society, and that with the deterioration of the Muslim society's foundation, the family. They link the family's decline with birth control and family limitation, which are in turn linked with lax morality and permissiveness. They ascribe these to dangerous Western imports, designed to undermine Islam and the Islamic way of life. Whereupon, they totally repudiate programs that might be instrumental in controlling their expanding population and simultaneously improving the economic and social conditions of their people.

Islamic proponents of natalism, like advocates worldwide, dismiss the population problem as "bunk" and, ostrichlike, deny the existence of overpopulation; for them the problem is mainly one of underproduction. From that point it is easy for them to equate azl (coitus interruptus) with wa'd (infanticide) and, by extension, to condemn birth control of all kinds. They disallow contraception for every reason except if the mother's life is endangered by pregnancy and delivery, and even that exception is becoming jeopardized in countries where fundamentalist forces have taken or are taking hold. Otherwise, they dismiss privation, starvation, famine, poverty, and extreme hardships as justifiable reasons for using contraceptives to limit family size. They invoke Muhammad's injunctions to marry, reproduce, and multiply, but ignore his and subsequent eminent jurists' cautions that marriage and reproduction should only be undertaken if economic, social, and health privations do not occur. They ultimately rest their case on fatalism. "He who does not marry for fear of having a large family has no trust in God"[28] and "If they are poor, God of His bounty will enrich them."[29]

Proponents of multitudinous births visualize strength in numbers, irrespective of quality. They see multiplicity as a means of strengthening the Islamic Empire and national power. Their advocacy of unlimited procreation, regardless of the costs to the individual (particularly to the woman), the family, or future society, and their condemnation of birth control are linked by a vision of glory, of Islam redoubt.

Abortion and sterilization are totally condemned by pronatalist extremists. They equate these acts (and contraception to a lesser degree) with genocide, the emasculation of life, and a rejection of the religious way of living and of things spiritual. They conjure up the fear that through the use of abortion and sterilization, attacks (largely by unknown, mysterious enemies) will be made to displace and eject their people from their riches and lands. They continue to play upon people's worst fears and deliberately or merely inadvertently, owing to their own ignorance, they cater to the ignorance of the masses. In effect they terrify uneducated and illiterate people by conjuring up bodily emasculation and revenge with such statements as "It [sterilization] is the prevention of reproduction through castration, through contraceptives or through the performance of an operation to the male or female to stop reproduction"[30] and "Consequently, to control births by preventing either husband or wife from begetting children is a crime for which full indemnity or blood-money has to be paid."[31]

Nonetheless, formal Islam's attitudes toward family planning, family limitation, birth control methods (traditional and modern), abortion, and sterilization are basically flexible and pragmatic. Though pronatalist, Islam has within it sufficient latitude and scope to mount an effective population-restraint program if its political leaders could really see the need for doing so. Some opposition would arise from conservative religious elements, but presumably, at the village level at any rate, their objections could be overridden by their spiritual leaders. Other obstacles would be created by the long-held myths and beliefs of villagers, which could be unraveled by education, information, and the use of convinced village leaders. More than Catholicism, Islam has a religious legacy that does not prevent the institution of population-oriented programs and their integration into social and economic development. But do its religious leaders have the motivation, will, and organization to introduce full-scale population policies? And will they interpret Islam sufficiently flexibly to allow women the freedom to decide how many children to bear and what modern, safe contraceptives to use without the approval of their menfolk?

NOTES

1. Perdita Huston, Message from the Village (New York: Epoch B. Foundation, 1978), pp. 44-45.
2. Ibid., p. 45.
3. Ibid., p. 54.
4. Ibid., p. 31.
5. Abdel Rahim Omran, "Islam's Natality Design," in Islam and Family Planning, report of the proceedings of the International Islam Conference held in Morocco, December 1971 (Beirut: International Planned Parenthood Federation, 1974), 1: 217, 225.
6. Ibid.
7. Ibid.
8. Ibid.
9. Ibid.
10. Dudley Kirk, "Factors Affecting Muslim Natality," in Family Planning and Population Programs, ed. Bernard Berelson et al. (Chicago: University of Chicago, 1966), pp. 561-79.
11. Omran, "Islam's Natality Design," pp. 233-34.
12. Sheikh Muhammad Mahdi Shamsuddin, "Islam and the Planning of Parenthood," in Islam and Family Planning 2:61.
13. Ibid.
14. Edwin Terry Prothro and Lutfy Najib Diab, Changing Family Patterns in the Arab East (Beirut: American University of Beirut, 1974), pp. 25-26.

15. Muhammed el-Mekki el-Naciri, "Family Planning in Light of Muslim Legislation," in Islam and Family Planning 2: 44.

16. Koran 2: 23.

17. el-Mekki el-Naciri, "Family Planning," pp. 44-45.

18. Ibid., pp. 51-52.

19. Ibid., p. 55.

20. Ibid., p. 59.

21. Abdel R. Omran, "Abortion in the Natality Transition," in Islam and Family Planning 2: 336.

22. Koran 23: 12-14.

23. Omran, "Abortion in the Natality Transition," p. 340.

24. Ibid.

25. Ibid., pp. 341-42.

26. Koran 4: 119-20 and 5: 90.

27. Muhammad H. Bahisti, "Rules of Abortion and Sterilization in Islamic Law," in Islam and Family Planning 2: 423-34.

28. Sheikh Abdul Rahman al-Khayyir, "The Attitude of Islam towards Abortion and Sterilization," in Islam and Family Planning 2: 345-61.

29. Koran 24: 32.

30. al-Khayyir, "The Attitude of Islam," p. 359.

31. Ibid.

14

CONCLUSIONS:
QUO VADIS?

The Prophet Muhammad said, "There is no compulsion in religion." Undoubtedly, his counterparts, Jesus and Buddha, would have agreed with him. Unfortunately, many of their followers in the past did not share that view. And many in the present do not, for compulsion in the name of religion not only still lives on but in many areas of the world is growing more and more vehement and virulent. Whereas 20, even 10, years ago a newspaper or magazine article on the political or social implications of religion would be rare, today they appear with amazing regularity, practically daily. They are an indication of the push and shove of modernization and custom, the turmoil and turbulence of people's confusion in a fast-changing, often incomprehensible, and sometimes frightening world. Modernization, or Westernization, is debited with evil, sin, apocalypse, corruption, and materialism rather than credited with improved health, expanded education, humane and humanistic practices, longer lives, and better food and water. From the debits arise bigots determined to right the wrongs by putting modernization on its ear and reverting to the "good old ways" of the rigid, religious path. For them, there is only compulsion in religion.

As might be expected, women are becoming the direct targets of that compulsion. And the gains (educational, economic, social, and political) that they have made over the last two decades could well be abrogated overnight. Already the situation has gone beyond the signs stage: in various countries already substantive efforts are being made to reduce women's status, to return them to another era.

The most obvious country is Iran, where under the dictates of the Ayatollah Khomeini, women's freedom has been severely curtailed in the name of religion. In Pakistan, where President Zia ul Haq has undertaken to Islamize the nation, the implementation of Is-

247

lamization has fallen into the hands not of the ulama (Islamic scholars) but of the maulvies, or local priests, who are renowned for their super- stitious beliefs and bigotry. While the federal shari'a court has stated that few of the central laws of Pakistan are repugnant to Islam and even allowed that women could serve as judges, the maulvies have prepared numerous antiwomen proposals. These include

> denying women the right to vote, or giving the female vote half the value of a male one; denying them the right to drive cars (as in Saudi Arabia); halving the bloodmoney paid for a female victim compared with a male victim; the death penalty for prostitution but for the woman only, not for the customer; [and] a proposal to set up an all-female university as a start to segregation in all higher education (again as in Saudi Arabia).[1]

So far the maulvi-backed Council of Islamic Ideologies and the Social Reform Committee have managed to get one antiwomen proposal implemented: the banning of Pakistani women from public sporting events, including school sports, the Asian Games, and Pakistan's na- tional games, even though the women said they were prepared to aban- don skimpy sportswear and play in the baggy shelwar trousers. An- other retrogressive step was taken when Pakistan's consultative as- sembly, the Majlis e Shura, amended the law of evidence to make the word of one male witness equivalent to that of two women.[2] It is contended by many that this distorts the Koran's specific injunctions and overall intentions. Lahore women protested this devaluation of their legal personality, but other than charges and injuries at the hands of the police, they do not know to what avail. Although many (educated) Pakistani men support the women (and their Women's Ac- tion Forum) and although President Zia is basically liberal and does not restrict the women of his own family, there is a strong likelihood that for political reasons he will capitulate to the pressure of the maulvies. It is unlikely that the maulvies, unconfined, will rest until their main enemy, the Westernized, educated Pakistani woman, is driven back into purdah, ignorance, and subjugation. If this occurs it will be contrary to the view of the founder of Pakistan, Jinnah, who said about women's rights: "We are the victims of evil customs. It is a crime against humanity that our women are shut up within the four walls of the houses as prisoners."[3]

But militant Islam is resurging not only in countries like Iran and Pakistan. It can be seen in countries as politically different as the Philippines, Sri Lanka, and Algeria. While in Algeria a good part of militant Islam is living in jails—the result of violent attacks on cinemas, bikinied tourists, and secular students—Islamic propaganda abounds and is growing. Those who would form an Islamic Algerian Republic would replace the Algerian national charter and constitution with the Koran and shari'a law; ban all political parties; and among many other exercises, abrogate women's rights and restrict female education to the elementary stage only. In contrast with General Zia, however, President Chadli Benjedid has stated that despite winds of "reactionary mysticism," no political philosophy exists in Algeria beyond the policies of Algeria's only political party, the Front de Liberation National (FLN). For the time being Algerian women's progress is protected, but they (and FLN politicians) will be subject to continuing pressure to yield to Islamization.

Religious reversionism is by no means confined to Islam. It has sprouted vigorously in Canada and the United States, particularly around reproductive choice and rights. In Canada Henry Morgentaler, who has attempted to provide safe medical conditions in Quebec, Ontario, Manitoba, and Saskatchewan for women requiring abortions, has been constantly harassed by antiabortionists. "Much of the antiabortion action has been tacitly and openly approved from Roman Catholic pulpits,"[4] and largely funded by fundamentalists and Catholic organizations. Yet almost three-quarters of the Canadian population (and 76.6 percent in Catholic Quebec) favors freedom of choice on abortion,[5] with the decision lying with the woman and her physician. In Michigan the Roman Catholic nun who directed the state's department of social affairs was ordered to resign her post by the Vatican. The reason for this action was that the agency, which oversees Medicare or government-paid health care for the poor, sustained the use of Medicare funds for abortions.[6] Legislative opposition and a federal ban on the use of such funds coupled with a diminution of funds for family planning and family-planning clinics are directly traceable to pressures from various religious sources to the particular detriment of indigent women and teenage girls.

No rational person can be in favor of abortion per se as an antidote to conception or as a form of contraception. By the same token, then, no one should object to contraception or the prevention of conceiving life if abortion can thereby be avoided. By providing one (contraception plus sound family-planning counseling and education), the other (abortion) could be largely minimized. But by condemning and preventing birth control, abortion becomes inevitable. The anguish of Pope John Paul II over the spectacle of "killing innocent creatures," of "destroying harmless innocent lives," is obviously acute; his concern for "the dignity of man—of his fundamental rights" (emphasis added) is deep-rooted.[7] But where is his anguish for living, suffering women? Where is his specific concern for their dignity and their basic rights, which include reproductive choice?

Certainly, he has assured "women in Italy and the whole world that the Church and the Pope pray for every one of them" and that "the Vatican would protect the dignity of every woman."[8] And he has gone further than other popes in calling for judicial equality between male and female workers through social legislation while urging that women who dedicate themselves to their families should not be subject to "psychological or actual discrimination" or "penalties in comparison with [their] counterparts."[9] But he still does not understand their needs in the area of reproduction, divorce, or remarriage; and he still undermines their status by not admitting them into full personhood in the church (by denying them ordination). His resistance to women's ordination has been paralleled by that of Archbishop Runcie of the Church of England, which also opposed ecclesiastical remarriage for divorced persons, although Runcie personally actually favored it.[10] The opposition to women's ordination and therefore complete equality is said to be based on "the conviction of the Church about this particular dimension [the call of men to the priesthood in accordance with prophetic tradition] of the gift of priesthood by which God has chosen to shepherd his flock."[11] While the pope denied that "the Church's traditional decision to call men to the priesthood, and not to call women, is not a statement about human rights, nor an exclusion of women from holiness and mission in the Church,"[12] nevertheless in many quarters that exclusion has been interpreted as an affront to women's equality and to human rights.

In contrast, Canadian Anglican bishops have increasingly accepted the theological argument that "when God became incarnate, He took upon Him 'our humanity', not just the half which we call male," and therefore Incarnation involves everyone. Accordingly, they find that continuing a practice that automatically excludes half of the human race from ordination because of their female sex is unacceptable. Indeed, some would affirm an English bishop's assertion that the "Christian Priesthood will never be complete until it includes both men and women."[13] Apart from these bishops, who testify that "such [female] priests have been a blessing to their dioceses" and are hard working, faithful, compassionate, and dedicated, many prelates have recognized that traditions (such as slavery) change and must change without necessarily undermining the authority of tradition. Others have admitted that they were slow to hear women's assurances of their call by God, while automatically accepting men's statements and working to have their call ratified by the church.[14]

The Anglican bishops and other clergy were enabled to come to their own decision as much by the General Synod's acceptance of women priests as by the conscience clause, which exempted them from pressure. As one bishop said: "The essence of the conscience clause is that we have mutual respect and understanding in love for one another. Our prayer will be that the priesthood of suitable women . . . may provide, under God, an enrichment for ministry in our world, whose every resource at our disposal should be utilized" (emphasis added).[15]

It is encouraging to see an Anglican bishop noting the need to use every resource at our disposal and a pope affirming the dignity of women and advocating equality between male and female workers. These are positive offsets to the fundamentalism of any religion that would set women back socially and economically. Will these positive affirmations be enough to counter regressive trends? What will happen if women's education and emancipation are curtailed? As Guy Hunter notes: "It is poverty which perpetuates poverty, and this truism applies as much to the mind as to the purse. Education, unless carried long and far, is powerless by itself to create the lively mind . . . [the process] will be greatly speeded up if women's education is not neglected."[16]

Women as much as men have been responsible for perpetuating myths, intolerance, and religiosity. They have been responsible for inculcating resistance to change and superstition in the next generation and for perpetuating ignorance. They have handed down customs detrimental to their own physical well-being and their children's. A case in point is the continued practice of female circumcision in Africa and the Middle East. While relatively well-educated and affluent African women might argue that the practice should continue because it is a rite of passage for young girls, a passage into womanhood and the human race, they fail to acknowledge the grave medical consequences (tetanus, dysmennorhea, perineal tearing, and obstetrical complications) that have afflicted a majority of the 74 million circumcised African females who are poor, rural, and without access to medical care.[17] While they may berate Western feminists for interference and say that it is none of their business if circumcision is practiced even in their own countries (Canada, Great Britain, or France) and that circumcision has an educational value for girls, they neglect to say that some of their most vigorous opponents are not Westerners but African, Arab, and Egyptian women and men. They neglect to say that the rites of passage will automatically lose their cultural context if they are performed in the sterile surroundings of a modern hospital or clinic, or that the educational value of rites of passage might be transmitted less harmfully through other equally symbolic but less physically painful means. Certainly countries like Norway, Sweden, and Denmark have every right to ban the operation within their own borders as not fitting within their own cultural and religious mores, just as they would have the right to prevent infanticide, stoning an illegitimate child, suttee, child or wife beating, or killing a prostitute or adulteress. Are women holding on to this custom through ignorance and lack of education, because they cannot come up with an alternative, or because of the obdurate intransigence of the older generation and their own fear of opposing a custom many do not want practiced on their daughters?

How can the restrictions imposed on women be loosened if women themselves actively condone and promulgate those strictures? While the major religions are undoubtedly male-dominated, patriarchal hierarchies, women to a large extent have been the willing handmaidens of those religions. Some might say that they have even collaborated in the repression of their own sex. Despite legislation to undo the damage of the worst proscriptions and myths, despite education to formulate understanding and new attitudes, despite the reform efforts of concerned individuals, many women still tolerate practices that hurt them and their daughters.

India is a case in point. Raja Ram Mohan Roy opposed suttee and had the Bengal Sati Regulation XVII promulgated in 1829 to make widow burning illegal and punishable. Pandit Iswarchandra Vidyasagar's efforts led to the enactment of the Hindu Widows' Remarriage Act XV in 1856, giving widows of full age the right to remarry upon their consent only. The Child Marriage Restraint Act XIX of 1929 restrained the marriage of children, prohibiting solemnization of a marriage of males under 18 and females under 15. It failed, however, to void child marriages if they did occur. The Hindu Marriage Disabilities Removal Act XXVIII of 1946 gave validation to marriage between the same gotra, or pravara, or to different subdivisions of the same caste. Later, in 1949, the Hindu Marriage Validating Act validated all marriages, whenever performed, between parties belonging to different religions, castes, subcastes, and sects, including Sikhs and Jains. These regulations offended a large portion of Hindu society but nevertheless eliminated or minimized the practices of suttee, female infanticide, child marriage, and widow isolation. But signs are appearing that such practices are being resurrected (suttee, infanticide) or being expanded (child marriage, widow isolation). Females may ultimately be the victims, but they also are active participants, and when victims acquiesce in practices harmful to themselves, change becomes even harder to bring about.

Legislation is obviously not enough to undo practices rooted in religious history unless it is forcefully applied and monitored. The situation of women somewhat parallels that of caste. Theoretically and legally, Untouchables no longer exist in India. But at least 105 million do. Untouchability was abolished by the Parliament of India on November 29, 1948; by the constitution of 1950; and the Untouchability Offences Act of 1955. Affirmative action was put into place to ensure Untouchables a quota of college places, government jobs, and places in Parliament, but they still "may be killed, maimed, dispossessed or humiliated by resentful higher Hindu castes."[18] As Britain's Minority Rights Group has documented, they are subject to numerous unlawful acts, yet little is done to enforce the laws.[19] To improve the lot of the Untouchables has not been in the religious tradition of Hinduism or higher-caste Hindus. Women are as much the perpetrators as the victims of caste distinctions and prejudice. But their attitudes will be no more changed by legislation than men's unless enforcement is vigorous, unless village leaders and priests are persuaded to help bring about tolerance, and unless a massive education campaign is undertaken commencing in the primary grades.

In India as in Islamic and Christian countries, the questing for a religion to satisfy individual needs is taking various shapes. In Assam it is Muslim-Hindu clashes; in the Punjab it is a demand for separation; among the Untouchables it is counterviolence against higher-caste Hindus and conversion to Buddhism, Christianity, and Islam.

Religion everywhere is in a state of flux, pushed and pulled by conservative and liberal forces. Whichever wins, traditionalism or reform, will have major repercussions for development and women. Women ultimately will have to decide for themselves whether they want to be part of development and modernization. If they do, they will need to resist being buffeted and manipulated by male-dominated religious forces. For most this will be difficult. They will need help and encouragement to develop an understanding that they can continue to be faithful adherents to their religions and yet expect to be treated as full, intelligent human beings.

Each religion has an innate flexibility and considerable scope for helping women to reach their potential. But will religious leaders be prepared to yield that option to women? Will they continue to resist women's full integration into development in all its multifaceted aspects: spiritual, educational, economic, social, and political? Will they be aided and abetted by the laity, politicians, development planners, and others, ignoring women's presence and needs and resisting their full incorporation into development? To paraphrase Mao Tsetung, will they be allowed to hold up half the sky in their own right? The world has changed, women are changing. Will they finally be given the right to participate in changing the world? That is the challenge of the present and the future.

NOTES

1. "The War of Zia's Moustache," Economist, April 2, 1983, pp. 55-56.
2. Ibid.
3. Ibid., p. 56.
4. "Religious 'Fanatics' Trying to Stop Abortion Clinic, Morgentaler Says," Toronto Star, April 9, 1983.

5. Ibid.

6. "Vatican Orders Nun to Quit Job over Abortions," Ottawa Citizen, March 28, 1983.

7. Pope John Paul II, speaking on abortion, London Times, May 11, 1982; November 4, 1982.

8. Pope John Paul II, speaking in Rome to mark International Women's Day, New York Times, March 9, 1981.

9. Pope John Paul II, New York Times, December 7, 1981.

10. "New Command in Canterbury," Time, September 17, 1979, p. 68.

11. Pope John Paul II, speaking in Philadelphia on the ordination of women, New York Times, October 5, 1979.

12. Ibid.

13. Bishop William Robinson, Partners in Priesthood (Ottawa: Archdiocese of Ottawa, n.d.). See also "Priests, Bishop Meet," Ottawa Citizen, June 2, 1979.

14. Robinson, Partners in Priesthood.

15. Ibid.

16. Guy Hunter, Modernizing Peasant Societies: A Comparative Study of Asia and Africa (Oxford: Oxford University Press, 1969), p. 292.

17. "Female Circumcision Necessary, Say African Women in Canada," Toronto Globe and Mail, April 22, 1983.

18. "An Upward Sweep Is Subversive," Economist, April 2, 1983, p. 56.

19. Ibid.

GLOSSARY

acharya	Brahmin who initiates and teaches the Vedas.
Agamas	A class of Hindu Tantric writings of medieval India that are sacred texts of the Saivites, or followers of Shiva
ahimsa	Nonviolence; nonkilling.
Ajivikas	Homeless, ascetic nomads, who eschewed worldly goods. Many eventually joined the non-theistic religious sect by the same name, which resembled Jainism but was founded by Gosala Maskarin and flourished during the sixth to third centuries B. C.
arahants	Lay followers of Buddhism who observed a high standard of moral discipline.
ashrams	A place of religious retreat or a hermitage, typically in India.
ashramas	Four stages of a Hindu's life. See varnashrama.
Atman	Means Self. The Upanishads point out that the Brahman and the Atman are the same.
Atman-Brahman	The subjective experience and thought, as opposed to objective experience and thought.
avatar	Human manifestation of a god or goddess; the divine appearance of deities in human form; humanity's saviors.
be-waquf	Ignorant; a state of ignorance.
Bhagavad Gita's Seven Concepts	Dharma, nonattachment, avatars, multiple ways of salvation, vision of God, devotion as the Supreme Way to Salvation, grace or God's help to attain eternal life.
bhakti	The intimate devotion to a personal deity as a supreme way of salvation; the intense personal love or devotion to God, evinced through puja and daily religious ritual at a public temple or private altar.

255

Bharata	The indigenous name for India.
Brahma	One of the Vishnu-Brahma-Shiva triad; the creator of the world.
brahmacharya	First, student phase of Hindu life; education, work, discipline.
Brahman	Absolute Creator-Reality, Supreme Being.
Brahmanas	Priestly writings or ritual books.
Brahmans (Brahmins)	Priests and educators, scholars.
casta	Class or caste.
chador	A head-to-toe covering worn by Iranian women.
chulha	An Indian stove, typically made out of clay, that is wood or charcoal burning.
circumcision	Female circumcision in its most limited form is nipping off the tip of the clitoris. Excision is removal of all of the clitoris and the labia minora. In its more extreme Pharaonic form, it is the cutting away of the clitoris and genitalia down to the bone, followed by infibulation, or the sewing together of the vagina so that only a small opening, to be broken open upon marriage or pregnancy, is left for menstrual flow.
devadasis	Temple girls. High-class prostitutes attached to the service of deities in Hindu temples.
dharm	Right behavior, including acceptance of one's lot and the observance of Hindu caste restrictions.
dharma	A person's basic duties in life.
dharmashastras	Legalistic treatises on social and individual behavior; brahminical rules.
Durga	See Kali.
Epics	Mahabharata and Ramayana stories of India's heroic period.
excision	See circumcision.
fatwa	Authoritative legal opinions on external legal matters by the ulama.

Gārgī	A Vedic woman who was an early philosopher of India.
ghail	Prohibition of sexual intercourse during nursing.
grihastha	Second stage of Hindu life: householder period of married, social, and public life.
hadith	Traditions or sayings attributed to Muhammad, partly interpreted and partly coined from sources other than Muhammad.
Harijans	The untouchables, who were named by Gandhi the Children of God.
haram	Forbidden, protected area.
harem	Secluded group of women.
Hegira (Hijrah)	The first year of the Muslim calendar and the beginning of the new Islamic era.
hinjras	Male transvestites.
ijaza	Authorization to teach to others what pupils had learned from a scholar.
ijtihad	Original free thought; reasoning.
imam	Leader in prayer: supreme leader of Shi'ites.
infibulation	See circumcision.
Islam	Submission to the immutable moral law of God.
Jahiliyah	Age of Ignorance, which predated the Hegira.
jati	Birth (and occupation).
jiwar	Protection (of the Kaaba's forbidden area).
jnana	Knowledge.
Kali	Also known as Durga; the goddess of destruction and fear.
karma	Fate, the law of moral causality based on reaping what you sow.
karuna	Compassion.
Kaur	Sikh term meaning princess and given to a female initiate in the Khalsa.
Khalsa	The "pure"; the militant company and brotherhood of Sikhs founded in the seventeenth century by Gobind Singh, the tenth guru.

Kshatriyas	Warriors, leaders, nobles.
Laisa minu	Muhammad's follower.
lingam	A representation of the phallus, symbol of Shiva, revered in Hindu temples.
madrasahs	Institutions for theological instruction with an official status, paid teachers, and often, students in residence.
makruh	Disfavorable.
manes	Spirits of the dead to be remembered and placated by relatives through offerings.
Manu-Samhita	Laws or Code of Manu; smriti literature ascribed to Manu of Manava and given an aura of sacredness.
maulvies	Local priests in Pakistan.
maya	The world of change or the insubstantial; the unreal nature of the visible world.
moksha	Salvation with and through Brahman, the Absolute Reality; freedom from reincarnation; the ideal of liberation.
mukti	Similar to moksha and apavagara, in Indian religion. Renunciation of reincarnation; freedom from karma and rebirth; the ultimate spiritual goal, devoting the soul's release from the bonds of transmigration.
nautch girls	Professional dancing girls attached to Hindu temples and first introduced to India by Muslim rulers.
panchayats	Governing councils of elders in Indian villages.
puja	Initially, image worship of specific theistic deities that required the construction of permanent altars or temples originally nonexistent in ancient India. Subsequently, ritualistic puja became individualistic worship and meditation practiced within the sanctity of individuals' homes, according to their needs, status, and character.
Puranas	In Hindu sacred literature, popular, encyclopedic collections of myth, legend, and genealogy.

purdah	Literally meaning (in Urdu or Persian) a veil or curtain. A divide to screen Muslim and Hindu women from the public, men, and strangers. In India it was particularly used to seclude women of rank from public view and to protect their reputation and property during travels.
qiyas (al-qiyas)	Analogous or analogical reasoning within Muslim jurisprudence, or syllogism within Muslim philosophy.
rishis	Saintly forest dwellers, philosophers, or seers of the early Vedic period.
saddhu	An Indian holy man.
Saivism	The worship of Shiva, the destroyer of the world.
samhitas	Hinduism's earliest sacred writings.
samsara	The world conceived as a constant, endless cycle of change, that is, birth–death–rebirth–death– ad infinitum.
sannyasi	A man who has renounced all ties to his family, caste, and the world. Fourth stage in a Hindu's life. See varnashrama.
Shaktis	Female counterparts of gods.
shramanas	Nonbrahminical teachers.
Singh	Sikh term, meaning lion, given to a male initiate in the Khalsa.
Sita	The heroine of the Ramayana, the story of Rama, her husband.
smriti	Literally, what is remembered.
soma	An intoxicating drink derived from the soma plant and often used in Vedic rituals; also sacrificial offering.
sruti	Literally, what is said/told; infallible, divine revelations received by the rishis; divinely revealed.
Sudras	Native population; workers and tillers of the soil; often enslaved or non-Aryan blacks.

sunna	Traditional lore; Orthodox Islam; Muhammad's hadith, which later constituted the voluminous collections of the sunna, passed on orally initially from collectors of hadith to their pupils.
suttee	Immolation of a widow on her husband's pyre, sometimes referred to as sati.
tapovanas	Forest schools of ancient India.
tirthas	Holy places, for example, Varanasi.
trimurti	Three in one; the triad of three gods—Brahma, Vishnu, and Shiva.
ulama	Plural of alim, or one possessed of ilm ("religious knowledge"); learned Islamic scholars or clerical class with religious authority.
Upanishads	Hinduism's highest forms of intuitive visions.
Vaishnavism	The worship of Vishnu, the preserver of the world.
Vaisyas (Vaishyas)	Merchants, traders, freemen; Aryan common folk; some Aryo-Dravidians.
vanaprastha	Third stage in a Hindu's life. See varnashrama.
varna	Color; the original basis on which Indian society was divided.
varnashrama	Four classical stages of life: brahmacharya, celibate student stage; grihastha, householder stage; vanaprastha, the stage when a householder lives with his wife but abstains from sex; sannyasi, when a man renounces all ties to family, caste, and the world.
Vedas	Early vedic writings; four collections of Vedic hymns: Rigveda, Atharvaveda, Samaveda, and Yajurveda.
wa'd	Early infanticide, usually of female children.
yajna	Sacrificial offering.
yoga	Techniques and philosophy of meditation; physical and mental discipline.
yoni	Representations of the vulva, revered in Hinduism.

SELECTED BIBLIOGRAPHY

The following references are supplementary to those already cited in the text. Many more could be given but space does not permit.

BUDDHISM

Anderson, Sir Norman, ed. The World's Religions. Grand Rapids, Mich.: Wm. B. Eerdmans, 1976.

Bellah, Robert N. , ed. Religion and Progress in Modern Asia. New York: Free Press, 1965.

Conze, Edward. Buddhism: Its Essences and Development. New York: Harper & Row, 1959.

Gaer, Joseph. How the Great Religions Began. New York: New American Library, 1956.

Humphreys, Christmas. Buddhism. Middlesex: Penguin Books, 1962.

Khantipalo Bhikku. What Is Buddhism? Bangkok: Social Science Association Press of Thailand, 1965.

Ling, Trevor. "Buddhist Factors in Population Growth and Birth Control." Population Studies 23 (1969): 53-60.

_____. The Buddha. Middlesex: Penguin Books, 1976.

Myrdal, Gunnar. Asian Drama. New York: Pantheon, 1968.

Potter, Sulamith Heins. Family Life in a Northern Thai Village: A Study in the Structural Significance of Women. Berkeley and Los Angeles: University of California Press, 1977.

Schecter, Jerrold. The New Face of the Buddha: The Fusion of Religion and Politics in Contemporary Buddhism. Tokyo: John Weatherhill, 1967.

Schumacher, E. F. Small Is Beautiful. London: Blond and Briggs, 1973.

Spencer, Robert F., ed. Religion and Change in Contemporary Asia. Minneapolis: University of Minnesota Press, 1971.

Young Womens' Christian Association. According to the Scriptures: The Image of Woman in the World's Major Religions. Geneva: YWCA, 1972.

CHRISTIANITY

Abrecht, Paul. The Churches and Rapid Social Change. London: SCM Press, 1961.

Biezanek, Anne. All Things New. New York: Harper & Row, 1964.

Boulding, Kenneth. Beyond Economics—Essays on Society, Religion and Ethics. Ann Arbor: University of Michigan Press, 1968.

Bromley, D. B. Catholics and Birth Control: Contemporary Views on Doctrine. New York: Devin-Adair, 1965.

Bruns, J. Edgar. God as Woman, Woman as God. New York: Paulist Press, 1973.

Bullough, Vern, and Bonnie Bullough. The Subordinate Sex: A History of Attitudes towards Women. Urbana: University of Illinois Press, 1973.

Cox, Harvey. On Not Leaving It to the Snake. London: SCM Press, 1976.

Daly, Mary. Beyond God the Father—Toward a Philosophy of Women's Liberation. Boston: Beacon Press, 1973.

Davidson, Robert, and A. R. C. Leaney. Biblical Criticism. Middlesex: Penguin Books, 1970.

_____. The Pelican Guide to Modern Theology. Vol. 3. Middlesex: Penguin Books, 1970.

Davis, Elizabeth Gould. The First Sex. Baltimore: Penguin Books, 1971.

Deen, Edith. All of the Women of the Bible. New York: Harper & Row, 1955.

Encyclopaedia Britannica. 15th ed. S.v. "Biblical Literature."

Ermarth, Margaret Sillter. Adam's Fractured Rib: Observations on Women in the Church. Philadelphia: Fortress Press, 1970.

Evans, Allan S., et al. What Man Believes: A Study of the World's Great Faiths. Toronto: McGraw-Hill Ryerson, 1973.

Figes, Eva. Patriarchal Attitudes: The Case for Women in Revolt. Greenwich, Conn.: Fawcett, 1970.

Foster, Theodora C. "Religion Restricts Women." Perception (Ottawa), vol. 3, no. 1 (September–October 1979).

Gage, M. J. Woman, Church and State. New York: Arno, 1972.

Greeley, Father Andrew M., et al. Catholic Schools in a Declining Church. Kansas City, Kan.: Sheed & Ward, 1976.

Hamilton, Mitchell P., and Nancy S. Montgomery, eds. The Ordination of Women: Pro and Con. New York: Morehouse-Barlow, 1975.

Hewitt, Emily C., and Suzanne R. Hiatt. Women Priests: Yes or No? New York: Seabury Press, 1973.

Heyer, Robert J. Women and Orders. New York: Paulist Press, 1974.

Hunt, Ignatius. The World of the Patriarchs. Englewood Cliffs, N.J.: Prentice-Hall, 1967.

Jewett, Paul K. Man as Male and Female. Grand Rapids, Mich.: Wm. B. Eerdmans, 1975.

Keller, Werner. The Bible as History. London: Hodder & Stroughton, 1963.

Komisar, Lucy. The New Feminism. New York: Watts, 1971.

Kung, Hans. Infallible? An Inquiry. New York: Doubleday, 1971.

LeFort, G. Eternal Woman, the Woman in Time, and Timeless Woman. Milwaukee, Wis.: Bruce, 1962.

Mendelsohn, Jack. God, Allah, and JuJu: Religion in Africa Today. New York: Thomas Nelson & Sons, 1962.

Plaskow, J., and Joan Arnold Romero. Women and Religion. Papers of the Working Group on Women and Religion. Chambersburg, Pa.: American Academy of Religion, 1974.

Robinson, John A. T. Honest to God. Philadelphia: Westminster Press, 1963.

Ruether, Rosemary Radford. Mary: The Feminine Face of the Church. Philadelphia: Westminster Press, 1977.

Van Der Meer, Haye. Women Priests in the Catholic Church? Philadelphia: Temple University Press, 1973.

Van Vuuren, N. Subversion of Women as Practiced by Churches, Witch-Hunters and Other Sexists. Philadelphia: Westminster Press, 1973.

Wahlberg, Rachel Conrad. Jesus according to a Woman. New York: Paulist Press, 1975.

Westoff, Charles F., and Elise F. Jones. "The End of 'Catholic' Fertility." Demography, vol. 16, no. 2 (1979).

HINDUISM

Ashby, Philip H. Modern Trends in Hinduism. New York: Columbia University Press, 1974.

Bancroft, Anne. Religions of the East. London: Heinemann, 1974.

Billington, M. F. Woman in India. New Delhi: Amarko, 1973.

Brent, Peter. The Godmen of India. New York: Quadrangle, 1973.

Buhler, George. The Laws of Manu. New York: Dover, 1969.

Carstairs, G. Morris. The Twice Born: A Study of a Community of High-Caste Hindus. London: Hogarth Press, 1961.

Corbett, J. My India. London: Oxford University Press, 1952.

Cormack, Margaret Lawson. The Hindu Woman. Westport, Conn.:
Greenwood Press, 1953.

Das, Devendra N. Sketches of Hindoo Life. London: Chapman &
Hall, 1887.

Dowson, J. A Classical Dictionary of Hindu Mythology and Religion.
London: Routledge, 1950.

Dube, S. C. Indian Village. London: Routledge & Kegan Paul, 1954.

Encyclopaedia Britannica. 15th ed. S.v. "Hinduism."

Field, H. H. After Mother India. London: J. Cape, 1929.

Forster, E. M. The Hill of Devi. London: Arnold, 1953.

_____. A Passage to India. London: Arnold, 1932.

Gandhi, M. K. An Autobiography. New York: Heiman, 1969.

Hate, C. A. Changing Status of Woman in Post-Independence India.
Bombay: Allied, 1969.

Hume, Robert E. The World's Living Religions. Rev. ed. New
York: Charles Scribner's Sons, 1959.

Kapur, Promilla. Changing Status of Working Women (India). New
Delhi: Vikas, 1974.

Karunakaran, K. P. Religion and Political Awakening in India.
Meerut: Meenakshi Prokashan, 1965.

Kaur, Manmohan. Role of Women in the Freedom Movement, 1857-
1947. Delhi: Sterling, 1968.

Koller, John M. Oriental Philosophies. New York: Charles Scribner's Sons, 1970.

Lannay, Richard. The Speaking Tree: A Study of Indian Culture and
Society. London: Oxford University Press, 1971.

MacNicol, Nicol. The Living Religions of the Indian People. London:
SCM Press, 1934.

Mehta, Ved. The New India. Middlesex: Penguin Books, 1978.

Mill, James. The History of British India. 1858. Reprint. New York: Chelsea House, 1968.

Morgan, Kenneth William, ed. Religion of Hindus Interpreted by Hindus. New York: Ronald Press, 1953.

Naipul, V. S. India: A Wounded Civilization. New York: Random House, 1978.

Nehru, J. Selected Writings. London: Probsthain, 1950.

Noss, John B. Man's Religions. New York: Macmillan, 1974.

O'Malley, L. S. Popular Hinduism. New York: Johnson Reprints, 1971.

Presler, Henry H. Primitive Religions in India. Columbia, Mo.: South Asia Books, 1973.

Rothfeld, Otto. Women of India. London: Simpkin, Marshall, Hamilton, Kent, 1920.

Roy, Manisha. Bengali Women. Chicago: University of Chicago Press, 1975.

Sarma, D. S. Hinduism through the Ages. Thompson, Conn.: Inter-Culture, 1973.

Sen, K. M. Hinduism. Middlesex: Penguin Books, 1961.

Singh, Ganda. The Sikhs. Amritsar: Shiromani Gurdwara P. Committee, n.d.

Singh, Teja. Guru Nanak and His Mission. Amritsar: Shiromani Gurdwara P. Committee, n.d.

_____. The Sikh Religion. Amritsar: Shiromani Gurdwara P. Committee, n.d.

Sivachandra, V. Hindoos as They Are: Bengal. London: W. Newman, 1881.

Srinivas, M. N. Caste in Modern India and Other Essays. London: Oxford University Press, 1962.

_____. Social Change in Modern India. London: Oxford University Press, 1966.

Watts, Harold H. The Modern Reader's Guide to Religions. New York: Barnes & Noble, 1964.

ISLAM

Badawi, Gamal A. Polygamy in Islamic Law. Takoma Park, Md.: Muslim Students' Association of the United States and Canada, 1976.

_____. The Status of Woman in Islam. Takoma Park, Md.: Muslim Students' Association of the United States and Canada, 1976.

Belyaer, E. A. Arabs, Islam and the Arab Caliphate in the Middle Ages. New York: Praeger, 1969.

Cooke, Hedley V. Challenge and Response in the Middle East: The Quest for Prosperity. New York: Harper & Row, 1952.

De Voto, Bernard Augustine. The Course of Empire. Boston: Houghton Mifflin, 1962.

Encyclopaedia Britannica. 15th ed. S.v. "Islam."

Epstein, Isidore. Judaism. Middlesex: Penguin Books, 1975.

Farrag, Osman L. Arab Women and National Development. UNICEF, reprint from no. 23, July–September 1973.

Fernea, Elizabeth Warnock. Guests of the Sheik: An Ethrography of an Iraqi Village. Garden City, N.Y.: Anchor Books, Anchor Press/Doubleday, 1969.

_____. A Street in Marrakech. Garden City, N.Y.: Anchor Books, Anchor Press/ Doubleday, 1976.

Gaudefray-Demombynes, Maurice. Muslim Institutions. London: Allen & Unwin, 1954.

Gibb, H.A.R. Islam: A Historical Survey. London: Oxford University Press, 1975.

Guillaume, Alfred. Islam. Middlesex: Penguin Books, 1975.

_____. Traditions of Islam: An Introduction to the Study of the Hadith Literature. Oxford, Conn.: Clarendon Press, 1924.

Hitti, Philip K. History of the Arabs. 10th ed. London: Macmillan, 1970.

Iranian Women's Organization. The Epic of Iranian Women. Tehran: IWO, 1972.

Kartini, Raden Adjeng. Letters of a Javanese Princess. New York: W. W. Norton, 1964.

Levy, Reuben. The Social Structure of Islam. Cambridge: At the University Press, 1957.

Lippman, Thomas W. Understanding Islam: An Introduction to the Moslem World. New York: Mentor, New American Library, 1982.

Mernissi, F. Beyond the Veil: Male-Female Dynamics in a Modern Muslim Society. New York: Schenkman, 1975.

Minority Rights Group. Arab Women. London: Minority Rights Group, 1976.

Mufassir, Sulaiman. Jesus in the Qur'an. Takoma Park, Md.: Muslim Students' Association of the United States and Canada, n.d.

Naipul, V. S. Among the Believers: An Islamic Journey. Middlesex: Penguin Books, 1981.

Papanek, Hanna. "Purdah in Pakistan: Seclusion and Modern Occupations for Women." Journal of Marriage and Family, August 1971, pp. 517-30.

Planhol, Xavier de. The World of Islam: A Geographical Analysis. New York: Cornell University Press, 1959.

Rahman, Fazlur. Islam. New York: Doubleday, 1968.

Roberts, D.S. Islam: A Concise Introduction. San Francisco: Harper & Row, 1981.

Roberts, R. Social Laws of the Quran: Considered and Compared with Those of the Hebrew and Other Ancient Codes. London: Curzon, 1971.

Rodinson, Maxine. Mohammed. Middlesex: Penguin Books, 1976.

Supreme Awqaf Council. A Brief Guide to the Dome of the Rock and Al-Haram Al-Sharif. Jerusalem: Supreme Awqaf Council, 1962.

Von Grunebaum, Gustare Edmund. Islam: Essays in the Nature and Growth of a Cultural Tradition. London: Routledge & Kegan Paul, 1955.

POPULATION

Appleman, Philip. The Silent Explosion. Boston: Beacon Press, 1965.

Biezanek, Anne. All Things New. New York: Harper & Row, 1964.

Brown, Lester R. In the Human Interest: Population Strategy for a Finite Planet: World Population and Food Supplies: Looking Ahead. New York: W. W. Norton, Aspen Institute for Humanistic Studies, 1974.

Chadrasekar, S., ed. Asia's Population Problems. London: George Allen & Unwin, 1967.

Concepcion, Mercedes B. "Female Labour Force Participation and Fertility." ILO Review (Geneva), vol. 109 (June 1974).

Dumont, René, and Bernard Rosier. The Hungry Future. New York: Praeger, 1969.

Erlich, Paul. The Population Bomb. New York: Ballantine Books, 1968.

Erlich, Paul, and Anna Erlich. Population, Resources, and Environment. San Francisco: W. H. Freeman, 1970.

Food and Agriculture Organization. Population, Food Supply and Agricultural Development. World Population Conference, E./conf.60CBP/25, 1974.

Hamilton, Michael P., and Nancy S. Montgomery, eds. The Ordination of Women: Pro and Con. New York: Morehouse-Barlow, 1975.

Hawkins, E. K. "A Family View of Population Questions." Finance and Development, vol. 10 (November 4, 1973).

International Bank for Reconstruction and Development. India's Population Policy: History and Future. World Bank Staff Working Paper no. 265, prepared by Ravi Gulhati. Washington, D. C.: IBRD, August 1977.

_____. Population Policy and Family Planning Programs: Trends in Policy and Administration. World Bank Staff Working Paper no. 411, prepared by Kandiak Kanagaratram. Washington, D. C.: IBRD, 1980.

_____. World Bank Atlas. Washington, D. C.: IBRD, 1982.

_____. World Tables 1976. Baltimore: Johns Hopkins University Press, 1976.

International Labour Organisation. World and Regional Labour Force Prospects to A. D. 2000. World Population Conference, E/Conf. 60/CBP/31, 1974.

Liskin, Laurie S. "Complications of Abortion in Developing Countries." Population Reports. Population Information Program, Series F, no. 7. Baltimore: Johns Hopkins University, 1980.

McNamara, Robert S. "The Environmental Dilemma: War on Hunger." AID Report, vol. 6, no. 8 (August 1972).

Molnos, Angela. Attitudes towards Family Planning in East Africa. Munich: Weltforum Verlag, 1968.

Muncie, Peter. Doctors and Dukuns, Puppets and Pills: A Look at Indonesia's Family Planning Program. Washington, D. C.: International Bank for Reconstruction and Development, 1972.

Myrdal, Gunnar. Asian Drama or an Inquiry into the Poverty of Nations. Vols. 1-3. New York: Pantheon, 1968.

Panitchpakdi, S. Human Resource Development and Foreign Aid: Financial Aid to Population Control, Education and Public Health. New York: South-East Asia Development Advisory Group, 1974.

Population Council. A Fact-Book. 5th ed. New York: Population Council, 1973.

Population Reference Bureau Inc. "Catholic Perspectives on Population Issues." Population Bulletin, vol. 30, no. 6 (1975).

Stanford, Quentin H., ed. The World's Population: Problems of Growth. London: Oxford University Press, 1972.

Stycos, J. Mayone. Human Fertility in Latin America. Ithaca, N.Y.: Cornell University Press, 1967.

Tan, Mely G. "The Social and Cultural Context of Family Planning in Indonesia." Unpublished paper, Djakarta.

Tata, N. H. "Population and Family Planning in Developing Countries." ILO Review (Geneva), vol. 109 (June 1974).

United Nations. Economic Bulletin for Asia: The Interrelationships between Economic Development and Population Growth during the Second and Third Development Decades (New York), vol. 24, no. 4 (March 1973).

_____. Population and the Family. World Population Conference, 1974.

_____. Status of Women and Family Planning in the Western Hemisphere. E/CN.61.

_____. World Population: Challenge to Development. Summary of the highlights of the World Population Conference, Belgrade, August 30-September 10, 1965. New York: United Nations, 1966.

United Nations, ECAFE. Integration of Women in Development, with Reference to Population Factors.

_____. Role of Voluntary Organizations in National Family Planning Programs. Asian Population Studies. Bangkok, August 1972.

United Nations Economic Commission for Africa. Data Base for a Discussion on the Interrelationships between Women in Development, Their Situation, and Population Factors in Africa. May-June 1974.

United Nations Fund for Population Activities. Law and Population. Population Profiles. New York: UNFPA, n.d.

_____. People in Population. Population Profiles, no. 4. New York: UNFPA, n. d.

_____. The Role of International Assistance in the Population Fields. World Population Conference. New York: UNFPA, 1974.

_____. The United Nations and Population: Major Resolutions and Instruments. Oceana, N. Y.: UNFPA, 1974.

_____. Women, Population and Development. Population Profiles, no. 7. New York: UNFPA, n. d.

World Health Organization. Family Planning in the Education of Nurses and Midwives. Public Health Papers no. 53. Geneva: WHO, 1973.

_____. Female Mutilation. Toronto: Globe & Mail, 1978.

_____. The Health of Women: How It Affects Their Needs and Status. World Conference of the International Women's Year, Mexico City, June–July 1975.

Worldwatch Institute. Filling the Family Planning Gap. (Paper no. 12), Washington, D. C., May 1977.

_____. Health: The Family Planning Factor. Prepared by Eric Eckholm and Kathleen Newland (Paper no. 10), Washington, D. C., 1977.

_____. Resource and Population Policy: A Time for Reassessment. Prepared by Lester R. Brown (Paper no. 29), Washington, D. C., May 1979.

_____. Twenty-two Dimensions of the Population Problem. Prepared by Lester R. Brown, Patricia L. McGrath, and Bruce Stokes (Paper no. 5), Washington, D. C., March 1976.

_____. Women and Population Growth: Choice beyond Child-Bearing. Prepared by Kathleen Newland (Paper no. 16), Washington, D. C., 1977.

Zeidenstein, George. Including Women in Development Effort. New York: Population Council, 1977.

WOMEN AND DEVELOPMENT

Abell, Helen C. "The Forgotten Familiars and World Food." Paper presented at a symposium on Canada and World Food, Carleton University, Ottawa, 1977.

American Association for the Advancement of Science. Culture and Population Changes. Document prepared by the Office of International Science. Washington, D.C.: AAAS, August 1974.

American Universities Field Staff. When Will Women and Men Escape the Mythic Strait Jacket? New York: Common Ground, January 1976.

Appadorai, A., ed. The Status of Women in South East Asia. Bombay: Longmans, 1959.

Barnes, Harry Elmer. Social Institutions. New York: Prentice-Hall, 1942.

Bauer, P. T. Some Economic Aspects and Problems of Underdeveloped Countries. Bombay: Forum of Free Enterprise, 1958.

Belloncle, Guy. "Listening to the Peasant." CERES, FAO Review, vol. 6, no. 3 (June 1973).

_____. Problems Raised by the Promotion of Rural Women in West Africa. Prepared for the Education Department, International Bank for Reconstruction and Development, 1975.

Berger, J. Women's Groups in Rural Development: An Evaluation. Nairobi: Food and Agriculture Organization, 1975.

Bergman, Arlene. Women of Viet Nam. San Francisco: People's Press, 1974.

Bernard, Jessie. Women, Wives, Mothers: Values and Options. Chicago: Aldine, 1975.

Boserup, Ester. Women's Role in Economic Development. New York: St. Martin's Press, 1970.

Boserup, Ester, and L. Liltencrantz. Integration of Women in Development: Why? When? How? New York: United Nations Development Program, 1975.

Boulding, Elise. Handbook of International Data on Women. New York: Halsted Press, Sage, 1976.

_____. The Underside of History: A View of Women through Time. Boulder, Colo.: Westview Press, 1977.

_____. Women in the Twentieth Century. New York: Halsted Press, Sage, 1977.

Brown, G. N. Conflict and Harmony in Education in Tropical Africa. London: George Allen & Unwin, 1975.

Buvinic, Mayra. Women and World Development: An Annotated Bibliography. Washington, D. C.: Overseas Development Council, 1976.

Canadian International Development Agency. The Integration of Women in Development. Ottawa: CIDA, 1976.

_____. International Women's Year. Ottawa: Cooperation Canada, 1975.

Cobb, G. B. "Women and Economic Development in East Africa." SAIS Review (Washington, D. C.), 1975.

Colombo-Sacco, Daniela, and Gloria Lopez-Morales. The Missing Half: Women 1975. Rome: Food and Agriculture Organization, 1975.

De Vries, Egbert. Man in Rapid Social Change. London: SCM Press, 1961.

Dia-Gaye, M. A. Role de la femme dans le developpement rural. Ottawa: Universite d'Ottawa, 1977.

Elmendorf, Mary. Nine Mayan Women: A Village Faces Change. New York: John Wiley & Sons, 1976.

Farrag, Osman L. "Arab Women and National Development." UNICEF, reprint no. 23, July-September 1973.

Food and Agriculture Organization. Arab Women in National Development. With the UN Children's Fund, Cairo, No. 29627, October 1974.

_____. Family Planning and the Participation of Women in Integrated Rural Development. With the International Planned Parenthood Federation, Cairo, No. 29629, October 1974.

_____. The Role of Women in Rural Development. Rome, No. 30323, November 1975.

_____. Status of Rural Women, Especially Agricultural Workers. Report to the Commission on the Status of Women, 25th sess., January-February 1974.

_____. Women's Leadership in Rural Development. National Workshop, Institute of Adult Studies, Kikuyu, Series 14, August 1974.

_____. The World Food Programme and Women's Involvement in Development. Rome, No. 29935, September 1975.

Foster, George McClelland. Traditional Cultures and the Impact of Technological Change. New York: Harper & Row, 1962.

Foster, Theodora Carroll. Canadian Women and Education. Ottawa: Match International, 1980.

_____. Sex Role Stereotyping in the Canadian School System. Ottawa: Canadian School Trustees' Association, 1982.

_____. Women and Agriculture in the Third World. Occasional Paper. Ottawa: EDPRA Consulting, 1983.

_____. Women, Marketing and Trade in the Third World. Occasional Paper. Ottawa: EDPRA Consulting, 1983.

Germain, Adrienne. "A Major Resource Awaiting Development: Women in the Third World." New York Times, August 26, 1975.

_____. "Poor Rural Women: A Policy Perspective." Reprint from the Journal of International Affairs, vol. 30, no. 2 (Fall-Winter 1976/77).

Geyer, Georgie Anne. The New Latins: Fateful Change in South and Central America. New York: Doubleday, 1970.

Gornick, Vivian, and Barbara K. Moran. Woman in Sexist Society: Studies in Power and Powerlessness. New York: Signet Books, 1971.

Harding, M. E. Woman's Mysteries, Ancient and Modern. New York: Putnam, 1971.

Hoskins, Marilyn. Women in Development: Income Generating Activities with Women's Participation. Washington, D. C.: Agency for International Development, 1980.

Ihromi, T. O., et al. "The Status of Women and Family Planning in Indonesia." Preliminary Report. Jakarta: Indonesia National Training and Research Centre, 1973.

Inter-American Commission of Women. The Woman in Latin America: Past, Present, Future. Washington, D. C.: Organization of American States, 1975.

International Bank for Reconstruction and Development. The Impact of Bank Projects on the Condition of Women in Developing Countries. Washington, D. C.: IBRD, 1975.

_____. Integrating Women into Development. Washington, D. C.: IBRD, 1975.

_____. The Integration of Women into the Development Process. Washington, D. C.: IBRD, 1975.

_____. World Development Report 1982. New York: Oxford University Press, 1982.

International Labour Organisation. Yearbook of Labour Statistics. Geneva: ILO, 1978.

International Planned Parenthood Federation. Family Planning and the Status of Women. London: IPPF, 1975.

_____. Half of Humanity. London: IPPF, 1975.

_____. Islam and Family Planning. Vols. 1 and 2. Beirut: International Islamic Conference in Rabat, IPPI, 1971.

Johnson-Sirlead, Ellen. "The Role of Women in Africa." Report of the seminar sponsored by the African/American Women Association at Howard University, Washington, D. C., February 1975.

League of Arab States. "Role of Arab Women in National Development." Paper prepared for the conference jointly sponsored by the League of Arab States, General Secretariat, Social Affairs and Youth, and UNICEF, Cairo, September 24-30, 1972.

Mead, Margaret. Male and Female: A Study of the Sexes in a Changing World. New York: W. Morrow, 1950.

Mill, John Stuart. The Subjection of Women. New York: Everyman's Library, Dutton, 1970.

Organization for Economic Cooperation and Development. "Meeting on the Integration of Women into the Development Process." Papers submitted to the Development Assistance Directorate by the International Bank for Reconstruction and Development, the Agency for International Development, and the Swedish International Development Agency, October 10, 1975.

Papanek, Hanna. "Women in South and South-east Asia: Issues and Research." Signs: Journal of Women in Culture and Society, 1975.

Patai, Raphael. Women in the Modern World. New York: Free Press, 1967.

Paulme, Denise, ed. Women of Tropical Africa. Translated by H. M. Wright. Berkeley and Los Angeles: University of California Press, 1971.

Peebles, Dana, and Theodora Carroll Foster. Women and International Development Cooperation. Ottawa: North-South Institute, 1983.

Riegelman, M. A., et al. Women in Rural Development: A Seven-Country Survey. Boulder, Colo.: Westview Press, 1976.

Saunders, Sir Alexander Carr. "Women's Role in the Development of Tropical and Subtropical Countries." Paper presented to the International Institute of Differing Civilizations, Brussels, 1959.

Schapera, Isaac. Married Life in an African Tribe. Middlesex: Penguin Books, 1971.

Smith, Prudence, ed. The Changing Roles of African Women: Africa in Transition. London: Max Reinhardt, 1958.

Southall, Aidan, ed. Social Change in Modern Africa. London: Oxford University Press, 1965.

Souza, Alfred de. Women in Contemporary India: Traditional Images and Changing Roles. New Delhi: Indian Social Institute, 1975.

Tinker, Irene, and M. B. Bramsen, eds. Women and World Development. Washington, D.C.: AAAS and ODC, 1976.

United Nations. Constitutions, Electoral Laws and Other Legal Instruments Relating to Political Rights of Women. New York: United Nations, 1966.

_____. Report of the World Conference of the International Women's Year. Conference held at Mexico City. New York: United Nations, 1975.

United Nations, Department of Economic and Social Affairs. Report of the Interregional Meeting of Experts on the Integration of Women in Development. New York: United Nations, 1973.

United Nations, Offices of the Secretary-general. Participation of Women in the Economic and Social Development of Their Countries. New York: United Nations, 1970.

United Nations Educational, Scientific and Cultural Organization. "Genuine Education for Equality." Paper prepared for the World Conference of the International Women's Year, Mexico City, June 1975.

_____. Study on the Equality of Access of Girls and Women to Education in the Context of Rural Development. Submission to the Commission on the Status of Women. New York: United Nations, 1973.

Ward, Barbara E. The Challenge of Development. Chicago: Aldine, 1967.

Ward, Barbara E., ed. Women in the New Asia. Paris: UNESCO, 1963.

Williams, C. Ebun. "Rural Women and National Development in Developing Countries." Paper prepared for the Seminar on Prospects for Growth in Rural Societies: With or without Active Participation of Women, sponsored by the Agricultural Development Council, New Jersey, December 1974.

Wollstonecraft, Mary. The Rights of Woman. New York: Everyman's Library, Dutton, 1970.

Worldwatch Institute. The Unfinished Assignment: Equal Education for Women. Prepared by Patricia L. McGrath (Paper no. 7), Washington, D.C., 1976.

_____. Women and Population Growth: Choice beyond Childbearing. Prepared by Kathleen Newland (Paper no. 16), Washington, D.C., December 1977.

INDEX

abbesses and abbots, 106 (see also bhikkunis; bhikkus)

abortion, 113-15, 231, 239-42, 244-45,
249; and antiabortionists, 183-84; in Canada, 183; Catholic opposition to, 183-84;
and importance of mother's life, 115; in
Latin America, 183; legal codes, 239-
40; legalization of, 240-42; as legalized
in Italy, 179; and public policy, 189, 190;
religion and, 187-88; in United States,
183

Abraham, 135, 144, 195

abstinence, 74, 77, 111, 120; benefits of,
235-36

abu-Bakr, 201

abu-Talib, 200

acharya, 44-45 (see also Brahmins)

Adam and Eve, 148, 173; as Everyman,
136; and treatment of women, 133-36

adharma, 57

Adi-Granth, 33 (see also Sikhism)

Adnanis, 195

adultery, 67, 125, 204, 207-8

Afghani-al, Jamal al-Din, 219

Afghanistan, 224

Africa, 208, 251

Agamas, 21, 53

agnostic school, 81-82

agriculture, 120-22, 195; and education,
107, 108; and women, 122

ahimsa, 42

Ahmad, Khurshid, 218

Ajivikas, 81, 104 (see also shramanas)

Akali Dal Party, 38 (see also Sikhism)

Akbar, 64

Akkadians, 195

Algeria, 219, 248

Ali, Imam, 201, 240

Ali Sadikin, 220

all-Ma'mum, 213

Allah, 197, 198, 199, 202-3, 205, 209,
228, 238

alsiqt, 238

Ambapali, 86, 87 (see also upasika)

Amin, Idi, 181, 232

Amin, Qasim, 219

Amorites, 195

Ananda, 86, 88-89

anatta, 84 (see also anicca; dukkha)

Anglican church, 146; and contraception,
184-85; and family planning, 184-85; and
marriage, family, and divorce, 177-78;
and moves toward greater equality for
women, 161-62; and tendency to deem-
phasize women's issues in discussions
with Roman Catholic church, 162; and
women, 133, 161-62, 185; women
preachers in, 151-52

anicca, 84 (see also anatta; dukkha)

animal veneration, 11

animism, 76, 79, 197; in Africa, 7

antiabortionists, 183-84

Aquinas, Thomas, 149; on women, marriage, sex, and contraception, 180, 181

Arabia, 194-95, 197, 201, 233

Arabs, 196, 197, 198, 199, 203, 208, 251;
Muslim, 195

arahantship, 102 (see also nirvana)

Aranyakas, 45

Argentina, 167

Armaeans, 195

Arjuna, 57

Arya Samaj, 38

Aryans, 11-15; aggression by, 12-13; and
cultural synthesis, 50; as educated, 41;
education of, 41-42; family life of, 16;
literature of, 13; and marriage, 13; and
marriage to non-Aryans, 24; patriarchal
system of, 16; stratification of, 14; and
subjugation of women, 18; and women, 12

asceticism, 83-84, 113, 120, 233-34; of
Hinduism, 11

Ashoka, King, 32

Ashoka Maurya, 92, 93-96, 99, 106, 121

ashramas, 43, 57

ashrams, 38

Asia, 109; educational level of girls in,
54-55 (see also Southeast Asia)

Assam, 253

atheism, 11

atman, 60

Atman-Brahman, 13, 47

Augustine, 149, 153; on contraception,
180; effect of, on Christian ethics, wom-
en, and population policies of nations,
154-55; on marriage, women, sex, childbirth, predestination, and Original Sin,
154-55, 180; on onanism, 180; on prostitution, 180

as intertwined with women, 15, 16; mixing of, 67; in modern India, 19; and reform, 30-32; and Sikhism, 33-34; strictures of, on women, 15; and subcastes, 16; and the "twice-born," 24
castration, 242
Catholic, 105, 115, 125, 221, 237, 249; missionaries, 35 (see also Christianity)
Catholicism, 215, 235, 238, 245 (see also Roman Catholic church)
Catholics, 115
celibacy, 43, 60, 73, 75, 77, 83, 111, 120, 153-54, 177, 179, 200, 206, 231, 233, 234, 242; Augustine, Jerome, and Thomas Aquinas on, 180; and family planning and population control, 182 (see also brahmacharya; marriage, family, and sex)
Chadli Benjedid, President, 248
chador, 229
Chaitanya, 37
Chanhu-Daro, 10
Charvakas, 48
chastity, 88, 234
Chelebi, Katib, 215
child marriage, 23-24, 26, 34, 35, 44, 65, 70-72, 91; as banned by Sikhism, 34; consequences of, 71-72; effect of Code of Manu on, 23; and inadequate legislation, 72; physical demands of, 71-72
childbirth (-bearing), 228, 234; and women, 237
childlessness, 205, 210
China, 96, 98, 208; and family planning, 188, 191
Chinese, the, 115
Christian: counterpart, 198; groups, 200; missionaries, 218-19; religion and customs, 196
Christianity, 7, 29, 83, 95, 124, 197, 200, 201, 233, 253; church attitudes of, 120; and development, 131; effect of, on Hinduism, 54; European, 115; and missionary education, 108; and Ten Commandments, 1; as theology, and women, 130-41
Christians, 207; Jewish, 144-45
chula, 10
church, the, 249; attitudes toward, and women, 140, 146, 149; 150-51, 153, 154-55; and contraception, 143; and development projects, 146; and divorce, 143; and family planning, 143, 154; and marriage and sex, 139, 154; membership in, by women, 143; moral leadership of, 132-33; and ordination of women, 143, 146; and preaching by women, 143; rebellion of women against, 179; and taking of theology degrees by women, 143; and women's family and property rights, 143 (see also Roman Catholic church)

Church of England, the, 250 (see also Anglican church)
church patriarchs, 140, 141, 143, 148; and attitudes determined by guilt and obsessions, 156; and attitudes toward women, sex, and marriage, 152-56; and inability to reconcile opposites, 155; on parenthood and infanticide, 154
circumcision: female, 127, 144, 251 [consequences of, 228; laws against, 228]; male, 144-45, 176
civil rights bills, 152
Clement of Alexandria, 153
Code of Manu, 17, 21-25, 26, 48, 51, 62, 65, 91, 103; and bodily defilement, 72-75; as code of conduct, 21; and duties of women, 62, 63; effect of, on development, 26-27; impact of, on education, 43; impact of, on women, 22-25, 51-52; as tool of Brahmins, 28
coeducation, 214, 220, 224
Comstock, Thomas, 188
conception, 116-17 (see also Buddha; Budhism, and population; gandharva)
concubinage, 33, 64
concubines, 18, 86, 201, 208
Confucianism, 98
contraception, 222, 223, 228, 230-31, 237, 239, 242, 244, 249; Anglican church on, 184-85; Augustine, Jerome, and Thomas Aquinas on, 180; Buddhism and, 111, 113-14, 115, 125, 126; Catholic church on, 168, 171, 172, 176, 177, 180, 181-83, 184-88, 191; and Catholic laity, 171-72; and Catholics versus Protestants and Jews, 185-87; and the church, 143, 154; as coitus interruptus, 175, 236; Hinduism and, 69; John Paul I on, 165-66; Judaism on, 171, 173, 186; and "Mater and Magister," 191; and Onan, 175; opposition to, 114-15; Paul VI on, 163-65; in Philippines, 168; Pius XI on, 180-81, 182; problems of, 98; Protestantism on, 171, 172-73, 177, 184-85, 188; and public officials and policy, 188; and souls, 115, 116-17
Corinth, 201
Council of Islamic Ideologies, 248
cow worship, 46, 58
customs, 4, 8, 12, 20, 109, 196, 197, 231, 238, 247, 248, 251, 252; and education, 55; and fate, 112; impact of, on women, 127; and values, 4, 7

Daly, Mary, 166
Dasa, 11
Dasyus, 11
defilement, 72-73, 75
deities (see goddesses; gods)
Denmark, 251
Deoband, 214

dependency burdens, 230
devadasis, 26, 70
devas, 94, 116-17 (see also conception)
development, 109, 219, 221, 223, 230,
232, 253; effect of caste on, 29-30; effect
of Code of Manu on, 26; effect of religion
on, 26, 58-59, 108, 126-28; priorities
for, 107
development aid agencies, 131
development planners, 144; and influence
of church, 131-32
Dev-gun, 60 (see also Rakshasgun)
Dhamma, Doctrine of, 80, 90, 92, 93-94,
96, 97, 102-3, 123 (see also Ashoka,
King; Buddhism; dharma)
dharm, 60-61
dharma, 29, 41, 57
dharmashastras, 21, 62
"Divini Illius Magistri," 160
divorce, 206, 208, 209, 219, 250; and An-
glicans, 177-78; and the church, 143; and
divorcees, 234; and Genesis, 136; in Hebraic law and custom, 177; in Italy, 179;
in Latin America, 178; and New Testament, 176; Paul VI on, 163; in Philippines, 168; Protestantism on, 184; Roman Catholic church on, 168, 178
Djebar, Assia, 220
dowry, 204-5, 206, 208, 234
Dravidians, 47
dukkha, 82, 84, 123 (see also anatta;
anicca)
Durga, 33 (see also Kali)

eating restrictions, 19, 28; and dietary
practices, 19, 42
Echeverria, Luis, 181
education, 228, 251-52; adult, 213; Arab,
213; and Buddhism, 102-28, 121, 122;
compulsory, 219, 222; effect of Code of
Manu on, 43-45, 52; of girls, 68; and
Hinduism, 41-55; level of, for girls in
India and Asia, 54-55; medieval, 213-15,
216; opposition to women's, 52, 66, 106,
107; palace-school, 213; and policy
makers and planners, 108-9; and population, 126-27; priorities for, 107; regarding family planning, 117; and student-
teacher relationships, 43-44; universal,
under Buddhism, 103, 106; universal female, 219-20, 222; vocational, 107;
Western and colonial, 108; and women
under Islam, 212-26
Egypt, 220, 228-29, 238
Egyptians, 219, 251
Eightfold Path, 85, 112
el-Badiyah, Bahithat, 219
elders, 95 (see also Theravadins)
elite: educated, 3; power, 2
el-Naciri, Muhammed el-Mekki, 235, 237
employment and education, 107, 108

England, 108
ensoulment, 240-41
Ephesians, and women, 144
Epics, 49 (see also Mahabharata; Ramayana)
Episcopalian church (see Anglican church)
equal opportunities legislation, 152
equality, as preached by the great religions, 7; and women, 7
Europe, 187
Evangelistic churches, 151, 178; female
preachers in, 151

Fahd, King, 221
family, 205-6, 208-9, 231, 233, 236, 243
family planning, 28, 100, 113, 114, 115-
16, 126, 222, 227, 228-31, 233, 235,
236, 238-39, 242, 243, 245, 249; and Anglican church, 184-85; attitudes toward,
117; in Barbados, 188; and brahminical
opposition, 28; among Catholics, Protestants, and Jews, 185-87; and celibacy,
182; in China, 188, 191; and the church,
143, 154; and clinics and bhopas, 60; effect of Buddhism on, 113-14; and feminists, 190; in India, 188, 190; and Judaism, 172-73, 186; and "Mater and Magister," 191; and opposition by in-laws, 66;
and opposition by priests, 59; and Protestantism, 172-73, 184-85; and public officials and policy, 188, 189-92; in Singapore, 188; in Sri Lanka, 118; in Thailand,
190; and Third World, 181, 183, 184,
187; and U.S. policy, 188; and women,
182, 189
fate (fatalism), 124, 205, 209, 210, 244
fathers, duties of, 70
Fatima, 201
Fatimids, 214
fatwa, 241
feminists, and family planning, 190
fertility, 58, 119; behavior of, 232, 239-
40; effect of Hinduism on, 75-76; and
ghosts, 60; and infertility, 58; and use of
Sapinda, 67
fertility rates, 229-30, 242, 243
fetal development, 240-41
Five Precepts, 113-14, 125 (see also Buddhism)
Four Noble Truths, 84
France, 34, 251
free enterprise, effect of Buddhism on, 107
French-Canadians, 221
fundamentalism, 143, 185, 251

Gamaliel, 142
Gambia, 230
gandharva, 116-17 (see also Khwan; souls)
Gandhi, Indira, 64
Gandhi, Mahatma, 10, 35, 36; and Un-
touchables, 15

284

Gārgī Vacaknavi, 17, 42
gau-mata, 62 (see also matijis)
Gemara, 151
General Synod, 250
Genesis, 133-34, 135, 137-38, 144, 148;
  and pronatalism, 173-74; and women,
  133-38
Gentiles, and church membership, 144-45
ghail, 235
Ghassanids, 195
Ghazzali-al, 237
Ghose, Aurobindo, 35
Gibbons, William J., 184
girls (see women)
Gobind Singh (see Sikhism)
God, 196, 198, 205, 206, 208, 209, 210,
  225, 236, 242, 244, 250
Godbey, W. B., 151
goddesses, 21, 46, 58, 60, 74, 199; earth-
  mother, 11, 16; pre-Islamic, 197, 198
gods, tribal, 197-98, 199
Gosala, 81
Gotama, 82, 83, 86, 92, 104 (see also
  Buddha)
gotra, 252
Great Britain, 251
Greeks, 146
Gregory of Nyassa, 153, 155
grihastha, 43, 75 (see also varnashrama)
guru, 69; modern, 127
gurudwaras, 34

Hadith, 196, 207, 231, 241
Hagar, 195
Halakhah, 151
Hanafis, 241
Hanuman, 74
haram, 199
Harappa, 11
Harijans (see Untouchables)
Harun al-Rashid, 213
health, 209
Hebrew (Mosaic) law and customs, 146-
  47, 148, 149, 151, 178; and divorce,
  177; and marriage, 176-77; and women,
  138,140
Hebrews, 195, 202
Hegira, 202
Hellenistic philosophy, 150
Hijaz, 197, 198, 200 (see also Mecca)
Hijrah (see Hegira)
Himyarite, 195
Hinayana, 96, 97, 98 (see also Thera-
  vadins)
Hindu: literature, 20-21, 45-48, 50;
  philosophy, 20, 50-51; rituals, 28; sac-
  red thread ceremonies, 28, 34
Hindu Marriage Disabilities Removal Act
  XXVIII, 252
Hindu Marriage Validating Act, 252
Hindu Widows' Remarriage Act XV, 252

Hinduism, 7, 10-39, 47-48, 50, 234-35,
  253; and abstinence from sex, 61-62; and
  birth, 57-58; as contrasted with Buddhism, 89, 113; and education, 41-56; effect of, on fertility, 76-77; and Laws of
  Manu, 1; and marriage, sex, and family
  responsibilities, 179; popular, 29; and
  population, 57-100; pronatalism of, 57,
  182; reform of, 34-37; similarity of, to
  Buddhism, 111; splinter movements of, 37
hinjras, 61
homosexuality, 61, 207; and religion, 187;
  and Roman Catholic church, 164
honor, 218, 234 (see also izzat)
hospitals, Canadian versus U.S., 240
"Humanae Vitae," 164; criticism of, 171
Huston, Perdita, 9, 117, 229
Huzzah-al, 198 (see also goddesses)
Hymns, 53

idolatry, 198, 203-4
ijtihad, 215
Illich, Ivan, 171
illiteracy of females, 54-55
imams, 130, 231, 243
India, 5, 11, 102, 104, 106, 112, 121,
  208, 214, 252; aboriginal inhabitants of,
  10; Bronze Age art of, 11; climate of,
  11; decline of Buddhism in, 95-96; educational level of girls in, 54-56; and
  family planning, 188, 190; impact of Islamic incursions in, 32; non-Aryan inhabitants of, 10-11, 12 [in Bengal region,
  10; in Tamil region, 10]; pre-Aryan, 10,
  14; pre-Vedic, 10, 16; reformers and
  leaders of, 34-37; Vedic, 13, 16
Indian Ocean, 194-95
Indo-European languages, 12
Indonesia, 119, 182, 238-39
Indra, 11, 46
Indus River Valley, 10
infanticide, 35, 64, 67-68, 236, 252; as
  banned by Sikhism, 34; female, 196, 198,
  203-4
infibulation, 34
international institutions, 131
International Women's Year (1975), 8
Iran, 6, 210, 223, 224, 226, 238, 247 18
Iraq, 220, 229
Irenaeus, 153
Isaac, 135
Ishmael, 144, 195
Islam, 7, 248, 249, 253; and abstinence
  from sex, 61; as contrasted with Buddhism, 113; effect of, on Hinduism, 54;
  effect of, on women, 32; impact of, on
  women, 194-210; incursions of, 32; jurisprudence of, 231, 233, 236, 238, 239;
  and the Koran, 1; and marriage, sex,
  and family responsibilities, 179; over-
  view of, 194-210; and population, 227,
  245; and pronatalism, 182

Islamic Algerian Republic, 248
Islamists, 225
Islamization, 247
Israel, 135
Italy, 249; divorce law in, 179; and legal-
ized abortion, 179
izzat, 217

Jabir, 236
Jacob, 135
Jahiliyah, 202
Jahwist, 135
Jainas, 81, 104
Jainism, 29, 37, 42; birth of, 48
Jakarta, 220
Japan, 96, 98, 106, 114
jati, 13, 15
Java, 49, 112
Jayawardene, Kumari, 126
Jehovah, 197 (see also Allah; God)
Jerome, 153, 154; and women, marriage,
sex, and contraception, 180
Jesus, 138-41, 142, 144, 148, 200, 202,
233, 247; and adultery, 138; and divorce,
138; and marriage, 140, 176-77; and
racism, 140; and serfdom and slavery,
140; and women, 138, 176
Jewish: dietary laws, 144; religion and
customs, 196; settlements, 200
Jews, 140, 144, 146, 173, 202, 207; versus Catholics on contraception and family planning, 186-87; and family planning,
187
Jinnah, 248
jiryan, 73
Jita, 33 (see also Sikhism)
jiwar, 199
jnana, 43
John XXIII, 163; attitude of, toward women
and men, 162; and "Mater and Magister,"
191
John Paul I, 165-66
John Paul II, 249-50; and emphasis on family, 168; social and economic views of,
165-66; views of, on priests in politics,
167; and women, 165-66
johur, 64 (see also suttee)
Jordan, 220
Judaism, 7, 144, 145, 197; and contraception, 171, 172-73; and family planning,
172-73, 186; and marriage, 172-73
Justin, 153

Kaaba, 197, 199
Kabir, 33
Kadijah, 196, 201
Kailavastu, 82 (see also Buddha)
Kali, 46
Kalinga, 93
kampong, 220

karma, 11, 20, 29, 60-61; within Bud-
dhism, 81-82, 112, 113, 116, 117
karuna, 125-26
Kathavathu, 95
Khalsa, 33 (see also Sikhism)
Khantipalo Bhikku, 124
Kharijites, 215
Khartoum, 227
Khazraj, 202
Khwan, 114 (see also Buddhism)
killing, 113, 114, 204 (see also Buddhism;
contraception; family planning)
kinship, 197, 199, 200 (see also women)
Kirk, Dudley, 231
Kisagotami, 83
Klausner, Joseph, 150
Koran, the, 195, 196, 200-3, 206-8, 209,
212, 213, 219, 222-25, 231, 233, 238,
240, 248
Koranic schools, 212, 213
Korea, 96, 98, 114
Krishna, 46, 57
Kshatriyas, 14-15, 42-43; education of, 45;
student-teacher relationships with, 43;
wives of, 17, 24
Kung, Hans, challenge to Roman Catholic
doctrine, 166
kuttab, 212, 213, 214
Kuwait, 229, 230, 238

"Laborem Exercens," social and economic
views of, 166
laisa minu, 233
Lalla, 53
Lat-al, 198 (see also goddesses)
Latin America, 227; abortion in, 183; attitude of males to marriage in, 174; birthrate and religion in, 187; influence of
Catholic church on attitudes in, 187-89;
machismo in, 174; marriage and divorce
in, 178-79; relations with Roman Catholic
church in, 184; social movements in, 167
Laws of Manu (see Code of Manu)
Leander of Seville, 153
legislation, 252-53
lesbianism, 61
levirate system, 175, 176
lex talionis, 28
Libya, 6, 219, 230, 238
lingam, 58
literacy, adult, 221; literacy classes, 212
lokayatas, 81

machismo, 174, 178; and the Roman Cath-
olic church, 174
Madhva, 37
Madinat al-Rasul, 202 (see also Medina)
madrasah, 214-17, 223-25
Mahabharata, 13
Mahaprajapati, 88 (see also Sanghas)

286

Mahayana, 53, 93, 96, 97, 98, 114 (see also Buddhism)
Mahinda, 96 (see also Ashoka)
Maitreyi, 42
Majlis e Shura, 248
makruh, 241, 242
Malaysia, 119, 229, 238
Maliki, 241
malnutrition of females, 19
Manah, 198 (see also goddesses)
manes, 28, 67, 68
Manu of Manava, 21
Manu-Samhita, 21, 51 (see also Code of Manu)
Mao Tse-tung, 253
marasmus, 68
Marcos, Ferdinand, and relations with the church, 167, 168
marriage, 119, 197, 200, 205-9, 217, 231, 234, 238, 244, 252; arranged, 34; by daughter purchase, 16; duties of, 65; early or child, 234, 251, 252; by forcible abduction, 16; Islamic rulings on, 206, 207, 233; by mutual consent, 16; polygamous, 208, prohibitions against, 204, 205, 209; types of, 70; widows and, 63
marriage, family, and sex: and Anglican church, 177-78; Aquinas, Thomas on, 180; Buddhism on, 179, 180; and the church, 139, 154; church patriarchs and, 152-56; Clement of Alexandria on, 153-54; Hinduism on, 179; Islam on, 179; Jerome on, 180; Jesus on, 140, 176-78; Judaism on, 172, 173, 176, 177; in Latin America, 174, 178; Old Testament on, 176; Paul on, 147-50; and the Pharisees, 176; Protestantism on, 172, 173, 177, 184; Roman Catholicism on, 174, 179, 180; Tertullian on, 153
Marshall, Sir John, 10
Mary, 154
matajis, 58, 62
"Mater and Magister," and acknowledgment of population crisis, 191
materialism, 206
materialists, 104; school of, 81, 82
maternal mortality and morbidity, 240
matriarchy, 12, 100, matrilineal descent and, decline of, 16; matrilocal system and, 12
Maududi, Maulana Abul A'la, 218
maulvies, 248
Maya, 20
Maya, Queen, 83
McNamara, Robert, 188
Mecca, 197, 198, 200, 202
Meccans, 203, 204
Medicare, 249
Medina, 200, 202
Meechai Veeravaidhaya, Khun, 117
menarche, 234

menstruation, 200
merit earning, 100, 106, 119
Mexico, 167, 181-82
Middle East, 251
Middle Path or Way, 83, 84, 85, 100, 104, 111, 113, 119
military leadership, 225
Minaean, 195
Minority Rights Group, 252
Mishnah, 151
missionaries, 108; and education in the Third World, 168, 169; and Original Sin, 169; Spanish, 168; and Third World women, 143, 144
Mitra, 11
mobility, 196, 197
modernization, 106, 107, 109, 119, 127, 219, 223, 225, 239, 243, 247 (see also reform)
Mohenjo-Daro, 10, 11
moksha, 20, 42, 92
monastic schools, 90, 103, 120 (see also Sanghas)
monasticism, 200, 234
monks, 85, 86, 89, 98, 118, 120 (see also Sanghas)
monogamy, 208
Morgentaler, Henry, 249
Morocco, 229
mortality rates, 229, 230
Moses, 138, 140, 142; and women, 139
mosque, 212, 213, 214
mothers-in-law, 66
Muhammad, 194-210, 222, 223, 233-36, 238, 244, 247; code of conduct established by, 204; and education, 212; and infanticide, orphans, and parenthood, 153, 154; and Jesus' teachings on women, 140
mujtahids, 224
mukti, 42 (see also moksha)
mullah, 220, 221, 224
Muslim, 32, 34, 64, 105; creativity, 213; family, 206; fundamentalists, 224; governments, and population policies, 230; jurisprudence, 196, 207, 208; law, 227, 228; man, 219-20; population growth, 227; society, 205-6, 219-21, 243; women, 220 (see also Islam; suttee)
Muslims, Orthodox and non-Orthodox, 196, 218, 222, 241-42
Myrdal, Gunnar, 4

Nabataeans, 195
Naga, 11
Nanak, Guru, 33; and women, 33
narodha, 84-85
Nash, Manning, 223
Nasser, President, 232
Nastika, 48
National Council of Churches (U.S.), and role of women in churches, 151

287

nautches, 26, 70
Nehru, Jawaharlal, 35, 36
Nehru, Pandit, 64
Neil, William, 150, 152
Nepal, 96
New Testament, 136, 153, 176
Nigeria, 182
nirvana, 84, 85, 89, 102 (see also narod-ha)
Noah, 173
nomadic life, 194, 196, 197
nongovernmental organizations, 108, 131
Norm, 104 (see also Buddhism)
Norway, 251
nun, 249

Old Testament, 136; and marriage, 174, 176; and women, 153
Omran, Abdel Rahim, 232, 240
Onan and onanism, Augustine on, 180; and contraception and levirate system, 175; Protestants on, 185; Padmapurana on, 65
Ontario, 249
ordination of priests, 250
Origen, 153; on sex, 154
Original Sin: Christian missionaries, and, 169; meaning of, 136; and women, 136, 137
orphans, 200, 201, 203, 208; inheritance of, 204
Ottawa, 227
Ottoman Empire, 214, 234
Ottoman law, 234

"Pacem in Terris," and concern for women, 162
Pakistan, 6, 219, 224, 225, 247, 248
Pali Canon, 93, 95, 97
Pancha Sila, 113 (see also Buddhism; Five Precepts)
panchayats, 21
Pandit Iswarchandra Vidyasagar, 252
Panikkar, K. M., 5
Parmatma, 60
Parrinder, Geoffrey, 147
Parvey, Constance, 152
Pastoral Constitution on the Church in the Modern World, and women, 162, 163
patriarchal fathers, 233
patriarchy, 12, 16, 199, 202; and Aryans, 16, 17, 18; patrilocal system and, 12
Paul, 95, 141, 142, 198, 201, 203, 233
Paul (Tarsus): character and background of, 142, 143, 152; on education of women, 160; on head covering for women, 143, 150; on male circumcision, 145; on marriage, 147, 149; on segregation of women in the synagogue, 145; on sex, 147, 148, 149; on women, 141, 146, 148-52

Paul VI: on church reforms, 163; and concern about Third World, 163-64; on women, divorce, and contraception, 163-65
Pauline epistles, 136
Perfection of Wisdom, 104 (see also buddhas; Buddhism)
Persian Gulf, 195
phallus: and phallic worship, 11; and fertility worship, 11
Pharisees, 141, 142, 145; and marriage, 176, 177; and women, 138-40
Philippians, and women, 145, 146
Philippines, 248; contraception in, 168; divorce in, 111; education in, 168; Catholic church in, 167, 187, 188
Philo, 153; use of Genesis to show inferiority of women, 155
Phoenicians, 195
Pitakas, 93, 95
Pius XI: on contraception, 180, 181, 182; and opposition to equality of women, especially in education, 160-61; and opposition to working mothers, 161
Pius XII: and emphasis on maternal role of women, 161; and reaffirmation of pronatalism, 161
policy makers, 3, 4, 117; attitudes of, toward family planning, 117
polyandry, 16, 17, 199, 204, 205; and Aryans, 16, 17; and pre-Vedic women, 17
polygamy, 16, 18, 33, 64, 86, 91, 199, 201, 204, 208, 218, 219, 223, 224; and Aryans, 16, 17
polytheist, 197
population: of Arabian peninsula, 194-95; attitudes on, 227; and Buddhism, 111, 127; growth of, and its consequences, 7, 115, 116, 120-22, 124, 125-27, 227, 229, 230, 242; and Islam, 227-45; policies of, 228, 229, 232, 239, 245
population limitation, reasons against, 67
pornography, public policy on, 189
Portuguese, 34
power: elite, 2, 3; holders and politicians, 3, 7
pravara, 252
predestination (see fate)
pre-Islamic: practices and attitudes, 194-97, 233-34; societies, 212, 234
priests, 98, 212, 221, 222, 231, 232, 238, 243, 248, 250, 251, 253; monopoly of, over education, 159; opposition of [to family planning, 59, 117-18; to female education, 99] (see also monks)
Prithivi, 46
procreation, 58, 63, 123, 231, 234-38, 243 243; as destiny, 65; reasons for, 60, 67, 112
pronatalism, 116, 119, 231, 238, 239; Buddhism on, 182; Genesis on, 173, 174;

ABOUT THE AUTHOR

Born in China and educated in Thailand, THEODORA FOSTER CARROLL returned to her native Canada to complete postsecondary studies. She received a B. Comm. (Economics) and an LL. B. from the University of British Columbia and undertook postgraduate studies in international law at Delhi University.

She practiced law in Vancouver before turning her attention to international development, working extensively with nongovernment organizations in Canada, the United States, and the Third World. She has been involved in a wide range of projects and programs in such areas as education, vocational training, health, women's participation, and community development, including development-education programs.

In Canada Ms. Carroll established and directed Oxfam-Quebec and ran the World Law Foundation in Montreal. In recent years she has consulted to such organizations as the Canadian School Trustees Association, where she wrote a report entitled "Sex Role Stereotyping in the Canadian School System"; the Canadian International Development Agency; and the Human Rights Institute of Canada. She also conceptualized, produced, and directed a six-part television series on the International Year of the Child.

While in Washington, D. C., she established and directed Oxfam-America and consulted to the American Civil Liberties Clearing House, the International Development Conference, and the Farmers' Union. She also worked for the American Society for International Law, preparing briefs on international law agreements.

Currently, Ms. Carroll is a partner in a private consulting firm, EDPRA Consulting Inc., in Ottawa, Canada. The company has undertaken projects for such institutions as the World Bank, the United Nations, and the North-South Roundtable. She has just completed a section on laws, customs, and practices for the North-South Institute's study on women and development, due to be published in early 1984.

Library